Bill Haley at 100:
Rockin' Around the World

Commissioned by the
Estate of Bill Haley

Bill Haley
David Lee Joyner
Chris Gardner

DLJ Music Services
Distributed by
IngramSpark

CONTENTS

INTRODUCTION
By Pedro Haley

My father never played guitar. I knew he could, but he didn't, not in front of me anyway. I grew up knowing him as Daddy, not Bill Haley. He was inducted into the Rock and Roll Hall of Fame in 1987. Mom sent me to accept the award and give a small acceptance speech. I was sixteen years old and my life was about to change. Before every performer was presented with the award, a film was shown to the audience that night at the Waldorf Astoria. When it was Daddy's turn, I saw something I had never seen before, images of him and the Comets performing live. The music I knew a little but the live performance was new. I was dumbstruck, absolutely floored by the images that showed the man I knew as a quiet old guy who watched baseball and boxing on TV, listened to Ray Charles, Hank Williams, and Agustin Lara on his record player and went fishing on the Gulf of Mexico on other days. I started playing guitar two weeks later. Now, I'm a professor of music and, a few people might say, pretty good on the guitar. However, my entire life seemed to be informed and predicated upon the ripples Bill Haley's life had upon my family. I have never forgotten the profound influence that night in 1987 had on my life. In 2010, after twenty-nine years of silence, my older sister and I were finally able to convince my mother to talk to a journalist about her life with Bill Haley. The sea change this instigated brought about my renewed endeavors to find someone willing to write a biography of my dad. There had been books written but I felt that a musicologist needed to write this and analyze the music. Frequently stated were the connections to rhythm and blues and country and western but as I became more knowledgeable about various styles of music, I realized that the great influence jazz had on the music of Bill Haley and the Comets had been completely missed by any of the writers. The music had always been the most important thing to my dad. I had read it interviews. Now I wanted a professional musician and scholar to write about the music and explain to a reading audience what was so obviously important to my dad.

In my sophomore year of college at the University of North Texas I took a class called The Development of Jazz and American Popular Music. Twenty years later I approached the professor of this class, David Lee Joyner, about the biography project. He was intrigued and a little surprised. I was elated to get his approval and we embarked on the project. Dr. Joyner met with my family to get the *imprimatur* from my mother and he conducted several interviews with her to lay a foundation for the book. As he continued his work David met and befriended Chris Gardner, a Bill Haley researcher, and with the Bill Haley Estate's blessing, brought the book project to a finish.

In 2025 we will celebrate the 100th birthday of my father. It would be fitting to celebrate this event with the release of an authorized biography of this important and tragically overlooked American musician.

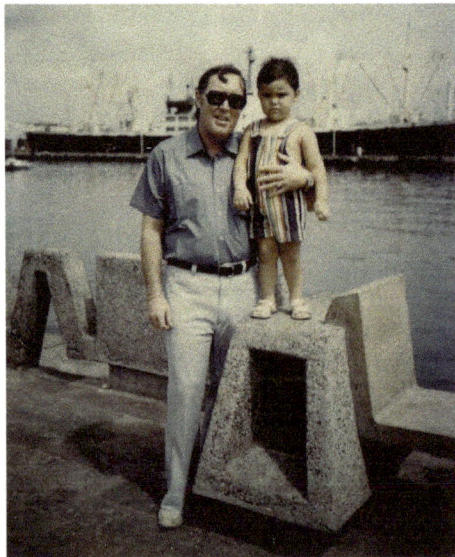

Bill Haley and Pedro, 1973

ABOUT THE AUTHORS

Bill Haley (1925-1981) was a singer, guitarist, songwriter and bandleader. In his early career, he specialized in country music, inspired by yodelers such as Elton Britt. Later on, he experimented with fusing swing, rhythm and blues, and country styles into a version of what would become known as rock 'n' roll. His career peaked with the release of his recording of "(We're Gonna) Rock Around the Clock" in 1954 and its appearance in the motion picture *Blackboard Jungle*, released in 1955. He was the first to take his music abroad with a tour of Australia, Europe, and Jamaica in 1957. While his popularity ebbed in the United States, he continued to tour the world and, in the rock 'n' roll revival of the late 1960s, had a resurgence in fame. In the last years of his life (c. 1979), he began an autobiography, intended as the catalyst for a biopic screenplay. He was inducted into the Rock and Roll Hall of Fame in 1987.

David Lee Joyner is a pianist, composer, arranger, lecturer, and educator. With degrees in composition and a PhD in musicology, he was Associate Professor of Music at the University of North Texas from 1986-2000 and Professor of Music at Pacific Lutheran University in Tacoma, Washington from 2000 until his retire-ment from university teaching in 2018. His history text *American Popular Music*, published by McGraw-Hill, has been in print since 1993. He has also contributed to *The Cambridge History of American Music*. He is now a freelance musician, regularly performing, com-posing and lecturing, while enjoying his home in the Puget Sound region of Washington state.

Chris Gardner lives in the UK and has been a Bill Haley fan since the early 1970s when the Rock 'n' Roll revival really kicked in. He has been researching Bill Haley's career and life since then, and over the years has provided countless sets of liner notes for LPs and CDs, articles for music magazines, and made the occasional appearance on national radio. His working career was spent with PRS for Music, where he rose through the ranks to become IT Director in the early 2000s. He was the first Managing Director of ICE Services, now a thriving business which manages copyright licensing on an international basis. Now retired, he is busy as a freelance musician, writing music, accompanying and conducting choirs and orchestras. For many years he was a member of the Stargazers, a well-known UK Rock 'n' Roll band, and is currently a member of the Dreamrollers. The father of four grown-up children, and now a grandfather, he lives in Hampshire, U.K., with his wife, Clare. Private passions include cricket and model railways.

FOREWORD
By David Lee Joyner

Bill Haley was a musician whose life and career were marked by contradictions. He wanted success, but did not do well with fame. He was a cowboy yodeler who became world-famous as a pioneer of rock 'n' roll. When his towering presence ebbed, Haley was still stuck with that label (and actually fearful of letting it go), which barred him from successfully returning to his beloved country music in the 1960s and '70s. He pioneered a style of music designed for the tastes of teenagers — but presented it to them with a middle-aged band that had cut its teeth on jazz and country music. He regarded his greatest rock and roll rival, Elvis Presley, with paternal affection, but was always tormented by his jealousy of him. In the last twenty years of his life, Haley was conflicted between his yearning for a stable family and home life and his sense of obligation to keep his band, the Comets, working and touring. He hated touring, particularly flying, but had his greatest and longest-lasting success outside of the United States. He was, in fact, the first to take rock 'n' roll on tour internationally. When Presley, ten years younger than Haley, died in 1977, Haley felt additional pressure to be, in his mind, the sole remaining torchbearer for "real" rock and roll.[1]

Haley was married three times and had children with each wife. He married Dorothy "Dottie" Crowe (1926-1983) in 1946 and they had a daughter, Sharyn Ann, in 1947 and a son, John William ("Jack"), in 1950. His second wife was Joan "Cuppy" Cupchak (1932-2025), whom he married in 1952. Together, they had five children: Joan Patricia in 1953, Doreen Debra in 1954 (who died in infancy), William Jr. in 1955, James Steven in 1956, and Scott Robert in 1960. He married Martha Velasco (1936-2025) in 1963 and they had three children: Martha Maria in

---

1 Bill Haley told the New York Post in 1969, "When I'm 75, if I can still hold my guitar and sing and you can still clap your hands, there will still be rock and roll!" Those are, in fact, the first words in his autobiography.

1963, Pedro Antonio in 1971, and Linda Georgina in 1975. All three marriages were prompted by unplanned pregnancies.

By the time Haley established his third family, burnout, self-reflection, a diminishing career, and his true love of Martha led him to a life that was more stable, isolated, and "normal." He spent the last third of his life in Mexico and south Texas, limiting his touring and recording and, between 1976 and 1979, he flat-out retired. Haley spent his days deep-sea fishing, dabbling in the motel and trailer park business, and going to the kids' ball games and plays. "I didn't know Dad, the entertainer," daughter Martha Maria told me in 2018. "I knew the man, the father. To me, he was just Dad. He wasn't anything more than that. I had no concept of who he was or how important or how famous or what he had done."

From around the time Haley resumed touring and recording in 1979 until his death in February 1981, neither an uptick in career nor a happy ending for the Haley family was in the cards, for the demons had come calling. The last two years of his life were a period the family refers to as "when Daddy was sick." Chain-smoking and escalating alcohol abuse took a toll on Haley's heart and mind, likely coupled with a mental illness that could possibly be traced genetically to his father, whom Haley always referred to as having "bad nerves." The painful end to Haley's life drove the family into deep secrecy about his final years, leaving it up to the sensationalistic speculation of journalists to fill in the blanks.[2] Even his final resting place is a closely guarded secret. In her grief and sense of protectionism, Haley's widow, Martha, was silent for three decades and the children followed her example.

When he died in 1981, the world took little notice. When the Rock & Roll Hall of Fame announced its first inductees in 1986, Haley was not among them; he wouldn't be added until the next year. His most famous recording, "(We're Gonna) Rock Around the Clock," didn't enter the Library of Congress National Recording Registry until 2017; when that finally happened, I wrote the accompanying essay.[3] In 1990, John W. Haley, child of Bill and Dottie Haley, along with John von Hoelle, published a well-researched and comprehensive biography of his father.[4] The book deals fairly and evenly with Bill's life across his three families; admirable,

---

[2] Haley's death certificate cites, "natural causes, most likely heart attack." The next portion of the death certificate reads, "Due to, or as a consequence of" and is left blank, but the many accounts of his chain smoking and acute alcoholism make a compelling case for their contribution to his assumed heart attack.

[3] David Lee Joyner, "'(We're Gonna) Rock Around the Clock'- Bill Haley and His Comets (1954)." *Library of Congress Index of Recording Essays* (added in 2017), https://www.loc.gov/programs/national-recording-preservation-board/recording-registry/index-of-essays/

[4] John W. Haley and John von Hoelle, *Sound and Glory: The Incredible Story of Bill Haley, the Father of Rock 'n' Roll and the Music That Shook the World* (Wilmington, DE: Dyne-American Publications, 1990).

considering that Jack must have pushed aside some bitterness over his father's absenteeism. I consider this biography the voice of Bill's first family.

Bill Haley, Jr., child of Bill and Cuppy Haley, has performed and recorded with his own band, named after the Comets, taking the role of his father in the band. He also produced a biography of his father[5] and is working on a documentary at the time of this writing. This is the voice of Bill Sr.'s second family and focuses on the years 1960-62 when, as Bill, Jr. describes it, his father finally didn't come home for Christmas. The narrative of Bill, Jr.'s mother, Cuppy, is a dominant voice in the biography, the result of more than twenty hours of recorded interviews with her son. The book also has the perspective of another family member who is a musician and has experienced performing Bill Haley's music: Bill and Martha Haley's youngest child, Gina, who has performed and recorded her father's music alongside Comets alumni and tribute bands.

The third family realized they may be a big part of the reason Bill had fallen into obscurity and something needed to be done. As journalist Michael Hall tells it, Pedro and Martha Maria said to their mother, "We want Daddy to be remembered and given proper credit, and your behavior [refusal to be interviewed] has been damaging to his legacy." Martha relented and the resulting article, "Falling Comet," appeared in the October 2011 issue of *Texas Monthly*. It was the first fruit of a now-forthcoming widow and her children. Martha tells of meeting Bill in Mexico, their flowering relationship, and their subsequent years together in detail that no one, even her own children, had ever heard before; however, Hall's article played up the dismal scene of Haley's last two years.

Now that the family had opened up to Hall, he suggested that they get serious about promoting Haley's life and career. Taking charge of the estate willed to Martha, Pedro set to work turning the spotlight back on his father's legacy. He went to Austin to seek out music business lawyers and procured a management firm, ALG Brands, to promote Bill Haley's brand, image, and intellectual property. Pedro also became executor of the estate in 2016. Royalties, mostly from recordings, continue to come in and have provided an income for Martha and put the children through college.

Preceding Jack Haley's biography of his father, John Swenson, a writer for *Rolling Stone* and *The Village Voice*, wrote a biography in 1982, a year after Haley's death.[6] The cover of the 1983 American paperback edition touted the book as, "the illustrated, first-ever biography of the world's first superstar of rock 'n' roll."

---

5 Bill Haley, Jr. and Peter Benjaminson, *Crazy Man Crazy: The Bill Haley Story* (Guildford, CT: Backbeat Books, 2019).

6 John Swenson, *Bill Haley: The Daddy of Rock 'n' Roll* (New York: Stein and Day, 1983; first published in the U.K. by W.H. Allen, 1982).

More recently, Austrian superfan Otto Fuchs published a staggering biographical work in 2014 (one he terms a "fanography"), totaling more than a thousand pages. Admirable in its energy and detail, it covers aspects of Haley's life and work that were missed by previous authors. Despite these few, but fine biography projects, more work remained to tell "the rest of the story."[7]

As Pedro Haley told in the Introduction, he was a student in my American popular music history class in the early 1990s. More than twenty years later, I somehow came to mind as Pedro was seeking a new biographer. "Why me?" I asked Pedro. "I'm not happy with the biographies that are out there. I want someone to talk about Daddy's music," he told me. "These other biographers aren't musicians." As jazz critic Francis Davis stated in the introduction to his first book, *In the Moment*, "Musicians presuppose that all critics are frustrated musicians. That's incorrect: the good ones are frustrated novelists."[8]

Pedro was also frustrated that previous writers had not adequately emphasized the importance of jazz in shaping the sound of Haley and the Comets. As he told Fuchs, "I think that my father's music has not been correctly interpreted. It is misunderstood. To my ears, it is so obvious that big-band jazz is an essential part of the Comets' sound."[9] Pedro felt this was something I could address. As a trained musician and music historian himself, I asked Pedro, "Why not you?" His response was direct and logical. "I'm too close to it. He was my dad." Therefore, one of the goals we set was to look at Bill Haley's life as that of a musician's and look at it with a musician's curiosity.

The Haley family was keen on guarding against salacious accounts of Bill's life. Now the question arises as to how to proceed with telling the personal side of a very private person, particularly in the sensitive later years, and do it in a way that would be acceptable to Bill and especially to Martha. How about hearing Bill Haley's story from Bill himself? The most guarded piece of Haley ephemera is his own autobiography. Every Haley author and authority knows about it and has written about it, but no one had ever seen it. The family kept it locked up tight.

The idea of the autobiography was at the urging of Haley's manager at the time, Patrick "Paddy" Malynn, who was promising Haley — and the world — that a biographical film based on the singer's life was in the works. Movies about early rock and rollers were certainly a hot topic in the 1980s. *The Buddy Holly Story* (1978) launched actor Gary Busey to stardom. Six years after Haley's death,

---

7 Otto Fuchs, *Bill Haley: The Father of Rock and Roll* (Linz, Austria: Wagner Verlag, 2011).

8 Francis Davis, *In the Moment* (New York: Oxford University Press, 1986).

9 Fuchs, pp. 945-946.

actor Lou Diamond Phillips ramped up his career in 1987's *La Bamba*, portraying Ritchie Valens. Two years later, Dennis Quaid played Jerry Lee Lewis in the biopic, *Great Balls of Fire*. Elvis Presley biopic movies, of course, are legion; the first notable effort was Kurt Russell's portrayal of Presley for a television film in 1979, produced by Dick Clark only two years after Elvis' death. That same year, Malynn had engineered a big comeback for Haley, had gotten him much better money for his gigs, and he had no reason to believe he couldn't pull off a movie, too.

Hugh McCallum, Haley's long-time friend and president of the Bill Haley Fan Club in England, probably took the initiative. He drafted a two-volume, 163-page outline for someone of Malynn's choosing to adapt into a screenplay. The title page reads: "The Bill Haley Story: An initial outline resume compiled for purposes of furthering discussions towards a film on the life story of Bill Haley." Running to 108 pages, the first volume is almost the same length as Haley's autobiography text, and covers the years up to when Haley had his triumphant rock and roll revival concert at Madison Square Garden in New York on October 18, 1969. It turns out there is also a "Volume 2" that extends the narrative to 1979, climaxing at the Royal Command Performance in London on November 26. Unfortunately, at the time of this writing, this portion is not in the possession of the family and McCallum was not willing to part with it, even as a digital copy.

Looking at them side by side, Hugh's outline and Bill's autobiography follow each other closely, strengthening McCallum's case that Haley may have used it as a guide for his own work. Further evidence that McCallum coached Haley on his own autobiography was a trip that McCallum and his wife made to the Haley home in Harlingen for that very purpose. The PDF I received has about 104 typewritten pages and a page and a half of Bill's handwritten manuscript. The handwritten pages made me suspect that Haley had not typed the manuscript himself. The typewritten manuscript is full of grammatical errors and clumsy phrasing, indicating that the typist transcribed Bill's handwritten notes without editing or any other intervention. Pedro said that Bill's then-teenaged daughter, Martha Maria, was the typist of a portion of it and she confirmed it when I interviewed her in October 2018:

Yeah, I think it was, it was in '79 so I was, what, sixteen years old, and so somehow or another he must have asked me to help him type up the notes and reluctantly I go, "Okay. Yeah, Dad. Alright." I think it was just the yellow notebook paper and he would just hand it to me and I would go off into whatever room we had the typewriter in. As a matter of fact, I'm not sure if I even finished the job. Something tells me that I probably did not type everything up. Probably, being sixteen, I had more important things going on in my life... you know, 1979 disco was Number One, disco was king. Donna Summer was calling me, and the Bee Gees.[10]

I was also interested in Bill's writing routine. Did he write in isolation, out of sight, or in the family common area of the house? Did he write in binge sessions or sporadically? Did he fish during the day and was writing at night? "He could have been," said his wife, Martha, "although he had an office. All in the kitchen. There was a little hallway that went into this little room, which he converted to his office. And he would go in there and nobody would bother him. That's probably when he wrote all this." Bill's daughter, Martha Maria, added: "Yeah, I think he probably wrote during the day." She insisted that she didn't know that the purpose of the autobiography was to provide fodder for a movie. "I didn't know anything about that. Did you, Mom? That they were talking about maybe making a movie?" "Oh, with Paddy? Oh, sure," her mother answered, matter-of-factly, revealing that she knew more than she earlier let on.

Nothing came of the movie during Haley's lifetime, but what of the autobiography? I'm proud to say that it will be presented here for the first time, with the blessing of the Haley estate. Haley's manuscript can now be analyzed on a number of levels: his historic viewpoint, the character of his narrative style, his level of detail and accuracy, his objectivity versus his self-promotion, and, of course, a first-person account of how he saw his own music and career.

He was certainly not lacking in eloquence. As a seasoned radio announcer and disk jockey, Haley's voice and elocution were pleasant and well-groomed; his many interview responses were articulate and well-rehearsed. Seeing him on camera, hearing him speak on radio, or catching his song introductions in concert is to witness poise at its best, a far cry from the mumblings of an Elvis Presley or the rantings of a Jerry Lee Lewis or Little Richard. He was a pro, but an elaborate narrative of his life was a project Haley himself probably would not have initiated.

He was not a narcissist and didn't particularly think about telling the world every detail of his life; some of it he was proud of and some of it he was not. Haley was a very private person, and it is interesting to see where he is forthcoming in his narrative and where he tends to hold back. He is refreshingly revealing about his own musical evolution and we get great insight into how scientific and methodical he was in his transition from cowboy country to early rock and roll. The time he spent as record librarian at radio station WPWA in Chester,

---

10 We, the authors, discovered from Bill's phone conversations with manager Rex Zario that, as Martha Maria lost interest in typing up Bill's notes, a commercial typing service completed the job.

Pennsylvania, played a critical role in his research as he absorbed the styles and artists of big-band swing, bebop jazz, and rhythm and blues, as well as the country music subgenres cowboy, bluegrass, honky tonk, and western swing. He is also very open about his distaste for touring, fan mania, intrusive interviewers, and the general hubbub typical of fame. Haley is forthright about the racism that was so prevalent in the 1950s and is clear, yet modest and matter-of-fact about the injustice he felt for his fellow musicians who were African-American and his own efforts, though tentative, to champion their cause.

As expected, he is more guarded about his personal life. He mentions his first two marriages and family almost in passing. Writing in 1979, we can only speculate if he was feeling guilt or perhaps some self-imposed pressure not to elaborate on his earlier married life now that he was married to Martha. Martha herself stated that she was not involved nor even inquisitive when Bill was working on the autobiography, so we can be assured that she wasn't standing over him and his notepad with the proverbial rolling pin at the ready.

Haley also seems reticent to admit his fatal stubbornness in his business decisions — his loyalty to inept managers, his insistence on pushing the unsuccessful and often lackluster original songs and albums that he and Comets members cranked out, and his naïve side-business investments and personal overspending. When discussing the illness and death of his parents, sister, and infant daughter, Haley's narrative style has a poised sentimentality rather than a wrenching, raw expression of grief. I find it similar to the style of the tragedy songs that Haley would have learned and performed as a country music singer. In fact, much of his narrative style is affable and "aw shucks" in the manner of a cowboy storyteller. You can almost picture him, Will Rogers-style, in his cowboy outfit twirling a lasso by a campfire and telling a tale of the Old West.

There are only a few moments in Bill Haley's writing that tend to raise the eyebrows. While clearly not a racist, he does throw in a bit of black dialect when quoting his dear friend, touring, and (briefly) recording partner Big Joe Turner, but it was a practice that Turner was cognizant of and typical of the hijinks he and Haley shared. (Martha told me Bill did a great Big Joe impersonation.) Writing in the late 1970s, Bill also permitted himself to use an occasional obscenity. His quote of saxophonist Red Prysock while they were on tour is priceless (p. 77).

In his words written in 1979, two years before his death, we would hope that Bill Haley would give us a fairly complete narrative of his life to that point, especially debunking all the speculation of his years in relative isolation and retirement. Unfortunately, his story only takes us to about 1960. My question to the Haley family was, "What do you think he would have told us if he had continued his story through the 1960s and '70s, through Bill's filter? Do you have any speculation what he would have brought to the surface and what he would have just kept down here [in Texas]?" Martha's reply was wistful. "He was so tired by then. He wanted just to fish and watch the baseball game."

Bill only wrote six chapters that, as previously mentioned, only take him up to about 1960. Following that, however, he provides a chapter outline indicating the topics he planned to cover next. The tantalizing list, presented here verbatim, suggests additional material covering the 1950s, and then beyond:

CHAPTER 7 GOING DOWN BUT STILL ROCKIN
SUBJECTS TO BE COVERED
    1. Meeting Buddy Holly Again
    2. Florida Tour with Jerry Lee — Everlys — Holly
    3. South American Tour.
    4. Almost Tragedy in Buenos Aires.
    5. August Allan Freed Fabian Fox Brooklyn
    6. October. European Tour Austria, France, Germany.
    7. Berlin Riot. Hamburg Riot.
    8. Two More Movies.
    9. Meeting with Old Pal Elvis
    10. Tour Cancellation in Spain.
    11. Corporation Failing Lord Jim Retires.
    12. Left Decca — Sign Warner Bros.
Chapter VIII THE BOOZIN HEARTBREAK (1960-1961)
Chapter IX PICKING UP THE PIECES (1962-1963)
Chapter X BACK TO ENGLAND AND HOW (1964)
Chapter XI VIVA [sic] LA ROCK AND ROLL (1965-1966)
Chapter XII ROCK AND ROLL REVIVAL (Madison Square Garden)
Chapter XIII VERA CRUZ, MEXICO (Slowing down — Loss of Best Friend and Retirement.)
Chapter XIX RETURN (Story of Royal Command Performance Show)

In addition to the chapters, Haley also offers possible book-title and cover art options that identify it as a work in progress, but clearly state his prominence and significance in the history of rock and roll: "WHEN I'M 75 IF I CAN STILL HOLD MY GUITAR AND SING AND YOU CAN STILL CLAP YOUR HANDS, THERE WILL STILL BE ROCK AND ROLL!"

THE LIFE AND TIMES OF BILL HALEY
THE MAN WHO INVENTED ROCK AND ROLL

WRITTEN BY BILL HALEY

OTHER POSSIBLE TITLES: ROCK OF AGES
THE TRUE AND UNTOLD STORY OF ROCK AND ROLL
SEND ME THE FLOWERS WHILE I'M HERE

SUGGESTED FOR BACK COVER OF BOOK
"NO MATTER HOW BIG I GET TO BE HE WILL ALWAYS BE THE
KING."

(ELVIS PRESLEY TALKING TO LORD JIM FERGUSON AS THEY
STOOD BACKSTAGE WATCHING THE BILL HALEY SHOW AT THE
AUDITORIUM FRANKFURT, GERMANY, OCTOBER 1958 — CHAPTER
VII.).

As I was setting up shop to begin research for this book, Pedro Haley kindly
provided me with contact information for some key Bill Haley experts, including
Hugh McCallum, Texas expert Denise Gregoire, former Comets guitarist Bill
Turner, German record company owner Klaus Kettner (who has curated
numerous releases of rare Haley recordings), and British Haley researcher Chris
Gardner. Already impressed by his spectacular liner notes for the German Bear
Family Records CD set, *Bill Haley: The Warner Brothers Years and More*,[11] it was
obvious, from looking at the extant research on Haley, that Chris was the go-to
guy for everyone, tapping into his 40-plus years of research and writing, though
he had never produced a full biography himself. As Pedro Haley said in my
interview, "Well, Chris Gardner is a gold mine." I quickly established a close
working relationship with Chris, albeit mostly through email and video
conferencing. Chris was so generous with his consultation and sharing of research
materials that I took the next logical step and asked him to formally co-author this
book, a proposal that he enthusiastically accepted. In May 2019, my wife and I
visited Chris and his family in Alton, Hampshire, England, where we had the
luxury of working side-by-side for a couple of days, sharing our interest in Bill
Haley research as well as our enthusiasm for vintage trains and composition. In
addition to being the foremost authority on Haley, Chris is an accomplished

---

11 Bear Family Records, BCD16157 (1999).

composer and conductor, the son of composer and Royal Academy of Music professor John Linton Gardner. We are truly "brothers from another mother."

This book is the next step in the Bill Haley autobiography effort. It is our intention to give Haley his voice and for our role to be as a guide for the reader, to offer historical and musical context, clarifying side notes, and factual correction as needed. We applied enough editing to make it more readable, but retaining Haley's character. That will be the first part of the book. Haley's narrative takes us to 1958.

As both Chris and I were concerned with narrative consistency after we took the reins from Bill after 1958, we decided on an "omnibus" concept, where we could allow our book to be a bit of this and a bit of that — Bill's autobiography, heavy annotation with correction and commentary, historical and stylistic context, and deeper analysis of the music itself. This is also where Haley's wife, Martha, comes into the picture. Since she was closely at Bill's side for the second half of his life, and since an elaborate narrative from her has been as elusive as Bill's manuscript, I will give her voice for that period, based on extensive interviews I conducted with her and her children in 2018 and 2019. In dealing with sensitive and personal details, we took the lead of Bill and Martha's own narratives, assuming that, if they were willing to formally reveal the information, then we had their blessing to write around it. Even if the intention is to focus strictly on Bill's professional activities and musical output, some of these "private" details have a direct bearing on that career and must be mentioned.

This book does not attempt to be a comprehensive and exhaustive biography, but directed and delimited by the Haley family narrative. In keeping with Pedro Haley's wishes and our own observations as musicians, we will look deeper into the workings and etymology of select Haley recordings. We will not validate them on their commercial success, but on their significance as musical efforts or as best illustrating a notable moment in Haley's artistic evolution.

Part 1 of this book is the story of Bill Haley's life as told by him up to 1958 and completed by us, the authors.

Part 2, "Haley in Context," puts him and his music in the broader setting of American popular music, such as country music, swing and jazz, and rhythm and blues. Most of the previous works on Haley have been too focused on Haley's own musical sphere alone without putting him in the larger context of his stylistic world from the 1930s to the 1970s.

Part 3, "Focus on Music," is a more technical analysis of Haley's music intended for the trained musician and the musically curious.

One last declaration I'll make here. We are not out to make a case for Bill Haley being the "inventor" of rock and roll. No one can definitely declare that any more than we can pinpoint the specific Italian who invented pizza. Scott Joplin was declared the King of Ragtime, but he didn't invent it. However, his 1899 "Maple Leaf Rag" did make it a popular phenomenon. W. C. Handy called himself the Father of the Blues on the strength of his published songs like "Memphis Blues" (1912) and "St. Louis Blues" (1914), but no one had less of a concept of real blues than Handy, and he sure didn't invent it. Rock and roll probably goes as far back as the 1940s recordings of Sister Rosetta Tharpe, if not earlier, but it is a fight we are not willing to wage. However, as Joplin and Handy lit the fuses of their respective genres with specific songs, Bill Haley and the Comets did record that iconic song that, once and for all, got rock and roll as a phenomenon really going, "Rock Around the Clock." As mentioned earlier, he was also the first to take rock 'n' roll overseas, both through live appearances and through the international showing of the film *Blackboard Jungle* that used "Rock Around the Clock" as its title music. For that, we can tentatively allow him to be "The Father of Rock and Roll." In fact, our calling is more to show that Haley was more than rock and roll. His early career as a cowboy yodeler is more deserving than a brief mention and treatment as something either short-lived or insignificant. Likewise, after the mountain-top career spike in the mid-1950s, he and the Comets dabbled, sometimes worthily, into easy-listening instrumentals, twist, Mexican popular music, and country rock. His struggle with the grind of the professional music life is an archetype and, though sometimes spectacular and often times mundane, is a window into an experience that many musicians have shared.

Happy 100th birthday, Bill.

POSTSCRIPT: As we were moving into the last stages of publication, we learned of the passing of Martha Velascao Haley on June 29th, 2025. She was the solid rock Bill needed and she raised three wonderful children that are now dear friends of mine. She made a significant contribution to this book by granting me hours of interview, something she hadn't done to that extent for anyone else. She was spunky *and* sweet, just the firebrand you would expect. THIS BOOK IS DEDICATED TO HER MEMORY. She's back with Bill in time for his centennial.

David Lee Joyner
Sumner, Washington
July 2025

The Haley family attending at a performance of Puccini's *La Boheme* at the Dallas Opera, March 9, 2025.
L to R: Gina Haley, Martha Haley, Pedro Haley, Martha Maria Haley-Castillo

PROLOGUE
By Bill Haley

It's Monday night, November 26, 1979 and I find myself, for the first time in more than six weeks, with a few moments to relax. I am backstage at THE THEATRE ROYAL, Drury Lane in London, England, where I have been invited to appear in the Royal Command Performance in the presence of Her Majesty Queen Elizabeth II. The show is the annual benefit performance in aid of The Entertainment Artistes' Benevolent Fund and, as befits such an occasion, some of the world's top artists from all fields of our business have been invited. For the past two days in rehearsals and sound checks, I have been in complete awe surrounded by such greats as Yul Brynner, James Mason, Carol Channing, Red Buttons, Elizabeth Welch, Millicent Martin, James Galway, Jim Davidson, Elaine Stritch and, in the dressing room across from this one, stars of the Bolshoi Ballet-- Vladimir Vasiliev and Ekaterina Maximova. Also, Amii Stewart, Bernie Clifton, and a great comedian, Les Dawson, all working and worrying for the past 48 hours to put together the show we were to present in a few hours. Producer Norman Maen proved to be the Rock of Gibraltar for all of us.

This is to be for me the climax of this six weeks' tour of Europe. My wife Martha and I had left home six weeks earlier and flown to Amsterdam, Holland to begin the tour which was mainly a promotion tour to try to let the public know we were still alive and carrying the banner of my life's work, namely Rock and Roll music, pure and unadulterated. The six weeks had taken us to Holland, Finland, Denmark, Sweden, then to Germany for 11 days and finally here to England for 10 days ending the tour with our show here. The tour had been going well but, as all tours go, we were tired by now of daily plane trips, hotels, different food, bad weather, and coupled with the fact that both Martha and I had come down with colds and we were missing home, the kids, and we were really looking forward to finishing the tour. I had the good fortune to be sharing the dressing room with a man I have admired for many years, but had never met, Mr. Red Buttons. Red and I had become friends after two days of rehearsing and had settled in to prepare for the show. He is a real pro in every sense of the word. Red had flown all the way here just to do this show at his own expense because he really cared and I shall always remember those two days we worked together preparing for this show. When I start feeling old and tired, which I sometimes do, my inspiration comes from grand people like Red Buttons.

It was now 5:00 p.m. and the show was scheduled to start at 8:00 p.m. My best friend and manager, Patrick Malynn, had taken Martha back to the hotel for her to change. My band, the Comets (1979) version, Mal Gray [band leader], Steve Murray [drums], Jerry Tilley [guitar], Pete Thomas [sax], John Gordon [bass guitar], and Chico Ryan [rhythm guitar] had all gone to eat, and the entire cast were off somewhere preparing for the show, and so as I sat waiting for wardrobe to alter the jacket I was to wear tonight, for the first time, it began to hit me what was I doing here on this show with all those show business giants, and for the first time the butterflies started.

Anyone who tells you that entertainers do not get pre-show jitters and moments of stage fright are not really telling the truth and I, even after 36 years of doing shows, always get that moment of fright before a show. But thank the good Lord for my good fortune and as I often have said through the ups and downs of my career, I have a little piece of gold I carry around in my back pocket and it has never failed ("knock on wood") to pull me through. It is a song called "Rock Around the Clock" and even after 25 years of singing this song, I still get a chill when we start the song and the reaction of the crowd seems to inject energy to the band and me, and we are off to our little world. But more than just performing the song the fact that I know that the song is part of me and the confidence it has given me all these twenty-five years, especially in bad times, I have been able to carry on knowing I could count on this song to pull me through. But tonight, somehow was different. I would be playing before a lady that I most admired of all the world (pardon Your Majesty) with the exception of Martha my wife, and I must admit for the first time I was worried about the reaction. I began to think really the importance of this show for me and my entire career, and my music and all that I believed in the future of the original style of Rock and Roll the way we tried to present it to the world. The danger was if our part of this show was received badly and we did not at least do fair, and as sometimes happens the critics would blast us, all the good work of this tour would be for naught, and I would have set back original Rock and Roll music a long way.

On the other hand, it was an opportunity for me to play our music before a vast television audience and a theatre audience the likes of which I had never had the chance to do before. So, in a nutshell, it was kind of do or die. If we won, we would have helped our careers, but if we lost - well by now you know this show meant all the marbles for me. My manager Patrick Malynn had plans to do a major motion picture in the near future about the Life and Times of Bill Haley and a good showing here would help these plans, but again a bust here might also kill the plans for this project. How I wished at that moment that my dear friend Rudy Pompilli were here with me tonight. Rudy and I had fought side by side for 20 years and he had become like a brother to me, not only on stage but in life as we had become inseparable through the years, until I lost him to cancer in February 1976. I had found it impossible to do shows without him and, after his death, it was indeed more than two years before I could again do shows, and only through the urging of promoters and fans and people like Hugh McCallum and my wife Martha, and finally through Patrick Malynn, who convinced me after Elvis Presley died that, unless I once again began to do tours, that everything that Rudy and I had worked for would be forgotten, did I again start on the road to where I am tonight. I somehow felt, as I have many times recently, that I had to try my best for Rudy and for what we had worked for all the years, and I thought how proud he would have been could he have only been here tonight.

As the time was passing, I slowly lit my Pall Mall cigarette, leaned back in my chair, and my mind began to review all that had happened down the long, long road from Highland Park, Michigan to the stage of the Theatre Royal Drury Lane London.

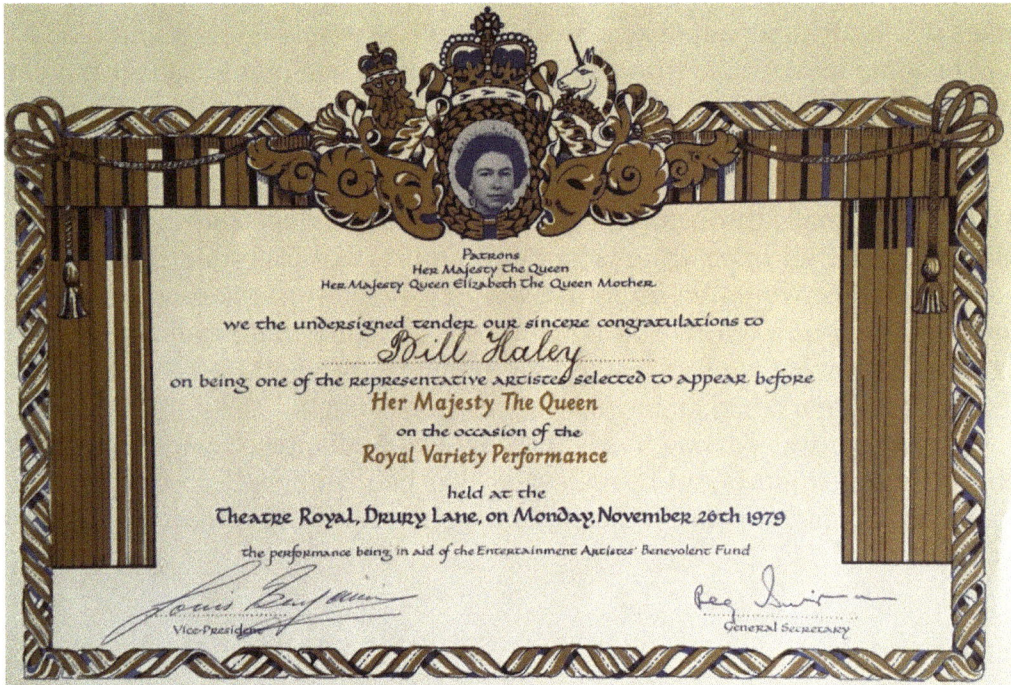

Patrons
Her Majesty The Queen
Her Majesty Queen Elizabeth The Queen Mother

we the undersigned tender our sincere congratulations to

Bill Haley

on being one of the representative artistes selected to appear before

Her Majesty The Queen

on the occasion of the

Royal Variety Performance

held at the

Theatre Royal, Drury Lane, on Monday, November 26th 1979

the performance being in aid of the Entertainment Artistes' Benevolent Fund

Vice-President

General Secretary

PART 1
The Bill Haley Autobiography

CHAPTER 1
The Early Years (1925-1943)

PLACE OF BIRTH   MICHIGAN DEPARTMENT OF HEALTH   682 6107

County of... *Wayne*

Township of.....................

or

Village of......................

City of... *Highland Park*   (No. *395 Florence* St.,.................Ward)

Register No...... *863*

(If birth occurs in a hospital or other institution, give name of same instead of street and number.)

FULL NAME OF CHILD... *William John Clifton Haley*   { If child is not yet named, make supplemental report, as directed.

Sex and ___: *male* | Twin, triplet, or other? | and | Number in order of birth *2* | Legitimate? *Yes* | Date of Birth *July 6 1925* (Month) (Day) (Year)

FATHER	MOTHER
Full Name *Wm Albert Clifton Haley*	Full Maiden Name *Maude Green*
Residence (P.O. Address) *395 Florence Ave.*	Residence (P.O. Address) *395 Florence Av*
Color or Race *white* Age at Last Birthday *35* (Years)	Color or Race *white* Age at Last Birthday *36* (Years)
Birthplace *Kentucky U.S.A.*	Birthplace *Lancashire England*
Occupation (And Industry) *Gas Station Attendant*	Occupation (And Industry) *Housewife*

Number of child of this mother.. *2* .... Number of children, of this mother, now living. *2* ....

CERTIFICATE OF ATTENDING PHYSICIAN OR MIDWIFE.

I hereby certify that I attended the birth of this child, who was. *Born alive* ...at. *2:30 p.* ..M. on the date above stated. (Born alive or stillborn.)

Have eyes of child been treated with } prophylaxis solution?.. *Yes* }

Surname or christian name added from a supplemental report.............192...

(Signature) *G. S. McAlpine*

Dated. *July 7 1925*   Attending   Physician (Attending physician, midwife, father, etc.)

Address. *11 548 Livernois Blvd Detroit*

Filed. *7-13 1925*   *Palmer Bowring*   Registrar.

I hereby certify that the above is a true and correct reproduction of the certificate on file in the Michigan Department of Public Health, Lansing, Michigan.

CERTIFIED BY: *George Van Amburg*

George Van Amburg
State Registrar

Bill Haley's Birth Certificate

Ifirst saw the light of day on July 6, 1925, when the good Lord saw fit to present to Maude Green Haley[1] and William Albert Clifton Haley an eight-pound-plus bouncing baby boy — or, at least, they said I was bouncing. This event took place in the Detroit suburb of Highland Park, Michigan. My father [also William, and known as "Will"] came from Kentucky — a Kentucky boy. He and some of the

Three Generations: Bill's first son and biographer, John "Jack" Haley, holds a portrait of his grandfather, Will, with his infant son, Bill. Photo from the 1980s.

Haley family had moved to the Detroit area before the outbreak of World War I. Dad had gone into the Army, and it was as a Corporal, stationed in New Jersey, that he had met Maude Green, a pretty young English lass. Mother was born and raised in Ulverston, England, where my grandfather, Johnny Green, had a bakery. The Green family emigrated to the United States and settled in Marcus Hook, Pennsylvania, where my grandfather and uncles went to work for the American Viscose Company.

It was on this occasion that Maude met William and they fell in love. When Dad finished his service, they were married and returned to Detroit, where, in 1923, my sister, Peggy, was born. Dad went to work for the Standard Oil Company and we lived in a small home on Whitcomb Street.[2] My recollections of this period, naturally, are non-existent. But, from stories told by Mom and Dad and other relatives, the only thing important and worth mentioning was my first appearance as an entertainer. One day, so the story goes, one of the neighbors called Maude to tell her that her three-year old son was coming down Whitcomb Street with no clothes on. She rushed out and grabbed me. My explanation was that I had been playing with the kids, and, as it was a warm day, decided to get rid of the clothes and came home that

1 Bill's mother's name is spelled "Maude" in his manuscript, but she is "Maud" on her (British) birth certificate. We will use Bill's spelling in his narrative, but will use the legal spelling in our captions and footnotes.

2 We can use official records to illuminate, correct, confirm and clarify Bill's story at this point. Maud ("Maude") was born on June 23, 1895. The Green family lived above the bakery at 39 Devonshire St, Ulverston, and emigrated en masse to the US in November 1912, the party including Maud's parents, aunts, uncle and siblings. The lure was the prospect of work at American Viscose, where her father John would become a foreman. Will Haley (b. 2/22/1890 in Firebrick, Kentucky), meanwhile, had been working for the Paige Motor Car Co. in Detroit when called up for War service. Based in New Jersey, he met Maud, whose father used his influence to get him a job at American Viscose. Will and Maud married in 1922, and Bill's sister Margaret Ann May ("Peggy") was born on May 20, 1923. Bill was born William John Clifton Haley at the family home, 395 Florence St., Highland Park.

Will, Peggy, and Maud Haley

way. The world's first streaker? Well, that introduced me to my first belting and ended my career as a nudist.

At the age of six months, I had developed a mastoid behind my ear[3] and they hadn't discovered it until almost too late. Mother called the doctor who operated on me on the kitchen table and saved my life. Tragically, it was not until age five, when one day I was playing on the front porch and put my hand over my right eye and told my dad that, when I did that, everything was black. At first, my dad thought I was joking, but, finally, when I kept telling him, he took me to an eye doctor. They found that indeed I was blind in my left eye. After examination, it was discovered that the operation at six months had not only removed the mastoid but, in the process, had cut the optic nerve to my left eye. It was later found to be irreparable and so, to this day, I am blind in the left eye. However, I think that it was a blessing in disguise. Although in the years ahead it kept me from an athletic career (boxing or professional baseball) and also from the Service, I have always striven a little harder to prove I was as good as the next fellow, and perhaps that has helped me in my career as an entertainer.

In 1928, Dad and Mom put a down-payment on a big white house in Garden City, Michigan. We moved there,[4] and here are my first recollections of the evenings when Daddy would play his mandolin and Mom the piano, and we as a family spent many happy moments listening to the Kentucky mountain songs that Dad played and the English folk songs that Mama played. I also remember the winters of Michigan. In those years, we had a lot of snow, and many mornings I remember arising early to help Dad shovel the path from the back door to the garage. Sometimes, it was so deep, we would tunnel all the way to the garage. I can remember when the family would go into the city on Saturday. Sometimes, the

---

3 Of course, one doesn't develop a mastoid, which is a bone of the inner ear. Haley likely had mastoiditis.

4 The April 1930 U.S. census lists the family as still living in Highland Park, so their house move was later than Haley says here.

snow on each side of the road was piled higher than the car. Dad sometimes remarked, "The snow was ass deep to a thirty-foot Indian."

These, of course, were the depression years of 1929-1932. And I remember that we, like everyone else, had fewer and fewer luxuries and Daddy lost his job. In 1932, Mom and Dad called a family meeting to tell Peggy and me we were going to sell our home and move to Pennsylvania. We were sad to leave, but, as kids, it was a big adventure for us. Later, I realized that, like a lot of folks at that time, Dad had lost the house and everything, so we packed our few belongings that we could take, and Maude, Will, Peggy, and Billy started out in Dad's Model T Ford across the mountains to Pennsylvania where Dad hoped to find work and start out again. We rented a small farmhouse near Booths Corner, Pennsylvania. As I had finished second grade in Michigan, I started in the third grade.[5] Dad could not find work right away, and I remember how we all pulled together. Daddy took a job digging ditches, farm work, and other odd jobs to keep us eating. But everyone was in the same boat in those years.

We were close as a family, and, between our own garden, raising chickens, and my paper route, we always managed to have food on the table. But mostly I remember the evenings when I would enjoy listening to Dad and Mom, our songs, and, on the radio: Big Slim[6] from WWVA in Wheeling, West Virginia, the *Grand Ole Opry* from Nashville, and *The National Barn Dance* from Chicago. Hence, I began to sing some of the songs, secretly practiced in front of a mirror, and I decided, at the age of seven, [that] I would someday be a singer. I remember looking at a guitar in a Sears Roebuck catalog and wishing that I could have one, but, as times were so hard for our family then, I knew it was impossible, so I got the idea to draw a guitar with strings on a big piece of cardboard. I did this, and for weeks I would secretly sneak out of the house, go out behind the barn, set up my stage, and practice my show. One afternoon, my sister, Peggy, caught my act, so to speak. She told Mom and Dad and they encouraged me to continue. I still remember my dad as he said, "Billy, you really want a guitar, don't you?" The Lord only knows how many hours Daddy must have worked, but that Christmas morning, under our tree, there was my first guitar.[7] In the days and months that followed, every spare moment that I could find after school was out and the chores were done were spent practicing my

---

5 Bill's school record has survived. He was in Grade 3 in 1933-34 attaining excellent marks in all subjects. The following two years he spent at the school at Booths Corner, with his attainment declining each year.

6 Hamilton (Harry) C. Aliff, "The Lonesome Cowboy."

7 There is evidence, in the form of a printed program, of Bill singing with guitar at the Bethel Junior Baseball Team entertainment in April 1938, which would date this episode to Christmas 1937 or earlier. (Elizabeth McCarrick and Faith McCarrick Diskin, Bethel Township, Delaware County (Arcadia Publishing, 2013).

guitar and singing all the tunes that I had heard Mom and Dad do.

These were good years for me. I proceeded through the third, fourth, and fifth grades, playing baseball, and I learned to smoke corn silk wrapped in newspaper, which made us kids violently sick, but it was the thing to do, and we did. Daddy, by now, had begun to work for The American Viscose Company[8] and we moved to Johnsons Corner, Pennsylvania.[9] There we rented a small farm. We had a cow, a horse, and raised chickens. Dad went all out raising vegetables, strawberries, and asparagus. I spent my days after school and weekends milking the cows, cultivating the fields, collecting the eggs, feeding the chickens, and daydreaming of the day I would be a singer and entertainer.

By now, I had progressed to singing for my friends at parties and for anyone who would listen to me. Those were the days of the outdoor hillbilly parks, where, on Sundays, local promoters would bring in country entertainers to sing on outdoor stages and those parks were a big success. The one nearest to our home was Sunset Park. Dad took us there on Sundays. We would pack a picnic lunch and spend the day listening to such greats as Roy Acuff, Ernest Tubb, and Hank Williams, etc.[10] If I had been fired with ambition before this, as I watched Hank Williams sing, I was positive that this was what I wanted to do.

At Johnsons Corner I completed sixth, seventh, and eighth grades in school. Along with my friends Maggie Roop,[11] Joe Ballantine, and Giggles Thompson, I passed the magical time of eleven, twelve and thirteen years. We walked, swam in the Brandywine River, and smoked my first cigar (again, we all got sick) so that ended that. Playing baseball, finding out about girls (*The Rustle in the Bushes* by Izzy Oner).[12] By now, I had become quite a businessman. Dad had become ill again[13] and could not work, so the job of helping the family was on my shoulders. I had a paper route and sold magazines like the *Saturday Evening Post*. I used to go door to door selling tomatoes, vegetables, strawberries, or anything that would make money for our family. In 1939, Dad and Mom bought a little plot of ground,

---

8 The American division of the British firm Courtaulds, established in 1909, a manufacturer of rayon and other synthetic fibers. The 1940 Census records Will's profession as "oiler" in silk manufacturing.

9 The1940 U.S. Census record indicates that the move took place sometime between 1935 and 1940.

10 Sunset Park opened in 1940, when Bill was already fifteen. It is doubtful that he would have seen Hank as early as he suggests here. Williams was not a national phenomenon until 1947 and his earliest verified appearance at Sunset Park was in 1950.

11 The Roop family lived next door to the Haleys according to the 1940 Census. "Maggie" was probably Elsie Marie, who is listed as being 11 years old.

12 Probably a play on the phrase, "Is he on her?"

13 The 1940 Census records that Will had worked only twenty weeks in the previous year. The reason for this might well be revealed in his death certificate (1955), in which manic-depressive psychosis (bipolar disorder) causing general marasmus (malnutrition), leading to bilateral pneumonitis are cited as the cause of death.

again at Booths Corner, and, for the first time since coming from Michigan, we began to work our own ground again.[14] I entered high school at Upper Chichester School in Boothwyn, Pennsylvania.[15] During 1939, 1940, and 1941, Dad's health again improved, and he was able to return to work and I to my schooling, guitar practice, girls, and dreams in general.

In the summer of 1941, Dad's nerves once again took a turn for the worse and he could not work. Even though I had completed the eleventh grade in school by then, we made the decision that I would have to leave school and go to work. I got a job near home, bottling spring water at the Bethel Springs Water Company. I worked forty hours a week for thirty cents an hour. But the $12 kept the wolf away from our door. Later that year, I took a second job working for Baldwin Locomotive Works in Chester, Pennsylvania. In December of 1941 came Pearl Harbor and the Second World War. My two buddies and I went to enlist. They were both accepted; I was rejected because of my eyesight. This was crushing news for me. I still remember my mother talking for hours in an effort to cheer me up. Although I worked in defense plants, did hundreds of shows for U.S.O. and service bases, the disappointment I felt at that time was a long time wearing off.[16]

Close to our home was a Friday-night auction sale ground,[17] and every Friday night merchants from miles around would bring their wares to sell. It was a big social event. People from the area gathered each Friday to buy food, vegetables, and clothing. There was a carnival atmosphere. I befriended a man who had concessions at the auction. His name was Bill Ormsbee. Bill offered me a job working in one of the concessions stands. One Friday night, Bill asked me to sing with my guitar, as it would attract customers to the games. At first, I was too bashful, and he convinced me to sing over his microphone in his little office, which I did.[18] After a few Friday nights of this, we set up a little stage, and I began

---

14 Given that the family was still living at Johnsons Corner in April 1940, this must have happened later.

15 The April 1940 Census indicates that Bill had completed Grade 8, but that he had not been to school since March 1, 1940. With Will unable to work, Bill, Jr. might have had to contribute to the family income and not attend high school at all. The eyewitness account of Amy Clark, an early girlfriend of Bill's (in an unpublished interview with Haley's son and biographer, Bill Haley, Jr.) indicates that Grade 8 was the last he attended.

16 Bill registered for the draft on July 7, 1943, the day after his eighteenth birthday. His draft registration gave his place of employment as the Baldwin Locomotive works in Eddystone. The registrar noted him as being 5'11.5".

17 Phillips Auction Sale at the Booths Corner Farmers Market, opened by local farmer Earl Phillips in the 1930s.

18 One legend suggests that, either as a prank or to circumvent Bill's shyness, Ormsbee secretly turned on the microphone that fed numerous loudspeakers throughout the building. Bill reportedly gave renditions of "Has Anybody Seen My Gal" and "My Old Kentucky Home." It is a good story, but it seems unlikely that Bill would have been overcome by shyness, given that his first known appearance in public had been in 1938, and (in his own words above), he would sing for "anyone who would listen to me."

to perform a few songs, along with a very dear old gentleman, Uncle Ben Guthrie, who played fiddle. For our performance we received $10 every Friday night and I was finally on my way.

Authors' Interlude: Ben "Pop" Guthrie was a local carpenter and former vaudevillian many years Haley's senior. Guthrie taught young Bill how to intersperse cornball humor between musical numbers and the two of them, profoundly mismatched in age, would exchange insults during their show to the delight of their audiences. Many years later, in 1969, Bill Haley gave Patrick Malynn (his manager during his latter-day career) and Hugh McCallum a private performance of his slapstick act from these early days. Hugh wrote about the evening:

> Bill backs up to the chair, sits down and then leaps into the air having sat on an imaginary tin-tack; for our benefit Bill gave us a 'running commentary' on the act — he brushes the chair with his hand, turns and smiles to the "audience" and stutters "h...ah...m'sorry about that..." he sits, gets the guitar in the right position and then without speaking again starts on a real fast guitar instrumental piece which is obviously designed to look "flash" — after perhaps 30 seconds he stops — looks at the audience and says "you ain't heard nuthin' yet" which he said was always received with laughter!! He then continues through the instrumental the name of which Bill couldn't recall; suddenly Bill plays a whopping huge "fluff" 'plunk" smiles shyly towards the audience — looks at the finger nails on his left hand and pretends to tear a raggy nail off with his teeth — and spits out a small piece of card which he had earlier slipped into the corner of this mouth which represents the nail!!![19]

---

19 *Haley News* Issue No.70, Bill Haley International Fan Club, October 1969.

As will be revealed in the next chapter, it is believed that Bill's first public appearance was on June 1, 1941 as part of an "amateur night." This followed an afternoon performance by Roy Rogers (misspelled "Rodgers" in the poster) at Radio Park. This advertisement has been clipped from the *Delaware County Daily Times* of May 31st.

CHAPTER 2
The Early Learning Years (1943-1947)

Authors' Introduction: This chapter covers Bill's formative years as a musician. The period was crowded with experiences, and Bill's memory does not always correspond to the evidence that can be found in documentary sources. We have let Bill's narrative stand, adding interludes which reconcile his story with known facts.

The job of working the concessions at the Booths Corner auction grounds also led to working for Mr. [Bill] Ormsbee on Sundays at a nearby outdoor country music park called Radio Park,[1] which was operated by Cousin Lee, a local radio personality (WDEL Wilmington, Delaware).[2] I continued singing and working concessions every Friday night at the auction and, on Sundays, working at Radio Park.

One Sunday, one of Cousin Lee's musicians did not show up, and the people suggested to Cousin Lee that he use me to fill in. I filled in on two shows, and the hometown crowd applauded enough to prompt Cousin Lee to offer me a job working for him six days a week on his 6:00 a.m. radio show[3] and personal appearances also. For this the salary was to be $30.00 a week. I rushed home to tell Mom, Dad, and Sister. They all agreed that I should try it since it was on the radio and a start for me. However, $30.00 was less money than I had been making, but as Lee agreed to let me sell photos, I picked up some extra money doing that. That was standard procedure for Country artists in those days. You bought 8 x 10 photos by the thousand and sold them, autographed, at a profit. That has kept many a poor entertainer from starving, because, many times, the only eating money would be derived from sales of the songbooks, pictures, etc.

---

1 Route 419, between Booth's Corner and Johnson's Corner.

2 "Cousin Lee," Arley Basil Ellsworth (1896-1971), was a former boxer and evangelist who traveled with Billy Sunday. He went into the radio business and formed a seven-piece band, Cousin Lee and His Boys.

3 Cousin Lee's 15-minute daily show went out at 7:30 a.m.

Cousin Lee (2nd on left in the back row) with His Boys (and including a few girls). Date unknown.

Authors' Interlude: Bill Haley's own account of joining Cousin Lee's band is at odds with two other eye-witness accounts. The first suggests that Bill's debut at Radio Park was on Sunday June 1, 1941 during an "amateur night" following the afternoon show, in which Roy Rogers made his first appearance in the East. Jack Howard, who would later become a close associate of Bill's, recalled,

> I went back to the park operator (Cousin Lee) and finally convinced him to give Bill a chance to perform on his stage... Over 10,000 people had come to see the first appearance in the East of Roy Rogers and the Sons of the Pioneers in person... Bill was called up to do a few numbers. He was so excited and elated that he had a hard time trying to make the words come out, but after the first couple of lines he began to feel that 10,000 people were no different than a hundred."[4]

Amy Clark, Bill's girlfriend at the time, would tell Bill Haley, Jr. that, "Roy Rogers was on the program one time with his horse Trigger... Bill was on that day too. It was quite a show. But I couldn't get over that they let Bill sing, as part of their two-hour show at WDEL.... It was special."[5] There is another factual conflict to point out. Newspaper accounts of the Rogers appearance make no mention of the Sons of the Pioneers accompanying him. Rogers left the group in 1937 to pursue his solo career as a movie cowboy. His horse, Trigger, became his sidekick only after that point. Therefore, Clark's account is correct; Howard's is not.

4 John W. Haley and John von Hoelle, *Sound and Glory: The Incredible Story of Bill Haley, the Father of Rock 'n' Roll and the Music That Shook the World* (Dyne American Publications, Inc., 1990), p.31.

5 Bill Haley, Jr., from unpublished notes.

LENAPE PARK

On the Historic Brandywine
Above Chadd's Ford, Pa.

JOHN V. GIBNEY, Manager
Phone Lenape 2386

TEXAS RANGERS

Hit of Old Fiddlers'
Picnic, in a concert

SUNDAY EVENING, AUG. 13

LENAPE SWIMMING POOL

Fun and Recreation with
Your Friends

Amusements for Kiddies
and Grown-ups, Too.

Free Table and Benches
for Family Picnics

An ad for the Texas Rangers' second show at Lenape Park, 1944.

The authors' research has not unearthed any more public appearances until a solo perform-ance at Willow Grove on June 18, 1944. Titled "Jest for Laffs" it seems to have been a comedy act. On August 5th, Bill and The Texas Rangers made an unadvertised appearance at The Old Fiddlers' Picnic in Lenape Park. A few days later, they would take on twice-weekly appearances at Phillips' Auction Mart (Booth's Corner) until September 3rd.

Thus, I packed my first suitcase and with my guitar, cowboy hat, and dreams, I moved (seven miles) to Wilmington, Delaware, to a rented room. Mama cried and Daddy was full of advice and I was full of dreams as off I went.

We would be at the studio at 5:30 a.m. all set up, rehearsed, and ready, so, when the red light came on, we would greet the airwaves with our music. Cousin Lee was an older gentleman and quite a master talker, and the first few months flew by for me. I studied every move and mannerism of the entertainer until I had learned a small part of what made him so successful, both as announcer and bandleader. Little did I know that I would still be watching and learning from other entertainers thirty-five years later. My big song in those days was "Put Me in Your Pocket,"[6] and, as it was the most requested song on the show, it wasn't long before I began to get a real big head and thought it was I who was the star, and not Cousin Lee. One morning, I arrived at the studio at 6:05 a.m. and Lee and the band were already on the air. I walked in the studio and began taking my guitar out of the case. As I did this, Lee finished singing his song, and on the air said, "Well, Silver

---

6 "Put Me in Your Pocket" is a sentimental country waltz often attributed to the Wilburn Brothers, though they did not record it until 1950. It was written by W. "Pappy" Lee O'Daniel and first recorded in 1933 by his Light Crust Doughboys, a Texas western swing band that gave a start for other western swing greats such as Bob Wills, Tommy Duncan, and Milton Brown.

Yodeling Bill[7] has finally arrived in the studio and, Bill, you won't have to take your guitar out of the case. You won't be needing it here this morning." I came to the microphone and said "Why not, Lee?" He answered, "Because you're fired." I left the studio stunned and heartbroken, but later realized that Lee had taught me a lesson that I remember to this day. My hat size decreased back to normal and I was a singer without a job.

Authors' Interlude: Bill's time with Cousin Lee was short and, in November 1944, he is advertised as a solo performer for a show at the Harrowgate Theatre on Kensington Avenue in Philadelphia. *Billboard* (December 16) reported that "Jack Howard and his cowboy stage show, featuring Kitty O'Brien and Bill Haley, are playing Saturday matinee at neighborhood movie houses in Philadelphia ... Kitty O'Brien, the singing cowgirl and protégé of Jack Howard, music publisher of cowboy songs in Philadelphia, has signed a contract with Hit Records, bringing folk tunes to that label for the first time. Kitty, who is playing theaters around Philadelphia with Yodeling Bill Haley, has written a song titled 'Could You Mend a Broken Heart?'"

Jack Howard was born on October 17, 1913, and, in 1943, established Jack Howard Publications, Inc. ("The Cowboy Publisher"). He functioned as manager and booking agent in the early years of Bill's career and, founded Cowboy Records in March 1945. The uncorroborated story behind the label is that it was funded by a Mafia loan, and supplied free copies of its discs for Mafia-owned jukeboxes. Evidence of this can be found in surviving copies of Cowboy Records' artist contracts which stipulated that the first 5,000 discs pressed would be "royalty free." In April 1950, Howard engaged Jolly Joyce as Bill Haley's booking agent, and would become an employee of Bill's corporation in the mid-1950s. When the corporation folded in 1963, he took over the management of Haley's music publishing and record labels. Until his death on December 1, 1976, he ran the Arcade Music Center, a small music shop at 2753 Kensington Avenue in Philadelphia.

I had been rooming with a fiddle player called Brother Wayne Wright, and, for a few days, I just sat in my room and sulked. I didn't dare go back home a failure, and also I had been taking home $20 every week to help out the family. I was really in a bad way. Wayne was not happy working in Wilmington and so we decided to team up as Brother Wayne and Yodeling Bill, the Red River Boys, just fiddle and guitar. Wayne came from North Carolina and was a great guy. We

---

7 This is the first mention in his autobiography of Haley as a yodeler. Young Bill was a self-taught yodeler, modelling the greats of the day, including Roy Rogers and the legendary Elton Britt, whom Haley finally met one day at Radio Park. Approaching him with a beer in his hand, the youngster asked the master for yodeling advice. Britt told him, "Son, never drink beer if you want to be a good yodeler. It gives you gas. A first-class yodeler only drinks whiskey! And if you can't afford good whiskey, drink port wine" (Haley and von Hoelle, p. 33). As much drinking as Haley did in future years, he never had a beer before a performance for fear of a hearty belch while singing.

hit it off right away. We went to Bridgeton, New Jersey, in Wayne's old car and auditioned there for WSNJ.[8] They agreed to give us thirty minutes a day and we would receive no salary, but were allowed to advertise our personal appearances and to sell pictures and song books, etc., on the air, and keep the proceeds. So, we started broadcasting. Wayne did the M.C. work, and he and I did duets, instrumentals, and I did the yodeling. We advertised that we were available for shows for local VFW,[9] church functions, fire companies, etc., on a percentage hour. We rented a room in a boarding house and began to plug away. However, our finances ran low after about six or eight weeks of this and our diet of peanut butter and bread began to get old. Wayne decided to take a day job and he began to lose interest. I began to think of greener pastures. I read in *Billboard* that a man named Fleetwood Jack was looking for a guitar player to work with his band. I wrote and received a reply asking me to come to Downingtown, Pennsylvania, to his home to audition.

I returned home to talk to Mom and Dad and they gave me enough money for the bus ride. I got off in Downingtown and began to ask directions and found out that Jack's home was about five miles out of town. So I, with my guitar, walked the five miles. When I arrived, I found Fleetwood Jack to be a grand man, full of ambition, ideas, and plans — but no money. The offer was a percentage of what he made. But as it was a chance to learn, travel, and sing, I decided to go along. We left for WMRF in Lewistown, Pennsylvania, about eighty miles away from my home. Once again, we started daily broadcasts and Jack made plans to open an outdoor country music park, again on a percentage basis. I found myself, along with Jack and Marjorie Lee (Jack's daughter), who sang with the band, working all day cleaning up the park, painting and doing odd jobs and broadcasting thirty minutes a day.[10] Again eating peanut butter and bread with an occasional hamburger. I didn't make much money that summer, but, as they say, necessity is the

---

8 Wayne William Wright (1922-1986) was a fiddler in the Cousin Lee band. Wright was a huge supporter of, and collaborator with, Haley over a period of five years. When Haley's luck was down, Wright and his wife would offer a bed and a home-cooked meal. The decision to team up as The Red River Boys probably dates from about January, 1945.

9 Veterans of Foreign Wars, who have gathering places ("posts") in cities and towns across the U.S.

10 The May 12, 1945, *Billboard* provides insight into the make-up of Fleetwood Jack's troupe. "Fleetwood Jack and His Nevada Ranch Gang are to be featured at the K.P. Ranch in Kishacoquillas Park in Lewistown, PA, starting May 20th and operating every Saturday night with the Mifflin Country Barn Dance Jamboree and stage-shows. The Nevada Ranch Gang includes Fleetwood Jack, manager and emcee, Fiddlin' Dusty, Marjorie Lee, Connie Castiglio and Conly Forrester, known as the Nevada Kid. Also joining the group for personal appearances and jamborees are The Red River Boys, with Brother Wayne, Yodelin' Bill Haley, and Slim Bradley, who have been the top-notch attraction on WSNJ, Bridgeton, NJ. The group will be heard over WMRF, Lewistown." Bill was also advertised as part of the show for an appearance with Fleetwood Jack for a one-night show at the Memorial Park Pavilion, Williamsport, Pennsylvania, in July 1945. At this time, he would also appear under the moniker "Smiling Jack, the Rambling Yodeler."

mother of invention and, somehow, we had to do seven or eight forty-minute shows starting at 2:00 p.m. The last show began at 10:00 p.m. I volunteered to do two shows all by myself, so I got experience being my own M.C., doing comedy, singing, and yodeling but, most of all, I gained more confidence in my ability to perform. I remember some of my awful comedy routine, talking about my girl: "I met her at a dance, and she asked me to take her home. I asked her, 'What's in it for me?' She replied, 'Just a little dust from dancing.' She was so skinny, if she put on a white dress and drank a Coca-Cola, she'd look like a thermometer running up and down! I bought her a bicycle and then I caught her peddling it all over town. I proposed to her in a garage and she couldn't back out," etc., etc.

"Big Slim" (Harry C. McAuliffe) the Lone Cowboy, who appeared for nearly thirty years on the "World's Original Jamboree" at WWVA in Wheeling, West Virginia.

Somehow the summer passed, and, one Sunday, our star of the day was Big Slim, The Lone Cowboy from WWVA, Wheeling, West Virginia. Slim was one of my heroes, and he was very kind to me. He gave me advice and, as I told him of my hopes and ambitions, he said that he had heard of a new Saturday network show that was starting called *Hoosier Hop* from WOWO in Fort Wayne, Indiana. He knew that a group called the Down Homers were looking for a man to sing tenor in their quartets and trios, and play guitar, yodel, and do solos. Slim said he thought that I was perfect for the job and he recommended me. He gave me the address to write to them and so I did. A week later, I received a telegram offering me the job plus train fare to Fort Wayne, Indiana, and an audition date. I said a sad farewell to Fleetwood Jack, to Marjorie, and the band. I returned home to spend a few days with my mom and dad and sister, Peggy. I also got clean clothes and a few good meals and, once again, they gave me some money and their good wishes. I boarded the train for Indiana. That was really my first trip (eight hundred miles) away from home, and it took twenty hours. I rode through the night with doubts and fears and misgivings crowding my mind.

Arriving in Fort Wayne about noon the next day, I stepped down from the train, not knowing what to expect. As I waited, one by one, everyone left the platform and I was all alone. I waited for a while and, when nobody came to meet me, I telephoned WOWO radio and asked for Shorty Cook or Guy Campbell, the names on the telegram. In a moment, a voice came on the phone and said, "Hello, this is Shorty."

I replied, "This is Bill Haley."

He said, "Where are you?"

I replied, "I am at the train station."

"Well," he replied, "we were there to meet the train and we didn't see you. Wait there and we will come to pick you up."

So, I waited and, in a few minutes, two men arrived and looked all around and started to leave. I called to them and asked if they were the Down Homers. "Yes," replied the shorter one. "I'm Shorty Cook, and who are you?" I replied, "Bill Haley."

The "Other" Bill Haley.

A blank stare appeared on both of their faces. Shorty said, "Well, you are not the Bill Haley we know." They went on to explain that there was another entertainer, about forty-five years old, from the Midwest named Bill Haley. That was the man they thought they were hiring for the job. They said they were sorry for the mistake and offered to buy my ticket back to Pennsylvania. I asked them to let me audition anyway, explaining that, after the long trip and quitting the other group, I felt I should have a chance at least. They finally agreed and we went to WOWO studios.

They put me in a studio and said, "Sing." After a few songs and yodel tunes, they came in and agreed to hire me and I became a Down Homer.[11]

Authors' Interlude: "The Other Bill Haley." Researching Haley's early career sent us up a few blind alleys as we discovered newspaper references from the late 1930s and early 1940s to a yodeler named Bill Haley who might, or might not, have been "our man." The information that unlocked the puzzle was Bill's revelation that the Down Homers had given him the job in the belief that he was someone else, a Bill Haley who was already well-known and established in Indiana as a yodeler. We re-examined the various morsels of information and concluded that there was a significant "other" Bill Haley working in the same field at the same time, in the same geographical area, so it was a lucky case of mistaken identity that led to "our" Bill Haley's first big professional break with the Down Homers.

In May 2013, the *Kentucky Explorer* published a short biography of the "other" Bill Haley, written by Joe Fothergill. This Bill Haley was born in 1909 in Blue Lick, Kentucky and was a first cousin of Red Foley, with whom he formed a yodeling duo. In 1931, they took jobs on different radio stations, Red on WLS in Chicago, and Bill on WCKY, which served Covington, Kentucky and adjacent Cincinnati, Ohio.

In 1937, this Bill Haley was working on KMOX in St. Louis, Missouri, and was runner-up in the National Fiddlers' Association national yodeling competition. In 1941, he was working under the moniker "The Singing Sherrif" and had moved to KFRU, Columbia, Missouri, leading a band called the Hot Peppers. In 1942, he was often being billed as "Yodelin' Bill Haley," having moved to WIBC, Indianapolis, Indiana, and building a reputation as an MC as well as a performer – hence the Down Homers being familiar with him. Calling himself "Neighbor Bill Haley," he challenged "Barefoot Ozzie" at a national hillbilly jamboree and string band, fiddlers, and yodelers contest in Muncie, Indiana, on March 14, 1943. A few years later, "our" Bill Haley would claim to have been the Indiana State Yodeling Champion in 1946, and, in an interview with Canadian broadcaster Red Robinson in 1966, he escalated the claim by saying, "In 1946, I won the National Yodeling Championship with guys like Elton Britt and Kenny Roberts."[12] Our attempts to find confirmation of any such achievement have revealed no evidence, and the possibility arises that our Bill simply allowed people to think it was he who had been a champion yodeler, and that he was therefore just basking in the "other" Bill Haley's glory. Furthermore, none of the known promotional material from this part of Bill's career makes any claims to champion status.

A new page in my learning started for me. The Down Homers was a group patterned after the Sons of the Pioneers and I had to sing tenor in the quartet on

---

11 In a recorded message to the 1999 meeting of the Vogue Picture Records Collectors' Association, Kenny Roberts described how he tutored Bill at this point in his career: "[Haley] was a fairly good yodeler and I taught him some of my yodels before I left and I taught him to play the upright bass fiddle, too, and he sang and yodeled in the group when I left for the navy, of course." While Roberts probably wanted to be known as the man who taught Bill Haley how to yodel, it seems unlikely that they met at this juncture. The comings and goings in bands such as the Down Homers were regularly reported in *Billboard* and other specialist publications. These suggest that the first replacement for Kenny Roberts was Bill Stallard (who also worked under the name Billy Starr). He, in turn, was replaced by Don Crenshaw, who was later replaced by Bill Haley.

12 The *Bill Haley Tapes* (Jerden Records, JRCD 7023, 1995).

tunes like "Tumbling Tumbleweeds," "Cool Water,"[13] "Apache Trail." etc., but Shorty and Guy Campbell were indeed veteran professional entertainers and, after a few weeks, I was holding my own. The *Hoosier Hop* was on the Blue Network, as it was called then. Later changed, I believe, to ABC, but, in any case, Mom and Dad could listen in on Saturday nights and hear the Down Homers and, even though I was far away, I would receive letters from home with encouragement and criticism, depending on my performance on the show.

After about seven or eight months (happy times, learning times), I was informed that Kenny Roberts was returning from the Navy and would soon be rejoining the Down Homers. Kenny was a great guy, a fine entertainer and yodeler. When he had left for the Service, it had created the job for me and, even though Shorty and Guy wanted me to stay, I by now had itchy feet to see the big wide world.

Authors' Interlude: Kenny Roberts, the Down Homers' yodeler and high tenor voice, was born in 1926 and became eligible for the U.S. draft on his eighteenth birthday (October 14, 1944). *Cowboy Music World* reported that Roberts received his questionnaire three weeks after his birthday, and that his physical had been set for December 7, 1944. He joined the U.S. Navy shortly thereafter, leaving a vacancy in the band. The magazine followed up with a report in its January/February 1945 issue that Roberts was serving at Sampson, N.Y. Bill Stallard was the first replacement for Roberts. The January 1945 *Cowboy Music World* reported that Don Crenshaw had joined the Down Homers, the March 3, 1945 *Billboard* describing him as a specialist yodeler who had been discharged from the Navy after twenty-one months of service and rejoined the Down Homers on WOWO. *Cowboy Music World*, in its July-August issue, reported that Roberts had been given a medical discharge and would be back with the Down Homers "in a few weeks," after a spell in hospital. The September/October issue confirmed that Roberts, as well as Lloyd Cornell, was back in the band. Bill was presumably no longer a member at this point. In November 1945, Haley is listed as "Yodelin' Bill from WSNJ, Bridgeton, N.J." in an advertisement for the Blue Hen Ramblers in York, Pennsylvania. We are left with the likely conclusion that Bill was a member of the Down Homers between July 1945 (at the earliest) and October 1945 (at the latest); that is, between his known appearance with Fleetwood Jack and the likely date of Roberts's return.

So, when Kenny returned, I once again rejoined Brother Wayne, and we went to Jacksonville, Illinois, to WLDS, and once again Brother Wayne and Yodelin' Bill tried to start our little operation. We represented the same formula we had earlier in Bridgeton, New Jersey. We worked hard, promoting and rehearsing, but things were not to be, and, as Wayne was then thinking of marriage and settling down, we once again parted. After about four months, Wayne returned to the east, and I headed west.

---

13 Bill is heard singing this song with the Down Homers on a 1946 transcription disc in the Bear Family boxed CD set, *Rock 'n' Roll Arrives...The REAL Birth of Rock 'n' Roll 1946-1954* (BCD16509). Bill fails to mention that, on this same disc, he sings a solo yodel number, "She Taught Me to Yodel."

Authors' Interlude: The Range Drifters were listed in the WLDS broadcasting schedule from February until April 9, 1947. The next section of Bill's narrative is then impossible to corroborate with published information. Singing for his supper and riding the freight trains, he was definitely "flying below the radar." However, it seems likely that what he describes next probably happened earlier than his time in Jacksonville.

I remember, during this time period in Jacksonville, Illinois, that I became more and more aware of the rhythm part of the music we were playing. My forte in music during that period was yodeling, and I knew, if I were ever to become a success, I would have to develop something different. So, as I listened to the fiddle tunes and watched the way Wayne would syncopate, I tried to pattern my yodeling after this. I spent hours with two spoons drumming on a table or chair, while yodeling to the different rhythms, and so the beginnings of my style began changing from strict country singing to rhythm, more suitable to the yodeling technique I was trying to develop.

As Jacksonville, Illinois, was only one hundred miles from St. Louis, I first went to St. Louis hoping to land a job. However, aside from a few nights as a sideman with pick-up groups, I had no luck. Money was very low, so I began "busking," a term used in those days meaning singing for your supper, so to speak. I would pick a small diner or restaurant and go in and approach the owner and offer to sing a few songs if he would allow me to pass the hat afterwards. Sometimes they would refuse, but usually would work out and be good for two or three dollars, plus supper. This was not unusual in those days, because of the large number of musicians who travelled.

I was hitch-hiking down Highway 66 on my way to Oklahoma City one day and decided to try to get a ride near a railroad crossing, since traffic had to slow for the crossing and thus presenting a better chance to get a ride. I met a man sitting beside the tracks and we began to talk. I found that he was also on his way to Oklahoma, and he asked me why was I hitch-hiking instead of riding the freight. I replied that I had never ridden a freight and didn't know how. He said that a train would be coming through shortly and, if I wanted, I could go with him. The train came through and stopped nearby to load. We climbed into an empty box car, and a new form of transportation was introduced to me. Tommy, my new friend, and I rode to the outskirts of Oklahoma City and parted there. I used the free train rides quite a few times in the next two years. They were cold and dusty, and you had to be ever on the watch for the railroad detectives. But, whether I was just lucky, or all the stories I've read about how bad a breed these men were, I don't know. The few that I saw were not a bad sort.

Over the next six months, I was to repeat the same routine many times through Missouri and Oklahoma, and finally headed for Shreveport, Louisiana. I had heard so much about *The Louisiana Hayride* and hoped to get on this show. I had no luck there. There was a waiting list of musicians anxious for a chance, since that was one of the premier Country shows at that time.[14] While in Louisiana, I got a chance work a three-night date with a local group. In the group was a black blues guitar picker named Willard Brown.[15] Willard was from New Orleans, and we struck up a friendship immediately. I had never heard this kind of blues. After the three-day gig, Willard was going back to New Orleans and said, if I wanted to go with him, I was welcome. So off we went, and for the next two months I listened, watched, and admired the Dixieland black blues plus white blues styles of the deep-South musicians. I had also become a fan of Bob Wills and the Texas Playboys, so, after a few goodbyes, I once again hit the rails and decided to try around the Dallas, Fort Worth area where Western Swing was predominant at that time. Whether it was my lack of experience at that time or itchy feet, I did not seem to be able to find the right spot, so drifted on through to Nebraska.[16] One night, as I was singing for my supper in a small restaurant, a short fat gentleman with grey hair approached me. After I finished, he offered to buy my supper and said he had a deal to offer me. He said, "My name is Doc Protho,[17] and I'm the owner of a medicine show. I travel this broad land and distribute a medicine to help all people, and I need a bright young man with talent like yours to assist me." After dinner, Doc took me back to see his operation, which consisted of an old pickup hooked on to an early version of what we know now as a house trailer. The complete back of the trailer folded down outward and

---

14 This recollection would have to be incorrect. The show did not start broadcasting on Shreveport's KWKH until April 3, 1948, and had no previous life as a non-broadcasted live performance series. (In 1948, it became a breakout forum for a budding Hank Williams and, in 1954, for newcomer Elvis Presley.)

15 Apprenticeship with black musicians was a significant factor in the development of the most legendary country music pioneers and should debunk any notion of country music being simply "white" music. The "Father of Country Music," Jimmie Rodgers, learned directly from the black musicians/rail workers of his native Mississippi. Bluegrass founder Bill Monroe openly credited Kentucky black musician Arnold Shultz with the blues influence in his music, and Hank Williams apprenticed with Rufus "Tee Tot" Payne in Alabama, influencing songs like his first big hit in 1947, the bluesy "Move it on Over." Like the other "Bill Haley," there are a number of southern blues singers named "Willard Brown" or "Willie Brown," the most famous of whom (1900-1952) was from the Mississippi Delta and shared the stature of his contemporaries Charley Patton and Son House. He was probably not the bluesman young Bill gigged with.

16 Bill's testimony here is notable. Many rock histories label Bill Haley and the Comets as a Northeastern "western swing band," probably basing their designation on the instrumentation and country roots of the group, which certainly bears a resemblance to Bob Wills, Milton Brown, Spade Cooley, and other Texas swing bands of the 1930s and '40s. It is significant that Haley did not gain traction in the Dallas/Fort Worth area and, from his later description, based his style and instrumentation on other factors. The western swing association may be reinforced by the emergence of the western swing/jump blues band, Asleep at the Wheel, that was founded in Chester, Pennsylvania, (Bill Haley country) in the 1970s.

17 The name used by this character is uncertain. He was named as "Doc Protheroe." in a much earlier mini biography of Bill which appeared on LP sleeves in the 1950s. His true identity, of course, is unknown.

became a small stage. He had two speakers, one on either side of the back of the trailer plus one on the roof, and a microphone permanently installed on the floor. As soon as he loosened the rope inside the trailer, the back would drop down, complete with small spotlight. Doc could flip the switch of an amplifier and, in record time, the stage was ready for his pitch — or show, as he called it. He explained that in a matter of thirty seconds he could close the stage and be ready to be off. At first, I did not understand the need for all this hurry, but, after watching him work a few nights, I began to understand that what he was doing was sometimes frowned on by dissatisfied clients or the local authorities, thus the need to exit town in a hell of a hurry.

Being young and relatively innocent, I agreed to join him, since the chance to perform and get paid was very attractive to me. We would pull into the outskirts of a small town and Doc, while driving with one hand and a microphone in the other, would announce to one and all that, in thirty minutes, there would be a free show in the town square featuring Silver Yodeling Bill, well-known radio personality, admission free. He then would park in the town square, drop the back of the stage, and I would step out and proceed to sing and yodel until we had a good-size crowd of people. At that time, I would introduce Dr. Protho with a message for all of you and promise to sing more after Doc finished. While Doc went into his pitch I would step inside the trailer and get a cardboard box with fifty bottles of Doc Protho's Elixir of Life medicine and step out to the audience to await the moment to start to sell.

I suppose a good description of the Doctor would be a slight resemblance to W. C. Fields. He used the same type dress and similar hat, only his voice was deeper, and resembled that of a typical old-time preacher. He had a stuffed groundhog, to which he had added a few patches of fur and had sewn a fifth leg to the underbelly. He worked this like a puppet, and, as he started his pitch, this "animal" would cross back and forth on the table in front of him as he stroked its fur and pulled the strings out of sight of the audience to keep it moving. His pitch would open on a talk about how this little animal, that looked so much like an American groundhog, was really from the deepest dark jungle region of Africa. After a few jokes about the animal, he would tell how it had been raised in the tall sharp-bladed jungle grass, amid wild ferocious animals, and how strong and healthy these little animals had to be to survive. Then he would say that if you give this little animal an aspirin tablet, he would become ill in a matter of hours and even might die. Then into the pitch: "Ladies and gentlemen, let that be a lesson to you. Never take aspirin to relieve your suffering. Now, I, as a medical man, have discovered a magic tonic that has proven effective in the relief of almost all aches and pains known to modern man. If you are suffering from neuritis, neuralgia, backache, arthritis, lumbago, or any of the hundreds of miseries, then I would like for you to try Doc Protho's, supply available here tonight. The demand is so great for this product and, as I will neither allow anyone else to sell it, allow stores to handle it, as I personally guarantee, each and every bottle to be one hundred-percent effective, I can only sell fifty bottles to each community. Ordinarily, the price is $1.00 a bottle; but, for this first time, as an introductory offer to you fine folks, we are not asking $1.00, nor seventy-five cents. To prove to you and to introduce you to this miracle medicine, we are asking only fifty cents a bottle. Now, Silver Yodeling Bill will pass among you, and you'll get a chance to meet him and purchase your bottle of Doc Protho's Elixir of Life."

With that, I would appear among the crowd, with Doc urging them on with, "Hurry, hurry, there's only a few bottles left." Usually in a matter of ten minutes I had sold all fifty bottles, and then Doc would call a short intermission. As soon as I would return and pick up my guitar and start to sing, Doc would drive slowly away as I thanked them and waved goodbye. One-half block away, I had my instructions to step inside the trailer and pull the ropes to bring up the stage, and we were off to the next town. At first the fast exit puzzled me because they seemed like nice towns and Doc would always make forty miles or so before we would stop for the night. All my questions were evaded, but I was to receive the answers to all of them sooner than I or Doc had expected.

After about two weeks of this, we set up in a small town and Doc did his usual pitch. I was in the audience, feeling like a veteran, smiling at the girls, kidding everyone, giving an autograph here and there, and calling out: "Only a few bottles left, folks." I felt a hand on my shoulder, and, turning around with a bottle of "Elixir of Life" in my hand, I saw the biggest cowboy hat I had ever seen in my life, and under it a man with a big badge on his chest that said, "Sheriff." At the same moment, out of the corner of my eye, I saw "W. C. Fields" Protho disappearing off the trailer stage with another cowboy hat by his side. We ended up in the local jail where we spent the night. During that time, "Doc" explained to me that he didn't have a license to sell his miracle water, and, too late, he remembered he had been in this town three months before. That had been the wrong timing, since the sheriff was just waiting for him to return. Thus, I understand why we exited these towns so fast. The next morning, we were taken before the local judge, where we got a good lecture and a promise to Doc that, if he ever returned, they would throw the key away. The judge levied a $50.00 fine, and told us to please get the hell out of town. I rode with Doc to the next town and told him that I must be on my way and wished him luck.

Authors' Interlude: The next section of narrative is supported by *Billboard* which, on February 2, 1946, reported that Haley was working for Slim McCarthy in the Oregon Rangers. A report in *Variety* on November 5, 1945 mentioned Haley emceeing a WLS *Barn Dance* show in Indianapolis, but this could well be the "other" Bill Haley, mentioned earlier in this chapter.

I had managed, out of my share, to save about $60.00, and with this bought a Greyhound ticket, "High Class". Now with money, I went to Chicago to try to get on the WLS *National Barn Dance*. While working in Fort Wayne on the *Hoosier Hop*, I had met a man named Slim McCarthy, who worked with a group called the Oregon Rangers. When I left, Slim had given me his address in Chicago, so, when I arrived, I called and, sure enough, Slim had returned to Chicago. I went to visit him and we decided to try to put the Oregon Rangers together again. We did, and I told Slim of my ambition to appear on the WLS *National Barn Dance*. We went to see the WLS Artists' Bureau and auditioned. Although we did not get on the radio show, we were hired to do the WLS *Barn Dance* road shows, which at that time toured the Midwest four and five days a week, working theaters and dance halls.

This began another period of learning for me. As I watched and listened to the greats of WLS and got to know such people as Lulu Belle and Scotty, Arkie the Arkansas Woodchopper, Mac and Bob, Georgie Gobel (another yodeler at that time), Pat Buttram (one of the grand men of our business),[18] and many, many greats of that time period. I remember they placed bales of hay in a semi-circle on the stage and we all sat on the hay. As the emcee announced each act, they would walk up and do their part of the show. I used to get a thrill watching as Mac and Bob, two blind entertainers, stepped into the spotlight and sang "Keep a Light in Your Spring
Window Tonight, Your Wandering Boy is Coming Home."

When I finally left Chicago, I had gained so much more knowledge of stage presentation and showmanship that I shall always be grateful for the time I spent on the road shows. One entertainer, "Salty Dog Holmes,"[19] particularly impressed me. His style was different, and I found myself starting to pattern my songs after him. Looking back, I now realize it was sort of a combination of hillbilly-blues-bluegrass, but the way in which Salty performed the songs was different.

---

18 George Gobel later became known as a mainstream comedian, "Lonesome George Gobel," famous for his flattop haircut, deadpan personality, and his big Gibson L-5 guitar that exaggerated his short stature. Pat Buttram, likewise, became a popular actor in westerns as a sidekick of singing cowboy Gene Autry and as the shyster Mr. Haney on the popular 1960s television series, *Green Acres*. He had a distinctive cracking voice that, in Buttram's own words, "never quite made it through puberty."

19 Generally known as Salty Holmes, he was famous for his "talking harmonica" and duets with his wife, Mattie, on his records for Decca in the 1940s.

As I said before, I had been searching for something just a little different and trying anything not really knowing what I was looking for. I found, in singing country blues, tunes that others would do slowly, by upping the tempo the whole concept of the tunes was changed. I had to do them faster because I yodeled on every tune, and, for trick yodeling, the tempo had to be up. Consequently, was born the idea of merging styles of music, an idea that would serve me well in years ahead. Also, this made my act just a little different, and, I suppose, you could say I had formed a little style of my own.

When the WLS road shows had a layoff period, I worked on Madison Street in one of the many small clubs. I still remember walking back to my room at 3:00 a.m. or riding the elevated, and how cold winter nights are in Chicago. But I wouldn't trade those memories for anything, because Chicago is a wonderful town and has always been one of my favorite places. As time was passing, I began to wonder exactly where my career was going, and if I was on the right track.

During all this period, I was still sending as much money as I could to Mom and Dad. They were writing letters of encouragement each week. However, I began to get homesick. It had been over two years since I had seen them. When I had a few days off, I decided to go back to Fort Wayne for a short visit to see my old friends Shorty Cook and Guy Campbell. They told me they were leaving Indiana to go to Hartford, Connecticut, for a regional network show, and that Kenny Roberts was leaving to go on his own. When they offered me my old job back, at a raise in salary, I jumped at the chance and returned to Chicago to say goodbye to Slim and my friends. With my suitcase and guitar, I boarded a train (this time I paid for the ride) and first went back to Booths Corner, Penn., to spend a happy week with my family.

Once again, I said goodbye to them and headed off to Hartford to rejoin the Down Homers. It was then 1946 and I, at twenty-one, considered myself a veteran with road experience. After talking to my mom and dad, I promised to try that year, and, if I didn't make it big in show business by the end of 1946, to return home and try another profession. I

The Downhomers with Bill Haley, 1946.

arrived in Hartford, filled with determination and ambition, and Shorty and Guy and the gang welcomed me back. We began broadcasting over the New England Regional Networks — WTIC Hartford, WBZ Boston, WBZA Springfield, and WJRH Providence — six days a week. For the next three or four months, things went well and, for the first time, I began to make a few dollars. Two of the Down Homers at that time were Bob Mason and Lloyd Cornell. Bob was from New Hampshire and, when he received an offer to go to WKNE in Keene, New Hampshire, he approached me with an offer of a partnership in a group. Since I was still on salary, it seemed a step forward, so, once again, my itchy feet prevailed, and I left the Down Homers along with Bob and Lloyd and we went to Keene, New Hampshire. We called the group the Range Drifters, and, once again, Brother Wayne joined us as our fiddle player. After three or four weeks of broadcasting, it was back to the routine of advertising to do shows for local organizations on a percentage basis. The dates were coming
in and we seemed to be on our way. However, we hadn't figured on the New Hampshire winters. That particular winter, they had a lot of snow and, time after time, we had shows cancelled because our group or the audience could not reach the halls due to the heavy snow.

THE RANGE DRIFTERS
BROTHER WAYNE   BILL HALEY   BOB MASON   LLOYD CORNELL
Heard Daily 1 P. M. WKNE

Authors' Interlude: The move to Hartford, Connecticut, can be fairly precisely dated. Bill was listed as a performer in a *Billboard* review of a show on March 16, 1946, in Chicago (a Buffalo Bill tribute organized by the Freemasons at their headquarters in Chicago), and then by the Hartford Courant as a member of the Down Homers for a performance on April 13 at the Center School auditorium back in Hartford. This evidence does not support the often-reported notion that Haley participated on the two picture-disc singles that the WOWO Down Homers made for Vogue Records. These are known to have been recorded in Fort Wayne, Indiana, in January 1946, before Haley made the move to Hartford to rejoin the band. Bill himself seemed to believe he had taken part in the recordings, and, for many years, avid Haley collectors believed it too, as a figure in the middle of the band's picture, which was reproduced on the disc, looked rather like Bill. When the original of this photograph in high resolution began to be available through Internet archives, it was immediately apparent the face was that of Bob Mason. The 1946 radio broadcast Haley made with the Down Homers (released in the Bear Family CD box set, *Rock 'n' Roll Arrives... The REAL Birth of Rock 'n' Roll 1946-1954*), includes performances of two of the songs from the Vogue sessions. The earliest evidence that Bill had left the Down Homers for the second time and revived the Range Drifters is a set of four recordings made by the latter at WKNE that have survived on an aluminium disc now held in the Country Music Hall of Fame Digital Archive. The meticulous catalogue entry gives the recording date as September 18, 1946, with the musicians identified as Bill Haley, Brother Wayne, and Lloyd Cornell and the songs are "Chime Bells are Ringing" (vocal by Bill Haley), "Orange Blossom Special" (violin solo by Wayne Wright), "When My Blue Moon Turns to Gold Again" (vocal trio), and "Mommy Please Stay Home with Me" (Lloyd Cornell vocal).

While in Keene, New Hampshire, I married a pretty young lady named Dorothy Crowe from Salem, New Jersey. We had been going together off and on since my Bridgeton, New Jersey, days and we decided to wed.

Authors' Interlude: Dorothy Ann Crowe was born on December 30, 1925. She and Bill were married in Brattleboro, Vermont (about fifteen miles west of Keene), on December 11, 1946. Their daughter, Sharyn Ann, was born in June 1947, and their son, John ("Jack") William Haley, on December 1, 1950. After the long winter in New Hampshire that Bill described above, the Range Drifters left that state for Jacksonville, Illinois. For a short time in the Spring, they were being advertised both in Jacksonville *and* in Vermont. It seems likely that Bill, and possibly Brother Wayne, had returned East and were working under the same old name.

The luck of the band did not improve and soon our money ran out, so all the band decided to look for greener pastures and we split up. Wayne and I went back to trying the Brother Wayne and Yodeling Bill act, and this time we located in Lebanon, Pennsylvania, at station WLBR,[20] and started all over to plug away. It was while in Lebanon that, really for the first time, I began emceeing my own shows.

---

20 The earliest reference found is for an open-air performance at Mount Gretna Park on May 18, 1947, where they are listed fourth on the bill as "Range Drifters – Bill and Wayne. These are the boys you have waited to see. Heard daily over WLBR – 7:05am."

Bill with his first wife, Dorothy, and their daughter Sharyn Ann who was born in September 1947. Photo from Summer, 1948.

After a long five months of struggling and promoting and trying everything we knew how to do, we once again had to admit defeat and Wayne and I had to go our separate ways. While at WLBR, I worked with many fine people. One young newsman was Chet Hagen, whom I was to meet again years later. Chet went on to a great career with network television news, producing news for a long time with the nightly *Huntley-Brinkley Report*. Chet is still very active and successful with country and western award shows, etc. Although we did not have great success or make any money in Lebanon, as Chet and I years later would recall, we did have our lighter moments. One morning, as I was broadcasting solo in the studio and singing the daily hymn, Chet decided to try to get me to "break up" in the middle of the song. I was in the middle of "The Old Rugged Cross," a beautiful religious song, and concentrating on the lyrics. As I looked up from the sheet music [at] the control room, there stood Chet Hagen, at first making funny faces, later using hand gestures. Then he left the control room, and, a few seconds later, walked into the studio and, seeing he had not succeeded in breaking me up, stood in front of the mike and unzipped his fly and poked his finger through his fly. With this, I almost choked with laughter, and, after explaining to my radio audience that I had a bad cold and apologizing, I finished the song. Later that morning, as Hagen was doing the news from the same studio, I took my cigarette lighter and set fire to his news script as he was reading it. He somehow finished, and so went the antics in the early radio days. All this, of course, took place at 6:00 a.m. and, as there was no one at the station except the engineer, Chet Hagen and I could get by with this.[21]

As the year 1947 was coming to an end, with the wolf again at the door, my spirits low, money gone, my marriage suffering, I decided to return to Chester to regroup my thoughts. Remembering my promise, I was seriously considering

---

21 Hagen garnered a number of Emmys for productions such as the 1962 NBC News coverage of John Glenn's orbit of the Earth and a 1963 special on the Vietnam War. He died on February 12, 2002. His true name was Chester Edgett Hagan, although he often used the "Hagen" spelling professionally.

giving up show business to try another career. Little did I realize at this low point that, far from retiring, I was only just beginning.

Authors' Interlude: Haley cites marital difficulties, and this move was not destined to mend them. Dottie and Sharyn Ann were living in Salem and, from November 1947, Bill would spend most of his time working more than fifty miles away at Radio WPWA in Chester. The marriage did not recover, and Dorothy and Bill divorced by mutual agreement on November 14, 1952, just days before Bill's wedding to his second wife, Cuppy, who was already pregnant with her first child. During the good times, Bill would honor his obligation to support his first family, including visiting them with lavish gifts at Christmas and hosting them during his summer residencies on the Jersey shore. However, Dorothy would eventually struggle to get maintenance payments and to keep the family housed and fed, and had no health insurance to help her when she succumbed to cancer. She died in relative poverty on July 25, 1983. We can also observe at this point in the autobiography that Bill routinely fails to acknowledge the existence of a number of the children whom he had by his first and second wives, such as the birth of his first son John "Jack" Haley, born on December 1, 1950, the co-author (with John Von Hoelle) of a biography of his father.

Bill and Wayne's partnership as the Range Drifters did not survive the year. They were advertised as appearing at Sunset Park, between West Grove and Oxford, Pennsylvania, on September 29, 1947, and Bill's next band, billed as "Bill Haley and Western Aces," were advertised in the Harrisburg, Pennsylvania, *Evening News* as appearing at Ray Garver's Auction Ground, between Hummelstown and Middletown, on October 28.

BILL HALEY   THE RAMBLING YODELER   STAR OF ABC-NBC
Featured with The Down Homers on New England Regional Network
WTIC-WBZ-WJAR-WCSH-WLBZ-5:30-6:00 AM DAILY

Photograph of Bill taken in 1946 when he was a member of The Downhomers.

CHAPTER 3
Chester, Penna. Years (1947-1953)

I returned to my home and, after a few weeks nursing my wounds and deflated ambitions and dreams, there followed long talks with Mom and Dad. They once again encouraged me not to give up my idea of being an entertainer, since it seemed I was only happy when I was writing songs, singing them, and entertaining.

I read in the local paper that a man named Lou Poller[1] was planning to open a new radio station in Chester, Pennsylvania, which was only eight miles from where we lived. Dad said, "Why not go see this gentleman and perhaps, with your experience, you could get a job?" I did meet with Mr. Poller, and immediately I liked him. So began a friendship that was to really start me on my way. This was Lou's first venture and he so impressed me with his enthusiasm, hard work, and plans that I regained my own spirit. The station was to open in six weeks, and, at that time, was under construction. As Mr. Poller ex-plained, there would be little money but, if I would help out, he would be glad to give me airtime. So, when the station went on the air, I began doing my *Bill Haley's Country Store* program in the early mornings and a live thirty minutes in the afternoons on WPWA.[2] I also helped as record librarian, cleaning up the station, opening supermarkets, part-time DJ, in the newsroom

Lou Poller, founder and owner of WPWA.

---

1 This is the correct spelling of his name, as per the *Delaware County Daily Times* of the day. He has frequently been referred to, incorrectly, as "Pollar."

2 WPWA launched on October 17, 1947, opening with Joe Pyne hosting *Wake Up and Smile* at 6 a.m. This remained the early morning program for some time. The Western Aces first appeared on November 17, 1947, with a daily slot from 3:30 until 4 p.m. *Country Store*, which Bill mentions here, is not listed in the schedule until 1950. Over the years, Bill and the band would be allocated a number of different time slots.

cafeteria, or anything else I could as our WPWA family began to take hold in Chester, Pennsylvania.

The Four Aces of Western Swing. L To R: Al Constantine, Tex King, Bill Haley, and Barney Barnard.

After a few weeks of broadcasting as a solo performer, I advertised on my program for musicians to form a group, and, in a short while, I had chosen three: Bashful Barney Barnard, Al Constantine, and Tex King.[3] Our first club date was at a small club called s's Musical Bar and we worked four nights a week, which

---

3 As we have already seen, the Western Aces had been in existence before WPWA started broadcasting. Barnard had been a member of The Range Drifters during 1947 and is unlikely to have had to audition at this point. Barnard played double bass, Al Constantine accordion, and Tex King guitar. They all took vocal solos and provided backing vocals as necessary. In an online biography by his brother, Richard (downloaded from the Internet by the authors in 2014), Barnard is described as an equal partner with Bill and manager of the Western Aces. It is also known that the operating license for Radio Park in 1948 and 1949 was held jointly by Haley & Barnard Enterprises. At the end of 1949, their partnership was effectively at an end and, in establishing a new band (The Saddlemen), Bill entered into a three-way equal partnership with his new band members, Johnny Grande and Billy Williamson (the latter a long-time close friend of Barnard's).

enabled me to pay the musicians and keep us eating, so to speak. On the morning radio show, I came up with the idea to band together ten small independent garages. After a lot of talking, I convinced each one to pay $10.00 a week to the station and we formed the Independent Garagemen's Repowering Association. We had small signs made that read I.G.R.A. This, my first sponsor for the *Country Store Show*, meant $100 a week: $50 for me, and $50 for the station. Added to this small income, I received a percentage of the things I sold, including baby chicks, song sheets, and many items that were sold those days by radio. All in all, things were looking up! Also, as I was allowed to plug our personal appearances on the daily show. It wasn't long before our club work became seven days a week. As I had to be at the station for the opening at 6:00 a.m., and as I didn't finish working in the club until 2:00 a.m., I asked Lou Poller if I could fix up a little office somewhere in the building with a cot, so I could come directly from the club to the radio station and sleep a few hours before the show. Lou gave me a room in the basement, and I wood-paneled it and put an old carpet down and bought a used desk; thus, my first office came to be.[4]

I settled into the routine of improving my radio work. My schedule was from 6:00 a.m. until 2:00 a.m. daily, with three or four hours of rest and twenty hours devoted to music, music, music. Helping out in the record library gave me a chance to study and listen to all the various types of music. I would listen for hours and hours to the early Roy Acuff, Hank Thompson, Cliffie Stone, and Bob Wills records. Also, I remember the Tiny Hill, Count Basie, and Big Joe Turner records used to fascinate me. I kept feeling the need for a style of my own in music. In our group, I had started featuring the backslap of the bass fiddle on all our Western Swing tunes. Now this was nothing new by far, since the backslap bass had been used for many years by many groups. However, as I had started to use a lot of tunes that were not strictly country, and because those tunes really needed drums, I would substitute the slap bass for drums, and, little by little through 1947-1948, the style of our group began to form.[5]

It was about this time that I first met a man named Jack Howard. Jack was a song writer and publisher from Philadelphia.[6] He spent most of his time going out

---

4 This "room in the basement" was in fact the coal cellar. Bill's band members, when they reunited as "The Original Comets" in the late 1980s, would tell the story of the morning coal delivery, down the chute into the basement, which would cover Bill and his cot with coal dust.

5 It is interesting to note the scarcity of drums in much of country music. The notoriously conservative *Grand Ole Opry's* de facto policy was to ban drums from its stage, a policy that very slowly and sporadically gave way as rockabilly and similar country styles pressured the Opry into acquiescence. (Bob Doerschuk, "When Drums Went Country," *Drum!*, March 2018.)

6 This would have been in 1944, as noted in Chapter 2.

Jack Howard on stage with Bill Haley during one of Haley's comedy turns. This picture probably dates from 1949 or 1950.

to radio shows plugging his songs and promoting in general. He would get the local acts to finance their own records and he then would press up to three or four hundred copies and mail them out to radio stations and hope for the best. We made our first two records, "Four Leaf Clover Blues," a song that I had written with Shorty Cook, and "Too Many Parties and Too Many Pals," sung by Tex King. These were released on Jack's label, Cowboy Records.[7]

We promoted the records on our radio shows and made ap-pearances in the local theaters and record stores. Although we didn't sell many, we started to learn the record-promotion game for the future. Our second record, also for Jack, was "Candy Kisses" and "Tennessee Border."[8] The results were about the same, but, since the cost of making the records was minimal, and we sold them on the radio show and on personal appearances, we made money with them. Somehow, we felt better because we were now full-fledged recording artists![9]

---

7 Released July 1948. On their Cowboy singles, the Western Aces were credited as "Bill Haley and the 4 Aces of Western Swing."

8 Released March 1949 (Cowboy CR-1202).

9 Haley does not mention the band's significant role in the 1949 Cancer Drive. As reported in the *Delaware County Daily News* on April 18, 1949, the sum of $16,000 was raised through a thirteen-hour continuous broadcast on WPWA. "From 6 a.m. until the station went off the air at 6:45p.m., Bill Haley and his Western Aces spearheaded a continuous programme of music, talks by prominent local residents, and messages from nationally-known persons... There were personal appearances by a number of entertainers, telegrams read from Milton Berle, Tallulah Bankhead and others, and recorded telephone interviews with such stars as Ray Bolger and Melvin Douglas."

The Saddlemen: Marshall Lytle, Billy Williamson, Johny Grande. Kneeling: Bill Haley

Taken in Salem, N.J. c. 1951-1952, this is Dorothy Haley with her daughter Sharyn Ann (born 1947), and her son Jack Haley (born December 1950).

In the year 1949, there came some personnel changes. Tex King, Barney, and Al all moved on.[10] I searched for replacements, and once again advertised on the program for new men. It was here that Billy Williamson and Johnny Grande joined the Four Aces of Western Swing, along with Al Rex. As I added the new men, I changed the name of the group to the Saddlemen.[11]

10 In reality, the band had an ever-changing line-up. Members of the Western Aces between 1947 and 1949 included "Bashful" Barney Barnard and "Big Al" Thompson (bass); Al Constantine (accordion); Smiling Joe Dennis, Tex King, and Slim Allsman (guitar); "Brother" Wayne Wright and Jimmy Maise/Maze, (violin — the spelling of his name varies); James Weidow, Arrett "Rusty" Keefer (later one of Haley's most frequent songwriting collaborators), Duke Snow, and Slim Bland (guitar); and Merle Fritz (steel guitar).

11 Despite Bill's simple statement here, quite a story lurks behind the change of name. Towards the end of 1949, the Western Aces (a.k.a. Four Aces of Western Swing) seem to have been disintegrating. Barney Barnard was indicted for a firearms offense and Bill is said to have smashed his hand in a drunken act of bravado at Luke's Musical Bar in Chester (an incident recounted in Haley and von Hoelle, pp. 57-59). Bill was continuing as best he could as a solo artist at Luke's Bar, and, at that low point — and, apparently, coincidentally — two young musicians named Billy Williamson (a fiddle and steel guitar player) and Johnny Grande (a classically trained accordionist and keyboard player) had heard about Haley and tracked him down with the intention of joining him in a new musical venture. Their meeting was successful and they found they shared a common ambition. They shook hands on an equal three-way partnership, called themselves the Saddlemen and launched in early 1950. At the beginning, their bass player was "Big Al" Thompson. Being hugely overweight, he would tire rapidly on stage and a more athletic player, Al Rex (real name Piccirilli) stood ready in reserve and eventually took over on bass.

Dorothy and I had drifted apart due to my schedule of twenty hours a day, devotion to show business, and lack of money. After three or four separations and two beautiful children, Sharyn Anne and Jack, our separation and divorce came about, and I, though down-hearted, for the first time began to realize the sacrifices I would have to make for any success I would achieve in show business.[12]

The early personnel at WPWA consisted of some very fine people; since we were working hard to make the station a success, we became very close. Lou Poller was always very thoughtful and encouraging. I remember Bob Johnson,[13] Ray Mulderic, and Paul Warren. A man who helped me so much was our engineer, Harry Simington.[14] These people were always helpful to me, with praise or criticism, whichever was needed. Since I spent all my spare time studying the various styles of music and experimenting with new songs on daily radio shows, I began to wonder if it wouldn't be possible to combine different styles of music. So, I began to try out all styles of songs on our radio audience: a Dixieland tune, then a slow love ballad, then a country "hernia song,"[15] then a country blues, then a "pop" song, then a "race" tune, as they were called in those days.[16] However, all these were done in our "Saddlemen" style and I could tell which ones were accepted and which ones were not, because, in those days, we always asked our radio audience to "keep those cards and letters coming." They did!

Looking back now, I realize how valuable those days were for me. I not only had the time and means to study my profession, but I had the audiences and airtime to experiment and to test ideas on the public. Although neither the audiences nor I realized it at that time, we were to soon hit the winning combination that would change the entire music world for three decades to come.

---

12 They were not legally divorced until Bill wanted to marry Cuppy in November 1952, and the divorce was granted shortly before the wedding. As with Dottie (and Martha in the future), pregnancy had motivated the marriage.

13 WPWA's program director.

14 The name is spelled "Simmington" in a newspaper report describing him as a crew member at Wildwood in August 1954 when Bill's fishing boat, *The Comet*, lost power and the Cape May Coast Guard was called to tow it back to harbor. This was believed by some to have been a publicity stunt.

15 This appears to have been common parlance in country music circles for a song which makes great physical demands on the singer, known colloquially as "a real nut-buster."

16 "Race" songs and "race records" were introduced in the early 1920s when blues singer Mamie Smith recorded "Crazy Blues" and sold thousands of records to the previously ignored African-American audience. Major labels such as Columbia and Victor (later known as RCA Victor) established subsidiary "race" labels to distinguish these products from their mainstream recorded fare, which was classical and Tin Pan Alley music. The marketing term "race" was changed to "rhythm and blues" (or R&B) after World War II. *Billboard*, radio stations, and record stores strictly categorized music into "pop," "R&B," or "country and western." These were formidable barriers for rock and roll pioneers like Haley and Elvis Presley to break down in the 1950s.

Now, remember this all was taking place in the late 1940s, and there was a lull in the music business. The days of the big solo vocalists had passed, and really the only thing happening was a movement towards what was called progressive jazz. This style, of course, did not catch on in a big way, but it presented an opening for a new style.[17] I remember Lou Poller talking to me and urging me to "get off my ass" and come up with something that was different. Although Lou was hard on me, I later realized that way he kept me moving and drove me on. I shall always be grateful for his and the WPWA family's faith in me.

The years 1949 and 1950 passed, with the Saddlemen playing various clubs, parks, country fairs, anywhere people would hire us, and also doing our daily radio shows.[18] We also made several country and western records,[19] which we recorded at the radio station. We were always experimenting, but nothing was to happen record-wise during that period. We began appearing in Gloucester, New Jersey, just across the Delaware River from the Chester, Philadelphia, area at a club called the Twin Bar. The owner was a man named John Anthony. John and I became good friends and we appeared at the Twin Bar six nights a week for a three-year period. Although we did not make much money, it provided us with steady work and a show spot for the band. Our audience at the Twin Bar consisted of many men from the Philadelphia Navy base. Since these men came from all over the country, we had to play all styles of music to answer their requests. Once again, our fate seemed to be to play several styles of music, but this fit right in with my experiments at the radio station. We had great success at the Twin Bar during

---

17 This assessment requires some qualification. By the end of the 1940s, swing big bands were certainly on their way out, and the solo singers that emerged from that era (i.e., Frank Sinatra, Perry Como, and Doris Day) were on the rise. Meanwhile, mainstream record companies were putting out trite novelty songs by the early 1950s such as Patti Page's "How Much is That Doggie in the Window?" and syrupy ballads that were of no interest to young people. Post-World War II "progressive" jazz had a following, especially among the college and beatnik crowd. So-called "cool jazz," in particular, was preferred by college-age young people — thus, the emergence of New York clubs that catered to this audience, such as the Village Vanguard, that featured poets, jazz artists, and folk singers. Within the country and western genre, the "western" part of the music was fading, with cowboy-themed songs being replaced by honky-tonk, a more emotionally and musically raw and intense style that emerged in the Southwest after World War II. In 1958, the newly formed Country Music Association in Nashville pressured *Billboard* to change the category's name to just "country." It would seem Haley was transitioning away from his singing/yodeling cowboy image in the nick of time.

18 On January 24, 1950, Bill signed a contract with Jack Howard as his personal manager and publicity agent. Howard was given a basic ten percent commission, with the percentage increasing as the fees increased.

19 These are covered in some detail in Chapter 17.

those years.[20] At the radio station at that time, a friend of mine named Jim Reeves (not the country singer of fame) started a new disc jockey show called *Judge Rhythm's Court*. Jim, as the disc jockey, was called "Shorty the Bailiff." He would play only "race tunes," as they were called then. It was a great show featuring all the great black artists of our nation.[21]

As a theme song to sign off his show Jim used a Doc Bagby record of a song called "Rock the Joint."[22] Since Jim's show preceded mine every day, I would be standing in the studio with my band and ready to sign on as the strains of "Rock the Joint" came through the speakers. We got in the habit of playing along with "Rock the Joint" as a warm-up until we signed on our show. One night in the Twin Bar, we had a full house and all were enjoying themselves. I decided, as a throwaway song, to do a few verses of "Rock the Joint." The reaction was immediate and the place really rocked! After repeating the song several times that night, I realized that maybe this was the combination I had been seeking for so long. I was getting closer and closer to what was to become known as the Bill Haley style, or later known as Rock and Roll. Remember, all this was a success only on a 250-watt radio station and in one little club. Also remember the tremendous separation of musical ideas at that time. A hillbilly band or radio show only played Country music, race shows only Race music, pop shows only Pop music. But, as I talked to the many fans who came to our shows at the Twin Bar and read the mail we received at our station, I wondered why music had to be that way. At about this time, I received a call one day at the station from a man named Dave Miller; he explained to me that he had a local Philadelphia record company called Essex and Holiday records and that he would like to talk to me about mak-

---

20 Bill's memory of the chronology needs correcting here. On New Year's Day 1951, the Saddlemen took on a residency at the Spigot Café at 17th and Market streets in Philadelphia. They were originally booked until January 16 and then extended to the end of the month for a weekly fee of $281.25. The job was arranged by Jimmy Myers (a name we will be seeing again), using Jack Howard's booking license. Myers knew Billy Ewer, who booked entertainment at half a dozen venues in Philly, including the Spigot. The Spigot was a well-known dive bar with chicken wire across the stage to separate the band from the crowd. They were lured away from there by John Anthony, owner of the Twin Bar, who offered them $350 per week after hearing about them from the Philadelphia Navy Yard sailors who frequented both establishments. They opened at the Twin Bar in May 1951 and remained there until October 1952. At this point, the band could begin to consider music as a full-time rather than a part-time job, while Bill was still working hard, broadcasting daily on WPWA and, of course, promoting the band on the air.

21 This program moved to WPWA in May 1949, having previously been on WVCH for a few months.

22 The song was co-written by Bagby, but he did not record it under his name. It was probably the Jimmy Preston and His Prestonians recording on the Gotham label that was played.

ing some records for his label.[23]

When Dave arrived at the station I found him to be a young man full of enthusiasm and a real eager beaver and he told me that when he first heard me sing he thought I was a black singer doing Country songs, and that his idea was to record me doing cover records of black songs. We finally came to an agreement. We decided to do one side a black song and a Country tune on the other. He said he would only use the name Bill Haley and not allow any pictures of me as he wanted to sell me to both black and white audiences. I agreed to this, because it was a way to further my ideas about selling to all people ---not just one set of fans. The first record we did for Dave was a cover of Jackie Brenston's record of a song called "Rocket 88," and on the other side we did "Tearstains on My Heart." The initial reaction was not overwhelming, but we sold about 10,000 copies in the Eastern markets. This was enough for Dave Miller to record other tunes with us.

During this period, my song writing leaned toward boogie tunes, I suppose influenced by the boogie craze recently passed, but anyway "Green Tree Boogie," "Sundown Boogie", etc., etc., etc. More and more, the word "rock" would crop up as I sat to write tunes. One evening, sitting at the station playing around with ideas for another song, I jotted down the title "Rock-a-Beatin' Boogie" and began the song with "Rock, rock, rock, everybody," then "Stomp, stomp," then "Romp," and then "Jump." I could not find the word I needed for the second line, and then, remembering the old song "Roll Me Over in the Clover," I tried the word "Roll." Now it seemed to fit... "Rock, rock, rock everybody... Roll, roll, roll everybody. Rock-a-beatin' boogie beat." I finished the tune, "Rock-a-Beatin' Boogie," but, aside from using it in our show, I did nothing with the song until I gave it to the Esquire Boys and the Treniers to record a year or so later. We were later to record this song ourselves, but I am getting ahead of the story. This song, recorded by the Treniers and Esquire Boys, was used many times by disc jockeys Buddy Deane, Bill Randle, Alan Freed, and many others. From the Rock & Roll opening lyrics came

---

23 David L. ("Dave") Miller (born July 4, 1925; died May 24, 1985), with his father, Albert, and brother, Paul, set up the Palda record label in Philadelphia in 1947. This would quickly evolve into a company run by Miller himself, encompassing a number of record labels, including Holiday and Essex, for whom Bill Haley made records between 1951 and 1954. Palda also operated as a pressing plant where Haley's earliest records on labels such as Cowboy, Keystone, and Center were pressed between 1948 and 1950. Central to the Haley story was the rivalry between James E. Myers and Miller (see Chapter 17). Haley's business relationship with Miller came to an end when Myers exploited Miller's failure to take up the option on his contract with Haley in March 1954. Stories abound of the "sex parties" that were allegedly run by the Miller Brothers during the late 1940s and early 1950s, but we have not directed our efforts towards researching this legend. In later years, Miller made his fortune recording the highly successful 101 Strings Orchestra.

the phrase and the name for our style, "Rock & Roll."[24]

Through 1951, we recorded such gems as "Stop Beatin' Round the Mulberry Bush," "Chattanooga Choo Choo," "I'll Be True to You," "Green Tree Boogie,"[25] and so on. In early 1952, due to the response of "Rock the Joint" on our club dates, we recorded "Rock the Joint" and a country song called "Icy Heart" at Bell Sound Studios in New York.[26] On the tune "Icy Heart" we used an echo, and the record came out fairly well. Everybody, including Dave Miller, was excited about it. Upon release of the record, the initial sales were so good that Dave asked me to go on a promotion trip to the Midwest to see and visit the disc jockeys and record distributors, and to promote the record. I had to make arrangements to transcribe my radio shows,[27] and to get someone to fill in for me at the club. After much scrambling, it was finally arranged, and Jack Howard and I set off by car to promote the Country side of the record, "Icy Heart." We went first to Pittsburgh, then on to Detroit, Cleveland, Cincinnati, and St. Louis. In all of these towns, we were promoting the Country side, "Icy Heart." Indeed, the record did get on the charts in the C&W field,[28] and I began to think of the doors this would open for me *in* the Country field.

While in St. Louis, we received a phone call from Nashville implying that perhaps we could get on the *Grand Ole Opry*. We were really enthused since this had been one of my dreams since childhood! We headed out of St. Louis on the way to Nashville. When we stopped late at night at a roadside café for coffee, Jack almost got us shot with his golden personality. Jack was near-sighted, and, when we finished eating, we got up to leave and, as we approached the cash register, dressed in our buckskin cowboy clothes which we had worn for promotion

---

24 Bill told this story so many times that he came to believe it, but he could not really claim to have invented the phrase "Rock and Roll." He did not add the introduction ("Rock, rock, rock everybody, roll, roll, roll everybody") to the song until he recorded it himself in September 1955, long after the phrase "Rock and Roll" had become common parlance. Neither the copyrighted sheet music nor numerous known early recordings and performances of the song (by Haley session musician Danny Cedrone's band, the Esquire Boys, as well as the Treniers, the Jodimars (made up of former Comets), and Freddie Bell and the Bell Boys (all of which have survived on commercial discs or YouTube) actually contained the phrase. It can also be noted that the Treniers had used the lyric "rock, rock, rock everybody" on their 1953 recording of "Rockin' is our Bizness."

25 "Green Tree Boogie," on Holiday Records, was recorded in 1951; the other tracks mentioned here were recorded in 1952 and 1953 for Essex Records.

26 This autobiography appears to be the only time Haley claimed that Bell Sound Studios were used for their recordings. Previously, his answers had varied from "the radio station" to "various places" or, simply, "I don't remember."

27 A radio "transcription" was the pre-recording of a show for later broadcast. At this time, shows were recorded to sixteen-inch discs and played on special phonographs. The technology was eventually replaced by tape recording.

28 There is no evidence of this in *Billboard*.

purposes, I noticed through an opening in the wall, behind the cash register, the business end of a shotgun protruding. I suppose the owner was suspicious of those two buckskin-clad characters. I paid the bill without saying anything to Jack except, "Let's get the hell out of here." I walked to the door. However, Jack had big eyes for the waitress and, as I said before, being near-sighted, he approached the register to talk to her. From behind the wall came a voice that told Jack, "One more step and I'll blow your head off." Little Jack set a new record leaving that diner and was very quiet for a few hours as we sped on our way to Nashville.

Bill Haley with Dave Miller (left) and Monte Kelly (right), pictured at the time of the great success of "Crazy Man, Crazy".

Buddy Deane, who would be a great supporter of Haley for many years.

When we arrived in Nashville, we started our disc jockey promotion. We received a call from Dave Miller and he said, "Bill, get off the promotion on 'Icy Heart' and start promoting the other side, since we have a hit record with 'Rock the Joint'." He said we should go to Richmond, Washington, and Baltimore on our way home. We began to promote "Rock the Joint" and, as we entered Richmond, Virginia, we stopped on the outskirts of the city to put gas in the car. Once again, Jack's personality shone. Jack thought it would be cute to ask the guy who was pumping the gas a question. He said, "My name is Grant and how far is it to Richmond?" The guy looked at Jack and said, "Mister, if your name is Grant, I'd advise you to stay the hell out of Richmond."[29] We finished our promotion tour in Richmond and Washington, but had no luck getting airplay on "Rock the Joint," since the stations would not play the record because they said it was not C &W or

---

29 This would be a reference to Ulysses S. Grant, Union general in the Civil War and later U.S. president, someone whom Virginians might begrudge, particularly since his Confederate counterpart, General Robert E. Lee, was also a Virginian.

"Race" and they could not find a show to schedule it. Thus began the battle to get airplay on our newfound music.

When we returned, Dave Miller explained that we had what was called a "juke box hit," but no play. The only two guys who were daring enough to play the record were Buddy Deane in Baltimore and Bill Randle in Cleveland. So off I went once again to visit these two gentlemen, who were later to become my friends. I would like to state for the record that these were the first disc jockeys to play Rock and Roll music and, although later more publicity was given to other disc jockeys, these were the pioneers.[30] I arrived in Baltimore early one morning and went to station WITH and, as I entered the studio, I met Buddy Deane for the first time. Here was a young man with a pet monkey that he called "Chumley." He had quite a smooth routine, which was proven later, because Buddy enjoyed many successful years with television audiences in the Baltimore-Washington area. Later he retired with his own TV station in Arkansas, but that morning Buddy interviewed me and played the record several times. Through his efforts alone, we started our "Rock the Joint" in this area. In Cleveland, the same thing happened, thanks to Randle,[31] a fine man, who later became known as the man who really helped Elvis and lots of others on their way. All the stories are true because Bill and Buddy were there at the beginning.

Bill Randle, another major supporter of Bill Haley.

Meanwhile, back in Chester at WPWA, a new radio personality was born, a gentleman called "Lord" Jim Ferguson.[32] He started a talk show every evening

---

30 The evidence of this statement can be seen in the regional chart placings listed in *Billboard* between 1954 and 1955. Baltimore and Cleveland were strong territories for Bill and the Comets. Other disc jockeys may have done more for Rock and Roll generally, but Randle and Deane were promoting Haley in the earliest days of the music.

31 On radio station WERE in Cleveland, Ohio.

32 Born November 20, 1904, died February 1, 1969.

James Ferguson (1904-1969), an eccentric and colourful man, who would become a partner in the Haley Corporation in 1953. A great showman and raconteur, his business acumen was highly flawed, and contributed to the dramatic decline and fall of the Corporation in the late 1950s.

called *Lord Jim's Personality Parade.*[33] Jim was a local Chester man who was a former lieutenant-commander in the Navy, a local fight promoter, and news columnist. He was well-known in the area. His show was on for one hour in the evenings and was a mild success. I was finding it very hard now to cope with all the new duties and problems that a mild success on records brought. As I returned to the routine of radio work, clubs at night, song-writing, and recording more songs, it began to become very evident that I needed a manager. After befriend-ing Lord Jim, I approached him with the idea of managing our act.[34] Now, in all fairness to Lord Jim, he had never managed a musical group before this.

To describe Jim for you would be to say he was a Sydney Greenstreet sort of character.[35] Jim stood about 6' 2", was, shall we say, pleasingly plump (to be kind to him), had a bald head and smoked a big cigar. After Doc Protho, I would say Jim was one of the best "B.S." men around. Those were, in those days, the qualifications of a good manager, since these men were in a class of their own. I don't mean to put them down; quite the contrary, they were usually fine men, and, without the Lord Jims and Colonel Tom Parkers of that day, there would not have been the Bill Haleys and Elvis Presleys. So much credit goes to these people. Jim agreed and we formed a corporation of Billy Williamson, John Grande, Jim Ferguson, and Bill Haley.[36] He also began sending out photographs, writing

33 This began broadcasting c. April 1950. At one time, the daily WPWA schedule read: 3:05 p.m. *Judge Rhythm*; 4:30 p.m. *Roundup – Bill Haley*; 5 p.m. *Lord Jim's Personality Parade*.

34 The earliest evidence of Lord Jim in this role is a press release on March 3, 1953, in the *Delaware County Daily Times*.

35 Sydney Greenstreet (1879-1954) was a rotund British actor who appeared in films in the 1940s, most notably in the Humphrey Bogart films *The Maltese Falcon* (1941) and *Casablanca* (1942).

36 A three-way partnership already existed between Bill Haley, Johnny Grande, and Billy Williamson, and it now became a four-way partnership, with Bill as the acknowledged leader. The partners had an equal stake in the risk taken and the profit gained.

The master guitarist, Danny Cedrone (1920-1954). A close friend of and highly trusted and regarded by Bill Haley, his life ended tragically when he fell down the stairs in a local restaurant having picked up some sandwiches for his family's supper.

press releases, doing promotion from Chester, Pennsylvania, on the strange new music that wasn't Dixie, wasn't Pop, wasn't Race, wasn't Country, but still was growing in popularity as time progres-sed. The next few records we did for Dave Miller were received about the same, since we had now established a small, but loyal juke box audience for our records. We would go to New York, to Bell Sound Studios, and using our radio group, adding Danny Cedrone on lead guitar and Billy Gussak on drums. Dave Miller, who was always very active and helpful, would try any gimmicks he could think of to create different sounds on the records. I also give much credit to Dave for his ideas and hard work on promotion in those early days of Rock and Roll. At that time, Dave was having fantastic success for a small record company. He had a hit record with a local Chester group called (of all things) the Four Aces on a song called "It's a Sin." They had started using the name Four Aces after we had changed our group to the Saddlemen. I was happy the name had brought them luck, because they were four fine young men, and they were very talented. Dave had signed Al Martino and had a hit riding with Al. He also had another fine talent in Dick Lee, so, as I said before, Dave was riding high with success.

Although things seemed to be happening for us, we were faced with the problem of breaking out into the world of big-time show business. Knowing that records were the way, I kept trying to write a hit song for us. Later, as the music and popularity progressed, and more writers and groups joined us, I received hundreds of songs and ideas, but, in those days, either we wrote our own songs or did copies of other songs.

One night, as I sat at the kitchen table, a new expression that had been going the rounds of young people came to my mind. Everything in those days was "crazy" — crazy tie, crazy shirt, crazy shoes, etc., etc., etc., so I jotted down, "Crazy Man, Crazy." Along with this I used the football cheer, "Go, go, go everybody." In a few minutes the song, "Crazy Man, Crazy" was finished. It is funny with songwriting. You can write a hundred songs, but, when you write a hit song, or at least it was true in my case, you know immediately![37] The next day I called Dave, and he also liked the song. We went again to Bell Sound and recorded "Crazy Man, Crazy", with another song I had written, "What'cha Gonna Do", on the B side.[38] Dave released the record and, as the arrangement included yells and screams and a big party effect, it was to shock the radio stations and record people of that day. The first reviews were terrible, but the record hit like the well-known "ton of shit." In a few weeks, it was way up on all the charts, except in radio play. This time, we were not to be denied and soon a cover record by Ralph Marterie, a popular big band of the day, was released and began to fight us on the charts for top position. About this time, Lord Jim got us a booking at a jazz club called Ciro's in Philadelphia.[39] For this club, we had to change the appearance and name of the group. We rented tuxedos and changed the name to "Bill Haley and the Comets" after Halley's Comet. We added a drummer, and, with Lord Jim and some of our country music fans to cheer us on, we opened at Ciro's. Now this was a very nice club that featured the top jazz groups of that time such as Louis Armstrong, Dizzy Gillespie, Buddy De Franco, Gene Krupa, etc., etc., etc. It was like walking onto the lion's den for us; but we tried anyway. Opening night, we had about thirty of our C&W fans who could pay the high prices, a few of the regular customers, and Lord Jim was there for our opening show. It was a disaster, as our music was not for that club. To make matters worse, Lord Jim, in an effort to pick up business, tried to drink his spirits up. He proceeded to cheer loudly after each song and, at

---

37 Marshall Lytle, Bill's bass player in 1953, was adamant about his own involvement in the creation of "Crazy Man, Crazy." In his autobiography, *Still Rockin' Around the Clock*, he recounts that, after a morning assembly performance at Eddystone High School, a kid came up to them and described their music as "crazy man, crazy." Back at Bill and Cuppy's apartment, "Bill grabbed a guitar. He struck a chord and said 'Crazy man, crazy. Crazy man, crazy. Crazy man, crazy, Man, that music's gone.' Then we started throwing lines back and forth. I would come up with a line and Bill would use it, and then he would come up with a line and use it. Bill and I basically wrote 'Crazy Man, Crazy,' our next big hit, in about 30 minutes right there in the kitchen... When we recorded 'Crazy Man, Crazy' on Essex Records...Dave Miller asked Bill Haley, 'Who's the writers [sic] on this, Bill?' and Bill said 'just Bill Haley.' And I went over to him and I said 'Bill, now you know that you and I wrote the song together.' And Bill said, 'Oh I know that Marshall, but I just want to take credit on this one myself.' He said, 'I'll take care of you on other songs.'" (Marshall Lytle with Michael Jordan Rush, *Still Rockin' Around the Clock* (Philadelphia: Michael Jordan Rush, 2009), pp. 54-58.) Bill gave Marshall co-writing credit on the next record, the song "Fractured", which came nowhere near duplicating the success of "Crazy Man, Crazy." Marshall felt hard done by for the rest of his life.

38 Dave Miller's memory was that most of the Essex tracks were recorded at Coastal Studios on 40th Street, New York City, where the legendary Tom Dowd (later of Atlantic Records) was the engineer.

39 This happened earlier than Bill remembers, and they first appeared at Ciro's in December 1952, returning there on January 23, 1953, *before* they had recorded "Crazy Man, Crazy." The booking had originally been inspired by the success of "Real Rock Drive", which was their first disc as "Haley's Comets."

the end of the evening, we knew we had a long way to go before we made the jump from Country band to whatever lay ahead of us.

Authors' Interlude: The change of the band's name and image was indeed a pivotal moment. As musical cowboys, their future was limited, but, as smartly dressed rock musicians playing a slick new style of music, the world would become their oyster. As with a number of such moments in the band's career, there was a long list of people claiming to have been instrumental in the change. Whereas musical influences are easier to untangle, in the case of the change of name and dress, we have only a list of people who claimed it was wholly or partly their idea, and no trail of evidence to provide a clearer narrative. The list includes Dave Miller, Bob Johnson, Bix Reichner, Sam Sgro, and Jimmy Myers. Once again, Bill's chronology needs correcting. The name of the band changed towards the end of 1952. They appeared on December 7, 1952, at the Lloyd Club as "the Saddlemen," and on New Year's Eve at Berky's as "the Comets." Between these dates, they had made their first appearance at Ciro's. The first single to reflect the new name, "Stop Beatin' Around the Mulberry Bush" and "Real Rock Drive", was released on Essex Records in early December as by "Bill Haley with Haley's Comets." The first single to actually use the billing "Bill Haley and His Comets" was "I'll Be True", released on Essex in late 1953. The name "Halley," associated with the famous comet, was often mispronounced "Hay-lee," whereas its original U.K. pronunciation was "Haul-ee."

So, for a short while, we returned to our Twin Bar[40] and our familiar surroundings. About that time, I had met a pretty girl, named Joan Cupchak, from Camden, New Jersey.[41] We married and Cuppy and I set up housekeeping in Norwood, Pennsylvania.[42] At about the same time, Lord Jim signed a six-month contract with Joe Glaser at Associated Booking Corp. in New York City. Once more we had high hopes, because Mr. Glaser was one of the best agents in the business. Joe was Louis Armstrong's manager and he explained to us that, even though we had hit records, the style was new and it would be hard to find showplaces for us. My friend, Bill Randle, was promoting a show at the Loews State Theater in Cleveland,[43] and Joe succeeded in placing us on the bill, which headlined Sugar Ray Robinson as a dancer and a singer (a good one, I might add). Sugar Ray, at that time, was venturing into show business. Also on the show was a beautiful young singer, just starting out on her great career, Miss Eydie Gormé. On the show also were Billy Ward and the Dominoes. We spent a happy week there, and the show was a big success. For the first time, we experienced the kids

---

40 By now the band had moved to the Broomall Nite Spot at 2107 McDade Boulevard in Holmes.

41 Bill had first met Cuppy at the Twin Bar, and they would marry on November 18, 1952, the day before the recording of "Real Rock Drive." Cuppy was pregnant with Joanie, born on March 26, 1953.

42 According to Cuppy, their first home in November 1952, after their honeymoon, was a third-floor furnished one-bedroom apartment in Collingdale, Pennsylvania. Their home in Norwood, where they lived right by the train station, came later.

43 The show opened on June 5, 1953.

dancing in the aisles to our "Rock the Joint" and "Crazy Man, Crazy." Here, at last, was our audience. We knew now where to direct our efforts, since we saw that, even though the older fans had not got the message, the young people, without a music of their own, were accepting this as their own music.

We returned to Chester, Pennsylvania, and, realizing we had to showcase the music, contacted local high schools and began to do free shows in the afternoons during assembly periods. This immediately paid off because the kids liked the music and began to send letters and cards to the local radio stations to play the records. During this period, a local Philadelphia TV station started an afternoon disc show with kids dancing. The name of the show was *Bandstand*, and a man named Bob Horn was the personality [host]. We made several appearances on the show, and this, along with the high school promotion and local radio promotion, continued the forward movement of our music.[44]

I met a young man who was class locally as a radio announcer and disc jockey, and we became friends. I went some nights with him to his record hops, at the Tower Theater in Upper Darby, Pennsylvania. He told me of his ambitions and dreams of becoming a big-time disc jockey and TV personality. I knew then that he would like it. Shortly after this period, when Bob Horn left the *Bandstand* show and they were looking for a replacement, this young man took over. His name was Dick Clark, and we were to do his *American Bandstand* show many times.[45] To this day, when I see Dick still going strong, I have a warm feeling. Dick deserves all the success he has had.

We now tried once again to break into the night club circuit. Joe Glaser booked us into one of the top Chicago jazz clubs. Though we had misgivings since we were following Dizzy Gillespie into this one, off we went to Chicago. Now, our record of "Crazy Man Crazy" was No. 1 in Chicago,[46] but, on opening night, we had about thirty people in the club, and they walked out. Once again, our spirits were crushed. Such comments as, "What the hell kind of music is that?" and, "Hey, kid,

---

44 For many years, WPWA broadcast an afternoon radio show called *Bandstand*. The music from the program was relayed to a paved area outside the building where teenagers would gather in the summer to hang out and dance to the music. This seems to have been the prototype for what would ultimately become the TV show, *Bandstand*, later known as *American Bandstand* on national network TV.

45 Haley appears to be remembering Clark's arrival a few years earlier than it happened. Horn was fired as host of *Bandstand* in early July 1956 after an impaired-driving arrest. Clark was hired as his replacement and stayed on as host until stepping down in 1989. (Tom Wilk, "New Book on 'American Bandstand' focuses on its Philadelphia Roots." *Philadelphia Inquirer*, July 3, 2019).

46 *Billboard* listed St. Louis as the only location where "Crazy Man, Crazy" reached No.1. It reached No. 10 on May 30 on the *Billboard* chart for Chicago. Despite Bill's memory of the Preview Lounge being a disaster, the band's residency there is reported in *Billboard* for two weeks at the end of September into October, whilst also noting that Lord Jim continued to broadcast his *Personality Parade* on WPWA via a telephone link from Chicago.

Looking more like an apartment block, this is the Hofbrau Hotel and Wildwood, where the Comets had a residency in 1953, when riding on the success of "Crazy Man, Crazy."

where's your horse?" greeted us after every song, and, at the close of the first night, I asked Lord Jim to talk to the manager to let us out of the contract, which he agreed to do. We returned to Chester, feeling like we were a rubber ball, bouncing one day on top, and the next day down to the bottom of the show-business ladder.

That summer, Lord Jim booked us into the Shelter Haven Hotel in Stone Harbor, New Jersey, and also into the Hof Brau Hotel in Wildwood, New Jersey, which was the seaside summer resort for the Philadelphia area. It was here that we began to hit our stride, as the young people and the college kids arrived and began to flock to dance to "Rock the Joint" and "Crazy Man, Crazy". We spent the summer playing to packed houses.[47] I began to realize the effect of our music as I watched the college students march down the streets chanting "*Go-Go-Go-Everybody — Crazy Man, Crazy.*" Our six-month contract with Joe Glaser had expired and we decided not to renew it, because the jazz clubs were definitely not for us. We began to look for another agency to secure bookings for us.

One day, a local Philadelphia booking agent named Jolly Joyce came to see us in Wildwood. After long discussions between Lord Jim and Jolly, we decided to give his agency a chance. Once again, we had an agent![48] Lord Jim, having been a lieutenant-commander in the Navy, had a natural love for the sea. While we were working that summer in Wildwood, Lord Jim took me deep-sea fishing and I was "hooked" from that day on. We bought a small 28-ft. fishing boat and Jim and I spent many happy days off the Jersey Coast, fishing and relaxing. Lord Jim also had the habit, as most good Scotchmen do, of nipping Johnnie Walker Red Label. He

---

47 June 25, 1953, appears to have been the last day that Bill broadcast his afternoon show on WPWA. Bill thus ended a career of more than five years of daily broadcasting, which had often involved more than one show a day.

48 Born Samuel Jacobs on April 9, 1901, Jolly Joyce started a one-man business in 1930 that still trades as Joyce Agency Entertainment Services Inc. On behalf of Bill Haley and the Saddlemen, Jack Howard signed an exclusive booking contract with Joyce on April 21, 1950.

would end each day sitting in his robe with a 12-oz. glass, filled with ice and Johnnie Walker Red Label. For the first time, I learned the taste of whiskey, as I would join him at the end of the day. This was to prove to be both helpful and harmful to me in the years ahead. But more of that later.

One evening, late in the season at Wildwood, I was visited by two songwriters, Jimmy Myers[49] and Max Freedman. They brought me a song they had written and said, "Bill, this song is just made for you." The title was "Rock Around the Clock".[50] If there ever was a case of a singer and a song falling in love at first sight, this was it! I tried the song out on the band, and from the first rehearsal, everything seemed to click. During the rest of the season, we did the song every show, and, from the audience reaction, I knew we had a winner. I couldn't wait to get to a studio to record the song. I had promised my good friend, Danny Cedrone, who did the lead guitar work for me on most of our early records, "Rock the Joint," etc., and was to do "Rock Around the Clock" with me, that I would write a song for his little group, the Esquire Boys. Also, I had befriended a group in Wildwood, the Treniers, and they too asked me for a song. I played my song "Rock-a-Beatin' Boogie" for both of them, and they both made a record of that song.

We finished our season at the seashore, and, before we left for Washington, we went to record again for Dave Miller. Now I had told Dave of my enthusiasm for the new song, and, as usual, Dave was very happy, but there was a situation of which I was not aware. For some reason, there were ill feelings between Jimmy Myers and Dave Miller. Dave was a highly emotional guy. When we were all set up, and had rehearsed to record "Rock Around the Clock," Dave came into the studio to check one of the musical parts. He came over to the mike where I was singing my part. It was the first time he had seen the sheet music. When he spotted the name Jimmy Myers as one of the writers, he screamed like a raped ape and took the sheet music off the stand and tore it up, saying to me that no Myers tune would

---

49 James Edward Myers, (October 26, 1919 - May 10, 2001) was a significant figure in Haley's career in the early to mid 1950s. After World War II, in which he served in the Far East, he worked his way into the local music scene as a songwriter and publisher and obtained a share in Jack Howard's Cowboy Records. In 1950, he was responsible for helping Haley's career, acting as a booking agent and facilitating his groundbreaking recordings for Keystone, Center, and Atlantic Records. His most significant achievement came in 1954 when he brokered Haley's contract with Decca Records, which resulted in the recording of "Rock Around the Clock" and what would be a five-year association with the label. In later life, Myers embarked on a career as a bit-part actor in Hollywood films and accumulated significant wealth as the publisher and co-writer (under the pseudonym Jimmy De Knight) of "Rock Around the Clock". In retirement, he moved to Bonita Springs, Florida, where he installed a museum commemorating the song's success. In the late 1970s, he attempted, unsuccessfully, to reunite Bill Haley with the musicians from the 1954-1955 Comets' line-up.

50 Authors' note: We have refrained from adding footnotes to the story of "Rock Around the Clock" here. Haley's narrative here is at odds with the other participants' versions of the story, and the subject is covered in detail in Chapter 18: Focus on Music (1954-1959).

be recorded at his recording session. I was heartbroken. Although I argued and pleaded, Dave refused. So, we were not to do our song at that time. This was repeated again, and eventually was one of the main reasons I left the label, because I felt so strongly about this tune.

We then went for a two-week booking at the Casino Royal and the Blue Mirror[51] in Washington, D.C. Finally, our first nightclub success took place. One night between shows, I was sitting in the dressing room relaxing when Lord Jim came in and said, "Bill, I want you to come out to the table with me and meet a friend of mine who is a great fan. He is a politician, and he would like to meet you." I was tired after the first show and tried to beg off, but Jim was insistent, so I put on my jacket and went with him. We arrived at the table, and I saw a tall good-looking gentleman sitting there and Jim said, "Bill, I'd like you to meet Senator Jack Kennedy."[52] We talked for about fifteen minutes, and the senator told me that he was a fan of Rock music and of Bill Haley. We admired the chorus line of the show, joking back and forth, and I found him to be a very nice guy. I then went back to my dressing room to get ready for the next show. It was not unusual for politicians to come to our shows, so I forgot about this meeting but, years later, was to remember it with pride. Again, I am getting ahead of my story.

After we finished in the Washington area, we went to Reno and Las Vegas[53] for the first time. For this, we added saxophone, and the band now was really beginning to shape up into what was later termed a Rock group. Having finished our four weeks at the Golden Hotel Reno and the El Cortez in Las Vegas, we returned to Chester. As 1953 came to a close, we again went to record and again Dave Miller threw out the song, "Rock Around the Clock". Since our contract with Essex Records was due to expire in early 1954, I began to think seriously of looking for a major record label that would let me do the song "Rock Around the Clock."

By now we noticed, as always happens with success, other groups were copying our style.[54] We were no longer alone, and after almost three years of campaigning with disc jockeys, free high school shows, and promotion trips, the doors were finally opening and our music was beginning to be accepted.

---

51 The chronology is wrong here. They were first at the Blue Mirror in Washington, D.C., between June 29 and July 4, 1953, and did not appear at the Casino Royal until January 19, 1955.

52 John F. Kennedy, the 35th President of the United States (1961-1963).

53 There are more misplaced memories here. They opened in Reno, Nevada, on February 23, 1955, and, a few days later, in Las Vegas.

54 We cannot be sure which acts Bill refers to here, but in 1953/4 they might have included Jimmy Cavallo (Syracuse, New York), the Esquire Boys (Camden, New Jersey), Murray Schaff and His Aristocrats (St. Louis, Missouri, and Wildwood, New Jersey), Sonny Dae (Indianapolis), and Charlie Gracie and Dave Appell (Philadelphia), all of whom were, musically speaking, heading in the same direction.

CHAPTER 4
The Emergence of Rock & Roll (1954-1955)

Authors' Note: In this chapter, Bill gives his account of the circumstances leading to the recording of "Rock Around the Clock." Our research, however, has revealed a number of different versions of the story from other participants and news sources. We have let Bill's account stand, and we attempt to consolidate the conflicting stories in Chapter 18.

As 1954 began, the record company problem became more worrisome to me. Although Essex had proven to be a good luck charm for me, and I for them, the fact that I was being stopped from doing "Rock Around the Clock" began to bother me more and more. So, I decided to try to reason one more time with Dave Miller. When I called, the company told me that Dave had gone to Europe to record. They didn't know when he would return. After several attempts to contact him, I gave up the idea. As the end of the contract was nearing, and since I felt loyalty to the company, I waited until the last week[1] for Dave to come back or call to talk about a new contract. He either forgot or was too busy; I never found out.[2]

---

1 Miller had an option to renew Haley's recording contract, provided he exercised it before March 8, 1954.

2 In an oral history recording made by the Library of Congress between 1986 and 1988, Decca producer Milt Gabler stated that Miller had been "neglecting Bill" in general, was more interested in "making fancy records with a lot of strings," and went on to put out budget classical records and an easy-listening series called 101 Strings. Miller in turn boasted to Gabler that no one could get a better-recorded sound from the Comets than he could. Gabler obviously took that as a challenge, saying, "If I couldn't make a record as good as that [Miller's extant Haley recordings] sound-wise or better, I'd quit tomorrow!"

James E. ("Jimmy") Myers, co-owner (with Jack Howard) of Cowboy Records, and President of Myers Music, Inc.

I went to Philadelphia to talk to Jim Myers, since I felt so bad because Jimmy and Max Freedman had been holding "Rock Around the Clock" from anyone else's recording it, or so they told me at the time. I was to find out years later that another group was advertised as the original record.[3] However, I went to see Jim and told him my plan was to look for another record deal and promised him that my first record for the new label was to be his song. Now Jimmy and I had been friends for a few years. He was a partner with Jack Howard in the Cowboy Record Company, and he also shared offices with Jack. Over coffee, Jimmy suggested, since he was going to New York that week on other business, he would stop to see a few record companies. A few days later, [he] called me to say that a few of the major companies were very interested. He suggested Decca Records, and said if we were interested, we should talk to a man named Milt Gabler. Shortly after this, Lord Jim got together with Milt Gabler and we signed with Decca Records.[4] Our first session was to be in New York on April 12th and so, finally, I was to have my chance to do my song. We then met with Milt Gabler, whom I liked immediately. We went through the material. Milt gave me a song that he liked called "Thirteen Women (and Only One Man in Town)." We returned to Chester to start rehearsals on the songs.

Once again, we used Danny Cedrone on lead guitar and, as "Rock Around the Clock" was the same tempo and resembled "Rock the Joint" somewhat, I suggested to Danny that we use the same guitar instrumental we had used on "Rock the Joint." This guitar instrumental was later to be tried by thousands of guitar

---

3 "Rock Around the Clock," backed with "Movin' Guitar," by Sonny Dae and His Knights, was released in March 1954 on Arcade 123. The small number of known extant copies suggests that only a tiny number were pressed.

4 Myers would claim that he had negotiated the deal Haley signed. He was certainly instrumental in getting the deal, and there appear to have been aspects of the agreement that were not embodied in the document that Bill signed. These gave Myers the right to nominate one side of each of Haley's first four singles, and to be the first recipient of advances and royalty checks. On renewal of the contract in 1955, royalties would then start to flow directly to the Comets' Corporation.

Milt Gabler (1911-2001), A&R head for Decca Records. He joined Decca in 1941 and had been responsible for recording a string of top-selling artists, including Lionel Hampton, Billie Holiday, and the Andrews Sisters. Pictured here, L to R: Gabler, producer Larry McIntire, and "unknown" engineer.

players as though it is a simple chorus, it proved so effective on these two records it became a classic chorus among rock guitarists.

After days of rehearsals, we were primed and ready to leave for New York City for our first Decca record session. Now, in those days, in order to drive from Chester, Pennsylvania, to New York City, you could cross the Delaware River by ferry boat and then to the New Jersey Turnpike and north to New York. We loaded amplifiers and musical instruments and all the men into two cars and started out. It's funny how fate sometimes directs things in one's life. It was almost as if the Good Lord chose that moment to slow us down, or charge us up, whichever the case. As the Chester Ferry crossed the Delaware River, and I approached what was to turn out to be the biggest recording session of my life, the boat struck a sand bar and there we were stranded in the middle of the river. Now, you can imagine our feelings as we waited for another boat to come and tow us off the sand bar. I had crossed this same river every night for over two years on my way to work at the Twin Bar and I had never had any problems. But, this one time, as I carried the song that was to become the National Anthem of Rock & Roll, and Decca with Milt Gabler waiting in New York with studio and engineers ready, we got stuck on a sand bar! After about two hours, they finally succeeded in getting us off the sand bar and we continued our trip.[5]

Arriving two hours late, and by now ready for a nervous breakdown, we got to the Pythian Temple[6] and walked in, with me expecting Milt Gabler to be furious because of the delay. It was at that moment that I began to realize why Milt Gabler had become one of the legends in the recording industry, and why he had so many great successes in his career with Bing Crosby, Louis Jordan, and many others. I'm sure, had he chosen that moment (and he had every right) to raise hell with me for being late, he might have blown the whole session, since my nerves were at the breaking point. Instead, Milt greeted me with a joke and a big smile and never mentioned our being late, which immediately put me at ease. Looking back now, the session went almost like magic. Within one hour we had rehearsed, got the sound checks, microphones set, and had recorded our "Rock Around the Clock." Our second song, "Thirteen Women," although a little bit more detailed, also went smoothly. After the session, everyone was elated. Milt Gabler, Lord Jim, Jimmy Myers, all the Comets and I left Pythian Temple with a satisfied feeling. I, as I've said before, had loved this song from the very first moment I had heard it. Of course, I had no way of knowing that day that this would become my little piece of gold for the rest of my life, and that it was to open the doors for all the artists — Pop, Country, Rhythm and Blues, Jazz, or whatever in the days and years to come. "Rock Around the Clock," so long overdue, was born! For the next three decades, millions of words would be printed about this song and its effect on the music world, a sample being a full-page story on Monday, November 26, 1979, from *The Sun* newspaper, titled "Rock of Ages" by Colin Dunne that, in part, says:

> Bill Haley, the star who invented teenagers, and goes on to give credit to "Rock Around the Clock" as the song that gave young people their own music. Haley's record of "Rock Around the Clock" has sold more than 27 million copies, beating everything except Bing Crosby's "White Christmas"; Bill is well into his third generation now. "Rock Around the Clock"? After all this time, he is the "Rock of Ages"; his music never did bring civilization crashing down. But it did, as he says, give the teenagers

---

5 Bill's story here is difficult to reconcile with the report in the *Delaware County Daily Times* (April 13) that the ferry had run aground at c.9:30 a.m. and was not re-floated until the evening tide. The Coast Guard stood by to remove passengers, but there was no report of anyone leaving the ferry. It seems, therefore, that the band must have been on another boat which was delayed by the disruption caused by the grounding.

6 The Pythian Temple at 135 West 70th Street in New York City was built in 1927 to serve as a meeting place for the 120 Pythian lodges of New York City, and later, for many years, housed a recording studio.

something of their own, and they have never been the same since; a modest gentle courteous man, he shrugs, "Let's just say I opened the door a bit." Opened the door? He kicked the cage open; and if you don't believe me, ask your dad.

This was a typical example of the power of this song, even after twenty-five years, as the National Anthem of Rock and Roll. The record was to be rush-released by Decca and we immediately started our record promotion, cross-country disc jockey visits, and record hop appearances. Although the record hit the charts, it was not the big smash success that we had hoped it would be. The initial sales were about 250,000 copies.[7] We then began to search for material for our second release. Once again, I went to the WPWA record library and began to listen to hundreds of old and new records.[8]

As I have said earlier, my favorite blues singer, of all that I had heard, was Big Joe Turner. At about this time, Joe had released a song called "Shake, Rattle and Roll" and the song was doing well on the black stations. As I listened again and again, I realized that here was a song that I could do, so I called Milt Gabler in New York.[9] After listening to the record, he called me back to say that, although it was a good song, it wasn't for us, because we would not get airplay because of the lyrics. I told him that I would rewrite the lyrics to take out the "blue" lyrics as they were called then, and he said, "OK, give it a try, and then let me hear it." I changed, "Get out in that kitchen and wash your face and hands," to, "Get out in that kitchen and rattle those pots and pans." Joe's great verse, "Wearin' those dresses, the sun come shinin' thru...can't believe my eyes all of this belongs to you," which to me, was the greatest in the song. I had to change it to: "Wearin' those dresses, your hair done up so nice...you look so warm, but your heart is cold as ice." Also, the verse,

---

7 "Thirteen Women" was initially promoted as the A side in Decca and BMI advertisements and at the band's appearances at Jack Downie's Chateau. *Variety* charted the record's initial success. On May 26, as well as in the following week, it was listed as Decca's third top-selling record; on June 2 it was at #17 in the Retail Disk Sellers listing (based solely on being the #1 best seller in Louisville, Kentucky). Within a fortnight it had disappeared from any of the lists.

8 Bill had left WPWA by this time, his last advertised broadcast being on June 25, 1953.

9 It is more likely that Gabler chose the song, especially at this early stage of the contract when he was the big-shot producer and Haley the rookie artist. In the 1980s Library of Congress oral history, Gabler made it clear that he took the lead on Haley's music, teaching the Comets riffs that jazz combos on New York's 52nd Street were using, choosing existing songs to cover, developing the recorded sound, even cleaning up the lyrics of "Shake, Rattle and Roll" (something Haley takes credit for here). He does, however, give the Comets credit for showing up to the April 12, 1954, session with their own arrangement of "Rock Around the Clock."

"I believed you were going to the devil and now I know," to, "I believed you were doing me wrong and now I know."[10] With these changes, I sang it for Milt. He gave us the go ahead, and again we went into the studio to do "Shake, Rattle and Roll," and, on the other side, one called "A.B.C. Boogie." Of course, we were then criticized for covering Joe Turner's record, but understand this was then, and still is today, standard procedure in the recording industry. We had just been covered by Ralph Marterie on our "Crazy Man, Crazy," and later our songs were covered many times by other artists. It's a dog-eat-dog industry, and, even though I did not agree with it, as the expression goes, "When in Rome, do as the Romans do."[11]

Cuppy and I had suffered a tragedy. Our first born, a beautiful little girl named Doreen, had died at the age of six months of spinal meningitis and, despite the success, we were both full of deep sorrow during that period.[12]

That summer, our "Shake, Rattle and Roll" was released and, in a matter of three or four weeks, we had a No. 1 million-seller,[13] as the record really busted loose! By now, we really had a proverbial tiger by the tail, resulting in offers for shows and promotion tours rushing in. We were swept up in the whirlwind of

---

10 Though Haley was to become a close friend and touring partner with Turner, his quote of the original lyrics to "Shake, Rattle and Roll" is incorrect if one goes by Turner's original Atlantic recording from 1954. The first line is, "Get out of that bed, wash your face and hands," and starting out "in bed" would have been a cause for offence to conservative sensibilities. Later in the song, the actual original line is, "I believe to my soul you're the devil in nylon hose." (The line as Haley quotes it is how he sings the verse during the 1969 Bitter End performance captured by Buddah/Kama Sutra Records.) With all of Haley's expurgation, he either intentionally or unintentionally let the blues code for male and female genitalia slip through ("one-eyed cat," "seafood store"); we suspect the former. As we will see in Chapter 6, when he spends time with Turner on a flight to Australia, he knew the meaning perfectly well. They both pulled one over on the censors with Haley, all the while, casting himself as the master editor of family-friendly music.

11 Indeed, the common practice of Tin Pan Alley songs was to have multiple recorded versions; there was no one definitive record. Rock and Roll would erode that practice, making the performance more important than the song itself; "Rock Around the Clock" is certainly a case in point. Haley probably also alludes to the well-worn historical accusation of the white man stealing and profiting from the black man's music. Benny Goodman has often been a suspect as "The King of Swing." In fact, Goodman, with full cooperation from black bandleader Fletcher Henderson and negotiated by record producer and civil rights advocate John Hammond, adopted the Henderson library and hired Henderson as his principal arranger, to the benefit of both. Likewise, Haley and Turner's long friendship and collaboration should debunk any notion of exploitation.

12 She was in fact their second-born, on May 30, 1954. Their first child was Joan ("Joanie" or "Junebug"), who had been born on March 26, 1953. Doreen died on July 21 1954 and was less than two months old. Her death certificate gives the cause of death as accidental asphyxiation, which is what is now commonly known as Sudden Infant Death Syndrome (SIDS).

13 It reached No. 7 in the U.S. record charts.

teen magazine, newspaper, television, and radio promotions, and the little gang from Chester were now in the national spotlight and our lives were no longer our own![14] [15]

Authors' Interlude: In July 1954, Decca paid Bill Haley a $26,000 advance from future royalties. After the relatively disappointing chart performance of "Rock Around the Clock," and, with "Shake, Rattle and Roll" not entering the U.S. record charts until August 7, it is hard to see what their confidence was based on. Nevertheless, the payment was literally life-changing for the partners. The amount of $6,000 was transferred to the corporation's account, and some was spent on new stage clothes for the band; $5,000 went to each of the four partners. In 1954, such a sum was well above the median annual income for an American family.

Bill, Johnny, and Billy all invested their share in new homes, with Billy and Johnny putting deposits on homes in Jeffersonville, while Bill commissioned a local building firm to start construction on his new home on Foulk Road on the same plot of land (No. 3190) at the intersection with Bethel Road on which his parents' home still stood. The house would be called "Melody Manor," and was probably named after a radio program that was broadcast daily on WVCH during the time Bill was working at WPWA (1948-1953).

The house was relatively modest, especially when compared to Elvis Presley's nearly 18,000-square-foot mansion, Graceland. Melody Manor, even after an extension in 1955, was a mere 2,000 square feet, with four bedrooms and a three-car garage. It sat on three acres of land, much of which Haley had landscaped to make a garden with a woodland walk and a stone-built barbeque. He designed the basement as a "den," with a well-stocked bar, where he kept the band's awards in a trophy cabinet and could relax with records or playing indoor games such as darts. The house really came alive at Christmastime, which Bill took very seriously. The dressing of the Christmas tree was an annual ritual, and Harry Broomall would be detailed to set up a Lionel train set. The Corporation's annual "Christmas Party and Brawl" was a joyous event during the good times.

Unlike Elvis, who lived in his dream home for the rest of his life, Haley lost his house with the collapse of his business empire in 1962, after mortgaging it and then defaulting on the repayments. It was bought by the Ketrick family for $30,000 at a Sheriff's Sale in October 1962. They would live in it until 2015, preserving many of the original features, and welcoming Bill Haley fans, to view it and be photographed in Bill's den. When they moved in, they had found the roof space filled with many sets of the band's clothing, and, at the back of a fitted cupboard,

---

14 In late August 1954, a syndicated article by Lionel Hampton appeared in a number of U.S. newspapers. Reporting from Wildwood, New Jersey, where Bill and the Comets were enjoying their customary summer residency, he wrote: "CRAZY, MAN, CRAZY . . . that's what you'll hear at the HOF-BRAU where BILL HALEY and the COMETS, famous for that particular recording, are featuring their dynamic and wailing sax man from Mayfair, North Philadelphia . . . JOEY D'AMBROSE [sic] a twenty year old tenor sax star . . . His rendition of 'Tenderly' is the end." Hampton himself had been part of the early evolution of rock and roll with recordings like "Flying Home" in 1942, which featured the new "booting" style of sax-playing developed by his tenor sax man, Illinois Jacquet. Hampton was one of a small number of jazz musicians who embraced rock and roll and he would go on to star in the Alan Freed film, *Mister Rock and Roll*, in 1957.

15 At this point in his narrative. Bill goes on to describe his first meeting with Elvis Presley, which was not actually until 1955. We have relocated those paragraphs to Chapter 12 which covers Bill's lifetime relationship with Elvis.

Bill's personal diaries from 1956 and 1957. In 2015, the house was sold to a new owner for approximately $450,000 and it has since been modified, with a few of the features of the den being preserved after local Haley enthusiasts had explained their historical significance.

A rare picture of the Haley family, taken in September of 1954 during the building of "Melody Manor." L to R: Bill's father Will, Bill's sister Peggy, his cousin Danny, his mother Maud, Peggy's daughter Sylvia, Cuppy, Bill, and Harry "Reds" Broomall. Photo credit: Billy Haley, Jr. Collection.

Things now began to explode so quickly for us that we just sort of went day to day, not really knowing what to expect. But, when we arrived in Baltimore to do a show for my good friend Buddy Deane at the Loew's Theater, for the first time I experienced exposure to big crowds and what can happen. The show had been sold out two weeks in advance, and, although Buddy had been announcing there were no more tickets, when we arrived there were lines of people four blocks long trying to get in, crowds at the stage entrance, and 4,000 screaming teenagers inside, anxious for the show to begin. We tried to enter the theater and, amid screams, pushing, and grabbing for souvenirs, it took four separate tries with the help of police and theater people for us to get inside the theater. In the process, I lost a bow tie, all the buttons off my coat, part of my shirt sleeve, and about six inches of skin that had been peeled off my arm, as I was banged by the crowd against the concrete wall going into the theater. As we did the show and I watched the reaction of the young audience, I began to realize that our show would have to be carefully planned in the future if we were to have crowds of young people jammed into halls and theaters like this.[16]

Now, remember this was the beginning of what was later to be called rock concerts. We had no idea what to expect, since the only crowd worthy of comparison to this had been the Sinatra days in New York theaters; but the kids then had been cheering the great Frank Sinatra, a solo vocalist. This was young people wanting to dance to the music they were listening to being played by a band of musicians.[17] And so, after Baltimore, we carefully tailored the show to build slowly to a climax of "Rock Around the Clock." For instance, the third song into the show we made an instrumental, which succeeded in quieting the jumpers and dancers, since we played it up-tempo, and then, halfway through, we put a drum solo which again quieted things down, and so on through the show.[18] We also began carrying two men[19] to serve as bodyguards or equipment men to help us in and out of the halls and arenas.

Also, about that time, more and more during interviews, the words "teenage rebellion" and "delinquency" began to creep in, and more and more the parents, good music stations, and jazz-oriented magazines began condemning our band and music as something from the devil. This, of course, only made the records and songs sell stronger.

Authors' Interlude: Here Bill describes a number of shows that he performed with Elvis Presley in 1955. We have moved the text to Chapter 12, where we consider the lifelong relationship between the two men.

In late 1954, Metro-Goldwyn-Mayer decided to make a film called *Blackboard Jungle* starring Glenn Ford and Sidney Poitier.[20] It was a film about teenage rebellion and, as they were looking for a song to use as a theme, they contacted Lord Jim and, at first, were going to use "Shake, Rattle and Roll" but, as this record had already been to the No. 1 spot, settled on "Rock Around the Clock" as the

---

16 According to the December 11 issue of *Billboard*, this was a record-breaking gig. Two concerts were performed and the 1,600-seat theater was sold out for both shows three days in advance. The gate amounted to $4,000, with the band taking $2,040 (approximately $24,000 in 2024 dollars) for the night.

17 This is an important point made by Haley. Even with his name in front, the act was a band, not a front person. Elvis Presley, by comparison, was a solo artist; his backing ensemble was rarely promoted with him under a name.

18 The drum solo also gave Bill the opportunity to sneak off stage for a cigarette. He was a non-stop smoker for his whole adult life. He would stick with this structure for his show for the rest of his career.

19 This presumably refers to Harry "Reds" Broomall and his nephew Vince ("Catfish") Broomall. Harry had been as Bill's best friend, acting as Bill's chauffeur and general factotum since the 1940s.

20 The film was based on the novel *The Blackboard Jungle*, written by Evan Hunter and published in 1954.

theme for the picture.[21] Jim okayed the deal, before we knew what the story was all about, although in retrospect I'm not sure, even had we known it, we would have refused the picture. However, just for the record, we had no idea of the contents of the film. One of our main problems arose at that time — which jobs and offers to take. Since they came from everywhere, we had to turn down eight or ten jobs for every one we accepted. We did our first major TV Network show about that time, Sammy Kaye's *So You Want to Lead a Band*.[22]

I was questioned more and more during interviews about how long I thought my music style would last. A typical answer was this one I gave in an interview for *The New York World Telegram* in January, 1955: "I don't know how long this music will last, but I know it won't be forever — maybe six months, maybe a year, maybe five years; but I'm sure I'll find something to replace it." Little did I know or dream what lay ahead.

Somehow during this hectic period, Billy Williamson, Johnny Grande, and I, along with my good friend, Rusty Keefer,[23] managed to keep writing songs. At that period, we came up with "Birth of the Boogie" and this, along with "Mambo Rock," became our first Decca release for 1955.

---

21 As with the legend of how "Rock Around the Clock" was recorded, there are plenty of claims to being instrumental in the choice of "Clock" for the film soundtrack. Of course, Jimmy Myers put a claim in. Apparently fed up with the lack of action on "Rock Around the Clock," he went on a personal tour to visit DJs, telling them to pick "Thirteen Women" out of their wastepaper baskets and to play the other side. The highly plausible story that now seems to have stuck, however, involves *Blackboard Jungle* writer-director Richard Brooks visiting the home of his lead actor, Glenn Ford, where Ford's son, Peter, was obsessively playing "Clock" on his record player. According to Peter in his article, "Rock Around the Clock and Me" (published in *Now Dig This* and *Goldmine* magazines in 2004 and later as the foreword to Comet Marshall Lytle's autobiography), Brooks borrowed several records from his collection; Peter clearly recalls "Clock" being one, and believes two others were "All Night Long" by Joe Houston and Big Joe Turner's version of "Shake, Rattle and Roll."

22 Aired on December 9, 1954. Rock and Roll made fitful appearances on national television in its early days, so there is certainly a case for Bill Haley and the Comets being "the first" in that respect. The band was booked for an appearance on Perry Como's show as early as June 14, 1953, though the authors cannot verify if it actually took place, and the Comets appeared on Milton Berle's and Ed Sullivan's national broadcasts in 1955. *American Bandstand*, described by Haley previously, started as a local Philadelphia show and was not picked up by ABC for national broadcast until 1957.

23 Arrett Marwood "Rusty" Keefer was born on June 14, 1913. A veteran of the *Grand Ole Opry* and resident artist at Philadelphia radio station WFIL, he began a long association with Bill Haley as a member of the Four Western Aces in 1949. He became what could be called a "house writer" for Haley's publishing companies, with many of the songs created within the corporation having the credits shared between Bill Haley, Milt Gabler, Keefer, and Catherine Cafra (Billy Williamson's wife). Rusty was the main writer/arranger for the *Rockin' Around the World* album, released in March 1958 on Decca, and is also known to have played guitar on a number of the Comets' Decca recordings. He continued to have a solo career in the Chester area for many years after the collapse of the Haley empire and Bill's departure for Mexico. He died on June 29, 1967.

In early 1955, with "Mambo Rock" hitting big for us, they released the film *Blackboard Jungle*. More and more people were using the term "rock and roll" for the style of music that we played, and so now and hereafter we had a name for our music. If before this there was much publicity about the youth going to the devil and this music destroying the morals of the world, when *Blackboard Jungle* hit the theaters, the people who didn't like the music had a field day. Young people needed a music of their own and Rock and Roll was it. Naturally, they identified with this film and flocked to the theaters to see it. The film opened with "Rock Around the Clock" and, as the film was a box office smash around the country, Decca reissued "Rock Around the Clock" and the record now skyrocketed to the No. 1 position on all the national charts and stayed No. 1 for ten straight weeks between July 9th and October 1st.[24]

At about this time, Decca merged with Universal International, the film company, and we were offered a chance to make a short feature called *Round Up of Rhythm*, and so our first venture into film-making. We filmed this and I did three tunes. One of them was "Shake, Rattle and Roll." Although this was less than a big start in the movie field, it was great promotion and enabled Lord Jim to now advertise us as Stars of Decca Records, Television, and Universal Pictures.[25]

In April, we were on a short tour of one-nighters on the East Coast. We arrived in Wilmington, Delaware, and the final week of this tour and, sitting in my dressing room, waiting to go on for the show, a strange feeling came over me. It was as if a voice was coming from somewhere telling me to go home and see my mother, as she needed me. I did my show and tried to shake off this thought, realizing that I had been and was under a lot of pressure and worried about her, Dad, and Peggy. By the time we had returned to the hotel, I had made my decision to cancel the rest of the tour and return home immediately. I told this to Lord Jim, and he talked and talked and tried to reason with me, but the feeling was so strong inside me, as

---

24 "Rock Around the Clock" was played over the opening titles. This was not the first, nor the only case of a song gaining its hit status by its placement in a hit movie. A case in point is Herman Hupfeld's "As Time Goes By," a modest hit from the 1931 Broadway musical, *Everybody's Welcome*, that exploded in popularity eleven years later after its placement in the incredibly successful 1942 film, *Casablanca*.

25 Decca Records had taken full control of Universal International in 1952 and the Comets' segment of *Round Up of Rhythm* was filmed in Hollywood in early March 1955 with the Comets driving there on their way home after a few days at the Golden Bank Casino in Reno, Nevada. The numbers performed were their two biggest hits to date, "Shake, Rattle and Roll,"and "Crazy Man, Crazy", plus the instrumental "Straight-Jacket." The last was a showcase for Joey D'Ambrosio's booting tenor sax, acrobatics, and general "fooling around" by the rest of the band. Had the film been made a few weeks later, it would no doubt have included "Rock Around the Clock." The music was specially recorded for the film and provides insight into the band's stage act before they added a lead guitarist. The performance of "Straight-Jacket" features rare footage of Bill Haley playing lead guitar in the intro.

if a voice was urging me on, that I convinced Jim that I must go. Amidst screams from promoters and agents and threats of lawsuits, the next morning I drove home.

I went to Mom's little house where she then lived alone. She seemed to be in good spirits and was surprised that I had time off. I went out that day and bought a puppy dog, since she said she was a little lonely and missed my dad. We visited all afternoon and she talked and talked of the old days and how proud she was of how my career was going. I spent the first few days visiting my dad again in the hospital, and my sister, who was now back home with her family. Then I prepared to return once again to touring. On the third evening, as I was getting ready for bed, the telephone rang. It was my mother. She asked me to come over, as she would like to talk to me. I found this a little strange, since Mom usually retired early. Nevertheless, I got dressed and walked the short distance from my house to her little house.

When I arrived, I found her sitting in the living room in her favorite chair, looking as pretty as I had ever seen her. She invited me to sit down and we began to talk about how she wanted me to look after Dad as she was so worried for him. In the middle of a sentence, she stopped for a moment and looked up as if she saw someone. I said, "Yes, Mom, you were saying?" She didn't answer me, and as I again said, "Mom, what were you saying?" a beautiful smile came over her face and she looked up and said, "Oh, God, here I come." Her head fell back against the chair with her eyes closed. For a moment, I thought she had fallen asleep but, as I walked over to her, I realized she had had another heart attack. I phoned the doctor immediately, called my sister, and rushed back and picked Mama up and carried her around the room in my arms. Although the doctor arrived in a few minutes and tried everything, it was too late and Mama had gone.[26]

I was shattered and heartbroken, but, somehow, I managed to get through the next few days and the funeral. I then had to face up to the difficult task of going to the hospital to tell my dad what had happened. All during that period, my father's health had not been improving. He had been suffering severe moods of depression and his doctors had advised me not to give him any news that might depress him further. I was really in a turmoil as I waited at the hospital to talk first

---

26 The death of his mother was one of the tragic events that dogged Bill's career at the time of his greatest success. However, his recollection needs modification in the light of the known chronology. On the night of April 24, Bill and the Comets were in Wilmington, Delaware, the last night of a tour that had begun on April 14. Bill had almost certainly planned to drive home that night, as home was little more than ten miles distant. Bill's mother was living in the small house in the grounds of Melody Manor and Bill's father at that time was in hospital. Maud's death certificate records her death at 1 a.m. on April 25, with rheumatic heart disease, first diagnosed in 1946, the cause. The next day the band had been due to begin a week at the Casino Royal in Washington, D.C. and Bill may well have cancelled at least some of that engagement.

to his doctor. It was decided that I must tell him, regardless of the outcome. I entered his room and, although he was thin, he seemed in good spirits. He began immediately to talk of his plans as soon as he went home. I let him talk for a while, and then, taking him in my arms, I told him what had happened. For a long while, he didn't answer me and then he reached out and took my hand and said, "Billy, she was a good woman and she was proud of you and I am, too. I want to go home now and try to help." But his shoulders sagged and the light had gone out of his eyes. As I left him that day, I knew that, for both of us, things would never again be the same. I managed to hire a housekeeper to look after Dad and, in a few days, I returned and brought him home to the little house at Booths Corner, Pennsylvania. After seeing him comfortably settled, and visiting my sister once again, it was back to show business.

With the tremendous publicity from the film and record, I was besieged with interviews from magazines, newspapers, and radio shows from all over the world. The main question dealt with how I felt about creating such a monstrous thing and corrupting the young people. I found myself defending our music against accusations from teachers, parents, priests, PTA presidents, civic leaders, etc., etc. I fought back as hard as I knew how to defend the music as not being immoral or vulgar, but, quite to the contrary, fresh, new, down-to-earth, danceable music for the young. All of this controversy, of course, only made the music more appealing to the world in general and the "youth" in particular. The music exploded in all directions. All record companies, anxious to jump on the bandwagon, opened their doors to the hundreds of fine young Rhythm and Blues and Country and Western artists. Talent that had lain dormant for so long because of musical prejudice now had a chance. The barriers in the music world began to crumble. Black and white music mixed beautifully and the happy marriage of Country and Western and Rhythm and Blues brought happiness and prosperity to the music business. The music that was to dominate the entertainment industry in a way heretofore unheard of was on its way up and my baby, "Rock & Roll," was here to stay.

I became increasingly concerned for Dad, since his health was not the best. He had another relapse and his nervous condition was ever more serious and required constant attention. To make matters worse, my sister, Peggy, now married and with two children, also became ill and was hospitalized with what they told us were digestive problems. So, I was quite worried for both of them. So it was, with a heavy heart, that I convinced my dad to enter a nursing home where he could receive better care. He reluctantly agreed to this, and I hoped that it could only be for a short while. This brief period at home kept me jumping with visits to my sister in one hospital, my dad in another, and my own home life.[27]

Our network TV appearances at that time included *The Milton Berle Show* and our first appearance on *The Ed Sullivan Show*.[28]

The Comets at that time consisted of six musicians including myself plus Lord Jim [Ferguson], our manager. Billy Williamson, Johnny Grande, Lord Jim and I were partners and the other three were on salary.[29] There came a time, as happens in mostly all groups, when the three musicians wanted to go on their own, and so as they left the Comets we replaced them with Ralph Jones, a fine drummer, Al Rex, on bass and, looking for a sax player, I went to see a very dear man who had been a great help to me, Lou Rosenberg, who was Secretary of the Local #484 Musicians Union in Chester. Two years earlier, I had asked Lou to recommend a saxophone player and he had, at that time, recommended a fine young man named Rudy Pompilli.[30] I had tried then to hire Rudy but, as he was then working for the Ralph Marterie big band and had a contract to fulfill, he

---

27 Here Bill again forgets his family, with the extraordinary omission of the birth of his second son, William John Clifton Haley, Jnr., on July 28th. Whether by luck or good judgement, Bill was at that time working close to home with two performances at Willow Park (where he had first made his professional public debut in 1944) on July 30th & 31st and an made an unpaid appearance at the Annual Bethel Jamboree to raise money for Bethel Township Hose Company on August 3rd.

28 The Milton Berle appearance was on May 31, 1955. As it was lip-synched, except for a brief, *a capella* rendering of the introduction to "Rock Around the Clock," the surviving footage shows Haley pretending to play Danny Cedrone's guitar solo. The Ed Sullivan performance (live on stage and with Franny Beecher on lead guitar) was on August 7, 1955, when the series was called *Toast of the Town*.

29 There were at this time four salaried members of the band — Marshall Lytle, Joey D'Ambrosio, Dick Richards, and Franny Beecher. The first three were dissatisfied with their remuneration of $175 a week (plus expenses) while the partners (Haley, Williamson, and Grande) were enjoying a far better standard of living. They plotted their departure, setting up as the Jodimars (named after JOey, DIck, and MARShall), with Frank Pingatore securing them a deal with Capitol Records. During the negotiation of their departure, Jim Ferguson held firm on their current terms while advising Haley that they were "trying it on" and would eventually cave in. They gave Bill a month's notice and, shortly after Labor Day in September 1955, collected their paychecks and walked out. The Jodimars never got near to emulating Haley's success and performed in Las Vegas and Reno nightclubs for most of the rest of the decade. Much later, In 1987, the three Jodimars, with Johnny Grande and Franny Beecher, reunited as "The Original Comets" for a tribute performance for Dick Clark, and, in 1989, they embarked on a second career that took them to all parts of Europe and the U.S., as well as making many CDs and TV and radio appearances. An attempt was made c.1978-79 to interest Bill Haley himself in joining a similar venture (Haley and von Hoelle, pp. 107-108).

30 The spelling of Rudy's last name is actually Pompilii, but it had been misspelled so many times that it became his stage name. It was his dying request, perhaps partly in jest, that his name be spelled correctly in the papers' (obituaries?). The authors choose to honor that request by using the correct spelling when the text is in our voice (footnotes, authors' interludes, etc) and use Bill's spelling when the text is in his voice, hence the inconsistency the reader will see. We will afford Rudy's brother Al the same courtesy.

(Above) Ralph Jones (on drums) and next to him Rudy Pompilii on clarinet, as members of the Four Horsemen and before they joined the Comets.

(Left) Al Rex (Albert Floyd Piccirilli), photographed c.1950.

Rudy Pompilii on stage with the Ralph Marterie orchestra during his brief tenure in the band in 1955.

would not take the job.[31] Rudy was famous in his own right. His style was to lie on his back on the floor and, among other things, remove his jacket as he played the sax. He was generally known for his showmanship with the horn, which was to say the least, unusual in those days.[32] Lou Rosenberg arranged a meeting and Rudy and I talked. He agreed to become a Comet and thus began a relationship that was to last over twenty years. We also decided to add a seventh man and hired Franny Beecher on lead guitar.[33] As the music exploded, Bill Haley and his Comets rehearsed and braced ourselves for what was to come. By then, the Esquire Boys' and Treniers' records of "Rock-a-Beatin' Boogie" had been out for some time. Since I had wanted to record it also, we did this song along with "Burn That

31 In 1953, Rudy was working as a member of Little Ernie and the Four Horsemen, a band he had joined soon after the end of World War II, and would not join the Marterie band until 1955. The authors' extensive research suggests that he was with them only for a few weeks in the summer of 1955, before accepting a second offer from Haley.

32 This story does not ring entirely true. "Walking the bar" was far from being "unusual," and was a common practice with R&B saxophonists. Haley's omission of his saxophonist Joey D'Ambrosio's role here may stem from his bitterness over the defection of D'Ambrosio, Dick Richards, and Marshall Lytle.

33 Bill forgets that Don Raymond (found working at Andy's Log Cabin in Gloucester, New Jersey) was the first replacement for Dick Richards. He left very quickly after an argument, allegedly involving a minor scrap with his boss (Haley and von Hoelle, p.110). Lytle, Richards, and D'Ambrosio made their final appearance with Bill Haley and His Comets at the Broadwood Hotel in Philadelphia on September 17, 1955. Three days later, they recorded their first record for Capitol. Franny Beecher was hired shortly before the three Comets left the band.

Guitarist Franny Beecher, pianist Buddy Greco, and bassist Don Sgro. Beecher and Greco were veterans of the Benny Goodman Orchestra. Greco went on to become a major singing star from the 1960s on.

Candle" on our next Decca session.

The awards came pouring in. We began to fill our walls with gold records, awards for New Rhythm & Blues personality of the Year, *Billboard* Triple Crown Award, *Downbeat* award as man who had done the most for Country & Western and Rhythm & Blues for the year 1955, Record of the Year, etc., etc., etc. Then *Blackboard Jungle* was released around the world [and] more and more offers came for us to travel overseas to England, Europe, South America, and Australia. We tried to ride the storm and keep our feet on the ground.

In October of 1955, we were on a one-niter tour of the Southwest and, as we left El Paso heading for Lubbock, Texas, in two separate cars, tired and anxious for this tour to end, one of the cars carrying the Comets had a flat tire. Lord Jim and I, in our car, arrived in Lubbock.[34] After checking into a local motel, we got ready and went to the auditorium to find a sell-out crowd. We met the promoter and prepared to do the show. We waited for the Comets to arrive. Show time was approaching and there was no sign of the band. We began to get nervous. Also, on the show as a warm-up group was a local duet called Buddy & Bob. As I stood backstage waiting, I really enjoyed this duo as they did their part of the show. When they had finished and the Comets still had not arrived, the promoter, who by now was frantic, came and insisted that I must go on whether the group arrived or not. I suggested I use Buddy and Bob to back me up. After a few hurried moments of rehearsal, ("Hey man, what key is 'Shake, Rattle and Roll'?" etc., etc., etc.), we went out and, for the next twenty minutes, we entertained the audience until the Comets who had been delayed by the flat tire arrived, and we finished the show. After the show, I thanked the young man for his help and said goodbye to young Buddy Holly.[35] The next time I was to see Buddy was in New York at the Decca building, when he and his Crickets were signed to Coral Records, and that started a friendship that was to last until his tragic death shortly thereafter.

Shortly before that, Lord Jim had received a phone call from Colonel Tom Parker, who was then managing Hank Snow. We were scheduled to do a short tour of the Midwest and Oklahoma with Hank Snow, Marty Robbins, and acts from the *Grand Ole Opry*. I was anxiously looking forward to this, because I knew these were great entertainers and I would be right at home with my own people, the Country Music fans. Tom explained to Jim that he was going to sign a young man from Memphis, and that he wanted to bring him along on the tour to give him some experience and exposure. He wanted to ask Jim if it would be alright with me. The young man Tom was referring to was named Elvis Presley, and I told Jim praise for this new young kid, and so I was quite interested to hear him do his show.

---

34 The tour opened on October 10, 1955, in Omaha, Nebraska, and the show in Lubbock was on the fourth night after shows in Lincoln, Nebraska, and Topeka, Kansas (and not El Paso). The tour combined Bill Haley, billed as "The Nation's No. 1 Rhythm & Blues Artist," with a country line-up headed by Hank Snow, which included the Rainbow Ranch Boys, Jimmie Rodgers Snow, and Sleepy McDaniel. The tour had been arranged by Colonel Tom Parker, who was then at the point of considering signing Elvis Presley. The shows were among the first for the new members of the Comets. According to *Billboard*, Haley was to receive $10,500 for the seven-day tour. On October 16, the show reached Oklahoma City where Elvis Presley appeared as an extra added attraction. The events surrounding this as remembered by Bill are described in more detail in Chapter 12.

35 The late arrival of members of Haley's band created a golden opportunity for Buddy Holly. "Hi Pockets" Duncan, a DJ on the local KDAV radio station, was pushing to get more exposure for local artists "Buddy and Bob [Montgomery]" with their bass player, Larry Wellborn, and had engineered them a spot on the show as the opening act.

The first night was a sellout, and after Hank and Marty had been on, and I was back in my dressing room I heard them announce Elvis Presley. As I watched the tall, good looking youngster do his show, to only mild applause, I could see great potential but he seemed not to be timing his tunes. We went on and did our part of the show. When I returned to the dressing room, there came a knock on the door, and in walked Elvis, and he introduced himself. He was, and would remain all the years I knew him, a very shy, polite, young guy. He told me that I was his favorite singer, and for many years, Elvis would repeat this. Whether he meant it or not, I never really found out; but, anyway, he told me of his ambitions and how thankful he was to be on the tour. He asked if I would help him with any advice I could. I promised I would. For the next two or three nights, as the tour rolled along to great business, Elvis and I had more chance to get to talk and joke and kid each other. As I got to know him better, I realized that here was a very intense and determined young guy who really was intent on making it big in show business. Please remember those were the days before Elvis had had big exposure, or any big records, and on this show were the giants—Hank Snow, an idol of mine and Marty Robbins, a giant in the business, even then, and of course our group with the #1 record "Shake Rattle & Roll." So it wasn't easy for this young man, just starting out, to go out every night to packed houses and entertain a crowd, there to see other artists, and impatient as the audience always is, while waiting for the feature attraction. Nevertheless, as the tour progressed, Elvis held his own every night. One night after he had done his show, I saw him standing backstage looking kind of down. I called him to my dressing room and asked him what was wrong. He told me that he was worried because he didn't seem to be able to get the audience where he wanted than and couldn't figure out what he was doing wrong. I encouraged him and explained that he was fighting all the hit records of Snow, Robbins and myself. I assured him of how proud we were of him, because he was indeed holding his own. I also suggested that he take out some of the slow ballads and add more up tempo songs such as his "Blue Moon of Kentucky" and "That's All Right Mama." He did change some of them, and whether it helped him or not, I don't know. However, years later, in Germany, he was to recall our days here and he thanked me. We finished our tour, and I didn't see Elvis again until Cleveland. As he was to go on to challenge me in the next few years for the "King of Rock" title, our paths were not to cross as much as we, as friends, would have liked to. But more of that later in the story. It is with great warmth that I remember this tour and young Elvis in his pink Cadillac, tremendous raw talent, and ambitions. I was indeed proud of him as he climbed the latter of success. Also all through this tour Lord Jim was taking lessons from the greatest Manager of our time, Colonel Tom

Parker. Tom and Jim smoked many a cigar together. Those were indeed happy days for all of us.

As the end of the year was approaching, we all returned to Chester. For the first time, I really began to feel the effects of the tremendous pressures and tight schedule I had been on. Milt Gabler called from New York and asked me to go there as he had a song called "See You Later, Alligator" for me to hear, and so off we went. The song was written and recorded by Bobby Charles. The record was out on a small label and, although it was creating some "noise" as they say in the big business, it was not happening big. Milt thought that, with a different approach, it would be a big song for us. We tried many different combinations. Then remembering that Franny Beecher did a comedy routine in a little girl voice on the show, we came up with the idea of opening the record with Franny in his little girl voice saying "See You Later, Alligator." We recorded it that way.[36]

At home, as the better money started to come our way, we had now expanded our organization with accountants, lawyers, and business managers, and everyone had advice about what we should do. We bought an old house in Chester[37] and remodeled it into offices and headquarters for our growing organization. I started to build a home on the same ground as my mother and dad's little place, at Booths Corner, Pennsylvania.

As the holidays approached and I reflected on all that had taken place and wondered what was ahead, Jolly [Joyce] called to say that Sam Katzman from Columbia Pictures had called and wanted to do a major motion picture about us called *Rock Around the Clock*. And so, with our records selling well, our baby, Rock & Roll, surging ahead at full swing and our first major picture ahead, we passed the holidays and got ready for 1956.

---

36 Originally entitled "Later Alligator" and first recorded by Bobby Charles, who wrote it under his real name, Robert Charles Guidry, the song had been released on Chess 1609 in October 1955.

37 A three-story building at 129 East Fifth Street (now demolished) that they bought in early 1956. It was refurbished and they moved in in May of that year. Before that, the corporation had worked out of rented offices at 112 East Fifth Street.

CHAPTER 5
The Year the World Went Rock and Roll Mad (1956)

After a few one-nighters to start the new year, we flew to Chicago and prepared to board the Santa Fe Super Chief for the trip to Hollywood.[1] We boarded the train in Chicago with what looked like a small army of people. Everyone connected with us came along — wives, relatives, managers, agents, etc., etc., etc. All was at the expense of the corporation, but we were so excited, we didn't mind.

As we settled in for the trip, Lord Jim brought me the screenplay. As I read it over, I found it was a fictional account of how the band had been found and how Rock & Roll music came to be. I objected to this, as it was nowhere near the real story. For instance, in the film, we were supposed to be from a town called Strawberry Springs and Alan Freed was supposed to have been the big break for us. We were to have two dancers as part of our group and, the way it would be filmed, it was their dancing that made the group. I discussed this at length with Lord Jim. Although he seemed to agree with me and said he would see what he could do about it, we were later so swept up in the Hollywood scene and we let it be filmed exactly the way it was written. This was a big mistake, because, after the film was released and proved to be a tremendous success worldwide, I would spend years explaining or trying to explain that, no, we didn't come from Strawberry Springs, the dancers were not part of the group, Alan Freed did not make us a big act, etc., etc. To this day, people still believe and writers write stories about the origin of Rock taken from this film.

It was a big trip from Chicago to Los Angeles by train, but it also gave us a chance to relax and prepare ourselves for the film. The first night out, I wandered

---

1 On New Year's Eve, Bill and the Comets performed at Michigan State Fairgrounds Coliseum in front of 6,500 people, with the band netting $2,500. According to Bill's 1956 diary, the journey began the next day, when the band traveled from Michigan to Chicago.

up to the club car where the gang had gathered to have a drink and play cards. As I picked up a magazine and settled into a chair, a tall gentleman carrying a pretty little child came in and sat down in a chair next to mine and we began to talk. His name was Charlton Heston and he, too, was on his way to Hollywood to do a film. I asked him many questions and, for the next few hours, I listened as this great actor told me stories and gave me advice. He is a fine man and, as I have watched his great career and rooted for him, I always remember that trip on the Super Chief.

Unknown man, Ralph, Rudy, and Bill, photographed in January 1956 on the Hollywood Walk of Fame. Following the success of the film *Rock Around the Clock*, Bill would himself become one of the stars on the walk.

We arrived in Los Angeles and lodged the whole troupe in the Hollywood Knickerbocker Hotel. The deal for the two Columbia pictures had been made between my agent Jolly Joyce and Sam Katz-man, and, as Jolly also handled Alan Freed and a group called Freddie Bell and the Bellboys, they were also set for the picture. Freddie Bell was from the Philadelphia area and we had worked with him a few times. We liked the group, so we were right at home with them. I met Alan Freed for the first time here. We hit it off right away, although, aside from a few shows later with him at the Brooklyn Paramount and one other film, we did not work together again, but he and I were to remain friends until his untimely death years later.

After settling in at the Knickerbocker Hotel, we went over to Columbia Pictures and met Sam Katzman. Sam was a short, flamboyant, typical Hollywood producer with beret, cigar, and cane. He won me over immediately. He introduced me to Johnny Johnston, who was to play my manager in the film, to Lisa Gaye,[2] who was to be the dancer with the group. We went into rehearsal, and, for the next two weeks, we enjoyed completely making the film. I had a few lines, but mostly our scenes were musical. During our time at Columbia, I met Tony Curtis and Kim

---

2 Lisa Gaye, true name Leslie Gaye Griffin (March 6, 1935 – July 14, 2016) went on to appear in the film *Shake, Rattle and Rock* (1956) and many other films and TV shows. She was the sister of Debra Paget, who was best known for her appearances in *The Ten Commandments* (1956), *Love Me Tender* (1956), and *The Indian Tomb* (1959).

On the set of *Rock Around the Clock*, the Comets apparently enjoying the company of Lisa Gaye, the featured dance in the movie. L to R: Johnny Grande, Rudy Pompilii, Lisa Gaye. Bill Haley, Frank Beecher and Billy Williamson.

Novak and many of the Columbia stars of that period. They were fans of Rock & Roll, and every time they would get a break in their shooting schedule, they would come over to our set to cheer us on. This, of course, gave us confidence, and it was a big help; also appearing in this film was a fine group called the Platters. We had a lot of good times with them and we were to work together many times in the future. We finished the film and said goodbye to Hollywood and Sam Katzman and flew back East to resume our schedule.

Authors' Interlude: Bill Haley kept a diary for the first half of 1956. It was published in issue No. 154 of the British magazine *Now Dig This* in 1996. Like this autobiography, it is in Bill's voice, and it is interesting to read his immediate day-to-day account of his Los Angeles trip to film *Rock Around the Clock*, even though it may not completely line up with his reminiscence above, written twenty years later. His pertinent 1956 diary entries follow:

Friday, January 6: Started work at 7 am on Columbia picture *Rock Around the Clock*. Said my first lines today and did the first scenes. This is a thrill. Producer Sam Katzman is a nice person.

Saturday, January 7: Started second day on picture at 9:30 am. Everything going well. Saw some re-runs on first scenes – I look terrible I think, but everyone is giving me compliments. Hope we get through this. Quite an experience. Glad to have Cuppy with me.

Monday, January 9: Reported 9:30 am for the third day at Columbia lot. Shot more scenes on picture. Today did "Rock Around the Clock" and "Rudy's Rock." That makes 5 songs so far we've done in picture. So far the picture is going great. This is a big break for us. Keeping my fingers crossed. To be early and up at them tomorrow at 7:30 am.

Tuesday, January 10: Reported at 7:45 am to Columbia lot for the fourth day. Picture going along well. Did "Happy Baby" and some retakes on "Rudy's Rock" and "Rock Around the Clock." Looks like about two more working days for us on picture. Off tomorrow, start again Thursday morning.

Thursday, January 12: Reported 7:30 am to Columbia lot for fifth day on picture. Worked till 7 pm – toughest day yet on picture. Did a lot of scenes. "Rock-a-Beatin' Boogie," "See You Later Alligator" and some talking lines. Got back to hotel at 7:30 pm.

Friday, January 13: Finish picture. $20,000 for picture.[3] Started 7:30 am on sixth day of picture. Had my big talking scenes today. Finished work on picture at 3 pm. Now it's up to the public whether we're movie stars or not.

By now, with *Blackboard Jungle* creating a sensation wherever it appeared, and Rock & Roll really starting to dominate the music scene, the demand for appearances of all the artists was so great that the problem of how to showcase this new style had not been solved. In Washington, D.C., there were two brothers, Irvin and Israel "Izzy" Feld, with a chain of drug stores and record shops. They came up with the idea of a big Rock & Roll package show. They contacted Lord Jim and Jolly and a deal was set for us to headline three tours of six weeks each.[4] The show would consist of Bill Haley & The Comets and eight or ten of the top record acts of the day. We would only play big arenas, and the show would be of at least three hours duration. It was to be called *The Biggest Rock & Roll Show of 1956*. Now, much has been written over the years giving credit to many people for the development of our music. Indeed, many people did help, but the Feld Brothers were there first with the big package shows. They were the architects. They gambled their time, money, and work. As it

---

3 The *Delaware County Daily Times* of March 1, 1956, quoted Lord Jim (who was known to exaggerate), "Bill Haley Back From 1st Movie; Got $40,000 for Six Days Work."

4 The deal was done towards the end of February, in the wake of a successful pilot tour between January 28 and February 5. Lord Jim continued to boast about the fees being earned by his boys, and the March 1 *Delaware County Daily Times* summed up the deal with the Feld Brothers as being worth "$10,000 a week for 21 weeks."

turned out, they were big winners, but they also could have lost everything on their first shows. From these shows came the blueprint for all the future promoters on handling publicity, transportation, overflow crowds, security, and the thousands of problems that promoters had. Irvin Feld was to go on to greater heights in show business,[5] but, when giving credit to men who were there at the start, certainly the Feld Brothers should be given a great deal of it for what they did.

Poster for the Feld Brothers' *Biggest Rock 'n' Roll Show of '56.* Haley and the Comets were the only white act on the show.

---

5 Irvin and Israel Feld purchased the Ringling Brothers and Barnum & Bailey Circus on November 11, 1967, for $8 million. It ended its 146-year run (since P.T. Barnum's founding) on May 21, 2017.

And so the first big tour was set with LaVern Baker, Frankie Lymon & The Teenagers, the Platters, Shirley & Lee, Big Joe Turner, and others.[6] We also used Red Prysock's big band and the publicity started to roll. Now, for me, the highlight of this moment was that I was to finally meet my main man, Big Joe Turner, and have the chance to work with the "Boss of the Blues." When we met on opening night of the tour, I found this gentleman to be everything that I hoped that he would be. Joe is a big man, about 6' 2" tall and heavy-set, probably close to 300 pounds and full of laughter, spirit, and fun. From the first moment we met, we struck up a friendship that lasts until this day.[7] As I have said earlier in the story, I had admired Big Joe for a long time on records; but now, as we became friends and I watched him work, I admired him even more. Our first days of the tour were met with sell-out crowds, with people lined up outside the arenas, not able to get in. We struggled with lighting, dressing rooms, the time of each act, and, after a few days, we developed a routine and the show started to click.

Although I have done hundreds and hundreds of tours and shows since, these first ones are the big shows that I remember, not only because of the audience, but the acts also. The thrills were there! The show opened with Red Prysock and the big band doing a medley of the current rock hits, and then out came Shirley & Lee with "Come on Baby, Let the Good Times Roll." Then, "Ladies and Gentlemen...The Boss of the Blues...Big... Joe ...Turner," the band went into a vamp and Joe came out, all 300 lbs., bouncing across the stage to the rhythm and go into "Now, when I gets the blues I gets me a rocking chair ... Flip, Flop and Fly," which would turn the audience upside down. Each act would build the crowd and then Frankie Lymon and the Teenagers with "Why do Fools Fall in Love" and so on until, after two hours or so, the Platters with "My Prayer" and "Only You" would set up the introduction of Bill Haley & The Comets. "Shake, Rattle and Roll," "See You Later, Alligator," and "Rock Around the Clock" closed the show.

Backstage, we all pulled together and there developed a friendly rivalry between all the acts to see who got the most applause. As each act went out, all the other performers were in the wings, cheering and applauding each other on. We were always in each other's dressing rooms. A typical evening would start with the dressing room door opening and a booming voice would announce "Have no feah, Big Joe is heah." In would come Joe with his bottle of Cutty Sark or Johnnie Walker, passing around the drinks. A familiar scene each evening was our buddy,

---

6 Bill would take part in three Feld Brothers tours in 1956. His narrative is sometimes inaccurate with regard to places and dates. As the importance of this chapter is not in the details, we have let his narrative stand.

7 Bill would often claim that other music stars were friends of his, but they were usually little more than acquaintances. Big Joe Turner, however was an exception, and the two men were indeed great friends for many years.

Red Prysock, who always dressed fit to kill and, in reality, was a fine-looking man with a great sense of humor. Before the show, he would stop by our dressing room with a little nip, then walk in and stand in front of the mirror. Straightening his tie and talking to himself, he would say "Man, I'm so motherfucking sharp, I scare myself." We would all laugh and out would go Red and, in a few minutes, another show would be on the way. So, the Big Rock & Roll show of 1956 rolled on through Boston, Providence, New York, Philadelphia, Baltimore, Washington, D.C., Pittsburgh, Cleveland, Detroit, St. Louis, and Omaha. At that point, we prepared to head south to our first problem with the racial situation.

Our show consisted of some sixty black entertainers and Bill Haley & The Comets. We not only did not have any racial tension among the entertainers or the working people on the tour, we never even thought or talked about it. Such has always been the case in show business, because entertainers develop understanding, respect, and admiration for each other, regardless of the color of the skin. However, ours was an explosive situation, since Rock & Roll was the marriage of black & white music and was accepted by both black and white audiences on radio, records, and television. Although we had no problems in the Northern and Midwestern cities, as the tour approached the Southern part of the country, we began to receive threatening phone calls, bomb threats, and telegrams, always from anonymous people telling us what would happen if we didn't stop the tour. Now, to say that we weren't scared would be a lie because, as was later proven, many people were injured or killed by bombs and shootings. You never knew what might happen. We had many meetings to discuss the problems. As I looked at these fine people and thought of all the joy they brought with their songs and laughter, and I thought of the huge crowds that night after night on this tour left the arenas happy, I wondered how anyone would want to destroy all of this. However, as has been well documented by now, this is the way the situation was and there really wasn't anything we could do but go on with our shows. The publicity was out and the arenas sold out and "the show must go on!"

Strangely enough, all the hatred and bitterness erupted before we arrived and after we left the arenas. Once the show was started, everyone really enjoyed it. It proved once again the important part Rock & Roll music was playing in bringing people together. I could fill this book with stories and incidents of this period, but just one or two recollections will show you how it was. In one of the first major cities of the South where we brought our show, they had strict rules about the black and white situation. First of all, no mixed audiences. So, there had to be two separate shows, one for white audiences only and the next for black audiences only.

Now this, although we did not like it, it did not in itself pose a problem. Our aim was for everyone to get to see the show. The problem was that black and white entertainers were not allowed to be on the stage at the same time.[8] Therefore, we had to call a short break after the last act had been on, to be sure they were off the stage before we could appear. This was only agreed upon after many conferences between the promoters, Lord Jim, and the city authorities etc., etc. At the hotel, we received many phone calls and letters with threats and promises that, if we went on, "you nigger lovin' bastards will get shot," plus many such threats. About an hour before we were to leave for the auditorium, the Sheriff's Department arrived at the hotel. The Sheriff advised me to cancel our part of the show because he said he could not guarantee my protection. He also said people were picketing the auditorium and, though he felt sure he and his men could break the picket line and get us into the auditorium, he was afraid something might happen during the show. Further, he said many threats had been made to shoot us and bomb the stage, and, even though most of these threats were idle ones, there might be some who would really try.

All of the other acts and the Comets had gone to the show early. There remained only Lord Jim and myself with the Sheriff and his deputies. The plan had been to wait until the last minute in hope that, after the show had started, maybe the crowd outside the auditorium would break up. I did a lot of thinking and, after realizing that I had to go to the show, I said, "Let's go." The sheriff looked at me and shook his head, as if to say, "Well, it's your neck, boy," and we left for the show. We pulled as close to the stage entrance as we could, but it was still about fifty yards to the door. The crowd was about fifty or sixty rows deep, blocking the entrance. They had banners and signs reading, "Down with Rock & Roll," "Bill Haley's Devil Music," "Bill Haley, Won't You Please Go Home." With six deputies surrounding me with clubs drawn, we started through the crowd. Shouts of "White Nigger," "Nigger Lover," "Haley, Your Ass is Grass," and many others too bad to print were hurled at us as we tried to push through the crowd. As it parted, the stones, bottles, and bricks were flying through the air. I caught a Coke bottle on the side of my neck and blocked another one as I reached up to cover my eyes. Somehow, we got inside and managed to get ready for the show. I remember

---

8 The challenge of racially mixed acts was certainly not the unique problem to the first generation of rock and roll performers, nor was it a unique problem when performing in the South. As the Swing Era emerged in the 1930s, white and black bands would "compete" at the Savoy Ballroom in New York, but typically alternated sets and on two different stages on opposite sides of the room. When Benny Goodman presented his racially mixed quartet starting in 1936, it created a bit of a sensation in magazines like Metronome. Producer John Hammond championed racial mixing on stage at his New York club Café Society at a time when, he stated, "New York was as segregated as Birmingham, Alabama." In the 1950s, the Dave Brubeck Quartet was still occasionally getting hassled for having black bassist Eugene Wright on stage.

saying a prayer just before we walked out on the stage. We tried to do the show, expecting any moment to be the last. The band really kept moving that night as none of the Comets wanted to get near me, in case someone was going to shoot. However, again, Thank God, all the threats were just that, only threats. After the two shows were completed, we waited for about an hour. Only then the police told us it was safe, and they got us back to our hotel. We received the usual phone calls and we left that town the next morning.

Apart from some minor incidents, things proceeded rather smoothly for the next several days until we arrived to the next-to-last town of our tour. Here again, there were bomb threats, but, by now, we had become used to them and had learned to take them lightly. Before leaving for the theater, Lord Jim came and said that the police had told him that tonight the threats might be for real but, as I said, by now I was numb from so many threats. So off we went. Arriving backstage just before our part of the show, we were preparing to go on. Big Joe came to me and said, "Billy Boy, I don't like the smell of this place, so be careful out there." Now, nothing ever disturbed Big Joe, so, when he said this, I really got shook. I told the boys in the group to be alert for my signal at the first sign of trouble. My signal would be to stop whichever song we were doing and go into "Rock Around the Clock." About halfway through the show, I glanced backstage and saw Lord Jim standing in the wings frantically waving to me. As soon as I could, I walked over to the side of the stage. Jim said, "Cut the show; the police say there is a bomb under the stage and is set go off right about now." Well...I rushed back to the mike and stopped the song we were doing, and we did the fastest version of "Rock Around the Clock" we had ever done. When we finished, we took a quick bow, shouted the news to the band, and we all made a mad dash backstage and out the stage door. As I rushed through the hallway on my way out, I passed the Platters' dressing room and called the news to them. I still remember Herbie [Reed] standing there in his undershorts as he was changing his clothes. He ran out into the street, still clutching his shirt, shoes, and trousers. The bomb squad immediately entered and searched the theater. Sure enough, they found a bomb under the stage and they managed to defuse it before it could go off. Those were some of the thrills of the first Rock & Roll Show of 1956.[9]

---

9 With the benefit of Bill's diary for 1956, we believe this paragraph describes the night in Greenville, South Carolina, on May 22, 1956. The report in the Greenville News the next day was at odds with Bill's narrative here. It reported that the local police received an anonymous phone call at 9:52 p.m. saying that a bomb, made of five sticks of dynamite and coupled to a timing device, had been planted in the hall. The police cleared the building and the second show that night was cancelled. This was reported to have been done in such a way that it would appear to be "just as if it had been planned that way." The building was cleared and searched, with no evidence of a bomb being found. The police guarded the hall overnight and would be making another search the next day.

And so we finished this first big Rock tour. I was truly sad to see it end, since we had made many friends through it all. But, since we had another one coming up in the Fall, of that year, with many of the same groups, we all went our separate ways, knowing we would work together again in a few months.

Now that the Feld Brothers tour had done sellout business, everyone jumped on the bandwagon. The following months saw many other promoters with package shows. To this day, they still follow the blueprint laid out by the Feld Brothers and that show. As we returned to our home base, "Saints Rock & Roll" was released by Decca, and we once again rode up the charts with still another hit. With all the activity of the tours, we had neglected our song writing and recording. So during that period we went back to the studios to do the *Rock & Roll Stage Show Album*. Following that, I tried to spend some time in the office, at our headquarters, to sort out the organization, that by now had grown completely out of hand. We had continued expanding with personal accountants, lawyers, business managers, promotion managers, two publishing companies, a custom sheet metal factory, a small record company, a booking agency, personal management of some other groups and real estate investments. Looking back now we had more managers than money to be managed. As we were constantly traveling, in those days, it was impossible to cope with all of this. It was rapidly getting out of hand. Our staff, at that time, had grown to some 60 people, working with us, and this was eating up any profit that was coming from the tours. My only consolation was in the thought that we were building for the future or so I hoped.

Before leaving I visited with my sister and spent a few days at home with my family. I also spent time with my dad, who was now in a nursing home. For hours I tried to cheer him up as best as I could. We talked of building him a greenhouse, since he loved to grow flowers. He mentioned that he would like to go and visit his sisters in Detroit but, underneath it all, we both missed Mama so very much. As we shook hands and I left, he said, "Bill, take care of yourself, and maybe, when you come back, we will play mandolin and guitar together like we used to." I said, "OK, Dad," and I was off to Canada on a short tour of one-nighters to Canada and northern New York State.. Once again, I entered the world of airports, hotels, security, thousands of fans, and what was called a glamorous life of the Rock & Roll King.

The tour rolled along and the Canadians proved to be as enthusiastic as the fans of the United States. We arrived in Edmonton, Alberta,[10] and, since we had a day off after we drove on West, Lord Jim and I stopped at a beautiful lake to do some fishing. We checked in at a lodge under different names, and, after lunch, we

---

10 See the "Authors' Interlude" below. Bill's memory is confused and he was in Winnipeg, Manitoba, not Edmonton.

rented a small boat and went out on the lake and began fishing. It was a beautiful sunny day and, just as I was starting to enjoy the quiet and beautiful surroundings, I looked back to the shore and saw a Royal Canadian policeman with his red coat walking toward the lakeshore and waving for us to come in. I had a feeling of foreboding disaster as I picked up the oars and rowed our boat back to shore. He asked if I was Bill Haley and when I replied, "Yes," he said they had been searching for hours to locate us because I had an emergency call from home. I rushed back to the lodge, my heart in my throat. I called home and my sister told me to come home immediately. My father was dying and only had a few hours to live. I told Lord Jim and we tried every way to get transportation. Finally, we succeeded in hiring a small private plane to fly us to the Minneapolis-St. Paul airport. We were lucky enough to catch a Northwest Orient jet to New York, and from there another flight to Philadelphia.

When we arrived at the Philadelphia airport, we were met by my sister and her husband. As I stepped down from the plane and rushed to meet Peggy, I could tell by the look on her face that I was too late. Daddy had died two hours before I arrived and, for the second time in this short period, my world came tumbling down. The next few days passed and somehow, dazed and bewildered and with a deep searing pain in my heart, I laid my Kentucky daddy to rest beside Mama and once again caught my plane back to Canada to finish the tour.[11]

We had a long night flight from Toronto to Vancouver and, since it was not a jet, it took what seemed forever. As I looked out the plane window at the flame coming from the exhaust of the engines, I remembered sitting on the steps of the little house with Daddy, and all the Kentucky mountain songs and Mama singing with us, and, for the first time in years, I broke down and cried my heart out. I don't think anyone noticed, or, if the few who were awake did notice, they didn't say anything. For the rest of the trip, I fought and fought to mentally brace myself to once again put on the tuxedo and walk out on the stage and "rock around the clock."

The first show was the toughest one of my life. Somehow, I got dressed and got ready. Vancouver will always be close to my heart because, that night they announced us, the 8,000 or so rock fans that were there seemed to be especially receptive. After "Shake, Rattle and Roll" and "Razzle Dazzle" had passed, and as I woodenly went through the motions, I began to look out at the audience. I saw those thousands of young faces enjoying what we were doing and I began to realize that maybe I had not lost everything. The applause and appreciation seemed to reach out to say, "We love you, Bill, and we are your family now." The

11 According to his death certificate, Will died of bilateral pneumonitis, caused by a general marasmus that had, in turn, been caused by manic depressive psychosis, commonly known today as bipolar disorder.

audience that night lifted me from the depths of depression and despair for the first time in days. My spirits lifted a little and, as I ended the show, I looked to the back of the auditorium and thought I could see Mama and Dad watching and smiling. As the tour wound on towards the finish, and I somehow managed for one hour a night to put on the show, I really knew the meaning of the songs "Laughing on the Outside, Crying on the Inside" or "Even tho' Your Heart is Breaking, Laugh Clown, Laugh." And so, we finished the tour and once again returned to home base.

Authors' Interlude: Since this is such a poignant moment in Haley's life and we do have access to his personal diary, it is interesting to examine his entries during this time. Note the pattern of his travel and concert data, and his assessment of crowd size and behavior. As stated in his autobiography, he was increasingly aware of the threat. These excerpts also provide an accurate sequence of the events of the second half of June 1956:

Friday, June 15: Off today. Traveled to Winnipeg, Manitoba for start of Canada tour.

Saturday, June 16: Had a parade in our honor. People treated us very good. Arena, Winnipeg, Manitoba. 4,500 people. Show went well. Now on to western Canada.

Sunday, June 17: Father's Day. Another sad day in my life. Today God called my dad to heaven. He is now at rest. Daddy, we all loved you so and we will miss you. God bless him and keep him. Drove 168 miles back to Winnipeg and waited for a plane for home.

Monday, June 18: Left Winnipeg at 1:30 pm. Flew to Grand Forks, North Dakota, from there to Fargo, North Dakota, from there to Minneapolis and caught a plane from there to New York. Train from there to Phila. where Cuppy met me. Back home at 2:30 am to see my daddy for the last time.

Tuesday, June 19: Dad's viewing tonight at 7pm. Everyone sent flowers and dad would have been proud. He looked wonderful.

Wednesday, June 20: Dad's funeral today at 2 pm. Now he is at rest beside my mother. My heart is heavy today. May God bless him.

Thursday, June 21: Off today.

Friday, June 22: Left Phila. Airport at 11 am, flew to Newark, from there to Toronto and caught 9:35 pm six hours late plane to Calgary, Alberta. Arrived there at 2 am. Missed my show and have to do one tomorrow morning to make up for it.

Saturday, June 23: Played 10 am show in Calgary, Alberta then drove to Lethbridge, Alberta and did two shows. Shows went well and this ends a bad, bad week.

Sunday, June 24: Traveled all day to Spokane, Washington. Beautiful trip. Off.

Monday, June 25: Broke out with hemorrhoids here. Put in a bad day. Spokane, Washington. 4,000 people here. Crowd very receptive and show went well. Transmission went out on our car.

Tuesday, June 26: Off. Waited till 7 pm for our car to be repaired. Then left Spokane and drove to Columbia River Valley, Washington and stayed here overnight.

Wednesday, June 27: Arrived 8 pm and had car trouble again. Vancouver, British Columbia. 4,000 people here. $4,250 for our end. Our biggest money to date. Show was received well. Crowd a bit unruly but everything went well.

Thursday, June 28: Left Vancouver at 9 am and drove to Olympia. Olympia, Washington. 2,000 people here. Just a fair date as promoter didn't do too good a job. Went well then left after the job and drove to Portland..

Friday, June 29: Did record promotion. Portland, Oregon. 3,000 people here. Job went well. Crowd behaved and enjoyed it.

Saturday, June 30: Arrived at Seattle at 1 pm by train. Did record promotion. Seattle, Washington. 3,500 people here. Once again, I felt that we could have done a lot more people if the promoter had worked. Oh well, live and learn. Everything went well though.

And so, we finished this first big rock tour. I was truly sad to see it end, since we had made many friends through it all. But, since we had another one coming up in the fall of that year with many of the same groups, we all went our separate ways knowing we would work together again in a few months.

Now that the Feld Brothers tour had done sell-out business, everyone jumped on the bandwagon. The following months saw many other promoters with package shows. To this day, they still follow the blueprint laid out by the Feld Brothers and that show. As we returned to our home base, "The Saints Rock 'n Roll" was released by Decca and we once again rode up the charts with still another hit. With all the activity of the tours, we had neglected our songwriting and recording. So, during that period we went back to the studios to do the *Rock & Roll Stage Show* album.[12] Following that, I tried to spend some time in the office at our headquarters to sort out the organization that by now had grown completely out of hand. We had continued expanding with personal accountants, lawyers, business managers, promotion managers, two publishing companies, a custom sheet metal factory, a small record company, a booking agency, personal management of some other groups, and real estate investments. Looking back now, we had more managers than money to be managed. As we were constantly traveling in those days, it was impossible to cope with all of this. It was rapidly

12 This paragraph is chronologically misplaced. "The Saints Rock 'n Roll" had been released on March 14, 1956; the *Rock 'n' Roll Stage Show* LP had been recorded in the last week of March 1956.

getting out of hand. Our staff at that time had grown to some sixty people working with us, and this was eating up any profit that was coming from the tours. My only consolation was in the thought that we were building for the future, or so I hoped.[13]

As the tremendous publicity of our music, records, and movie *Blackboard Jungle* increased, I found myself more and more confined to hotel rooms. Each time we tried to go out, we were mobbed by people and reporters. Although I realized that this is all part of being a public figure, it began to wear on my nerves. For the first time, I started to become a little depressed. Lord Jim and I spent many hours discussing ways to get away for a few hours of relaxation and different ways to sneak in and out of hotels and theaters and disguises to use. This was to come in very handy in the days and months ahead.

Rock Around the Clock, our first picture, previewed in Washington, D.C., and we went to appear at the preview.[14] The opening was a smash success! As it opened in theaters all over the country, with kids jamming the theater and dancing in the aisles, and from all reports, the picture was a great success. I was trying to get myself back on the track.

We left once again for Hollywood, this time to film our second Columbia picture called *Don't Knock the Rock*.[15] Once again, I worked with Alan Freed and some fine groups. It was while making this film that I met Little Richard. He also had a part in this film. At first Richard was a little distant, since I had covered his

---

13 In May 1956, the Comets' Corporation moved into a newly purchased office building at 129 East 5th Street in Chester. Over the next few months, it was refurbished to meet their needs, including the equipping of the basement as a "state-of-the-art" recording studio. The full extent of the corporation, as described by Bill here, was put in place over many months between 1956 and 1958.

14 Bill places this a bit late in his chronology, as his 1956 diary indicates he had seen a sneak preview in Washington on February 27, 1956, and attended the public premiere on March 14.

15 They arrived in Hollywood on September 17, 1956. It is remarkable how little Haley has to say about the nature and quality of his two Katzman films, save for his complaints as to *Rock Around the Clock*'s depiction of how the Comets (and rock and roll) got started. The first film is actually a pretty good movie, with an intriguing villainess played by Alix Talton and some spectacular dancing. Haley's acting is wooden and terrible, as he would be the first to admit. *Don't Knock the Rock*, on the other hand, is a terrible, preachy, apologist movie, though Haley's acting improves and there are more wonderful musical performances, protagonist Alan Dale's notwithstanding. Haley's involvement in the film appears to have been secured at the last minute, with *Billboard* (September 15) reporting that Jolly Joyce had signed the deal "this week." The film at that time was going to be titled *Hi Fi*. A week later, it had been changed to *Rhythm and Blues*. Following the filming, the title changed yet again, to *Don't Knock the Rock*. Haley had not yet recorded the song; his later recording was played over the opening title, but the final scene of the film was given to Dale, who had already recorded the song for Coral Records. An indication of how Bill Haley's business model had developed since making *Rock Around the Clock* in January was that his company, Valley Brook, published five of the six numbers on which he featured, as well as the theme song. Nevertheless, the film was less successful than its predecessor, and the earnings may have been disappointing.

Bill and the Comets here on the film set of *Don't Knock the Rock*, miming to a specially-recorded version of Franny Beecher's feature number, "Goofin' Around."

On the set of film *Don't Knock the Rock* in September 1956, Alan Freed is pictured with Little Richard and Bill Haley.

record of "Rip It Up",[16] but, before the film was finished, we became friends and this friendship also has lasted through the years. He was and is a great entertainer, and that film was to help both of us with our careers.

When the film was finished, we returned once again to the East, where we were greeted with the news that our records had now, helped at first by *Blackboard Jungle* and now with the great success of *Rock Around the Clock*, broken wide open all over the world. For instance, in England in the year 1956, we were in the Top 30 for fifty-one out of fifty-two weeks, and for eight weeks we had five of the Top 20. In Australia, we were having similar success. It was about this time also, as more and more publicity rolled off the presses, that the titles began to flow. We were referred to as "The King of Rock and Roll," "The World's #1 Rock and Roll King," "The Father of Rock and Roll," "The Crown Prince of Rock," "The Originator of Rock and Roll," "The Glenn Miller of Rock and Roll," "The Man Who Started It All," and many more. Our next release was "Hot Dog Buddy Buddy" and "Rockin' Thru the Rye."[17] Another hit was on the charts! We received many offers from all over the world and Lord Jim said it might be kind of a vacation if we did travel overseas. It would be a chance for me to rest and clear my head. Little did we know what lay ahead for us, but we signed for a three-week tour of Australia for January of 1957 and also, following this, a six-week tour of Great Britain.

Now for the first time I was being challenged for the title "The King of Rock & Roll" as another artist had exploded on the scene to challenge me. Guess who? Yes my old buddy, Elvis, had come on like gangbusters as they used to say. RCA Records had mounted a tremendous publicity campaign and Elvis Presley records were bombarding the charts. I felt that Decca should match the RCA promotion, so Lord Jim and I went to New York to have a conference with the powers that be at Decca. We pleaded our case, but ran up against a stone wall. We were told that the company had a policy of treating all their artists equally, and if they gave us extra promotion, they would have to do this for all the others. I had great respect for my record company, and especially for Milt Gabler; and although I still felt that they should match the promotion of RCA for Elvis, there was no other choice for me but to go along with their decision."Rip it Up" was rush-released to coincide with the new film and this record also went up the charts.[18] By now, Rock & Roll had blossomed into full bloom and, due to the tremendous crowds, there was great concern for the safety of the people who were jamming theaters and

---

16 Released by Decca on August 6th, 1956.

17 These were released in June 1956.

18 It had been recorded on July 12 and was released by Decca within two weeks, some months before the film came out.

auditoriums. Everywhere we went, I was receiving orders and advice. As our final tour of 1956 was coming up, "The Biggest In-Person Show of 1956," I tried to clear my head. I was told to keep the act short, then the next moment to lengthen the act, next to put in more slow numbers, then don't play too wild as the kids would riot, then play only the million-sellers, then try to talk more and so on until, finally, I was more confused than they were. There was the constant problem of police protection and security at hotels and theaters. We ran into the problems now of hotels not wanting to give us rooms, lest the fans found out where we were staying. The press was always wanting exclusive interviews, which was a necessary part of the promotion.[19]

The anti-Rock & Rollers were now at full blast and were saying I was the "Devil's Advocate," the perverter of youth, and so, with all of this happening, we joined Irvin Feld and Company to hit the road once more. This tour included my old buddies, Big Joe Turner, LaVern Baker, Frankie Lymon and I was to meet for the first time such great acts as Clyde McPhatter and the Drifters, the Clovers, the Flairs, a young man with his first hit record, Chuck Berry, Ella Johnson, Shirley Gunter, and Buddy Johnson's Big Rock Band.[20]

This show was as great as the first one we had done. During the six weeks, I had a chance to regain my balance a little and many hours were spent with me playing guitar and Big Joe singing blues songs backstage. We killed many a bottle of Johnnie Walker Red as Joe told me stories of the old days in Kansas City. A great friendship had developed between Joe Turner and I and, when he mentioned wanting to travel with me, I managed for him and LaVern Baker to go along with us on our coming tour of Australia. Since Joe was afraid to fly, he had a million questions about Australia that I, of course, could not answer because I also had never been there. However, Joe seemed to think I was an expert and so, as a joke on my part, when he asked me how the weather would be in January in Australia I told him I supposed it would be cold, as it was winter, and for him to bring along

---

19 This was Bill's third and final Feld Brothers' tour, a tour of the Eastern Zones and the Midwest. For part of the tour, they were joined by Vic Lewis and his Orchestra from the U.K. They would have been completely unknown to the American audiences and they were there in exchange for the forthcoming Haley U.K. tour. The U.K. Board of Trade's post-war regulations demanded that for every American act visiting Great Britain, a British act would visit the United States and earn the same amount of money. Lewis reported in the U.K. music press that each act only did four numbers, and also remarked on the large number of different-colored stage costumes that traveled with the Comets. Lewis' orchestra would be one of the support acts for Haley's 1957 U.K. tour.

20 Yet again, Bill fails to mention a significant event in his private life. His and Cuppy's second son, James Stephen, was born on October 8, 1956. The schedule for the Feld Brothers' show seems to have been planned around it. It opened on September 28 for three nights in Hershey, Toronto and Montreal, which were followed by a two-week break. It resumed on October 14 in Richmond, Virginia, and then ran, with few breaks, until December 1.

plenty of warm clothes. I supposed that he wouldn't take me seriously, but ...more of that story in the next chapter.

The tour finished in the middle of December and, once again, we said goodbye to all of our gang, in particular to LaVern Baker and Big Joe. We all returned to our homes to prepare for January and the trip to Australia. Our Decca record of "Rudy's Rock" had been released and we had still another hit riding as the end of the year drew near. As the holidays approached, and I had a few moments to reflect on all that had happened, I felt suddenly very tired. True, as an artist, it had surpassed my wildest dreams on the one side, but the loss of my mother and dad nullified any elation I might have felt. My life was no longer my own, and the only rest or sleep I was getting was with the help of a bottle of Johnnie Walker. I realized that I had developed a shell around myself and was keeping the hurt inside; but, under the circumstances, there was nothing else I could do. It seemed there were now two Bill Haleys: the one the world saw as the King of Rock & Roll and the one that, for a few hours a day, could relax in a hotel room away from the crowds.

That Christmas Eve I walked outside and, as I prayed for strength in the days ahead, I asked myself, thinking of this tiger that I had by the tail, "Well, Haley, how do you feel?" and the answer was, "I'm Scared."

Authors' Interlude: 1956 was a momentous year in Haley's career, involving four major tours and covering most of the North American continent. Having left his diary behind when he had left his Boothwyn home, Melody Manor, he had no accurate references available when he wrote his autobiography. Thus his narrative is unreliable, at least in terms of places and dates.

Bill undertook four major tours during the year, three for the Feld Brothers (under the banner of "Super Attractions"), and one, promoted and booked by his own Corporation, which took in parts of Canada. He and the Comets were on tour for c.100 nights during the year, and on the Super Attractions tours he was the sole white act in an otherwise black line-up.

We have let his narrative stand, in preference to a major restructuring of the chronology. There are sources on the internet for those who want to know the detailed chronology of these tours.

https://rnrhistorian.blogspot.com/2016/02/biggest-in-person-show-of-1956.html

https://rnrhistorian.blogspot.com/2016/02/the-biggest-rock-n-roll-show-of-1956.html

CHAPTER 6
After #1 Where Do You Go? (1957)

In early January of 1957, we boarded our plane for the first leg of the trip to Australia.[1] As we flew to Los Angeles where we were to meet the rest of the people, I sat back and for the first time it dawned on me — I was taking Rock & Roll halfway around the world to far-off Australia and I wondered how it would be accepted. Lord Jim had always said he wanted me to travel around the world and prepare for the years to come because, as he said that, and later was proven to be right, if we built a world market for the band, when the lean years come, we "would always have places to work." As we flew west my spirits started to lift and I looked forward to once again joining my friends, Big Joe, LaVern Baker, the Platters, and Freddie Bell and the Bellboys.

Upon arrival at the Los Angeles Airport, we were met by the whole gang and, after hellos and greetings, I looked around for my main man, Big Joe, who was nowhere in sight. Shortly after, I was paged to go to the main entrance. There I spotted a large gentleman dressed in a beautiful black overcoat with a grey Homburg hat, scarf, and gloves and it took me a moment to realize that this was Big Joe. He called, "Hey, Billy Boy, here I am." Suddenly I remembered our conversation about the weather in Australia. I, of course, had brought along only summer clothes as the seasons are reversed; when it's winter here in the United States, it is summer there, but I suppose Joe had not asked anyone, so he assumed

---

1 They left on January 3, 1957, at 11:58 p.m. from Los Angeles after a sixteen-hour wait at the Ambassador Hotel. They had arrived in Los Angeles at 8 a.m. on the Santa Fe Super Chief (This information is according to Haley's 1957 diary, published by the British magazine, *Now Dig This*. (#155, February 1996) In an interview with veteran Canadian rock and roll disk jockey Red Robinson on May 31, 1966, Bill revealed the commercial details of the tour: "The price we received was $77,000 for ten days and round-trip fares to go down to Sydney, Australia.... Big Joe, I think, got $15,000." Later in the tour, while suffering from laryngitis, Bill didn't turn up for one show. He claimed he was sued by the promoter and, he told Robinson, "There went about $30,000 of the 77!"

it was cold there and had dressed as if he were going to the South Pole. He was already sweating as I greeted him. Of course, it was already too late for Joe to change wardrobe, so I just kept quiet and hoped for the best. We soon boarded our flight for Honolulu, Hawaii, where we were to change planes for our flight to Australia.

Upon arrival in Hawaii, I began to get my first taste of just how popular Rock & Roll had become outside of the continental United States. There was a big crowd of fans and press to meet us at the airport and, for the short one-day stopover, we were kept busy with press receptions and parties. The record company and movie company had arranged all this and we were treated royally. We met the mayor, civic leaders, and fan club people. That night they gave us a big party, where the food and drinks flowed freely. We got to bed late, but, somehow, we all managed to be at the airport the next morning early to board our Pan American Super Stratocruiser that was to take us on to the Fiji Islands, "our first stop," then New Zealand, and finally on to Sydney, Australia.

This was before the jets were flying that route and, as the flight was too long for non-stop service, they had to make all those stops. The Super Stratocruiser was a beautiful plane for its day, a big bird with comfortable seats and a lounge in the belly of the plane and so, as soon as we boarded, we all searched out the lounge and staked out our seats for the journey. We said farewell to Hawaii and all the new friends we had made in our short stay. As the big plane left the Islands, Joe and I settled in our three seats in the lounge (one seat for me and two for Joe as...well... remember his size?).

We started to make our plans for the show coming up in Australia. Now, as I have said before, Joe Turner was nervous about flying, so he was asking me a thousand questions about the plane and the trip and, of course, I was just as nervous as he was, but I didn't tell him this. We called the flight attendant and she gave us some brochures on the places we would stop and, as we read them, Joe and I began to relax. We read, for instance, that our first stop was to be in the Fiji Islands, which was the only landing spot in that part of the Pacific Ocean, and it was here that the expression came from, "One thousand miles from nowhere," as it was at least one thousand miles to the nearest land. We also read that the island we would be landing on was a small one and, after a few Scotches, Joe began making me laugh with his usual beautiful humor and comments like, "I hope the captain can set this big bird down on those palm trees."

We were soon joined in the lounge by Lord Jim and some of the gang. Somebody brought a guitar and, as the drinks flowed, we all sang a song. I began to kid Joe about the beautiful lyrics in some of his tunes and such expressions of undying love as, "Like a one-eyed cat peeping in a seafood store." I said to Joe, "Now, that is really an expression of longing and wanting."[2] We laughed about this, and Joe, going along with the kidding, as he always did, said, "Now, Billy, them other cats don't know how to write love songs and sing about feelings, about pretty little mamas. You got to write and sing them like you see them." Joe, of course, saw them and sang them just a little different from anyone else. Which was why he was and is a great star and "The Boss of the Blues."

As the flight continued, Joe entertained us with such Joe Turner-isms as, "Here comes my baby, flashing a new gold tooth. She is so small, she can Mambo in a pay phone booth," from "Flip, Flop, and Fly"; also, "You're so beautiful, but you got to die someday, all I want is a little lovin' before you pass away," and the great line from "Cherry Red": "I want you to boogie my woogie 'till my face turns cherry red." Who else but Joe could express suspicion of a girlfriend like Joe does when he sings, "How come my dog don't bark when you come knocking on my door? The way he wags his tail looks like you been here before!" He really broke me up with the lines from one of his tunes... "There goes my baby up a tree... shakin' and wigglin' her toes at me... let me put my glasses on... ain't had such fun since you been gone." And so, the hours on the long flight passed and, after we had dinner, we talked and Joe reminisced about the old days in Kansas City and New York. He spoke about all his old friends, and especially about his friend, Pete Johnson.[3] How I wish I had tape-recorded those hours, as they are indeed happy memories for me.

As I look back, I realize how important my friendship with Big Joe was to me at that time of my life. I relaxed with him and the drinks and laughter at that point worked wonders for me after all the tensions of the past year. As I've said, I had withdrawn into a shell, but Joe's humor and friendship helped me regain some of my old spunk and I shall always be grateful to him for this. Just after dark, the captain announced we would be landing in Fiji in a few minutes. , we could see the beautiful Fiji Islands in the twilight. As we circled to land, the stewardess told us they had radioed the news to the the captain that there was to be a big welcome for us at the airport. Indeed, there was! We landed and, as we taxied up to the small terminal, we looked out of the plane window and there waiting for us

---

2 Of course, this is the surface meaning of the line from Turner's "Shake, Rattle and Roll" that he and Haley counted on, carrying on the age-old tradition of pulling one over on polite company.

3 Pete Johnson (1904-1967) was well-known as Big Joe Turner's piano player, and also as the piano duet partner of Albert Ammons, specializing in boogie-woogie.

was a small group of people dressed in the local Island dress with lighted torches.[4]

As we came down from the plane, we were greeted with cheers and signs of welcome. After greetings, it was explained to us that our movie, *Rock Around the Clock*, even on this little island in the Pacific, had opened to great success. Everyone wanted to meet us, so this group had dressed up and arranged a party for us. We only had about two hours' layover, just enough time for the plane to refuel and prepare for the rest of the trip. We were taken a short distance to a beautiful nightclub lounge and served samples of the local food and drinks. Of course, by now none of us needed more to eat or drink, but the surroundings and the people were so nice and sincere, we all went along with it.

They wanted a song, and someone produced a guitar. For the next hour, we did a small Rock & Roll concert right there on the little island. This was the first time that Joe and I did "Shake, Rattle and Roll" together. Happily, we were to repeat this many times in the years ahead.[5] All of the gang did a song for them. Then they sang and danced for us until the announcement came that the plane was ready. After goodbyes, we were once again aboard the "big bird," as Joe called it. We took off and, as the plane banked, we could look down and see our Fiji friends with their lighted torches waving goodbye as we continued our journey.

All through the night, and into the next morning, we flew, stopping only for fuel in New Zealand. About noon of the next day came the announcement we were finally approaching the Sydney airport. My first impression, looking out the window of the plane, was what a beautiful city this was. We passed over Sydney Harbour, and it seemed to me all the houses had red roofs, or maybe, after the long flight, it just appeared that way. We landed at the Sydney airport and here we were welcomed by a mass of people. I later read there were two thousand people and press, but I seem to recall many more than that.

---

4 They arrived in Fiji at 10 p.m. on Saturday, January 5.

5 This statement is simply tantalizing, as Bill is not generally known for giving impromptu performances. . No evidence has been found of such performances taking place, and certainly no evidence in the form of a recording. There are many occasions when the two artists were together and it would have been possible. The most likely is probably their reunion in 1965 in New Orleans (described in Chapter 9), where it is conceivable that, in the excitement of the moment, Bill might have invited Joe to join him on stage from the audience. Bill, however, was not known for such impromptu displays in his performances and seemed to prefer his shows to run like clockwork to a prescribed "script." Fortunately, There is also footage of Turner lip-synching to his 1966 Mexican recording of "Feelin' Happy" on an episode of *Discotheque Orfeon a Go-Go*, with the Comets, led by Haley, backing him. At one point, Turner can be seen giving his friend a warm smile.

This was the first chance the Australian people had to see Rock & Rollers and they made the most of the opportunity. After clearing customs and immigration, we were hustled into a reception room where we met our promoter, Lee Gordon, the record company [Festival Records], and movie people. After a brief reception, we were asked to pose for pictures. Now, as I recall, we had to climb two flights of stairs outside the terminal for the photographers to get the pictures they wanted. As we started to climb, I looked around for Big Joe, because I wanted him in the pictures with us. Joe, who was very careful with all his personal belongings, had picked up his two suitcases. Since his hands were full (not wanting to trust anyone to carry the bags his booze was in), he had put on his hat, scarf, and big overcoat, and was struggling up the steps behind me. I waited and, after we had made the first landing, Joe, who by now was really sweating and huffing and puffing, called to me and said: "Hey Billy, wait a minute, Hot Damn Sam, I got to rest a minute." We paused and I offered to help Joe with his suitcase, but he refused, and, after a few seconds, we started up the second flight of stairs. It must have been 100 degrees that day and, as I said before, we were outside and the Australian sun was unmerciful. As we progressed, Joe was complaining about sweating out all that good Scotch we had consumed. Finally, with the sweat pouring down from under his beautiful grey Homburg into his eyes, he let out a yell and dropped his suitcases. Looked at me and said: "Billy, I'se the onlyiest cat in Australia with an overcoat on." It finally dawned on Joe that the seasons were different. We finished the climb and, after all the photos were finished, we escaped from the crowds with the help of security. Off to the hotel in Sydney, where we rested and prepared to leave for Newcastle, where the tour was to open the next day.

That evening, they had set up a rehearsal hall for us to run through the show. All the group had gone to the place and Lord Jim and I were just preparing to leave the hotel to go to a television station before going also to the rehearsal when the phone rang. It was the Australian director of the orchestra that was to do the back-up music for the Platters, LaVern Baker, and Big Joe. He was calling me from the rehearsal hall. He was beside himself and wanted me to come over right away. Big Joe was raising hell and hollering for me. As soon as we had finished the television interview, we rushed over and, as we came in, I could hear the commotion from the stage.

The leader rushed over to me and, in a broad Australian accent, said: "Mr. HyLee, please speak to Mr. Turner; he is awfully mad at something. I cawn't make out what the problem is. Please, please help us out!"

I went over and calmed Big Joe down and said, "Hey, baby, what's happening?"

Joe, who was really excited, said to me, "Billy Boy, these cats ain't makin' it and I been layin' it on them for two hours, and ain't nothin' shakin'."

The orchestra leader replied to me, "What the bloody hell is he talking about?"

Joe says: "I been tellin' them over and over they ain't puttin' it down and how am I goin' to pick up on it if the cats ain't puttin' it down?"

I then explained to the leader that Joe was using musician's talk to say he wanted the heavy backbeat, which they were not used to playing. After a few more words, we finally got it straightened out but, between Joe's jazz expressions and the Australian accent of the leader, it was mostly sign language for a while. Before the tour ended, Joe had them all talking like him, and he was doing all right with his Australian accent.

We opened the first night and the arena was a complete sell out, with thousands outside trying to get tickets. After many encores, the show was off to a big start! The show opened with Freddie Bell and the Bellboys doing their "Giddy up a Ding Dong" from the [*Rock Around the Clock*] movie, and Freddie went over just great. Then came "The Boss of the Blues." Big Joe bounced out and now, with the cats puttin' it down and Joe pickin' up on it, he had 'em rockin'. Next came my favorite gal, Miss LaVern Baker; she did kill them with her "Jim Dandy" and "Tweedle Dee." Next came Tony Williams and the Platters with their great hits like "Twilight Time," "The Great Pretender," and "My Prayer." Then came Bill Haley & The Comets! The whole show lasted about two hours, and the fans and the promoters were very happy. The opening reviews were good, too!

From Newcastle, we went on to Brisbane and Adelaide, from there to Melbourne and then back to Sydney. About midway thru the tour, I developed throat trouble, since the climate was very dry. I began to get hoarse. They had to fly in a throat specialist, as we were performing every night and could not afford a night off with all of the arenas sold out. After steam treatments, medicines, and every known remedy was tried, the voice improved a little. One day, as the doctor was leaving my room, I spied Big Joe walking down the hallway with a newspaper rolled up and tucked under his arm. I asked him what he had in the newspaper. He laughed and said, "I just went out and got me a hoagie." Now, for those of you not familiar with the word "hoagie," it's the name for an Italian sandwich, served on a small loaf of Italian bread, and really quite delicious. At first it didn't hit me, but, after thinking about it for a minute, I realized that in Australia they probably didn't have hoagies. Later that day, when I saw Joe again with his newspaper, I cornered him this time and said, "Joe, let me have a piece of your hoagie." Well, his hoagie turned out to be a quart bottle of Johnnie Walker, and this was Joe's way of

Left: LaVern Baker dancing for joy on the stage in Sydney.

Below: Bill Haley running on stage on the same occasion. He had just gotten over a throat infection that prevented him from singing for a few days.

bringing it back to the hotel; needless to say, we all helped Joe "eat" his hoagies!

In Melbourne one afternoon, I was in my room at the hotel. I needed Lord Jim for something and I called him to ask him what he was doing. He said that he and Rudy [Pompilii] were working with two secretaries sending out newspaper publicity and pictures of the tour. Now, knowing Lord Jim and Rudy, I was a little suspicious of this activity, so I went over to their suite to see what was happening. When I entered, indeed, they were working and there were two pretty secretaries that Jim had hired. Or, he said he had hired them. There were newspaper clippings and envelopes strewn all over the room, cigar smoke and liquor glasses all over, and they were all on their way to getting as drunk as a fiddler's bitch. About that time, Big Joe was passing by and, as I had left the door open, in walks Big Joe. He looked the situation over and announced, "Have no fea'! Big Joe is hea'!" and he poured himself a drink. We all laughed and Joe went to the bathroom and returned with a towel wrapped around his neck and hanging down in front like a bib. I said, "Joe, what is that for?" Joe got down on his knees and started across the floor towards the young ladies, saying, "Well, it's lunch time, Billy Boy, it's lunch time." Never a dull moment with my boy Joe around.

After Melbourne, we flew back to Sydney where we spent the last three days on tour. We had broken attendance records everywhere in the country, and Sydney was no exception. The arena in Sydney held 16,000 fans, and, for our three-day stay, we had over 50,000 paid admission, which broke all previous attendance records there. During the two weeks of that tour, because of the crowds, I had not been able to get out of my hotel room at all. When we arrived in Sydney, the promoter managed for us to go out of the city to visit an Aborigine village in the outback, I jumped at the chance. We travelled about one hundred miles out, and then we were taken up a long path through the brush to a typical native village. The huts were very primitive, and the people were mostly all tall and serious-looking. We went inside one of the huts and were looking at some of the handiwork of the natives. When I looked out the window, I found that we were completely surrounded by them. Our guide told us not to be afraid because they were just curious to see old "Rock & Roll" himself. Magically, every one of our crew disappeared and I found myself alone. The next thing I knew, they had lifted me onto their shoulders and were marching down the path chanting and singing their own type of music. I still remember looking about for help and seeing Lord Jim, Lee Gordon and Rudy waving and laughing as I passed by. However, after about two hundred yards, they put me down and returned to their village, and we went back to our car to return to Sydney for our closing show of the tour.

Backstage that night, there was kind of a sadness among all of us. It was closing night of this little tour and we were all proud of the attendance records we had broken. We knew we had opened the way for all the other Rock & Roll acts to follow, but we realized it might be some time before we would work together again. The acts did encore after encore that night, as 16,000 screaming and happy fans said goodbye to each act with their screams and applause.

After the show, we went to a farewell party given for us by the promoters. The first thing the next morning, we were back at the airport aboard our "Big Bird." Once again, there were lots of long faces as we flew over Sydney Harbour and the red rooftops and headed out over the blue Pacific on the way home. We had all promised to return soon, but it turned out to be many years before I would return to Australia.[6]

The first leg of the journey was uneventful and most of us were tired from the two solid weeks of the tour, so we slept all the way to New Zealand. After refueling in New Zealand and taking off again, the stewardess came to me and said, "The captain would like to meet you." In a few minutes, he came back and we talked for a few moments. He asked if any of us were nervous flyers. I said yes, that Big Joe and I in particular were. He said, "Then I have a little bad news for you." He told me there was a big storm up ahead and it was too high for us to go over and too low for us to go under and too wide for us to go around. So, he was going to fly through it! He suggested that I tell the boys about it and said for Joe and me to go down to the lounge and fasten ourselves in with our seatbelts. He said he would have the stewardess bring a big bottle of Scotch, compliments of the captain. And to hang on! Joe and I broke out in a cold sweat at every little bump, so you can imagine what this news did to me. I didn't tell Joe about the storm, but I did tell him about the free booze and he immediately joined me. We secured ourselves in and began putting the booze away.

After thirty minutes had passed, we weren't feeling any pain and, when the first rough weather hit us, it didn't affect us at all. We had a guitar and we were singing and joking. For the next hour, that big plane was thrown around like a matchbox and, at one point, we hit an air pocket and the plane dropped a long way. Everything was thrown all over the plane. Several people who hadn't fastened their belts were banged up. There were spilled drinks, food, and suitcases all over the plane. By now, of course, Joe and I were completely bombed out. We were singing and, when all this happened, Joe hollered, "Whee! Just like the roller coaster; do it again!" However, the Good Lord was on our side and we made it through the storm and landed in Fiji, where some minor repairs were made.

---

6 This would be 1973-1974.

We flew on to Hawaii, where we had to leave the plane for repairs. Later, when they told Joe and me how bad it had been, we were glad the captain had given us the advice that he did. In Hawaii, we all gathered at the airport to say goodbye to the Platters, LaVern Baker, and Big Joe. They were going to Los Angeles. Our group, along with Freddie Bell and his group, were going to San Francisco to continue on to New York. I said goodbye to them and thanked them for the great job they had done. Big Joe and I went for a final cup of coffee before we were to leave. The waitress was a very pretty girl and Joe, with his usual humor, said, "Hmmntha's a double diveeny." I asked what he meant by that. Joe went on to explain that, if a girl was pretty, he called her a "diveeny." A very pretty girl was a "double diveeny." A really very pretty girl was a "trawswaw," and the best was a "triple trawswaw."[7] Leave it to Big Joe! I said goodbye to my old friend, and I could tell, even though he did not say much, that Joe was truly sorry to see us all leave. Indeed, it turned out to be a long time till I was to see or have the pleasure of Big Joe's company again.

We flew out of Honolulu and headed for San Francisco where we were greeted with the news that a giant storm was spreading snow all across the northern half of the country. All the major airports were closed and the San Francisco airport would soon be fogged in. Therefore, we were rushed aboard a TWA Super Constellation, which was the last one out going to New York. I still hadn't gotten over the storm coming from New Zealand, so I began to feel worse and worse about flying. But, as our schedule was tight, there was nothing else to do. However, the flight was a pretty good one until we arrived in the New York area. There we found that the airport was fogged in. The pilot circled for what seemed to be an eternity. By then I was a nervous wreck. I died about three times as we made several approaches and had to climb again. Finally (and thank God for men like him), the pilot brought us in safely, and we were back in New York.

We were met on our arrival by some press and our agent, Jolly Joyce. He introduced me to a newspaper man who had come over from London to do interviews. He was to go with us on the Queen Elizabeth in a few days when we sailed for England. His name was Noel Whitcomb and he was with *The London Daily Mirror*. We did a short interview and then headed back to Chester, Pennsylvania, to prepare for the England trip and to try to sort out the many business problems at the office. I was quite happy with the results of our first trip

---

7 Bill did not forget this and he used the phrases "double diveeny" and "triple trawswaw" to describe "Skinny Minnie" when he re-recorded that song for Sonet Records in Sweden in June 1968.

of the new year. As I prepared for the trip to England, I felt some of the old spirit returning.[8]

In planning those tours for early 1957, as we had looked at the schedule, we had selected going by boat to England. We thought it would be a five-day ocean crossing, and we would utilize that time to rest before starting the British tour. It seemed to be good thinking. However, as we arrived in New York for the boarding, I began to have my doubts. It seemed that everyone had decided to go with us. Indeed, there were managers, press agents, wives, some children, advisers, accountants, and reporters. They were all there, and ready to go! We managed to, somehow, get everyone on board, and, aside from a last-minute panic scene when I lost my passport, we were finally all aboard (the passport was later found buried in one of my suitcases). The Queen Elizabeth was one of the most beautiful ocean liners in the world. It is still one of my fondest memories to have sailed the Atlantic Ocean, crossing on both this ship and her sister ship, the Queen Mary.[9] The whole gang set out to enjoy every inch of her. The food was wonderful and the service the best. The first day out, the Comets and all the gang were all over the ship exploring the gymnasium and the theater and having tea and generally being the tourists that we were.

We sailed from New York on January 30th,[10] and were scheduled to arrive at Southampton, England on February 5th. I really hadn't had time to give much thought to what lay ahead of me on this trip. On the second day out, I kept running into that reporter, Noel Whitcomb. He kept interviewing me, and, after about the third or fourth interview, I cornered Lord Jim, who was having a gay old time, and asked, "Jim, why am I doing so many interviews with this fellow Whitcomb?" Jim replied that, as he worked for *The Daily Mirror* and, as they were one of the sponsors of our tour and had paid for him to fly over and come back to England with us, we were to do a series of interviews with him for a feature story. It had become the policy of my manager, agent, and all those around me not to let me know ahead of time what was planned for me in case, I suppose, I would say "no" to certain things. Sometimes, they would just OK things and spring them on me at the very last second, leaving me in the position of either going along or appearing to be a jerk if I refused. However, I chose to believe that, at this stage of the tour,

---

8 Haley's diary entry for Tuesday, January 29: "Slept all day and rested and played with the kids. Started to pack to get ready to leave for European tour. What a life." From January 30: "I hate to leave. Nerves are real bad. Glad Cuppy is going with me."

9 In March 1965, Bill and his third wife, Martha, would return on the Queen Mary from another European tour, sailing from Cherbourg.

10 Thursday, January 31st, leaving at 10 a.m., according to Haley's diary.

they really didn't know what was ahead of us. It seemed that, on my every move aboard ship, there was a photographer taking a picture of me: eating, walking on deck, and even photos of me getting up in the morning in my cabin. Now all of this was under the guise of being for one story or article for a magazine. I was later to find out that this was sold to the British public in daily front page stories as our ship crossed the Atlantic. The only point I'd like to make here, and I am not blaming the newspaper for this, but my management should have known about it and capitalized on it. Had I known, we would have done much better stories and it would have better prepared me for the tour. Nevertheless, on the third day out, a way was found to slow down this activity. We hit a bad Atlantic storm and for the rest of the crossing the ship was tossed about on large waves and seasickness was the order of the day. Fortunately for me, I have always loved the sea and, as I've said before, I have spent what little spare time I had getting out at sea fishing, so the storm didn't bother me. It did give me a few free moments to walk around the ship without photographers and reporters.

Aboard the Queen Elizabeth on that trip were many famous people, as there always were in those years. On that trip were Jennifer Jones and Victor Mature,[11] among others. I did get to meet Victor Mature, and found him to be a great guy. He was going over to make a movie and he had a fine time. They were raising hell with him about playing his record player too loud and having a ball. I didn't get to meet Jennifer Jones, since she stayed rather secluded. I was disappointed, because I was a great admirer of hers. But then you can't have everything!

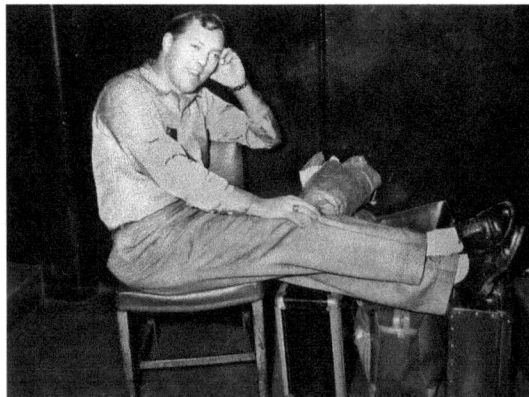

Bill Haley the world traveller sitting on his luggage.

11 Jennifer Jones (1919-2009) was a formidable film star in the 1940s, winning the Academy Award for Best Actress for her leading role in *The Song of Bernadette* (1944). Two years before Haley shared her voyage to England, she received her fifth Oscar nomination for *Love is a Many Splendored Thing* (1955). Victor Mature (1913-1999) is probably most famous for his Bible-themed movies, *Samson and Delilah* (1949) and *The Robe* (1953).

Finally, on the night of February 4th, we stopped in Cherbourg, France,[12] to allow the passengers [for Europe] to disembark. It was there, finally, that the press, en masse, caught up with me and I began to learn some of what was ahead. Now, of course, as I have said before and have written about, I was no longer a virgin when it came to crowds, police, welcomes, and all that, but nothing (and I mean nothing) could even come close to the mass hysteria that had been building for months in England. I had not had time to read of the riots in cinemas or the extent to which Rock & Roll had gripped that part of the world. That press conference aboard the Queen Elizabeth was dominated more by asking questions of the reporters than by their questioning me. They told me of the thousands of fans waiting for the ship to dock at Southampton and of the great welcome waiting for me in London. I learned that a special train had been arranged by *The Daily Mirror* to take us with our fans on the two and a half-hour ride to London. After the short crossing from Cherbourg to Southampton, the mighty Queen Elizabeth docked at Southampton and I prepared to disembark, quite confident and still not believing all the stories about the mass popularity of our music. One newspaper account of what took place went like this:[13]

Mr. Bill Haley, the American bandleader who originated rock & roll, arrived at Southampton yesterday on the Queen Elizabeth and was mobbed by 5,000 screaming young people who had been waiting for hours for the "King of Rock" to arrive. It started in Southampton when the Queen Elizabeth moored. Inside the gates, it began when about 200 enthusiastic dock workers and fans crushed in for autographs. They were an indication of the frenzy to come. "Nowhere in the world have I seen a welcome like this," panted Haley, as he, flushed, and with clothes rumpled, was pushed and shoved into the special rock & roll train that was to take him to London. In the crazy 25 minutes before that, he had run a gauntlet of a mob of thousands of fans who broke through an arm-to-arm police cordon at the gates of the Ocean Terminus and surrounded the car taking Haley to Southampton station. They brought the car to a halt. They climbed on the roof and banged on the windows. Another large crowd of rockin', rollin', stampeding teenagers, waving banners, waited at Southampton station gate. Teenagers clawed at Haley as police vainly struggled to get him from the car to the train. They pushed and clawed for souvenirs, getting all the

---

12 Tuesday, February 5, according to Bill's diary.

13 Bill's typewritten manuscript does not provide references for this or the other quotations from newspapers and magazines, and we have been unable to determine the original sources.

buttons off his coat, his tie, and his grey suede gloves. "Go, man, go" and "Crazy Man, Crazy," they shouted and raced up and down the platform looking for Haley's carriage. At last the Bill Haley train chugged slowly out towards London and chaos.

There were many accounts of the arrival in London after the train trip of two and a half hours, with the tracks lined all the way with fans carrying placards and signs welcoming Bill Haley to England. One account went:

Five thousand hero-crazed teenagers smashed through police cordons at London Waterloo Station to give Bill Haley, master showman of the new Rock Age, the stormiest welcome any celebrity has ever received in Britain. Police cordons were smashed. Women screamed and fainted as 5,000 screaming, shouting, elbowing, hero-crazed fans swept across the station. Platform 11 was like a scene from a Technicolor film packed with chanting cats swaying in Rock & Roll outfits. As the train from Southampton pulled in, the Technicolor film changed to a battle scene from *War and Peace*. The second Battle of Waterloo was on! The roar of 5,000 voices shook the glass ceiling of Waterloo station, 100 feet above their heads. Uniformed police and CID[14] men guarded the ten-yard path between the door of Haley's carriage and the black car waiting to whisk him to his hotel. The car sped off between rows of police. Then it happened! The fans realized that Haley was getting away; within ten seconds they had surrounded his car. A solid wall of bodies hundreds deep! The Haley car stopped dead. The mob pounded on the windows, some of them managed to climb on the roof, to be swept aside by police. Police jumped on the front and back and sides of the car and helped push a way through the wave upon wave of shrieking rock-intoxicated teenagers. For the next fifteen minutes the battle raged on and finally Haley was free and speeding across Waterloo Bridge to the Savoy Hotel. This was ten times the size and twenty times the noise of a Liberace or Johnny Ray welcome. "Welcome, Bill Haley, to Britain."

These were some of the newspaper reports of the arrival and they were pretty accurate. My personal view of all this, even though I was smack dab in the middle of it, was really rather limited. At first, I was overwhelmed, and later, as it dawned

---

14 Criminal Investigation Department. "Detectives" in common parlance.

on me, the situation created a necessity of just trying to stay alive and getting to safety.[15]

At Southampton, in the crowds of well-meaning people, I was banged up quite badly in the melee. At one point, something hit me in the ribs and I thought I felt a couple of them go but, aside from a few scratches and ripped clothes, and, as it later turned out, only bruised ribs, physically I came through it not too much the worse for wear. The train ride was wonderful and it was there that I met a young man named Hugh McCallum, who was later to become my International Fan Club president. But much more about Hugh later in the book.[16] At Waterloo Station, they really finally got to me. Now, don't get me wrong, I was probably the happiest man alive; because never in my wildest dreams, after all the years of struggles, did I think anything as big as this would happen to me. However, unless you have been through something like that, it's hard to understand the feeling. Usually, with proper security and planning, those situations were manageable. But remember that we were the first, and I suppose someone had to show the way.

There had been nothing like the enthusiasm of the young Rock fans before, and so everyone was caught by surprise. As I left the train at Waterloo Station, again I was thrown to the mob and once again there was mauling, kicking, pushing, and punching and into the car. There is nothing quite like being in a car surrounded by thousands of people hanging on the windows and rocking the car to really shake you up. There were two worries for me. First, as is natural and honest I suppose, was fear for our life and limb. Second, fear for the people who were being crushed outside the car. I had been through crowds in and out of many places, but this was unbelievable.

When we finally arrived at the hotel and I had a few moments to relax, I met with Mr. Leslie Grade and all of his people.[17] Leslie was a fine gentleman and we were to have a wonderful relationship with him and his organization. He was the man responsible for bringing our tour to England. We went over the itinerary for the tour, the length of the show, and the acts that were to appear with us on the

---

15 Haley's diary entry on Tuesday, February 5: "Docked at Southampton, England at 2 pm and all hell broke loose. 5000 people almost killed us."

16 Bill never got as far as writing about Hugh. Having spent several years as vice-president, Hugh took over the running of the International Bill Haley Fan Club in May 1964, running it until Bill's death in 1981. During those years, he became a close and trusted friend of Bill's. He traveled with Bill on a number of his U.K. tours, and holidayed with him, Martha, and their family in the U.S. on more than one occasion. As mentioned earlier, In 1978 and 1979, Hugh worked closely with Bill on the production of a 168-page summary of the key events in Bill's life, in preparation for a proposed life story film that never got made. Bill's autobiography, in turn, was enabled by this work of Hugh's.

17 Leslie and his brother, Lew, were well-known show business entrepreneurs and were the promoters of Bill's U.K. tour. Lew's ITC Entertainment produced many iconic British TV series that became popular worldwide.

show. I had wanted to bring the same show to England as we had used in Australia. Had we done this, I feel certain that the whole outcome of the tour would have been different. Unfortunately, I had been overruled by the powers that be and they had set up a show that they believed would be perfect for the British public. I think this was the first big mistake of the tour. As fine as these acts were, and they were the best, and with great people, too, it was not the kind of music the kids were expecting.

We had Vic Lewis and his big band, a pretty lady and great singer, Miss Irma Logan, and a great guy, Desmond Lane, who played penny whistle. As I said before, I don't mean to put down these fine entertainers, but, "Hey, man," as Big Joe would have said, "those cats weren't putting it down," and so how could the kids pick it up on it? They had stormed the cinemas and watched the movie *Rock Around the Clock*, and now we were going to give them a show that had over one hour of big band music? According to their standards, this was Mom and Dad's kind of music. They were asked to wait and then, finally, when we would appear, our part of the show was limited to thirty-five or forty minutes. I argued and tried but to no avail. The show was set and planned that way and for many reasons, I was told.[18] First and foremost, there was the problem of security. The police had to know exactly, to the minute, what time I would go on stage and what time I would come off, since they had to have their men ready to take us in and out of the theaters because of the great crowds that were expected outside the theaters and hotels.

Waterloo Station had taught everyone a lesson and it served as advance notice of many scenes such as this to come, and so, with some misgivings, we prepared for our opening show February 6th at the Dominion Cinema, Tottenham Court Road. We left the hotel by the back way and, as we approached the theater, we saw mobs of people in the streets and, after circling the theater three times, we finally sneaked in through the manager's office amid screams and mobs rushing to the car. When we arrived backstage, the show had already started. There were hordes of people backstage and after pictures, autographs, and handshaking, I finally found myself in my dressing room, ready to start our tour. Just before our part of

---

18 What Haley might not have known was that the British Musicians' Union and the American Federation of Musicians had made an agreement in 1955 that allowed American performers to visit the U.K. only if an equal number of British musicians, earning equivalent fees, were allowed into the U.S. Musical exchanges had taken place in previous years: Freddy Randall for Louis Armstrong, Ted Heath for Stan Kenton, and the Vic Lewis Big Band for Bill Haley and His Comets in 1956. These measures had been put in place to protect the British economy in the wake of World War II. The Musicians' Union saw rock and roll as a threat to the livelihood of its members and had resisted tours by acts of that style. By 1957, the rules had been relaxed and Bill's visit was allowed. To mount the sort of show that Bill is suggesting here, involving other top U.S. performers, would have required the placing of many U.K. acts on equivalent U.S. tours, something that would obviously not be attractive to the U.S. promoters at the time.

the show, I was again visited by the Chief of Security and the men from the Grade organization. They impressed on me that the show must run forty minutes or less, but, in any case, no longer as they had all the men set and ready for our exit. I didn't like to do shows under those conditions. Any entertainer likes to have freedom to stay on with his audience as long as the show is going well, but it seemed that those days were indeed gone forever.[19]

Cuppy and Bill Haley at the Hammersmith Palais for a reception organized by the *Daily Mirror* for Bill & the Comets. Jolly Joyce can be seen in the background.

They announced Bill Haley and the Comets and we walked out to meet the first British audience. They were wonderful, and, when I say enthusiastic, that is the under-statement of the year. From the first song they were up and dancing in the aisles and rockin' an' rollin'. We did the show in exactly forty minutes, and, when I finished "Rock Around the Clock," they were screaming for more. I went back onstage to take a bow with the intention of doing an encore, since they were threatening to take the theater apart. As I came off after the bow, I was grabbed by security and hustled bodily out of the side door where about twenty security and policemen were holding back the crowd. Off we went to the hotel, which, by now, was also blocked off with fans at the front entrance, so we had to go into the hotel through the service entrance. I realized then that I had become a virtual prisoner of the Rock fans. It was to be almost thirty days before I had a chance to return to a normal life, and this only came about when I was back home. They kept the rest of the Comets in the theater until I had gone and then, one by one, they bought them back. The show had gone over well and I was indeed proud of my band. They were all good men. Billy Williamson [steel guitar], Johnny Grande [piano and accordion], Al Rex [double bass], Franny Beecher [guitar], Ralph Jones [drums], and Rudy Pompilli [tenor saxophone] worked hard on this tour as they always did but, due to the mobs of fans, it was an exceptional effort on their part.

---

19 In hindsight, this is ironic, because the latter-day Bill Haley would keep his show short, sometimes as little as twenty minutes, believing in the adage of leaving an audience wanting more. There was a common complaint through the 1970s from his fans that his show was not long enough and he did not sing enough of the songs himself.

Bill surrounded by female fans at the Dominion Theatre, Tottenham Court Road at the beginning the UK tour.

The next day, the reviews of the show were mostly good, with the exception of the complaints that the show was too short and we didn't do any encores. I once again took this up with the tour managers and again got the same answer — because of security, we could not take a chance of someone getting hurt. Of course, I couldn't explain this to the audience and, even though I knew that this would eventually hurt us, there was nothing I could do but go along with them.

The next day, we tried to outsmart the crowds by going to the theater early. We did manage to get in all right but, after the show, they were waiting for us at all exits. The captain[20] of the police force who was in charge came up with the idea to dress me as a policeman. We did this, and I have to admit I got a kick out of walking right out through the crowds with my British "bobby" hat on. This worked once or twice on the tour, but the fans caught on to that too and we had to come up with other plans. This included wearing disguises and sending someone out the stage door dressed in my coat and hat while we went out the front door. In one theater, we went down under the street, through the sewers, and came up through a manhole inside the courtyard behind a theater. When the audiences got too rowdy inside the theaters and would rush backstage and outside to the stage doors when we neared the end of the show, the best idea of all came about. As soon as we finished "Rock Around the Clock", the orchestra would play "God Save the Queen". As everyone stood at attention, we would make our escape from the cinema.[21]

---

20 A In British parlance, this was probably a "sergeant."

21 It is amusing that Haley thinks this was introduced simply to get him out of the theatre safely, but it was statutory requirement in the UK for theatres and cinemas to play the National Anthem at the end of a performance. The audience was expected to stand and not to leave the theatre until it had finished playing.

Our first three days were in London and, after that, we were off to the Gaumont in Coventry, and next the Odeon Cinemas in Nottingham, Birmingham, Manchester, Leeds, Sunderland, and Newcastle followed by Bradford, Glasgow, Liverpool, then Cardiff, Plymouth, Southampton, then Croydon and four days in Ireland, finishing the tour on March 2nd and scheduled to leave for home on March 3rd. We traveled by bus as we left London, and, for the first time, I was able to see some beautiful England. I have to admit I fell in love with that country and its people. My mother came from near Liverpool, as I've said earlier in this story; when I was a small boy, she had told me so much about England. Now I was seeing it for myself.

Arriving in Coventry, we found a repeat of the London mob scene. After the show that night, we returned to the hotel and, after I had retired, the telephone rang. It was the manager of the hotel asking me to come down and say hello to the fans. He said they would not leave the front of the hotel. I asked him how many there were. He replied, "Thousands of them." I, of course, couldn't take the chance and refused him. After several more phone calls, we compromised. I had to go out on a balcony on the fourth floor and wave to them. As far as I could see, there were hundreds of fans all singing, "See You Later, Alligator," and other of our record tunes. I waved to them and they cheered and shouted until, finally satisfied, they left and I was left with a nice memory.

In Glasgow, Scotland, we played a tune for the audience that was written especially for this part of the world, "Rockin' thru the Rye".[22] The reaction was great and the tour rolled on. By now it was very evident that the short forty minutes we were doing was not satisfactory, but it was impossible to change. We were in each town for only for one night and all the security and timing for the police, hotel, and theater managers would have been thrown off had we changed. Of course, after all the advance publicity and the two movies, *Rock Around the Clock* and *Blackboard Jungle*, all the hit records, plus the fact that this was the first Rock & Roll show the kids had had a chance to see, they really were disappointed that we were in and out so fast. In Liverpool, I went to visit close by Ulverston, where my mother's cousin was still living. As usual, the press got wind of this and I'm sure I scared poor Annie Bannister half out of her wits when we arrived in a big car with a large group of press and camera crew. She was happy to see me and, I think, even happier when we left, since she wasn't used to all that publicity.

---

22 This song, credited jointly to Bill Haley and Rusty Keefer, was an adaptation of the traditional Scottish tune, "Comin' thro the Rye" and words by Robert Burns (which, in turn, were based an older anonymous text). The song was an enormous hit in the U.K., reaching No. 3 in the charts, despite having apparently been banned from being broadcast by the BBC on the grounds that it did not uphold traditional British standards.

As the second week of the tour ended, we returned to the London area to do some dates. One night after the show, I was met at the Savoy Hotel by record company executives and Val Parnell[23] and Gary Crosby.[24] We were presented with a gold record, as the first artist to sell one million records in the United Kingdom alone. Of course, this was for "Rock Around the Clock." Also, I was presented with a gold watch from Ted Lewis, then the head man at the record company.[25]

The last week of the tour was spent flying to beautiful Ireland, where we did two days at the Theatre Royal in Dublin, and then to the Hippodrome in Belfast. Then we flew back to London to say goodbye to all our friends. Finally, completely exhausted, we left on March 3rd on Pan American and flew back across the ocean with mixed emotions about the tour.[26] I felt as if I had never really had a chance to entertain the fans, and it was proven true later. Our record sales fell sharply after the tour, and it left me with a bleak and helpless feeling. It was to be seven years before I again saw England. We returned home to Chester, Pennsylvania, and we all took a few days off to be with our families.

Authors' Interlude: It is fitting to wrap up the narrative of this legendary Comets' tour with a few choice entries from Haley's 1957 diary:

> **Friday, February 15:** Theater, Sunderland, England. Shows still all sold out. Crowds behaving. This is nerve wracking. Counting the days now till it's over.

> **Wednesday, February 20:** Odeon Theater, Liverpool, England. Show sold out. Met mom's cousin today, Mrs. Anne Bannister. And the tour moves on.

> **Friday, February 22:** Odeon Theater, Plymouth, Wales [actually England]. Beautiful scenery in this part of England. Cuppy went back to London. I miss her.

> **Sunday, February 24:** ...Good to be back in London with Cuppy. Almost seems like home.

---

23 Managing director of Associated Television (ATV).

24 Son of Bing Crosby and Dixie Lee, who was in London to sing on Parnell's TV show, *Sunday Night at the London Palladium*.

25 U.K. Decca, which released Haley's discs on its Brunswick label.

26 A few more dates had been added at the end and the tour ran until March 10. Bill and Cuppy, with the other partners, their wives and children, including the Joneses and "Catfish" Broomall, sailed back to the United States on the Queen Elizabeth, arriving home on March 15. Some of the band flew and were back on March 11.

Tuesday, February 26: Gaumont State, Kilburn, London. 2 shows — sold out. Played to 27,000 people in 3 days. Really tired now, wish it was over.

Wednesday, February 27: ...Crowds outside theater of about 4000 people. They scare me.

The organization in Chester had been expanding and there were a thousand and one problems that we had to work on.[27] We realized that now we must slow down the pace. For the last two years, we had all been constantly traveling and, as always happens, you cannot be two places at once and our home lives were suffering. Billy talked about going in to recording. Johnny thought he would like to try management. Lord Jim had started collecting oil paintings. He had bought an old building at Booths Corner, Pennsylvania, to start an art gallery.[28] He was

Back in the States following the UK tour, Bill and the Comets are seen rehearsing for their appearance on the Ed Sullivan TV Show on April 28th. This featured their upcoming single, "Forty Cups of Coffee" and an uptempo performance of "Rudy's Rock." Designed to boost the band's profile following a long time abroad, disappointing sales of "Forty Cups of Coffee" indicated that, in his absence, Bill Haley had been somewhat forgotten.

---

27 The Delaware Daily County Times (March 15) interviewed Bill upon his return from the U.K. His offices are described as being in the process of being "converted to house two music publishing firms, a talent agency, an art business and a management concern, along with some real estate enterprises." Haley reports that, with an eye on future musical trends, he had considered buying the U.S. publishing rights in two hundred calypso numbers but was advised against it by the British publisher. The paper goes on to report that Haley's firm belief was that rock and roll had not yet reached its peak.

28 The gallery, known as Lord Jim and Bill Haley's Art Gallery, was situated on the corner of Foulk Road and Naamans Creek Road. It opened in the summer of 1958. Lord Jim boasted in a press release that the Comets had amassed a collection of some 1,000 paintings with an estimated value of $20,000, and that $7,000 was being invested in improving the premises. By the end of the decade, the business was known simply as Lord Jim's Art Gallery, and Bill eventually reclaimed his equity in 1963 when facing financial difficulties on other fronts. Lord Jim ran it for a couple of years more and, in 1965, appears to have made a failed attempt to find new shareholders for the business.

talking more and more of retiring, since he was somewhat older and, I guess, the road life was tiring for him. We found that we had lost a lot of money on the England tour as we totalled all the expenses for hotels, fares, etc., etc., etc., for the big gang that had taken the trip. Our generosity was starting to catch up with us.

It was recording time again and we spent the next month getting ready to do the album *Rockin' the Oldies*,[29] in which we took some of the big tunes of the past and did them in the Comet fashion. This album included such tunes as "Carolina in the Morning," "Moon Over Miami," "Apple Blossom Time," and "Miss You." It turned out to be a fair album and a good seller for us. Decca released "Rockin' Rollin' Rover" and "You Hit the Wrong Note, Billy Goat" and, although this was not a number one record, it hit the charts[30] and so we were still doing O.K., record-wise. We were trying to work as little away from home as possible during this period. However, in June, we took a week in Jamaica at a theater.[31]

We flew to that lovely island and did find a few moments of relaxation. The theater was nice and the people on this beautiful island were Rock and Rollers, too. They were very enthusiastic and the week passed quickly with few incidents. I do remember one evening at the hotel there. As we were getting ready to leave for the show, we were all waiting on the main patio by the pool for the gang to gather. Now, there was always a lot of good-natured horseplay among groups and Lord Jim and Johnny Grande were usually at the head of this. That night, Johnny came to meet us as we all sat there. He was dressed to kill in a beautiful white suit with his hair all combed and his white shoes and his diamond ring flashing. As he approached us, Lord Jim got up and walked over to him and said, "Here, Johnny, let me fix your tie." All the while, he was backing Johnny up towards the pool as he straightened his tie. When he had him in the right place, he gave a push and John did a back dive into the pool. John climbed out, amid the laughter of everyone there, vowing vengeance and here's how he got it... That night after the show, when Jim was sitting at the pool bar, John paid some of the local lads to go out in the fields and catch two giant rats. He then took them to Jim's room and released them. About 3:00 a.m., when the bar closed, Jim, by then pretty well stoned, came back to his room and, without turning on the light, lay down on his bed to sleep. In about five minutes, the whole hotel was awakened by a screaming, cussing Lord Jim. He stormed out of his room in his shorts shouting: "Grande, you little bastard. I'll kill you for this." But John wasn't through yet.

---

29 The sessions were at the end of March 1957. Rudy Pompilii was reported to have been recuperating from a hernia operation and was replaced by Frankie Scott, who took part in at least one set of live shows, too.

30 No. 60 on *Billboard*.

31 The weeklong engagement at the State Theater, Kingston, started on June 17, 1957. The shows were targeted at U.S. service personnel posted in the Caribbean.

Lord Jim always prided himself on wearing beautiful hats. Every night at the theater, he would arrive and hang his hat in my dressing room, then he walked around the theater to check the crowd and see what lady to charm that evening.

John was inventive, to say the least. He bought some slices of Limburger cheese[32] and had cut up some pieces. He came to my dressing room and got Jim's hat and spread this cheese all around the inside band of the hat. After the show, Lord Jim, who had been lucky enough to get a date with a lovely Jamaican lady, returned and picked up his hat and put it on and proceeded on his date. Johnny tagged along behind to watch the fun. In the warm Jamaican climate, it didn't take long for the heat from Jim's head to increase the already foul-smelling cheese to an unbearable odor. Jim, who was standing talking to his lady, began to sniff and fidget. Since Johnny was standing close by, Jim turned and said, "Jesus, Johnny, why don't you go take a bath?" But John persisted, and again Jim, by now convinced that the odor was from John, said, "Man, get the hell out of here, you stink." By now, John was splitting his sides and, a few moments later the lady, who could no longer stand it, excused herself and said goodnight and Jim had struck out again. Returning to his room, he discovered what had happened, and so he paid for shoving John into the pool.

We left on another Rock & Roll package show that summer.[33] Elvis was really hitting his stride. Such new acts as Jerry Lee Lewis, Ricky Nelson, Bo Diddley. The Everly Brothers and Tommy Sands were bursting upon the scene, and we worked with many of them. Once again, we toured all across the States for six weeks. That tour, as the previous Rock packages, did sell our business everywhere we played. The music scene was changing rapidly. Elvis was really hitting his stride. Such new acts as Jerry Lee Lewis, Ricky Nelson, Bo Diddley, the Everly Brothers, and Tommy Sands were bursting upon the scene, and we worked with many of them.

---

32 This Belgian cheese has a reputation of being the smelliest cheese in the world.

33 We have not been able to find evidence of such a tour taking place. Bill and the Comets continued to do big business in many parts of the United States, but not in the context of a package rock and roll show. Bill might be referring to "The Big Gold Record Stars" tour of February 1958 that featured Haley along with the Everly Brothers, Buddy Holly and the Crickets, the Royal Teens, and Jerry Lee Lewis.

Decca released a country song that I had done for them as the "B" side of "New Rock the Joint". The song was called "How Many" and this also hit the charts for us.[34] However, that was in the Country & Western field as well as pop charts. For a short while, I considered offers to return to the Country & Western field, which was then and still is today, after Rock, my favorite kind of music. I resisted the temptation, however, because our position as the Rock & Roll originators and our future bookings would not allow this. As the year drew to a close, I sat down to analyze that things were now getting out of hand and it was becoming harder and harder to control the large crowds such as we had seen in England. Rock & Roll had now grown to gigantic proportions, not only at home, but now was spreading around the world. As Jim told me, I had better get used to the idea of not being the only King of Rock & Roll anymore. He reminded me that the public is fickle, and, as he said, "Bill, you have been #1 for all this time, you've done it all. You've been to the top, and after #1, where do you go?" The answer, of course was ...Down.

---

34 "New Rock the Joint" was a re-recording of the Essex track, "Rock the Joint," with revised lyrics and arrangement, recorded in July 1957. Despite the modifications to the song, this contravened the terms of Bill Haley's contract with Palda Records, which, until April 1959, restricted him from re-recording any of the songs he had recorded for their Essex Records label. Such a provision was, and still is, standard practice in the music industry. Although often referred to as "New Rock the Joint," and identified as such on the 1958 compilation album, *Rockin' the Joint!*, the label for the original Decca single 9-30461 shows simply "Rock the Joint" as the title. Neither it nor "How Many" made the *Billboard* chart. Dave Miller is not known to have raised any objection to the re-recording.

CHAPTER 7
Going Down, But Still Rockin' (1958-1959)

Authors' Note: The following manuscript, written on a legal note pad in Haley's own hand, gives us another glimpse into the process of the creation of his own story. We will honor Haley's proposed chapter outline and succeeding chapter topics,[1] but not attempt to emulate his "voice." Instead, the narrative will consider Hugh McCallum's biographical outline (which was written in conjunction with Haley), our subsequent interviews with Haley's wife, Martha Velasco Haley, and our own research. As all researchers know, primary source accounts offer no guarantee of factual accuracy. As with Bill's autobiography, we will correct and enhance information throughout. The short narrative that follows here was handwritten by Haley.

To start the new year of 1958, Decca released "It's a Sin" and "Mary, Mary Lou" and, after a few weeks of promotion, we saw that the initial reaction was not over-whelming and, as we were worried about record sales, Lord Jim and I went to New York to have a conference with Milt Gabler to try to come up with some new ideas for recording. Milt, as always, was glad to see us and we had a nice lunch and discussed various songs and ideas and, as we were leaving, Milt said, "Bill, before you leave, I want you to say hello to one of Coral Records' hot new artists." (Coral Records was a part of Decca and had their offices in the same building.) Milt left and, in a few minutes, returned with a tall thin curly-haired lad wearing glasses and said, "Bill, say hello to Buddy Holly."

At first, I didn't remember having met Buddy a few years before, but then I remembered the skinny kid that had helped me out on the show back in Lubbock, Texas. Buddy remembered, though, and we both laughed as we recalled that day. He had come a long way from Lubbock and we spent the rest of the afternoon visiting and I found out that we were to do a series of shows together in the South

---

1 These are detailed in our Foreword.

later that month.[2] We said goodbye and left New York to return to Chester where, for the next two weeks, we went over material, and I sat with Rusty Keefer and we tried to write some new tunes. Rusty came up with an idea to write a song about skinny girls, as everyone was always writing about the pretty ones. The opening line, "My Skinny Minnie is a crazy chick, six feet high and one foot thick," gave us our start and, two hours later, we had our song, "Skinny Minnie."[3] Also, we wrote "Lean Jean"[4] and, with those two songs ready to record, we prepared to leave once again. This time our opening show was to be Jacksonville, Florida. It was a mini Rock 'n' Roll package show and was to feature our group, Buddy Holly and the Crickets, Jerry Lee Lewis, and the Everly Brothers.[5]

I received a phone call from my sister's doctor one evening during this period. He said he wanted to talk to me. I went to see him and I knew right away by the look on his face that he had bad news for me. He told me that my sister had developed cancer and had only six months to live. He said he had known it for some time, since they had operated on her earlier. He said he could not bring himself to tell her or her husband, and so he had waited until I returned from overseas to tell me, so I could tell her husband. He said it was incurable and there was no way to save her. I was crushed and numb as I left the doctor's office. How could this be happening? First my mother, then Dad, and now my beautiful Peggy. She was only 34 years old, right in the prime of her life, and with two young children and a good husband. My heart was breaking as I called her husband, George [Gray]. Later, I met with him to tell him the news. We decided not to tell Peggy and the doctor gave her the story that her liver was bad and that he would be treating her for this. We then settled in to pass the time. Although we tried every doctor and medicine we knew of, we knew there was no hope. This was a terrible blow to me and once again the blues took over and I threw myself back into working. My spirits were at such low point; I just went through the motions of entertaining.

---

2 By January 1958 Bill could not have failed to be aware of Buddy Holly's success with "That'll be the Day," a US No.1 hit record towards the end of 1957. This meeting with Buddy was therefore presumably at least a few months earlier than Haley suggests here.

3 In Chapter 18, we will see that Milt Gabler also claimed to have had the idea for this song.

4 The songwriting credits on this song indicate the Corporation's *modus operandi*. Stella Lee was an established songwriter, with previous success with the Mills Brothers' "Queen of the Senior Prom" in 1957. The Comets Valleybrook Company bought the song from her. Johnny Grande, Ralph Jones, and Rudy Pompilii were added as co-writers and thus 87.5% of royalty income would stay "in house."

5 This was the "Big Gold Record Stars" tour, on which the Royal Teens replaced the indisposed Jimmie Rodgers. The tour opened on February 20, 1958, at the Kellogg Auditorium in Orlando, Florida, and reached Jacksonville on February 22.

Authors' Note: Bill Haley's autobiography ends here. The remainder is guided in part by Hugh McCallum's biographical outline. This portion McCallum entitled, "The Final Years of Fifties Rock N' Roll (1958-1959)."

This tour placed Haley in the midst of the second wave of early rock and rollers (those after Haley and Elvis Presley). It had a different flavor to those he had made in 1956, and Bill had lost top billing to the Everly Brothers. Jerry Lee Lewis pointed out that Haley was the only one that did not have a hit record at the time, but he was also uncharacteristically respectful, apparently saying, "but it's only right. You're the boss cat. Without you, we'd all be driving trucks." The Comets now began to receive bad press:

> The most disappointing group of all was the Haley combine, which opened with a good swinging rocker. Following this, Haley introduced various members of the group who performed a series of nonsensical hits which had no real place in a rock and roll show. One man, for example, got up to the mike and sang a rather ridiculous item in a voice. If this is rock and roll, then let's get back to the good old solid rhythm and blues.[6]

This comment was probably directed at Franny Beecher, who was known to have performed "You Made Me Love You" in a high voice. This bit of showbiz kitsch sat awkwardly next to the new generation of rock and roll stars on stage. However, the more modern-sounding "Skinny Minnie"[7] became the band's biggest hit in three years and gave Bill a tremendous morale boost. After its initial success in the Spring of 1958, cover versions started appearing from 1964 onwards, by the likes of Gerry and the Pacemakers and Tony Sheridan. The song, with its follow-up, "Lean Jean," sparked the idea for the album *Bill Haley's Chicks* and Bill and the Comets cut the remaining tracks in three Decca session in June 1958.

"Skinny Minnie" drove a modest revival of fortune and the band appeared on national TV with Buddy Deane in Baltimore as well as on *American Bandstand*. However, just as they seemed to be rebuilding their brand in the USA, they left for South America from April 22 to May 20 (six days in Sao Paolo, four in Rio de Janeiro, three in Montevideo, two weeks in Buenos Aires, followed by a short trip to Chile). The band would net $65,000[8] for this month-long tour. In Buenos Aires, the Teatro Metropolitan was besieged by a crowd and Bill travelled to the show

---

6 *Billboard*, March 10, 1958.

7 Recorded in February 1958.

8 *Billboard*, February 24, 1958.

in a fire tender, protected by club-wielding police. Having circled the theater and finding no safe way in, they had to run the gauntlet to enter. A fan grabbed Bill by the necktie while the police pulled him the other way. He passed out, but following a medical examination, was allowed to do the show. He would then stay in the theater between shows.

Bill and the Comets in South America. l. to r. unknown, Paulinho Machado de Carvalho (a major promoter of foreign acts in Brazil who brought Nat King Cole to the country in 1959), unknown, Johnny Grande, Al Rex, Bill Haley, Billy Williamson (largely hidden) and Ralph Jones.

Bill on stage in Sao Paolo.

On May 6, Jack Howard reported to Bill that "Skinny Minnie" was doing better than other recent releases and he was shipping a lot of sheet music. However, he had had to pay a tax bill and make a payment for "compensation." The letter ends with evidence of the grim reality now encircling them: "Sure wish you were back home as I am running out of matches to keep the home fires burning." Dates in Chile were cancelled which sparked a demonstration by 10,000 fans at Santiago airport. Dates were added in Buenos Aires. Bill was to become infatuated with a woman called Dani, whom Alex Valdez, the promoter of the tour, had engaged to "look after" him. Later in the Summer, Bill would entertain them at Melody Manor and on the Atlantic Coast, which put him on course for a "trial separation" from Cuppy that autumn.

Dinner at the Waldorf Astoria, NYC in the Summer of 1958. L. to R: Jim Ferguson, Dani, Bill Haley and Joe Olivier. Bill was thought to have been having an affair with Dani at this time.

Buoyed by the success of "Skinny Minnie" and the substantial earnings from the South American tour, Bill expanded his business. In July, at a low point in his relationship with Jolly Joyce, he established the International Artists' Agency. Planning to end his relationship with Joyce, he talent-spotted in South America. James Fettis, an employee of the Corporation, who would run the agency, recounted how they "came back with a piano player that they thought was a genius. Haley said, 'You're going to book him, right?' I said, 'I can't book that guy. He stinks.' The guy was smart enough. He had a year's contract and I don't think he worked more than two weeks of the year."[9] The Corporation's second-quarter 1959 earnings and tax statement lists a "Hector J. Alaya" and the monthly payments to him of just $100 suggest he was on a retainer, rather than busy working.

Bill brought back original recordings of "Joey's Song" and "Chiquita Linda," which he would cover with the Comets later in the year. On New Year's Eve, Atilio Bruni and his trio appeared at Tommy Green's Lido in Wilmington, Delaware, billed as "discovered by Bill Haley on his recent South American Tour." Top of the bill were the Kingsmen, a contract-breaking spinoff from the Comets, also handled by the new agency.

Advertisement for a performance by Attilo Bruni, one of Bill Haley's "discoveries" in South America.

---

9 Swenson, pp. 116-7.

On his return from South America, Bill had found that his sister had been hospitalized. "I spent many hours visiting her at the hospital and it broke my heart again to see my beautiful sister wasting away," Haley writes. "We talked of our childhood and I did my best to cheer her up. She remained bright and optimistic about the future, not knowing of course what was wrong."[10]

Peggy died on June 21, 1958. In Bill's own words, "My dear sister Peggy passed away and now, of the original Haley gang, I was the only one left. After the funeral, a great emptiness was inside me and I once again found myself at the same cross-roads of having to put on the face of the entertainer — bright, cheerful and full of pep, while inside, somehow was eating me up. 'Even though your heart is breaking, laugh clown, laugh'...again..."[11]

The success of "Skinny Minnie" proved to be superficial and the Corporation was now in the red. The business had diversified into steel fabrication, publishing, recording, record production, an artists' agency, and an art gallery. None of the ventures turned a profit, with everything dependent on the band's Decca royalties and personal appearance fees, both of which were now reducing. The Comets moved their fan club operation into top gear and, having recently acquired an interest in a printing company, began publication of a magazine (The Comet) which appeared sporadically for a few months. Over many years, the club was run by "Carol Gray," who, although she had briefly done the job, would become whoever happened to be on hand in the office to sign a membership card or a letter to a fan.

In the summer of 1958, Al Rex became the first of the "September 1955" Comets to quit. "When we came home, this is what burned me up, I went down to the office in Chester to get my salary, and there was no goddamned money!"[12] He would be replaced by Rudy's cousin, Al Pompilii.

During October and November, Bill and the Comets toured Europe. After six shows in Italy, Pope Pius XII died, the nation went into mourning, and shows were either cancelled or poorly attended. Lord Jim wrote to Sam Sgro at the office, "In Rome, we were cancelled out and the following day played to half-full houses due to people thinking it was still a holiday of mourning. For this reason, we lost money in Italy."

---

10 This is a section of Bill's autobiography moved from 1957 to a more likely point in the story.

11 These words have also been moved from another part of the autobiography.

12 Swenson, p.116.

The band moved on to Paris where they gave three shows, with the remainder being cancelled because of the disorderly behavior of the audience at the Paris Olympia. Shows in Algiers and Tunis were quickly arranged, which Bill told Hugh McCallum involved "a battered old plane, a long stopover in Marseilles with no interpreter, and a drunken pilot in a storm." Brief visits to France, Austria and Germany followed, the band arriving in Frankfurt on October 23, where Elvis Presley, then stationed with the US Army, was a surprise visitor.[13]

Backstage in Strasbourg, France on November 7, 1958. L. to R: Rudy, Bill & Franny.

On October 26, they played the Berlin Sportpalast. Here a few hoodlums, hell-bent on trouble, managed to ignite a fully-fledged riot. The band played until it was no longer possible, and then fled the stage. It took half an hour to restore order and, in the process, dozens of people were arrested. Newsreel footage reveals the audience storming the stage, rows of smashed seats, the grand piano turned upside down, and police using water cannons. The riot was emulated in Hamburg and in Essen, where the Comets' show was filmed from behind the stage to identify troublemakers.

Onstage in Essen, October 28, 1958.

13 A highly detailed account of their meetings in Germany, as well as the entire 1958 European tour will be found in the book *Bill Haley & His Comets – Rockin' Around Europe 1958* by Klaus Kettner (Hydra Records © 2024 Hydra Records, München, Germany).

East German newspapers started a propaganda war, claiming Bill Haley was an American attempt to demoralize East German youth. The Comets, of course, became famous because of this and were suddenly in demand for TV and film appearances. They pocketed a substantial fee of $12,000 for a cameo appearance in the film, *Hier Bin Ich, Hier Bleib Ich* (*Here I Am and Here I Remain*), alongside star Caterina Valente, performing "Vive La Rock and Roll" and "Hot Dog Buddy Buddy." This was filmed in Berlin in mid-November. Comets' drummer Ralph Jones remembered that Valente arrived on set in a black leather jacket carrying a wooden club. "Where's the Haley rock concert?" she asked. Jones said the whole band cracked up, except Haley.[14]

The Comets were also filmed performing a third number, "Whoa Mabel!," a song from the album *Bill Haley's Chicks*. Still photographs of the shoot have survived, but seemingly the film footage has not. Haley's subtitle for this part of the chapter was "Two More Movies," indicating that he, at least, believed they made another movie in 1958. The facts have remained obscure. While there have been persistent rumors of a second film having been shot in Germany, and provisionally titled *Rock 'n' Roll in Heidelberg*, detailed research by German Haley expert Klaus Kettner, in the course of writing his book *Rockin' Around Europe 1958*, revealed no evidence of its existence. However, Haley's own draft life story does mention the band making a second film, described as a "small 'one song and a few lines' one in Austria."

While there was a cultural void for teenagers after World War II, the United States was at least intact. By contrast, London and Berlin suffered terrible damage. As that generation of youth grew into their teen years, their physical comfort as well as sense of identity had been seriously compromised. In London, the "teddy boy" subculture emerged among the working-class youth in the early 1950s and its rebellious tendencies latched on to the threatening energy of Haley's rock and roll, particularly as it was associated with the movie *Blackboard Jungle*. It also offered a "last hurrah" before the post-war regime of compulsory National Service claimed young men for eighteen months on their seventeenth birthdays. In the post-war divided city of Berlin, the pre-Wall East Berlin youth were bitter over their squalid living conditions and all young Berliners had lived with violence and repression as the country tried to get back on its feet. They brought this pent-up hostility to the Sportpalast the night the Comets performed.

---

14 Haley and von Hoelle, p. 187.

Jolly Joyce took a dim view of the Comets' European tour having been booked without reference to him. He launched a lawsuit claiming $100,000 for breach of contract, and commission on recording royalties to which he had been entitled, but never collected. Jim Ferguson was sent back from Germany on the day before the riot at the Sportpalast to deal with this. He told the U.S. press on his arrival that his parting words to the band had been, "You won't have any trouble in Germany."[15] The band moved on to Spain, appearing at the Sports Palace in Barcelona on November 21. This was reported as a tumultuous performance with an audience of 3,000. The local governor took a dim view, however, cancelling the next three shows because of disorderly behavior in the crowd. This appears to have been the end of the tour. The band flew back to the U.S. from Madrid on November 26, leaving instruments in lieu of unpaid hotel bills. With Joyce's lawsuit gathering momentum, and being on a "trial separation" from Cuppy, Bill stayed in Europe with Joe Olivier, whose multilingual skills were useful. They travelled back to Brussels, but after a few days Bill was broke and Sam Sgro sold some land owned by the corporation and wired money for their return flight.

Charlie Levigne (right of picture), Joe Olivier (in his stage clothes) and Bill in Liège towards the end of the European tour.

Sam Sgro, a friend of Jim Ferguson's, who was to become the "last man standing" at the demise of the Haley Corporation.

15 *Delaware County Daily Times*, October 27, 1958.

Far from being their financial savior, the tour had lost money and left a "black hole" in the corporation's finances. The partners had exhausted legitimate lines of credit, and turned to the Philadelphia mob, from whom they borrowed a five-figure sum. Although Lord Jim seems to have been generally blamed for it, Johnny Grande remembered that all the partners had signed it off.[16] Over the next few years, the partners would abandon the organization, leaving Bill to carry the huge millstone around his neck. He discovered that simply paying the interest (the "vig")[17] would cost him up to $5,000 a month and he would not be free of the debt until the late 1960s.

The last month of 1958 was occupied in attempting to mend the business, with the Comets seemingly making no personal appearances. Cuppy and Bill achieved a temporary reconciliation. The key people in the corporation (Bill, Johnny, Billy, Sam Sgro, Jack Howard, Charlie Le Vigne, Bob Hayes, and Cal Peltzman)[18] met to take stock of the situation and develop a strategy. Their in-house booking agency got busy promoting the other acts on their roster, of which The Kingsmen were the most successful. The partners secured the services of the attorney Charles B. Seton (who would work for Dick Clark during the 1959 Payola hearings) to handle the Jolly Joyce litigation, and Bill went to see Milt Gabler to ask for an advance on record royalties.

Jolly Joyce's lawsuit was settled out of court and on March 31, 1959 he would be contracted as the band's booking agent for another three years. Booking commission would be capped at ten percent and there would be no entitlement to commission on disc sales. Bill would then remain signed to the Joyce Agency until 1974.

---

16 In conversation with David Hirschberg, the manager for the Original Comets (Lytle, Ambrose, Richards, Beecher, Grande) in the 1980s and 1990s.

17 Abbreviation for "vigorish": an excessive rate of interest on a loan, typically from an illegal moneylender.

18 Sgro was brought into the organization by Lord Jim. He remained for many years and had become the senior staff member by the time the corporation collapsed in 1962-63. Howard had been an associate of Bill's since the 1940s and ran a number of his own businesses including the Arcade Music Shop in Philadelphia, Arcade Records, and Arcade Music Publishing. Le Vigne was a Haley employee for many years. His role is clouded in the mists of time, and Johnny Grande would describe him as "well-connected." He was known to have acted as a part-time bodyguard for Cuppy when she was in town alone, and he traveled on many of the Comets' domestic and overseas tours. Hayes was a good friend of Lord Jim's and started as Valley Brook Publishing's Midwest representative. Ultimately, he replaced Lord Jim as Bill's principal factotum and he remained with the organization into the 1960s. As we will see in subsequent chapters, he would eventually sue Haley in the early 1960s for unpaid salary. Peltzman was the latest in the line of accountants who looked after the Corporation's financial affairs.

Surviving documents indicate that the corporation was maintaining cash flow by borrowing large sums from the bank in the form of advances against record royalties. While royalties from U.S. Decca were by now much reduced ($38,000 for 1957, compared to $114,000 for 1956), royalties from the rest of the world, delayed for around two years by international royalty processing, were still increasing. Global Decca royalties peaked in the first half of 1958 at $122,000. However, from there, they would decline sharply.

In January 1959, Bill was back in the studio recording a number of tracks including "(Now and Then There's) A Fool Such As I" and a highly original arrangement of "I Got a Woman," a song made popular by Ray Charles. The latter was released in mid-February and enjoyed good airplay, while "Fool" was held back as a probable next release. Bill then heard that "Fool" was about to appear on Elvis Presley's next release and Decca agreed to rush-release "Fool," dropping the promotion of "Woman." Bill had thought that there would be room in the charts for two quite different versions, but he was wrong. "Fool" achieved only regional success. "Woman," meanwhile, was completely lost as a potential hit in the process.

Jim Ferguson's role in the corporation was reduced and he continued alone with the art gallery. Much of his role in the corporation would be taken up by Sam Sgro, his best friend. Ferguson continued to run his art gallery until the mid-1960s and would return to work for the corporation in a promotional role in the early 1960s.

The Comets continued to work hard with one-nighters and an increasing number of night club residencies. The corporation, however, was in serious trouble. A new accountant produced a set of books which he handed over to Bill with the advice that he should "leave the country!" Meanwhile, a surviving document from the period reveals that the failing corporation still had more than twenty people on the payroll.

In August, after the failure of another single (a cover of Louis Jordan's "Caldonia," backed by the guitar instrumental, "Shaky"), Bill persuaded Decca to let him record a tune that he had brought back from the South American tour, "Joey's Song" (an instrumental). Bill's faith turned out to be well-placed and the record reached No. 46 on the *Billboard* chart. Nevertheless, as Bill would tell Hugh McCallum, the corporation was in jeopardy unless further cutbacks were undertaken and new capital raised.

Bill's Decca contract was due for renewal at the end of 1959. The company turned down a request for a large advance of royalties and Bill decided to find a new label. Bill worked out his final obligation to Decca Records with the album

Strictly Instrumental in the fall of 1959. According to Johnny Grande, it was something in which Bill took little interest, apart from playing a few percussion instruments.[19]

Towards the end of the year (the date is not known, and could have been any time between September and December) and after a nail-biting negotiation between Bob Hayes and Warner Brothers Records in a New York Hotel, Bill signed a contract with the fledgling label. A cash advance of $50,000 provided the corporation with some valuable breathing space, and the deal guaranteed $150,000 over five years, with a five-percent royalty rate.

---

19 Johnny Grande, in conversation with Chris Gardner in 1989.

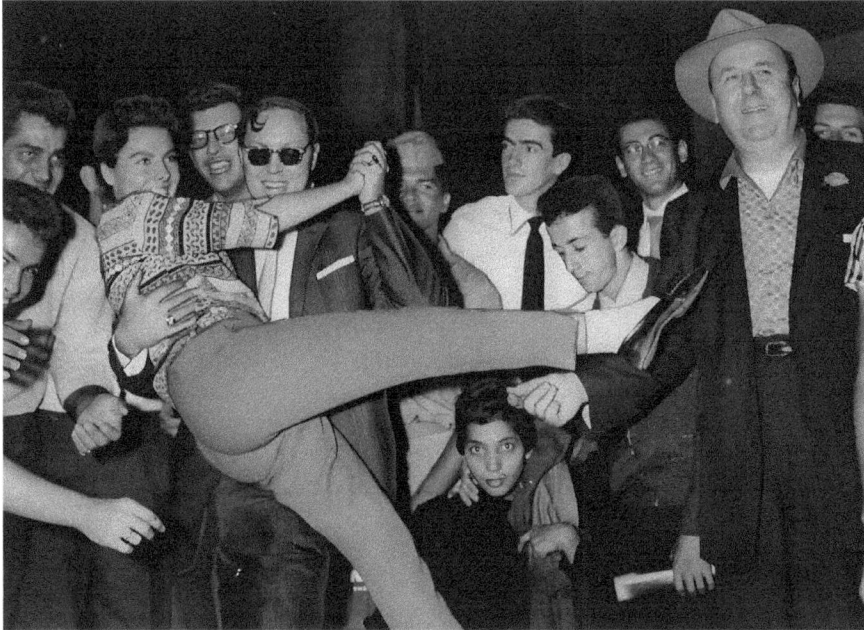

A picture from the South American tour of 1958. Bill dances with a young female fan. On the right, "Lord" Jim Ferguson smiles for the camera whilst fulfilling his role as Bill's "minder".

CHAPTER 8
From Heartbreak to Triumph (1960-1964)

Authors' Note: Although Bill's autobiography ends in early 1958, the Haley family preserved his 1961 diary, thus extending our ability to describe events in his own (admittedly shorthand) words during that period. We have also used the life-story narrative written by Hugh McCallum in collaboration with Bill in 1979 and 1980.

Bill was optimistic as 1960 dawned. Signing with the Warner Brothers record label represented a new beginning for the struggling Comets. However, things quickly went sour. Bill had signed with Warner's secondary East Coast office, but the company's primary headquarters was in Burbank, California and there was a rivalry between the two. Haley was being used as ammunition.

The Burbank office ridiculed the entire batch of East Coast recordings– a hodgepodge of Comets remakes, covers of songs by other rock 'n' roll artists, instrumentals, and country songs– and wanted to throw them all out. West Coast Warner's displeasure with Haley's recordings stemmed from the fact that they were attempting to rebrand him as a country singer, recording him in Nashville with the country-politan, candlelight-country formula of production, backing him with strings and without the Comets. This placed Bill in a conflict. Rock 'n' Roll was his baby and he did not want to risk the perception that he had abandoned it. At this same time, Bill Haley and the Comets were steering away from youngsters, whom they had obviously lost to Presley, the Everly Brothers, industry-manufactured teen idols, and the like.

Haley's first Warner recordings were produced by George Avakian, a former Columbia Artist and Repertoire Director who produced many jazz and classical albums for that label. In a fax to Chris Gardner in March 1999, he revealed that "Haley was extremely easy and pleasant to work with." He went on to explain that Warner Brothers were very "California-orientated" and that it was not them who appointed him as New York A&R Director. Avakian would leave Warner in

Producer George Avakian (on Bill's immediate right), during the first Warner Brothers East Coast recording session.

October 1960 and another producer would finish the Haley sessions.

Bill was motivated by an urgent need to pay off ever-increasing debts, and while his roots in country music were deep, he decided against Warner's offer. Had Bill followed through on WB West Coast's wishes, his career might have taken a positive turn and led to a viable return to his beloved country music. Instead, he concocted "rock and roll for grown-ups" that neither impressed his new label nor his audience. Bill's response did not please the record company, used to getting their way, and the relationship deteriorated to the point where Warner Brothers told him they would only do the minimum required by contract. They released his two new albums with little promotion. Once the $50,000 advance had been eaten up, Bill was back where he started, with little prospect of receiving any recording royalties in the foreseeable future, and tied to a useless contract for the next five years.

Warner's early strategy was typical of other record labels at the time, when the men in charge of A&R had older ideas and tastes in music and were resistant to, or incapable of, being purveyors of the new rock 'n' roll that was steadily gaining market share, indicating that young music consumers were now a force to be reckoned with. Mitch Miller, a classical oboist and head of A&R at Columbia from 1951 to 1967, called rock 'n' roll "musical baby food"[1] and said that "the reason kids like rock 'n roll is their parents don't."[2] It was his policy to exclude rock artists; they would remain absent from Columbia's catalog until Clive Davis succeeded Miller as president of the label. In the 1950s and 60s, Dean Martin, Frank Sinatra and the like were still as big or bigger than early rock 'n roll artists, so Miller's strategy was to double down on the tastes of mainly white, urban, middle-aged, middle-class consumers, providing them with a steady supply of crooners, novelty songs, easy-listening instrumentals, jazz, and classical music. Of course, this would not be sustainable in the long run, as his replacement by Clive Davis attests.

Warner Brothers would start out with the same philosophy. The fledgling record label, founded in 1958, hired James B. Conkling as its first president.

---

1 Barry Levine, "Anti-Rock Stance Hurt Mitch Miller," albanyherald.com, 10/9/2015, updated 5/11/2020.

2 Brainyquote.com/mitch_miller

Conkling was Mitch Miller's presidential predecessor at Columbia and shared Miller's conservative tastes, issuing similar fare of easy listening (Henry Mancini), novelty (Spike Jones), and Warner film and television soundtracks. Everything was a commercial failure. Warner contract actor and teen idol Tab Hunter's recording of "Jealous Heart," recorded years later by Bill Haley, was Warner's only charting single (No. 62) in 1959.

Like Columbia and Warner, Nashville intended to address the rock 'n roll "issue" by leaning even harder on the broader adult easy-listening audience. Nashville's Music Row veered away from the twangy honky-tonk style for one that more closely mimicked easy-listening records. They featured more velvety-voiced singers such as Jim Reeves, Eddy Arnold, and Tennessee Ernie Ford and backed them with studio string sections and backup vocal groups, all recorded in a wash of deep reverberation. Until the late 1960s, it proved quite successful. In a famous anecdote, a reporter asked Chet Atkins (who, among others, produced Elvis Presley) what the "Nashville Sound" was. Atkins answered by rattling the change in his pocket.

By the end of the 1960s, Bill's faithfulness would finally pay off in the form of the Rock and Roll Revival spearheaded by Richard Nader. His "music for grown-ups" would not be the adulterated music he made for Warner Brothers, but a return to the Comets' original style.

In mid-March, the Comets went to Mexico for the first time. They traveled by train, arriving in Mexico City to an ecstatic welcome. They were mobbed on arrival, and Bill was carried shoulder-high to a waiting car. The Comets' shows in Mexico enjoyed a great response and they made brief appearances in two movies, *Juventud Rebelde* (Rebellious Youth) and *Besito a Papa* (A Kiss for Daddy), lip-synching to recordings.

Returning home, Bill took stock of the continuing deterioration of the corporation's finances. Cutbacks were made and staffing reduced. The remaining staff worked harder, and while they received pay raises to compensate, there was sometimes not enough in the bank to meet payroll. Lines of credit had been exhausted and by early summer the corporation was on its knees. Holes in the roof of the office building had made two floors unusable and the IRS was making large demands for previous years. Bill told Hugh McCallum that he had been deceived into believing money had been set aside to pay the taxes. He was angry, bitter, and mentally drained, soon discovering that he was the only one of the partners prepared to mortgage his own home.

Bill's survival strategy became "work, work, work." The consequences of defaulting on his payments to the mob were unbearable. If necessary, he would take bookings that would involve several shows a night. Most of the band were married with families and by the middle of the year Franny Beecher, Rudy Pompilii and Ralph Jones had had enough.[3] They were replaced by Johnny Kay (Kaciuban) on guitar; Al Dean (De Nittis), previously a member of the Tyrones,[4] on saxophone, and Ed Ward (Warminski) on drums.

Ralph and Rudy reunited with Little Ernie, and also, with Franny Beecher, worked briefly as the Merri-Men, using their Comets' credentials to record two instrumentals for APT Records. The A side, "Big Daddy" (Frank Pingatore), was a robust, rocking sax-led instrumental, very much in the style of the erstwhile Kingsmen, whilst the B side was an insipid take on W.C. Handy's "St. Louis Blues," which aped the style of contemporary pop music with its use of a "straight eighths" beat. Both sides featured Little Ernie on electric organ, an instrument beloved of the pop groups emerging at that time.

Franny's replacement in the Comets, young guitarist Johnny Kay, was the first musician to come into the band from a rock 'n' roll background, rather than jazz or hillbilly, having previously led his own group, Johnny Kay's Rockets. In an interview with David Hirschberg, Kay recalled how he joined the band:

I received a call from a man claiming to be Bob Hayes, manager of Bill Haley. He said that Bill had heard of me and wanted to "catch the group" [the Rockets] as soon as possible. Frankly, I was doubtful that the voice on the phone was Bill's manager, thinking rather that it was a prank being pulled by a friend. I told him that we would be at a nearby VFW Post on Saturday, he said that Bill would be there to "catch the act." Bill and Mr. Hayes did in fact make it to that Saturday gig, staying for two numbers and leaving before the set was finished. I remember saying to the guys in the band, "Oh well, I gave it a shot!" To my surprise, exactly one week later, Bob Hayes called again and asked me to come to Bill's office in Chester, PA, for an audition. This was May of 1960 and I was only 19 years old. I was sure that it was all a dream, and that I could pinch myself and wake up. But no — the following week I went and auditioned. When I arrived at the office, I heard the sound of a guitarist auditioning for the right to be a "Comet." I don't know who he was, but he was definitely a jazz man, and he played wonderfully. Then came my turn to do my stuff. Bill Haley, John Grande and Bill Williamson were ready to play. They all greeted me warmly, asking if I was nervous. They needn't have asked that question;

---

3 The death of his father, Filideo on August 12, was undoubtedly a contributory factor for Rudy.

4 The Tyrones, a band led by the DeNittis brothers, modelled themselves on Freddie Bell and the Bell Boys. They were signed to Bill Haley's publishing and management companies in 1958.

gone in Mexico now. It's all dirt, Mafia, drugs, killing each other for drugs."[7]

Describing herself as a "tropical singer," Martha had her own act with her own orchestrations of boleros, mambos, and other Latin fare that would appeal to the

An early picture of Bill and Martha, date unknown.

Mexican nightclub audience, songs such as "Callate Corazon," "Ojo Traidores," and "Ipso Calyp-so." "There were also mariachis and ranchero singers," she added. A flyer from the Cine Royal includes Martha "Velazco" as a headliner. Her photo has her striking a dance pose, wearing a glittering costume that shows a lot of leg. The caption describes her having "an overwhelming voice that interprets Boleros." Martha was considered a *vedette* in the Mexican cabarets, defined by *Wikipedia* as a female nightclub entertainer "with a physical presence, personality, and charisma that captivates the public" and who could sing, dance, and act.[8] In the Mexico City theaters such as the Teatro Arbeu or the Teatro Principal, vedettes Lupe Vélez and "the white kitten," Maria Conesa, reigned supreme.

In 2018, Martha recalled her first meeting with Bill:

> When he was in the top, he went to Mexico City, and there was a line of people that went around the block for three blocks, people waiting to go and see him. And, from then on, when he went to the nightclub, he got a lot of offers to go into the nightclubs, because it was only two shows a night. He was a novelty there. "Bill Haley! He's going to be at so-and-such a club!"

7 All the quotes from Martha Haley, unless otherwise noted, are from an interview by David Lee Joyner at the home of Martha Maria Haley Castillo in McKinney, Texas, on October 6, 2018.

8 Pedro Haley fondly recalled in his interview with Otto Fuchs: "…she let me take a peek at a box of her memorabilia from the days before she met Dad and it proved to me that she was very beautiful, very sexy, and very popular." (Fuchs, p. 943.) In an interview with David Lee Joyner on December 15, 2019, Martha confirmed that "*vedette*" was a correct term for her in those days.

My story starts on February 10, 1961, which is when I met him in Monterrey [Mexico]. He came into the bus, a double-decker bus, and at that time I was very gregarious, you know, a typical woman. All the things I was saying in Latin, you know, and then he asked Rudy, "Hey, Rudy, how do you say in Spanish, 'Shut Up!'"? Rudy, he was Italian, and he more or less understood a little bit of Spanish. He said, "I don't know." The problem was the language, because I didn't speak a word of English when I met him and he didn't speak a word of Spanish.

The next night, we were going to perform. He was pissed off at me because the promoter of the tour said that he needed to let me sing with the band because Mexican men were used to looking at the legs and all that stuff. They didn't pay to see a bunch of guys play instruments, so the guy told him you are going to have to let her sing with you. Bill said, "Well, we've never done that. We're not gonna..." The promoter said, "Please do it, at least two songs." "Okay." I practiced with the boys in the afternoon, songs that we could put together with the Comets and myself because I was really not a rock singer. I was a tropical singer, tropical music and all that. He wasn't there and they told him she wants to sing this and that two songs. [One was a song by Paul Anka, but she couldn't recall the title.]

So anyway, the following night we were all getting ready and we're all waiting our turn between the curtains, and so he is standing there with the band boy looking at where he's performing, and I walk by and he notices me. And he goes, "Hey, who's that?" And [the band boy] says, "She's the one who's going to sing with the band." "No way!" And then he takes a [closer] look! "Okay." Anyway, it gets to the time that I have to perform and there are some pictures where he is already smiling, and his band behind me. That was it! In the meantime, the show is not over, so I'm watching the rest of the people working and I'm watching between the curtains and then here he comes to my back, and he says, "La Senorita, Eres muy hermosa," meaning, "You are very beautiful." That is what the band boy [José Luiz] had told him [to say], because he went and asked him, "Teach me some words I can tell her." And I turned around and I laughed because it was funny for me. After everything was over, he says, "Can we go out for coffee?" So, we all went. We couldn't say anything to each other because he didn't speak Spanish, I didn't speak English, and José was the one we sat in the middle and he spoke English and he explained to me what Bill was saying. That was the first night. After that, he asked Oscar, the person who was sitting with me on the bus, he asked for that place. We went to the next place where we were going to work which was the next town because it was a tour by bus, you know, from town to town to town. That was the Mexican way.

From Monterrey, we went on to Reynosa and the beginning of a tour of Mexico. I had to go to Chicago to do two days of shows. I went back to Mexico City to take the plane to Chicago. I did my thing I was supposed to and I brought him a carton of Pall Mall cigarettes, which was his smoke, and a bottle of Johnnie Walker, which is what he drank. Unbeknownst to me what a mistake I was making, because he smoked one cigarette after another. I came back from Chicago and it was Carnival, and that was in February. Bill was staying in an apartment in Mexico City. I got in touch with him and I talked to José Luiz, the band boy, and he explained to me where they [the Comets] are. I got all prettied up and I took the taxi and went to see him to take him his gifts. From then on, we started going out every day and every night. I would go up to the theater where he was working and, from there, he worked at a nightclub. He did two shows in the theater and one in the nightclub. By that time, we were madly in love with each other. Madly. Then his tour was over, they came back to the States, and he did impossible things to book another tour of whatever it was in Mexico to come back and see me.

As Bill's relationship with Martha developed, the partners were still grappling with their situation. Billy Williamson wrote to Sam Sgro from Mexico, instructing him to raise money by selling the corporation's office building in Chester. He explained that the operation would move to Bill's home, Melody Manor: "We will have a better office set up for our needs at Bill's. You will be able to work without all the big deals dropping in off the street corner out there too." A letter from Sgro outlined an immediate crisis faced by the corporation. He was required to submit its tax records. Their accountant had not been paid since October 1960 and was refusing to co-operate. There was no money to pay the payroll tax for the second half of 1960, nor did he have the money that should have been withheld from employees and deposited in the bank by Johnny Grande to cover the first two months of 1961. The corporation was under threat of being put out of business. He closed the letter stressing that "real co-operation ($) is needed." Sgro found that the dilapidation of the building made it impossible to sell and it was not until October 1962 that it finally sold, at a much-reduced price, in a Sheriff's Sale. Sgro was Lord Jim Ferguson's best friend and had been a loyal Haley staffer for many years. He was now the man in the hot seat and the stress was becoming unbearable. He parted company with the corporation in the late Spring of 1963. Like many people, he was owed several months' salary.

Despite these homeland issues, the band was continuing to do strong business in Mexico, and Bill's February 25th diary entry records an audience of 100,000 at Xalapa, which he notes were the "largest crowds we ever worked to."

Johnny Kay described the Mexican shows: "The shows in Mexico were vaudeville. It was like going back thirty years. Comics, dancers, dog acts, you name it. The shows lasted about ninety minutes and we did about twenty, combining Bill's hits with twist tunes."[9]

In fact, the Comets made little effort to produce or cover Mexican popular music; it was not their mission. The only accommodation was the few songs Haley sang in Spanish ... with Martha's coaching. "His Spanish was terrible," she remarked years later.

On April 28, Bill and the Comets undertook what would be their final recording session for Warner Brothers with "Flip, Flop and Fly," a cover of a 1955 Big Joe Turner song in the same vein as "Shake, Rattle and Roll," and the instrumental "Honky Tonk," a cover of the 1956 hit by R&B keyboardist Bill Doggett. Again, with little promotion from Warner, the resulting single made no impact on the market.

In June 1961, Martha visited Bill while the band were appearing for a fortnight at Madeira Beach, Florida. Bill and the Comets' annual summer residency the following month was at Tony Mart's (described by *Billboard* as a "resort nitery") in Somers Point, New Jersey. Bill took his second family (for the last time) for their customary summer holiday. His diary marks July 5, 1961, as a "three-star" day, saying, "Made deal today thru' Jolly Joyce to get out of Warner Bros. contract." Bill entertained George Goldner of Gone Records[10] at one of his shows and signed a deal on the spot on July 13, with the diary note, "Signed with Gone Records for 3 years. I hope is good." A few days later, he traveled to New York to review material and chose "The Spanish Twist" for his first single on Gone.

Later in the month, he flew to Mexico City for appointments with several record companies, signing very quickly with local company Orfeon in a deal

---

9 "A Comet's Tale", *Now Dig This* June 2010, p. 10.

10 George Goldner (1918-1970) started in the music business in the late 1940s, running a string of dance halls in New York and New Jersey. This gave him the springboard to launching Tico Records, which recorded a number of Latin American performers including Tito Puente. As dancers' tastes changed in the 1950s, he set up Rama for whom he recorded the Crows and the Cleftones before signing Frankie Lymon and the Teenagers, who had a crossover hit in 1956 with "Why Do Fools Fall in Love?" After losing a lot of his businesses as a result of his gambling habit, he set up Roulette Records in 1957, before selling his share shortly afterwards and establishing Gone Records. The label operated for a few years before being sold to Roulette, then owned by Morris Levy, and for whom Bill would record a live album in 1962.

covering Spanish-speaking territories. Having done this, he flew back to New York for his first session for Gone, held late in the evening of July 22, recording "Spanish Twist" and "My Kind of Woman."

The very next day, he left for more than a month in Canada. "Boy, am I tired," he wrote in his diary. He had a residency at the Oyster Barrel in Quebec City, where, he wrote on the second night, "things are picking up finally." On August 3, 1961, he noted that he "received word today that US taxes are now paid in full." This is hard to understand in the context of his not finally settling with the IRS until many years later. He continued with the warning, "Look out Hayes, am on my way back."[11] On August 13, he moved on to the Montana Inn, journaling it as a "Big success. Owner very happy. Very tired. Can I make it???? Of course I can." He starts counting down the shows he has left to do. At the Hotel Four Seasons and the National Theatre in Montreal, his shows are all sold out. On August 27, his diary conveys his relief: a cartoon of a plane flying carries the commentary: "Thank God FINISH FINALLY Wow."

In September, Bill and the Comets embarked on a ten-night residency at the Ali Baba Supper Club in Madeira Beach, Florida, the fourth time they appeared there. In October, they traveled to Latin America, spending the rest of the year in Mexico, Nicaragua, Panama, Puerto Rico, and Venezuela. The day before leaving for this tour the band had been in New York recording two instrumentals for Gone, "Riviera" and "War Paint."

In Mexico, the band recorded twenty-four tracks for Orfeon, including Bill's first Spanish vocals, on "Cerca del Mar"[12] and "Cielito Lindo." The determination to learn the language was driven by his desire to be able to communicate with his new love, Martha. She elaborated on this time period:

> [Bill] managed to get another tour in Mexico and here they come again. We couldn't be separated. There was this guy; I don't know how he met him. I guess it was on one of the tours. César[13] was his name and he spoke English and had a low, gravelly voice. César was a promoter and managed to get another tour and here he comes, and we stay together for the time the tour lasted. The time for them to go back arrived and here we go again, the same thing with the phone. So finally, one day he told me he got a contract in a nightclub called...Rio Rosa, I think, something like

---

11 A reference to Bob Hayes, who had resigned on March 31, 1961, one of many people harassing Bill for unpaid salary.

12 His diary also noted that he had recorded this track, in Spanish, in Canada on August 1. It is understood that this original recording had been unusable.

13 César Alvarez, promoter of Haley's early visits to Mexico.

that. He was working there and I was also working because I needed to work. I was out of Mexico City on a tour and I came back and I found out where he was and I started going to the club to see him. César, in the meantime, was working to see if he could get another tour out of Mexico City. And I think he did and I was included.

Time goes by and he finishes his contract there and he has to go back home. He has concerts to fulfill. He couldn't take it anymore, so he separated. One time, I don't know how or through who, the question [came from Bill that], if he sent me my ticket, would I go to meet him? I said "yes," and asked how I was going to do this. I don't have a passport or nothing, and [friends] tell me, "Well, go and get a passport!" Okay, I did go and get a passport and then I went to the Embassy, to the Consulate, and got a visa. By then, Bill was working, but he fixed it in a way that, when he finished that job that he was doing, that he was going to go to Florida, which is where I was going to meet him.[14] And it was perfect, you know. From then on, I took a trip with him everywhere he went, every concert he had I went with him. But then I needed to send money home because my family depended on my job a lot, so Bill started giving me money to send so I wouldn't have to go back home.

In Mexico, Bill quickly became "The Twist King." "All he had to do was change the beat a little bit," commented Martha. "It was money, paying the Comets' salary." Over the next few years, he would record a series of albums for Orfeon emulating the latest dance crazes such as the Madison and the Go-Go. His records, including "Twist Español" (a Spanish-language version of "The Spanish Twist") and "Florida Twist" (a mostly instrumental track co-written by Rudy Pompilii), became massive hits in Mexico, with the latter taking on a life of its own as a party and mariachi band standard. Bill happily told Hugh McCallum that Chubby Checker drew a crowd of 400 in a Mexican theater where 2,000 had enjoyed Bill Haley a few weeks previously. In speaking of Orfeon Records, Martha said, "They are such crooks. They never paid us royalties. We tried with a lawyer [to sue for royalties]; they just laughed at us." Hugh McCallum relates wryly that there would have to be a good few more bottles of Scotch to help forget the problems.

Bill's diary for 1961 concludes with this memorable piece of advice to himself for 1962: "Don't be a sucker like this year." While the rest of the band made it home for the Holidays, Bill was late, phoning Cuppy, making out that he was being

---

14 Martha flew to Florida at the end of August to be with Bill for his ten days at the Ali Baba Supper Club.

delayed by bad weather. He finally arrived in New York by plane on Christmas Day and Cuppy knew at this point that there was "someone else" in Bill's life. After Christmas, he drove to Quebec City where the band had a month's residency. On January 4, Martha flew from Mexico to be with him. She recalled:

> I went to Canada and to all the North and I remember that it was snowing. I took a shower and washed my hair and I went out and my hair froze! It was like a helmet. I went back to the hotel and finally it began to thaw out. It was really hideous.

Working away from home was also taking its toll on Franny Beecher's marriage. He quit the Comets at the end of the month. At the end of January, after a few days at Melody Manor Bill was off again playing dates in Minneapolis, Milwaukee, Cedar Rapids, and Hallandale, Florida.

Haley's contract with Gone Records expired after two single releases and, in March, Bill and the Comets recorded a live twist album for Roulette Records at the Roundtable Club in New York City (*Twistin' Knights at the Roundtable*). His Orfeon "twist" records were selling well in Mexico and "Florida Twist" topped the Mexican charts in March. For the Roundtable dates, Haley persuaded Franny to make an appearance. Cuppy went to one of the shows to see if their romance could be rekindled, but Bill displayed little interest and did not react when she danced with another man.[15]

Haley's absences from home were becoming more frequent and obvious, as other band members would be back home with their families. Soon, he was gone for good, living a nomadic life in motels, small apartments, staying with friends, or living in trailer parks. He defaulted on the payments for the loan he had secured against Melody Manor and this set off a chain of events that culminated with his family being evicted in July.

Bill now spent as much time as possible in Mexico. He also took a significant step to liberate himself from the monthly financial straitjacket of loan repayments, negotiating a deal which would see him work off his debt by performing for minimal fees in hotels and clubs, such as the Showboat and El Cortez, operated by the mob. It would take several years to repay the money, but he had started to chip away at the mountain.

In early September, Bill went to Hamburg for three weeks at the Star Club, for a much-needed fee of $25,000. There he shared the stage with several British bands who would ultimately become famous, among them the Searchers, the Swinging Blue Jeans, the Bachelors, and Gerry and the Pacemakers.

---

15 Haley, Jr. and Benjaminson, p.168.

In Chester, the corporation was all but finished. The office building was sold in October 1962 while Bill was in Germany.[16] Everything was becoming too much for Johnny Grande, who followed Franny in quitting the band, and leaving the partnership when he got home after the tour. Like Bill's, his marriage had become broken. He continued working as a Cordovox[17] demonstrator, performing in a lounge duo with drums He would not be replaced in the band. The fee from the Star Club allowed Bill some time off and he spent the next month in Mexico with Martha. The band's business would now be carried out through expensive, long-distance phone calls, which allowed Bill to be "difficult to contact" if he wanted.

Occasionally, work would take him to the East Coast of the United States and provide an opportunity to tie up loose ends in his home area. Martha, meanwhile, had become pregnant, and their thoughts turned to marriage. Of this time, Martha said:

> I was so worried because of my family. How was I going to come home with news like that? But I was already twenty-six when she [Martha Maria] was born. I was twenty-three or twenty-four when I met [Bill]. And how am I going to tell my mother and my father? How am I going to tell them? We Latin people don't just say, "I'm pregnant." It's a very serious thing and very shameful. When you do it outside of marriage, you embarrass your family, the name, and all that stuff. And so, finally, when I came back from that long tour all over the United States, I'm already three, four, no five months pregnant, and my mother knew as soon as she saw me. "Ah, yes, the gringo! What happened? What happened?" I say, "Mother, I'm already twenty-three, twenty-four..."

> Bill was beside himself because I was going to have a baby by him. I stayed home and, at that time, my father had died a few months before — no, weeks — before I came with the big news. He never found out because he died in August and Martha Maria was born in February. But when I was pregnant with Martha Maria, Bill needed to get in touch with me more often, and so he told me, "Is there any way that you can pay somebody to help us?" and the one was César [Alvarez]. César said, "Well, let me see what I can do. Leave it to me, I'll fix this." And he did. I don't know how he did it, how much he paid, I don't know. And then he gave us a phone.

16 Bill did not receive any benefit from the sale as the building had been seized *in lieu* of money that he owed the bank. The building was never renovated and decayed gradually over many years until demolished for new development.

17 Between 1960 and 1962, Farfisa developed the first generation Cordovox vacuum tube accordions that used tubes in a suitcase-sized module for tone generation. They were later developed as electronic instruments.

The company came and they hooked up the phone. Ah, what a relief! Then he could call me anytime. At that time, all we'd hear is, "I love you and miss you," and, "When are you coming?" Just a few things. But then I remember when I came home, he made me swear to him that I was going to write, but I said, "Bill, how am I going to write to you when I don't know how? I can hardly say a few words in English and you think I'm going to be able to write?" And he said, "You'll find a way." And I sure did. I bought four or five dictionaries, and through them I would find the word. You can't imagine what I went through writing him the letters. I would manage to get them through and send them and then he'd write me and I would have somebody read them for me. I still have those letters, by the way. I don't know what he did with mine, probably just burned them or whatever. But I have his letters.

In November 1962, Bill asked Cuppy for a divorce. Without adequate arrangements for child support, she refused. Bill arranged a divorce in Mexico, which carried no legal weight in the U.S. Martha's view of the situation was:

I don't know what he did in his divorce and I don't want to know. He was taking care of it and, even if I knew, I didn't want to be in a racing game. As a matter of fact, I never thought that he would marry me. I don't know if he had started in on somebody else and that's it for him, I don't know. We got married a month before Martha Maria was born. That was when he left his wife and he started the divorce and all that and by then I didn't know all troubles he had. I knew he did, but I didn't want to know.

December was spent in Mexico, with more recording for Orfeon. Bill and Martha spent Christmas together, planning their imminent wedding. Right after Christmas the Comets flew to Costa Rica for a few days and on January 14, Bill and Martha were married. Bill was aware that as well as being a tax fugitive, he was now a bigamist in the eyes of U.S. law. Expecting his first child with Martha within weeks, he made another trip home to tie up the loose ends. He met Cuppy and, while she would not grant a divorce, she did give her written agreement not to contest his marriage to Martha. She was badly in need of a car, and Bill paid for a cheap second-hand model. He promised regular support payments of $500 a month, which Cuppy related were received sporadically, and sometimes not at all.[18] Lord Jim helped him by borrowing money from local banks, with the Art Gallery as collateral. Sam Sgro got wind of the visit and appealed for his unpaid

---

18 Haley Jr. & Benjaminson, Chapter 35

salary. Bill wrote him a substantial check which Sam banked immediately, but found the account already emptied. Bill did give Sam a smaller sum for dealing with persistent claims of his ex-employee Bob Hayes.

Bill and Martha's first child, Martha Maria Haley, known by her pet name "Martita," was born in February 1963. Martha recalled:

He came right after she was born. He was working in Canada and he flew all the way from Canada to Mexico City to see her. He flew in and he took a taxi. I don't remember how, but he had his guitar in one hand, his briefcase in the other, and he showed up at my house. We open the door and he says, "Here I am with my guitar and my ass." He left [his New Jersey family] home and he never went back after that. After Martha Maria was born, it was touch-and-go because he needed to work, he kept on working to keep the band working. He couldn't stop working because of the band.

We had to take off from Mexico City back to the States and Martha Maria was three or four months old and I left her with my mother to go with him, because if I didn't go with him, he wouldn't go. He says if you're not going with me, I'm not going. Nowhere. I had to be with him constantly. I guess he felt secure with me, I really don't know. The only thing I can think of is that we loved each other so much that we couldn't be separated. I started going on tours with him everywhere and my mother took care of her. Then we'd come back and stay fifteen days, a month at home, you know. And sometimes I would tell him, "You go and I'll stay here with Martita and Mama and all that and, okay?

In March, Bill and the Comets signed a deal with Harold B. Robinson's Newtown label in Philadelphia. Robinson's main business at the time was secondhand car sales. He had started Newtown Records in 1962 and The Blue Belles' "I Sold My Heart to the Junkman" gave him his first hit. Over a few sessions in early 1963, Bill and the Comets recorded around a dozen tracks, including "Tenor Man," a feature number for Rudy Pompilii, borrowed heavily from the 1961 Fats Domino hit "What a Party" as well as something they had also recorded for Orfeon in Mexico as "Que Pachanga." Bill was again frustrated by the lack of promotion.

Bill's work schedule would involve several weeks at the Showboat and Nevada clubs in Las Vegas, repaying more of his debt. Martha has vivid recollections of the interminable road trips this would involve:

We used to travel by car because, at that time, he wasn't doing too good. He was having problems, having troubles, I was guessing. I didn't know anything. It was useless for him to tell me because there was no way for me to help him. I didn't know what the Internal Revenue was. I didn't know, didn't want to know. I didn't want to be nosey. Even if he had told me, I wouldn't have known what he was talking about. All I knew is that I needed to be with him and he needed me to be with him to take care of him, to take care of his clothes, his uniform, that everything was fine and ready to go, and keep him company in the car driving. We drove thousands of miles. I had to be there talking to him, singing to him and all that to keep him awake.

He hated flying. He flew only if it was completely a necessity to fly. We traveled all over the United States. There was no place, no state, no town that we didn't go, because he had to pay the contract. He used to tell me, "I have to do it because, if I don't, I'm going to lose my band. And, if I lose the band, I'm going to be done. So, even if I only get their salaries, I have to keep them working." They needed the money because they had to support their families. It was years like that.

One thing that stays in my mind, in Pittsburgh. He was performing and we stayed in a motel, and the following morning we got up to go on with the trip, and when we came out to get in the car, the car is gone. According to Bill, I understand that the Internal Revenue had taken the car. I didn't know who the Internal Revenue was. And I said, "They stole it?" He said, "No, no, no. Okay, don't worry." I said, "Where can we go without the car?" So, he calls somebody in Pennsylvania on the phone, I don't know who or where. All I know is that in a few hours he had another car. And I remember the car was a brand-new black Dodge Pioneer. We drove that car over two hundred thousand miles, and, at that time, it was hard to get that kind of mileage because the United States was making lemons. Two hundred thousand miles and God was with us. And he used to take care of it, check it all the time and all that.

The band was in Germany in May and June, playing military bases, as well as two weeks at the Star Club, again earning $25,000. The Liverpool bands, however had moved onto greater things. During the year, the IRS had called for an audit of the corporation's financial records. Bill failed to co-operate. He no longer had any

U.S. property interests and his two main sources of income were royalties from Decca Records and live appearance fees. The former were an easier target for the IRS, and they issued a garnishee order which choked off that source of income, but which of course would contribute to paying off his tax debt.

Shortly before Christmas, the Comets joined Bill in Mexico and recorded another LP (*Surf, Surf, Surf*) for Orfeon. In early January they had three weeks at the Showboat in Las Vegas. Bill was averaging 80,000 miles a year on the road at this time and his 1961 Dodge was on its last legs. Martha recalled,

> [Bill] knew the car was just about to go, so he says, "Martha, we gotta get a new car," and I say, "Well, I don't know, okay." So, we go to a car dealer and he got a used Lincoln Continental and he traded in the Pioneer. They didn't know what they were getting. And so, we get into the car and it was beautiful, clean, and all that stuff, and we took off. And later on — I don't know how he found out — the transmission, something had happened to it. And so, we drove that car everywhere; we put miles on that Lincoln Continental. There was no other way of transportation; that was the only way that he would go anywhere. We drove that car until it was time to buy a new one.

In Vegas, Bill signed a contract with Guest Star Records to record the album *The Rock-a-Round the Clock King*.[19] This gave him the money for the Lincoln, which was immediately put through its paces with journeys to San Antonio, Denver, Texas, Quebec City, Montreal, and Toronto.

On April 27, the last of Bill's original partners, Billy Williamson, left the band after an engagement at the Hotel Russell, just outside Montreal. By now disillusioned with the music business, he never touched his guitar again, refusing interviews and an invitation to re-join the Original Comets in the late 1980s. Steel guitarist Nick Masters[20] joined the band, would later switch to lead guitar, working with the band (on and off) until 1974.

In late May, Bill and the Comets flew to Germany for two concerts at Berlin's Waldbühne amphitheater. There was a rapturous reception from an audience of 30,000 over the two shows, which also featured Little Richard. Decca Records became interested in Bill again and wanted to re-sign him. Bill agreed to a single 45-rpm disc — a cover of Jim Lowe's 1956 hit, "The Green Door," backed with a new song, "Yeah! She's Evil" — which was recorded in New York on June 16. Ultimately this fine record was not a hit and although a follow-up was discussed in

---

19 See Chapter 20 for more on this session.

20 Nicholas Mathias Nastos, born June 26, 1936, died April 28 1995.

November, it did not materialize. Bill worked through the summer in Atlantic City, Montreal, and Somers Point, New Jersey, and by the end of July, a British tour was in the offing. The Comets would share the billing with Manfred Mann, then the top act in the UK. Hugh reported that Bill had briefed his band as an army officer would address troops before a battle, noting that the Comets beat the British bands hands-down in experience. What then happened was little short of a sensation. Bill and the Comets upstaged the British acts and, after just two nights, were promoted to be the closing act. The band also appeared on two top TV shows ("Thank Your Lucky Stars" and "Ready, Steady, Go").

Bill and the Comets on September 13, 1964 in Birmingham during an appearance on the TV show *Thank Your Lucky Stars.* Back row (L to R) Nick Nastos, Rudy Pompilii, Bill Haley, Dave Clark (the show's compere), Dave Holly. Front row (L to R) Al Rappa, Hugh McCallum, Johnny Kay.

Bill would later tell Hugh McCallum that, when he returned to America, he was disappointed to find he was doing the same sort of gigs he'd been doing for the last couple of years. In this context, Martha Haley had harsh words for Bill's long-time booking agent:

> Jolly Joyce prostituted Bill. As long as he had his $300 commission, he didn't care how much he holds him for. He's the one whose price went down. And that's why [Bill] would take all the jobs that Jolly would come up with because he needed to keep the boys working. If it hadn't been for Jolly Joyce, his pride would not have dropped so much.

In the 1960s, Bill Haley proved to be an avid cameraman. This photo was probably taken in Europe, companion name unknown.

CHAPTER 9
Viva La Rock and Roll! (1965-1969)

In February 1965, Bill signed a recording deal with the ABC-Paramount label, whose president, Sam Clark, had been a childhood friend. The Comets were joined by Ernie Henry (organ), Milt Hinton (bass) and Panama Francis (drums) to record a number of songs in modern dance idioms such as "The Jerk." Bill had high hopes for the first single ("Burn That Candle"/"Stop, Look and Listen"), and (as usual) blamed lack of promotion for poor sales.

Martha travelled with Bill on his next European trip. After the work was done, they enjoyed a short European tour on an economy budget, traveling third class by train to Switzerland, Rome, and finally Cherbourg, sailing on the *Queen Mary* to New York because it was cheaper than flying.

During 1965, Bill and Martha moved to Del Rio, Texas, as Pedro Haley explained,

This is the town my dad decided to make home after returning to the U.S. from Mexico with Mom. Several things about this. It fits right in with his romantic perception of the West from his cowboy/John Wayne/Gene Autry conception. It's isolated, giving him the privacy he liked, close to Mexico for Mom, *et al.* Just another example of the iconoclastic character of Daddy in that he didn't choose to move back to Philadelphia, NYC, Kansas City, Nashville, etc. He didn't even choose a city or even a large town. Very telling. He loved West Texas. I still have very fond memories of a stop in Alpine, TX, on way to Los Angeles on vacation. He bought all the way in to the "Judge Roy Bean-Pecos Bill-Gunslinger-Badlands" aesthetic of it.[1]

---

1 e-mail correspondence with David Lee Joyner, October 23, 2018.

Because work had become less frequent, the Comets now began working without Bill as a self-contained unit in the New Jersey/Philadelphia area. Seven musicians would leave the band during 1965 and Rudy sometimes struggled to meet the contractual demands for a specific number of musicians for a performance. At one point, the band played for a week with a bongo player instead of a drummer. Rudy, privately, would use the phrase "no-hope has-beens" to describe some of the players he had to recruit.

In October the band played two weeks at the *Whisky-a-Go-Go* on Bourbon Street, New Orleans, working solidly, "forty minutes on and twenty off." Big Joe Turner, then living in New Orleans, tracked Bill down. In 1974,[2] Bill reminisced about their historic reunion, which clearly raised his spirits:

> I lost track of Joe... I was working in New Orleans some years later and I got a phone call, a very strange phone call when I was working one night at the *Whisky-a-Go-Go* and it was Mr. Joe Turner, who had retired at that time from the business,[3] ... I got Joe to come down and got him back on the stage with me at the Whisky-a-Go-Go and the audience went mad to see Joe Turner and Bill Haley together. Rudy Pompilli and myself talked to Joe and we took him to Mexico.

As 1966 dawned, Bill signed a deal with Orfeon/Dimsa for another four albums. In January, he recorded two of them, one of them a "Big Joe Turner" album. Joe recorded twelve titles with the Comets, but Orfeon "pulled the plug" after just two EPs had been issued. Uncharacteristically, Bill, who would often leave the Comets to their own devices, was in the studio all the time Joe was recording. Turner joined the Comets on the *Discotheque Orfeon a Go-Go* TV show, lip-synching to his recording of "Feelin' Happy." In a golden pantomime moment, Bill literally falls off his pedestal and the two old friends can be seen on stage laughing their heads off. The remaining two contracted albums were never recorded: sessions would be booked for April 1967, cancelled by Bill at short notice, then penciled in for October, before again falling through.

One of Bill's last Orfeon recordings, "Land of a Thousand Dances" (a cover of a Chris Kenner song made famous by Cannibal and the Headhunters and, later, Wilson Pickett), was doing well in the Mexican charts as Bill and Martha drove back to their new home in Houston. Bill had little desire to work at this time and

---

2 Interviewed by Brian Matthew on *My Top Twelve*, May 5, 1974 for BBC radio.

3 Bill remembers wrongly: Turner's career was still going well at this time, especially in the U.K. and Europe.

began to refuse dates that he would normally have accepted, even though his finances were still in the red. Martha would admonish him with "Come on, you stupid Gringo! Work while you can!" Bill began four months of work, traveling to St. Paul, Kansas City, Redwood City, Sacramento, Salt Lake City, and Hollywood. He flew to Germany in September for another tour of U.S. service bases. Financial cutbacks in the Army meant the option to extend the tour was not taken up, and Bill spent several idle days in Frankfurt, hoping for more work.

Patrick Malynn, at that time an employee of the British Dumont Theatrical Agency, and who would later become Bill's European and UK Manager, tracked Bill down at his hotel. Bill accepted two nights at the Alhambra Theatre in Paris, as second billing on a show which included the Walker Brothers, Spencer Davis and The Pretty Things. Martha remembered,

Paddy Malynn was an Irish boy. Very smart and a big mouth and all that. I guess they didn't know each other but, when they met, they became very, very good friends... Paddy kept telling him, "Bill, you are giving yourself away... we need to do something to get the salary up." Paddy started dealing with people in Europe and he started bringing the price up.

Patrick Malynn would remain Bill's manager outside the U.S. until Haley's death in 1981, and his experience and ability to drive hard deals would be instrumental in Bill's success in Europe from 1966 onwards.

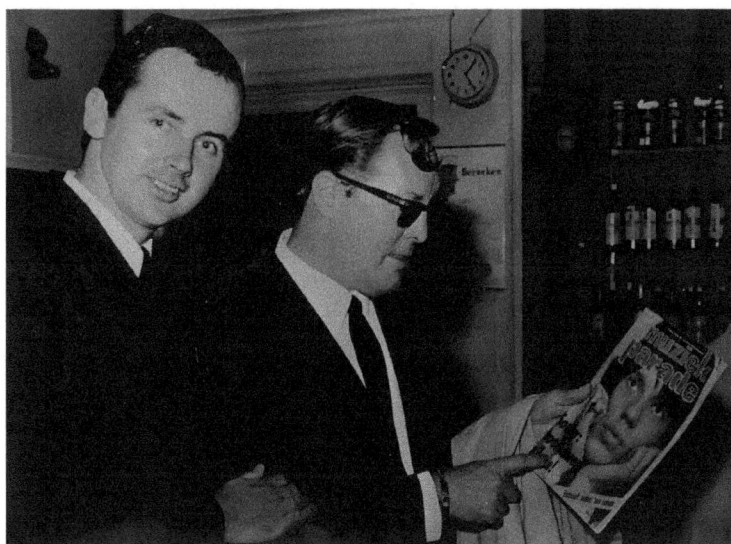

Patrick Malynn and Bill in Amsterdam, 1966.

While pleased to have work, Bill just wanted to go home and he spent his time writing letters to Martha, as he could not afford the phone calls. He made a decision: this would be the end for Bill Haley, the last show.

At the venue, there was a small, dirty dressing room for the band. Bill was taking a cigarette in the corridor when one of the Walker Brothers swaggered past and, without stopping, asked cockily, "Bill Haley!!! Are you still alive?" In Patrick's version of the story, there was "a little tear in the corner of Bill's eye". Bill would later paint the scene for Hugh McCallum, who would write,

Bill sat down and all but cried: he was so desperately unhappy. His spirit could go no lower. Never in his forty years could he remember being so dejected. He was now more determined than ever this would be the last date he would ever do.

Rudy tried to console Bill but he wanted to be alone. With a few minutes to go, they could hear the noise of the audience. There was a rhythmic chant that got gradually louder. It sounded like "*Beelally, Beelally, Beelally, Beelally!*" Of course, it was his name in a French accent! Bill had tears in his eyes, overwhelmed with emotion. Rudy and Patrick came in and told Bill the crowd was frantic. There were waving banners proclaiming, "Bill Haley — The King," "Long Live Rock 'n' Roll," "Long Live Bill," and so on.

The band assembled on stage. And when the lights came on Bill could see that the crowd were not fans from the 1950s, but teenagers. His mood lifted and he was uncharacteristically generous with encores. The following acts endured a barrage of "*Beelally!, Beelally!*" For the second show the promoter gave Bill top billing.

Interviewed by the British press, Spencer Davis was unreservedly complimentary and full of admiration for what Bill "had done to them." Scott Engel begrudgingly conceded that Walker Brothers had been humiliated. As Bill said to Hugh many years later, "I found out I was indeed very much alive!"

UK pop star Spencer Davis and Bill Haley, taken backstage at the Alhambra Theatre in Paris on April 9, 1966.

Bill and the Comets' itinerary for the next few weeks filled up. They worked the Paris Elysées Top 10 Club for several days, appeared live and on radio and TV in London, Dublin, Hamburg, Geneva, and Amsterdam. The band then flew home and took a few days off. News of their success reached the States and resulted in a full schedule of personal appearances for the end of the year in Milwaukee, Dallas, and Vancouver. Working on his life story in 1979, Haley pinpointed the show at the Alhambra as the beginning of the "Rock and Roll Revival" and he was reminded of the title of one of his old records, "Vive la Rock and Roll." In mid-August of 1967, the band played at JD's Lounge in Phoenix, Arizona. At the end of their booking, Bill stayed in Phoenix to record the ballad, "Jealous Heart." A more contemporary song, "Rock on, Baby," was cut for the B side with The Superfine Dandelion.[4] The recording of "Jealous Heart" was very close to the version by Trio Los Panchos in Nashville in 1966. Martha Haley recalls,

We went somewhere looking for this trio because this Mexican trio, Los Panchos, they were big in the '50s, and they recorded that song and it was so beautiful. When I heard it, I said, "Look, Bill, listen, this is a beautiful song." I didn't know the song originally was American, "Jealous Heart," but they did it in Spanish, and with the trio it was beautiful. And I said, "Look, Bill, you should cut a record with the trio singing this song in Spanish like Los Panchos." And we went...I don't remember where we went...we went to this Mexican place where I knew we would find the trio, and we did. That's the one you are talking about.

---

4 A psychedelic rock band based in Phoenix, who made one studio album before disbanding in 1968.

To further replicate the Trio Los Panchos sound, Musil wanted to overdub more vocal parts, but Bill liked the bare sound of the single voice: "...it sounded fine to me. I hope they don't overdub too much with voices, etc." Bill felt a complete break from his band might make a hit, and so none of the Comets was used on the session. As the story goes, the tape was sent to RCA Nashville's producer, Chet Atkins, to have the additional instrumentation added and perhaps be released on RCA itself, but Atkins decided instead to give the song to Latino/country crossover singer Freddy Fender. Martha stated, "[Bill] did cut the record, and he made the mistake of sending the recording to Chet Atkins. He [Atkins] gave it to Freddy Fender and he had a big hit with it. Bill had a three-day drunk. I think he even called [Atkins] when he was drunk and he cussed the hell out of him." Haley was often later quoted as saying, "I will never work with Chet Atkins again."

This is a colorful story and plays into the narrative of Haley being passed over by the country music business in the 1960s, but particular facts threaten its credibility. Born Baldemar Garza Huerta in San Benito, Texas, in 1937, Freddie Fender had an early hit with his signature song, "Wasted Days and Wasted Nights." He was arrested on a drugs offense and spent three years in prison from 1960 to 1963. He spent the remainder of the 1960s in Louisiana and Texas as an auto mechanic and college student. His career picked up in 1974 with "Before the Next Teardrop Falls." He never recorded for RCA.

Atkins, on the other hand, was a producer and artist *exclusively* for RCA in Nashville for thirty-five years, moving to Columbia in 1982. It is highly unlikely that Bill's 1967 Phoenix recording was sent to Atkins, or that Atkins gave it to Fender. There is no evidence of Fender having *ever* recorded "Jealous Heart." It is more likely that the story is a convoluted mix of truths: some rejection by Atkins in Bill's career, the stalled release of the recording by Musil or other responsible party, and a mix-up as to who the Latino artist was, if any, who benefited from this misdeed.

On October 4, 1967, a legal case, brought by Bob Hayes against Bill Haley and his Comets, Inc. was heard. It was a large claim for unpaid salary dating back to the early 1960s. Hayes provided a description of the work he had done for the Corporation as personal assistant, and, as he described it, at Bill's "beck and call" at all times. He claimed to have been responsible for travel arrangements, worked seventy hours a week, often paid less than his salary, and sometimes not at all. Bill put up no defense and judgement was given in favor of Hayes and compensation of $32,302.80 was awarded. The case was so flawed and delayed that there was no practical chance of Hayes ever collecting the money: the Comets' Corporation had long since ceased to exist...

In January 1968, Bill and the Comets played at the Blue Jackets Inn on the Naval Air Station in Jacksonville, Florida, with their act consisting mainly of modern pop music. The contract for these dates has survived and makes interesting, if sobering, reading. The band was to play for six nights, four hours nightly, for a total fee of just $2,100. The required entertainment is described as a "Dance Musical and One Show," indicating that the band would play several dance sets, and that Bill would join them for one show at the end of the evening. While it is known that many versions of such a contract typically existed for various nefarious reasons, this must represent one of the lowest points in Bill's career. We can also read the reminiscence of rhythm guitarist Bill Faye, later known as Billy Moon and a member of the Comets who played this gig. He published it on the Internet many years later:

> One tour took us to Florida, and worked some Navy bases. Another took us across the U.S. and to Vancouver, British Columbia. I'll always remember that tour, because along with (I believe) the bass player at the time, traveling with all the band's equipment, in a station wagon, we got stranded in a blizzard in the middle of nowhere, somewhere in South Dakota. We were late for the gig. The rest of the band was ahead of us, riding in a Cadillac, and arrived a day earlier. We had to put all the band's stage jackets on to keep warm after the car quit until we were rescued by an eighteen-wheeler, who brought us back thirteen miles to a town that put us up in different farms for the night.[5]

In marked contrast to America, in Europe — and especially in England — there was new interest in 1950s Rock 'n' Roll. The transfer of the Decca Records catalog to MCA in 1968 prompted the reissue in the U.K. of "Rock Around the Clock" and it entered the record charts yet again. Bill and the band toured Europe for two months, playing to "standing room only" crowds in Holland, Ireland, Austria, West Germany, Denmark, Sweden, and, on May 1, a capacity crowd of 7,000 at London's Royal Albert Hall. While in Sweden, Bill signed with Sonet Records, and in late June 1968 re-recorded his classic songs on three albums.

He came down to Earth with a bump on his return to the USA. He was performing at the Newport Club on Miami Beach when IRS agents entered the premises and seized his contracted earnings in lieu of unpaid tax bills. This would ultimately be resolved and is detailed in the next chapter.

---

5 This page was downloaded many years ago and is no longer available on the Internet.

Bill and Rudy, photo taken from the back of the stage at London's Royal Albert Hall on the night of May 1, 1968.

Bill and Dan Haegquist in Stockholm, on the occasion of Bill signing a recording deal with Sonet Records, June 20, 1968.

After the short spell in Miami, followed by a break in Mexico, Bill was on the road for the final months of 1968. On October 22, for United Artists, the band recorded two Christmas songs and a single in the country idiom, Tom T. Hall's "That's How I Got to Memphis," backed with "Ain't Love Funny, Ha Ha Ha" (Fred Burch), and, with time to spare at the end, an impromptu rendition of Joe Turner's "Flip, Flop and Fly" (with a high-spirited Moe Wexler guest-performing on piano). Yet again, however, Bill felt let down by lack of promotion. The single was reviewed favorably but sold poorly.

In 1969, Bill again toured Europe, visiting Norway, Sweden, Lapland and England, enjoying the Rock 'n' Roll revival in Europe. On his return, he received a call from Richard Nader, a New York City-based disc jockey who had hit on the idea of presenting concerts with the oldies acts from his youth. He had spent years failing to persuade promoters, before finally taking the risk himself, borrowing $35,000 and hiring the Felt Forum at Madison Square Garden for a concert on October 18, 1969. Bill definitely wanted "in" and accepted. Nader also signed a number of other fifties acts.

Bill traveled to New York ahead of the show to take part in the promotion. He found the press and media were largely cynical about his chances. His last time in New York City had been 1962, when, heavily in debt, he was simply trying to keep himself afloat by working as a "twist" act at Morris Levy's Roundtable Club.

His feelings as he stood at the side of the stage were voiced by Hugh McCallum: "He had never felt more nervous and scared. He tried to calm himself with thoughts that this was what the last ten years had been spent campaigning for — all those little clubs, ...Paris... with the snide backstage comments, the traveling, playing below rates to get work to keep the Comets and his life and music alive."

M.C. Scott Muni took the microphone, introducing Bill as "The man who started it all, the originator, the King, the King of Rock 'n' Roll...Bill Haley and the Comets!" In Hugh's words:

Bill walked on to a deafening reception. As he walked to the front of the stage, his eyes became accustomed to the glare. He could see that everyone was standing. He bowed, smiled, waved. Then again, and again... The noise grew louder than ever. He went to begin the show but it was impossible. The noise was overpowering. He looked at Rudy. As corny as it sounds now, it was the most appropriate gesture in the world, at that time, to embrace each other. Rudy raised his arms in a "V" for Victory salute and both men raised each other's arm. As if it were possible, the sound got louder. For 8½ min-

[as was later reported in the press], Bill received a standing ovation. Eventually, he was able to begin the show.

In a photo syndicated to many newspapers, Bill on stage at the Felt Forum, October 18, 1969, Madison Square Garden, New York City.

The Village Voice reviewed the Felt Forum concert, saying of Bill, "...in recent years he had been playing in Europe and South America, had heard about the rock revival in these far-off places and would not believe it until it happened in New York. Now here he was headlining a sellout show." The magazine, however, was not wholly complimentary: "Haley's group looked tired and not really with it and they futzed about with lesser hits and a couple of songs that weren't really theirs until going out with the big one, what people had come to hear." Unfortunately, this habit of not giving his audience what they really wanted would bedevil Haley throughout his later career. Nevertheless, one aspect of Haley's success was revealed in a letter from Rudy to McCallum in which he says that, although Chuck Berry closed the first show, he had had difficulty controlling the audience once Bill and the Comets had been on stage and requested that he go on *before* the Comets for the second show.

Shortly before Christmas, Bill quickly secured a week for the band at The Bitter End on Bleecker Street in New York City. Three shows were recorded and condensed into the album *Bill Haley's Scrapbook* on Kama Sutra Records. On stage, he was clearly enjoying himself as he told the story of the evolution of rock and roll:

Down through the years, since rock 'n' roll started, the country and western music keeps coming back in, all the time. I'm not making this a documentary for country and western, but it's a part of it. The same for rhythm 'n' blues: all the great Rhythm 'n' Blues artists and songs. The marriage of the two is what I think makes the music so interesting and so appealing to so many people. There are so many great artists from both fields. Right after we started it, the artists who were considered hillbilly, or country and western, they came out. All of a sudden, we had a fellow named Elvis Presley, who came along from the country and western field, and Carl Perkins, and a hillbilly boy, Pat Boone. From the rhythm 'n' blues field, boys like Chuck Berry, Fats Domino, and all these great artists came along right at that era, and we all teamed up. A little later, even the saxophone players, who at the beginning used to call us hillbillies. [Indicates to Rudy, standing next to him] This guy was one of them. When we first started, Rudy was high-class, I was a hillbilly singer, and Rudy was working with a guy named Ralph Marterie. We were both from this little town, and he would even talk to the hillbilly. Yeah, we were bums!

Another highlight was an astonishing honky-tonk vocal by drummer Bill Nolte on the Dallas Frazier song, "There Goes My Everything," replete with gorgeous vocal harmonies by members of the band. At its conclusion, the audience erupted in rapturous applause and an enthusiastic Bill exclaimed, "I *knew* you liked country and western!"

As Scott Muni announced Bill at the first show on November 29: "*He* was there at the beginning. *They* were there at the beginning. They *are* the beginning and the end: Bill Haley and His Comets!"

Nick Masters (Nicholas Matthias Masters, 1936-1995) was a long-standing but "on and off" member of the Comets from 1965 to 1974. He would play a significant role in keeping the Comets working as a band when Bill Haley reduced his own workload during periods in the 1970s. He first joined the band as a steel guitar player, graduating to a twin neck, and eventually to a standard electric guitar. He is photographed here in Varberg, soloing in typically ebullient style, during a 2-3 week tour of Sweden in July 1969.

CHAPTER 10
The Revival Years (1970-1978)

On February 10th, 1970, after a few weeks in Florida and the Bahamas, the band joined the traveling Richard Nader show in Orlando, incorporating a flight to New York to appear in the TV program *The Show* on the 24th. There they performed for a small audience of college students who asked Haley about the origins of rock and roll. Haley's enjoyment in his new role as the ambassador for the music was painted on his face throughout the show.

Bill was now finding he could take things more easily, and in mid-April he ducked out of performing to spend five months with his family, while the Comets continued to work near to home as Nick Masters and the Country Showmen.

Bill would continue to work for Nader for a couple of years. Of all the artists on the shows, Bill was the one who had least changed with the passage of time, both in terms of appearance and musical performance. Whilst artists like Little Richard, Jerry Lee Lewis and Chuck Berry would throw tantrums, "no shows" and other such *prima donna* behavior, Bill's reputation for simply delivering the same classic hits over and over again stood him in good stead, and of course resonated with his more mature audience as well. However, in October 1970, Bill would make a remarkable album for Sonet in Nashville. *Rock Around the Country* was produced by Sam Charters[1] and represented a return to Bill's country roots. (See Chapter 22.)

---

1 Samuel Barclay Charters IV, born August 1,1929, died March 18, 2015. *Wikipedia* (accessed February 22, 2021) described him as "an American music historian, writer, record producer, musician, and poet." Charters' 1959 book, *The Country Blues* (reprinted by Da Capo Press in 1975), was a monument in early blues research and spearheaded future comprehensive blues research by scholars such as Paul Oliver, David Evans, William Ferris, Robert Palmer, and others.

During the mid to late 1970s, when Bill Haley was not working, the Comets, led by Nick Masters, worked the Philadelphia area under various names, initially as "Nick Masters and the Country Showmen." This picture was taken in 1976 when the band was being promoted and managed by Jolly Joyce as "Bill Haley's Comets" and mainly working the Kingston, PA area From L to R: two unknowns (saxophone and drums), Nick Masters (lead guitar), Ray Parsons (rhythm guitar), and Rey Cawley (bass guitar).

In June 1971, Haley's long-running dispute with the IRS was finally settled. In 1961, they had garnished his Decca royalties, claiming he had not reported income from record sales in 1959 and 1960. An audit had been attempted in 1963, but Bill was in Mexico. This resulted in expense claims being disallowed, tax being due on gross estimated income, and a gross liability of $140,000.

In an attempt to resolve the tax issues, Rudy Pompilii had first made contact with Henry Bloch, founder of the H&R Block Company and a one-time Haley fan, in the late 1960s. Andrew Hoesch, an employee of the company, was assigned on a "no win, no fee" basis. He prepared a compromise solution based on "doubtful liability" and on behalf of Haley, made an offer of $25,000 to clean the slate. It took the IRS two years to react and now, at a meeting between Hoesch and the IRS, Haley's accounts were audited within four hours. The IRS was satisfied that up to 1960 the Corporation *had* properly reported its royalties. Hoesch was then able to knock $16,000 off the IRS estimate, the IRS abated another $111,000, and were prepared to settle for a payment of $13,000. Hoesch then demonstrated that the Decca royalties garnished by the IRS were greater than the liability. Bill thereby received a settlement payment of approximately $8,000.

An appearance on the nationally televised *Andy Williams Show* in the new year 1972 was another boost for Bill's profile. A Nader tour followed, an appearance on *The Dick Cavett Show*, and a grand finale at Madison Square Garden in front of an audience of 20,000. In early February 1972, the band appeared in Wisconsin, Chicago, and Minneapolis. In contrast to the current trend, on February 12, the *La Crosse Tribune* described Haley's appearance as "bombsville," with "one of the smallest audiences ever seen for a national act." Bill rejoined the Nader tour in March with Bo Diddley, the Crests, Gary U.S. Bonds, the Platters, and Screaming Jay Hawkins. The shows on April 23 and 24 at Cobo Hall in Detroit were filmed for the movie *Let the Good Times Roll*. The intense rivalry between the top artists on the Nader shows was apparent at Massey Hall, Toronto on May 19. Jackie Wilson strode on stage while Bill was in a second encore of "Rock Around the Clock." Bill and the Comets abruptly left the stage, and the promoter was so angry that he cut the power to Wilson's microphone and his performance ended before it had begun.

The poster for *Let the Good Times Roll*. This film did more than anything to bring vintage Rock 'n' Roll to a mass audience and resuscitated the careers of many 1950s stars. There was always contention for top billing between Bill Haley, Jerry Lee Lewis, Little Richard, Chuck Berry, etc. which would be dealt with by subtle changes to the advertising. Note that here Bill was kept happy by being a "special guest star"!

In late June, Bill joined the "Legends of Rock 'n' Roll," which played four nights in Californian cities. Cornell Gunter and the Coasters topped the bill, which also featured Bobby Rydell, the Platters, Danny and the Juniors, and Del Shannon. The aggregate attendance was 42,000 and Bill's biggest thrill was that Big Joe Turner joined the show for two nights. Bill, Big Joe, Zola Taylor (of the Platters), and Bobby Lewis got together one night to talk about the "great old days." This would be the last time Bill and Big Joe would enjoy each other's company.

Bill also made a quick hop to the UK for a show at Wembley Stadium in August. The audience fell far short of expectation and the show was plagued by disputes between Little Richard, Jerry Lee Lewis, Chuck Berry, and Bill Haley over billing, which had delayed confirmation of the line-up. These were resolved and, regardless of the playing order, Bill emerged as the generally acclaimed hero.

Toward the end of the year, Bill recorded the LP *Just Rock & Roll Music* at Woodland Sound Studios in Nashville. According to Swenson, Haley's drinking problem, which had been getting worse for years, had reached crisis proportions. He showed up to the sessions so drunk that, allegedly, Sam Charters had to point him in the direction of the microphone. Swenson claimed Haley was banned from recording in Nashville as a result.[2] Singer Donna Fargo reportedly attended one of the sessions and, according to Swenson, witnessed some of Haley's drunken behavior with great sadness.[3]

It is well-known that Bill developed a dangerous drinking habit in later life. For the most part, it appears not to have affected his career. However, when Bill introduces Lord Jim Ferguson in his autobiography (Chapter 3 of this book), we find this portentous paragraph:

> Lord Jim also had the habit, as most good Scotchmen do, of nipping Johnnie Walker Red Label. He would end each day sitting in his robe with a 12 oz glass, filled with ice and Johnnie Walker Red Label. For the first time I learned the taste of whiskey, as I would join him at the end of the day. This was to prove to be both helpful and harmful to me in the years ahead.

Alcohol, and particularly Johnnie Walker Red Label (Scotch whisky), features in Chapter 5 covering 1956, and involving Big Joe Turner. We have also found it mentioned in McCallum's text, particularly in less happy times, such as the low period in 1966 before the "rock and roll revival" began. Other texts, notably Bill Haley Jr.'s biography, *Crazy Man, Crazy*, and John Swenson's book, *Bill Haley: The Daddy of Rock and Roll*, which are frequently referenced in this work, have covered the subject in depth and in uncomfortable detail that we do not feel the need to repeat. The subject will return in this book at various points, including Chapter 11, which describes Bill's final days.

Alcoholism was a subject about which Bill would rarely talk in public. However, interviewed by Brian Matthew for the BBC Radio 1 program *My Top Twelve* (broadcast May 5, 1974), he said, "I've had the years when I've had my bad luck and I have gone through the alcoholic thing also and I fought it for a long time." In response to being asked whether anyone helped him with it he replied at length:

---

2 Swenson, pp.146-149. While Haley never recorded in Nashville again, a ban seems unlikely as Nashville was known to tolerate other artists with similar reputations.

3 On the other hand, in a phone interview with David Lee Joyner in 2018, pianist Bobby Wood recalled that the session went without incident, that Bill was quiet, but respectful and amicable. In many instances, Bill was on his best behavior when Martha was around, and his drunkenness in the workplace was more likely to occur when she was not.

You know, I don't think anyone can help you when you're like that. Of course, I suppose it depends on your character. I had to beat myself down. I think I finally had to see myself enough times at the bottom and finally you have to reach down and get hold of those boot straps yourself. I've had the tragedy and I've had the happiness, so I don't need to paint a picture that Bill Haley has been 'goody goody' all his life, because I haven't! But I think with me it's a case of having something in life which means something to you. I've always had this thing of loving my music, loving what I do, and being able to travel and wanting to get out there and do it.

From April 13 to May 27, 1973, Bill Haley and the Comets again joined the Richard Nader touring show. Bill's first son Jack went to the show at the Spectrum in Philadelphia, found that Bill was a "no show" and tracked him down to a nearby motel, too drunk to perform.[4] This might well have hastened the end of Bill's involvement in with Nader. The shows continued until early June, and included a return to Madison Square Garden on June 1, but the last occasion on which Bill appeared was at the Cobo Arena in Detroit on May 18.

Haley received a boost with "Rock Around the Clock" being used as the theme music for both the TV show *Happy Days* and the film *American Graffiti*.[5] Ultimately, these would result in the recording again entering the charts around the world. As Bill said to Hugh McCallum, "Around the end of 1970, I was feeling near the top. But drink and other problems dragged me down. By the end of 1973, I couldn't have gone down much further. But 1974 was a real shot in the arm."

On December 26, 1973, Bill and the band travelled to Australia and New Zealand. Events there would take an odd turn. Martha remembered this in Adelaide:

I noticed that he was not himself. I remember one particular day he stayed talking to the audience for an hour and a half. Talk and talk and talk. What was he saying? I don't know because it was an open field and I couldn't hear. And so finally, when he was done, he was done. The following day in the newspaper they were commenting, "Why was he talking so much?" Nobody knew, and I didn't know either.

---

4 Haley, Jr. and Benjaminson, Chapter 39 (although citing a different show).

5 The band made new recordings of "Rock Around the Clock" and "See You Later, Alligator" for the TV series, whereas the feature film used the original Decca recording.

The next day the Adelaide press criticized Haley "for lapsing into monologues during the show about his 'beautiful Mexican wife' and 'lovely family.' After waiting seventeen years and getting only seven tunes and a load of repetitive boozed-up crap talk, even the most loyal Haley fans must today be looking for a new idol."

In Australia for the second time, in December/January 1974. Haley and the Comets performed in a rainstorm at Randwick Racecourse. Other photographs of the event show stewards holding umbrellas above the individual band members. For Bill and Martha, this was the start of a long period of time of being away from home, lasting until May.

Bill then travelled to the U.K. for an extended tour lasting from February to May. This, coinciding as it did with the twentieth anniversary of its recording, sparked the re-entry of "Rock Around the Clock" into the U.K. Top 20. The show at the Hammersmith Palais in London was recorded and released by Antic Records. By the end of the tour, Bill and Martha had been away from home for the best part of five months. "Rock Around the Clock" had re-entered the U.S. charts, peaking at No. 39 in *Billboard* and No. 36 in *Cashbox*. In June, *Billboard* reported that global sales of the record had topped 22 million. It would be listed in the *Guinness Book of World Records* as the biggest selling record of all time, citing an "unaudited" sales figure that by 1989 had surpassed 43 million copies.

That summer, Bill would break his contract with the Joyce Agency, embarking on a well-paid tour of the U.S. Northwest and Canada. Jolly Joyce had recently retired and the agency was being run by his family. Haley and Joyce's relationship had been volatile, but had endured, with a few "break-ups" since April 1950. In 1974, Haley had been seduced by the promise of a greatly improved fee by Merv Goldstein, whom he took on as manager. Bill Turner, lead guitarist at the time, remembered a $10,000 nightly fee, compared to the $1,500 to $2,250 that Bill was getting from Joyce. One of the highlights was a gig at the Seattle Raceway with an audience of 50,000. With everything going well, Bill bought Rudy Pompilii a new saxophone. Turner has detailed memories of working with Haley in his hotel room:

Bill Turner, the Comets' lead guitar player from July 1974 to December 1976.

He took out his guitar and played me the arrangement of "Guitar Boogie," plus a couple of things for my solo on "Memphis." Then he asked me if I knew "12th Street Rag" and we played it together, right there in the room. That very night on the stage, he announced, out of the blue, "Now here's Billy T. Turner with the '12th Street Rag!'" Whoa! I just wheeled around to the band and yelled out, "Key of G!"

About Haley's singing, Turner recalls:

His voice held out well. I also noticed that he would stand quite a distance from the mic when singing, like a real old-timer from the radio days, which was probably why his throat would bother him at times. He didn't let the mic do all the work for him. Another thing I noticed was what a heavy smoker he was. I mean one right after the other.[6]

---

6 Bill Turner in e-mail correspondence with the authors.

In Sacramento, with the tour going well, Haley bought himself a new white Mercury station wagon. Turner remembers that Martha had been traveling with Bill, and her influence had kept his drinking in check. However, from Sacramento Bill travelled with the band by plane to Spokane, Washington, while Martha and the children presumably travelled in the new car. Haley got completely drunk on the journey and, in doing so, contravened the terms of his agreement with Goldstein. Goldstein stayed with the tour, but he would never book Haley again. The Jolly Joyce Agency (now run by Sandra Shekell) discovered that Bill had undertaken this tour and took out an injunction that effectively prevented him from performing again in the United States. In November and December 1974, touring Europe, Rudy complained of chest congestion and would sit in the dressing room, trying to cough it up. On his return, he was hospitalized with pneumonia and, a short while later, diagnosed with terminal lung cancer.

Bill and Martha returned to Mexico for Christmas at home. At this point, we should give an account of their home life between 1969 and 1976. In 1969, the Haleys were in Juarez, a large city conjoined with El Paso, Texas. The agglomeration straddled the USA/Mexico border. On June 25, 1971, their second child, Pedro Antonio Guillermo Haley, was born. Martha crossed the border into the U.S. to give birth so that their son would have dual citizenship.

One of Bill's great passions was ocean fishing and, in 1974, they bought a small house on the coast in Vera Cruz, a seaside town on the Gulf of Mexico, whilst keeping the house in Juarez. Martha picks up the story at this point:

> He became an avid fisherman.[7] When we lived in Vera Cruz, he would get up at five in the morning. He had two fishermen that were very close to him, but they were village men and they taught him how to fish, just with his hands. They used to go to the open sea and fish there. One time, they took Martha Maria and she caught a marlin. She caught one and he used to get them all the time. And we had a convent on the back of our house and we used to give them fish. He would get all the fish in the ocean and he wouldn't eat a piece of fish, and Pedro's the same. They hate fish. We used to have a station wagon then. He came up to the top with these big fish and we used to take them over to the convent so the nuns would dispose of it.

---

7 Martha's statement here is a bit shortsighted. Bill's love of fishing began much earlier. In his autobiography, he talks about his introduction to the sport with "Lord" Jim Ferguson. In the early 1950s, he also had his own fishing boat, "The Comet." His return to fishing, now that he was geographically and financially more in a position to do so, may have been new to Martha, or her terminology of his "return" might be misleading. It is heartwarming that he named his boat in Mexico "Martita," the pet name of his daughter Martha Maria.

On April 23, 1975, Linda Georgina ("Gina") Haley, Martha and Bill's youngest child, was born. At that time Bill was enjoying a considerable uptick in his royalty income from the *American Graffiti* film and *Happy Days* television show, both featuring his music. He decided to invest in a hotel in Vera Cruz with the aim of securing his financial future and facilitating a more relaxed lifestyle, at least from his point of view. Martha's viewpoint was quite different:

He would leave me alone there with the three kids, fighting the electricity company, the phone company, with the gas, everybody — "It's broken. It's not working" — and I was the one there fixing everything. And it was a big home. He wasn't there. I used to stay back at the house, and at one o'clock, all the stores closed for siesta to eat and then open up around three or four and then stay open until nine at night. And I hated all that. It was so hot!

We came back from Vera Cruz, sold the house in Juarez, and then he decided we were going to move to Vera Cruz, you know, the whole family and everybody. And that's when we bought that big house on the ocean. And then I got to the point where I told him, "Look, either we move from here and go back to the States, or give me a divorce. I'm not gonna put up with this anymore." But, by then, he had already bought a motel that was half-built and they didn't finish it so he bought it. My brother and him had become very good friends, and my brother was very hard-working and he had a lot of brains for business. They bought the hotel and they started rebuilding it, you know, finishing it. I don't know how much the hotel cost; I'm there in my house with the kids.

As Martha relates, the rate of inflation escalated. The alterations were becoming more expensive, problematic and falling behind schedule. She struggled to maintain a decent family home in the midst of it all. This all placed a demand on Bill to make more money, whilst he was facing the decline in Rudy's health and the effect of that on his present and future career. Martha struggled too, for obvious reasons, and, amidst a degree of domestic strife, the decision was made to abandon the hotel development plan and move somewhere where they could establish a more suitable family home.

One night on the West Coast tour in 1974, and out of the blue, Bill had announced that Rudy was going to record a solo album. This was a surprise to Rudy and it would become a race against time as Rudy's health declined. Despite that, in February 1975, Rudy would record his solo album. Titled *Rudy's Rock: The Sax That Changed the World*, it featured Philadelphia-area musicians but, crucially, not Bill.[8] It seemed that he could not face the world without his best friend and right-hand man. He had always had someone close to him as a buffer between him and the rest of the world, and for some time it had been Rudy. The album was a disappointment. Rudy was not allowed to use the musicians he wanted as Sam Charters, the producer, was working as cheaply and as quickly as possible. The musicians were basically those who worked for Bill's then bass player, Jim Lebak.

Rudy's illness placed a question mark over everything and Bill would not go back on stage until October 1975. Tours of many countries were discussed but not finalized. Bill was enjoying increased royalty payments, he was no longer in debt, and he could afford to take things a bit easier. The band however, effectively fell apart.

In October, Rudy made his final tour with Bill and the Comets, to South America, wearing a wig to hide the effects of cancer treatment. His health was now seriously affecting his playing, but, as a consummate musician, he was able to adapt solos and riffs to give himself literally more breathing space. On video, Rudy's undying dedication to the task of being Bill's right-hand man shines through the darkness of the moment. The tour was planned for three weeks, but was cut short after two when the deposit money for the third week did not appear. Back home, Rudy continued to pursue his love of performing as his health steadily declined. At one of his final performances, at The Captain's Table, he was joined on stage by Franny Beecher on guitar, and on November 16, 1975, he married his girlfriend, Ann Swan.

Rudy died on February 5, 1976. There would be a last "hurrah" for Bill Haley in the coming years, but, in the meantime, the loss of Rudy, for so long his best friend and confidant, was more than he could bear. He did not attend Rudy's funeral in Chester. Martha attributed his absence to the difficulty in traveling from Vera Cruz, his inability to deal with the grief, and the prospect of meeting old enemies. Allegedly, this pair of best friends had a pact that, if either of them were to die, the other would not play any more music. In 1979, Bill related:

---

8 This album is discussed in detail in Chapter 22.

Rudy passed away almost three years ago now, of cancer... I lost the spirit. I remembered the promise. I just couldn't bring myself to do it. I laid the guitar down, and, after a period of about a year and a half, I started to look at it a bit differently. Gradually, I began to feel I should go on, for what we had worked for. Consequently, this is the comeback tour...the first live tour I've done since that time. I kind of feel Rudy would want me to do it.[9]

Initially, it had seemed Bill would not be keeping the bargain, and the band was told there would be a tour. It was, however, cancelled at short notice for health reasons. Bill had low blood pressure and a slow pulse, and his doctor had forbidden touring. No one believed this, Bill was incommunicado, and no compensation was offered. On February 24, 1976, a newswire from United Press International reported that the Comets' manager, Sandra Joyce Hart, of the Joyce Agency, was suing him for $250,000. Hart claimed that, despite being exclusively signed to her, he had taken work from other agents, and that she had lost the commission as a result.[10]

Bill owed Sonet an album and travelled to FAME Studios in Muscle Shoals, Alabama, to work with Sam Charters on the LP *R-O-C-K*.[11] Bill used Jim Lebak (bass guitar) and Ray Parsons (rhythm guitar). The rest were local musicians. According to Charters, an attempt was made to come up with more modern material, but the album was primarily remakes of songs dating back to the 1950s. Rudy's absence weighed heavily on the session, which resulted in the saxophone parts being re-recorded. Bill was not happy with the musicians and had to be talked into recording "Mohair Sam," during which he wryly remarked, "So now we know what they do."

Effectively retired from music Bill was enjoying the peace and quiet and looking forward to the realization of his dream of owning a hotel by the sea. However, as Martha explains:

---

9 Bill Haley speaking in the UK TV documentary *Format V*, broadcast March 15, 1979.

10 Based on a commission of 10-20%, this implies gross earnings of between $1.25 and $2.5 million ($6 - $12 million at 2025 values).

11 We cannot date this session with confidence. Ray Parsons told Hugh McCallum that it was "a couple of weeks before Rudy died." Other sources suggest it was later in the year.

At that time, I think Paddy [Malynn] came to visit us in Vera Cruz and he told Bill to get ready because he was lining up jobs. At the same time, inflation came up and all the stuff they were buying to finish the hotel doubled in price, and that's when Bill said, "We can't go on like this. I'm running out of money and Martha wants to leave me. We need to do something." So, we left. My brother stayed on and sold the hotel the way it was, and that's when we ended up in Harlingen [Texas]. Vera Cruz, Tampico, that is on the eastern shore, the Gulf of Mexico. That's where we stayed and we found a very nice home in Harlingen, which is the house where he died. It was humble, but it helped us to come down and to relax. He could go fishing. He used to get up at five in the morning and go fishing in the Gulf at South Padre Island and Port Isabel.

When he had to go out on tour, I would have to go with him. We had a girl, a very nice girl, that we had brought from Vera Cruz and she stayed in the house with the kids and she managed the house nicely.

In 1976 they left Vera Cruz for the orderly peace and quiet of Harlingen, Texas, where they would live until Bill's death in 1981.[12]

The Haley home from 1976 in Harlingen, Texas.

---

12 Based on Martha Maria Haley's handwritten record of where the Haley family lived between 1969 (when she was six years old) and 1981.

A photograph taken in 1976 on Bill and Martha's arrival at Vienna Airport by Herbert Kamitz, one of the world's most avid Bill Haley fans. The picture shows Patrick and Martha on their way to a waiting limousine to be driven to their hotel.

A European tour was set up for November and December of 1976. Malynn was angling to recruit a band of British players for the tour. Bill Turner and Jim Lebak were the only two members of the most recent Comets' aggregation available and they set about gathering musicians to work with them, keeping the British takeover at bay. Malynn stressed that this was an important tour. Bill's contract with Sonet would soon expire and it was considered essential to maintain the label's interest. Everything was riding on a show at the Victoria Theatre in London towards the end of the tour, which Sonet executives would be attending.

Bill Turner observed that,

[Haley] was getting bad reviews all throughout the tour. It had nothing to do with the band, oddly enough (though he swore it did), which was badly divided and everybody going in different directions, musically. The criticisms were aimed squarely at Haley, who the articles in the press said was (if I may paraphrase) merely going through the motions, doing the same clockwork routine...etc. Some of the titles of the articles were particularly damaging to Haley! One was called "How to Betray Your Fans." Another was titled "Bill Haley — All That's Left is the Curl." One embarrassing article reported an irate German fan ripping his ticket stub up outside after the show, exclaiming "...same five songs...!" The ticket prices were supposedly very high, as well.[13]

Martha explained her husband's mood:

---

13 Bill Turner, in correspondence with Chris Gardner.

He was so tired by then. He was fed up with everything. What he wanted was just to fish and watch the baseball game. He worked the last tours and the last jobs just because he needed to do them, not because he wanted to be on stage and all that stuff. Which is probably what happened to all of the big acts. They get fed up, because I don't think they enjoy all of the noise.

Whilst Haley was in London, news broke of judgment in the U.S. in favor of Sandra Joyce Hart to the tune of $240,000. The Joyce Agency said it would collect this amount from Bill's U.S. assets. Bill did not defend the case, never made any payment, and was never to perform again in the U.S.

According to Turner, the band found it more difficult to sell to promoters for several reasons: last-minute cancellations, repetitive shows, with Haley himself only singing a few songs. Sonet, however, renewed Bill's recording contract. In due course, they would invest heavily in a new album, but not until 1979, as Bill effectively now went into retirement. He did nothing musically in 1977 and 1978. He sold the unfinished hotel in Vera Cruz, and purchased the Val Verde Trailer Park, a going concern in Donna, Texas, midway between Harlingen and Van Allen. He would occupy himself in running the business there. Martha's attitude was ambivalent:

One time, he was driving up and down the border highway, the one that is from McAllen to Brownsville, and he saw a trailer park for sale and he bought it. "Bill, what are you going to do with that?" "Well, I'm going to take care of it." So, he bought a trailer park and I'm gonna manage it. I did it for a while. Bill managed that and then my brother helped him, and then I told him, "Bill, this is too much for you. You're driving back and forth every day;[14] it's too much. You're not that young anymore and there is no need for you to be doing this." But he liked it because he liked to talk to people. He never told them who he was, with a baseball cap on and all that. I think that's when he sold the park and I don't know if he was good or bad because, when he sold the park, he began to act different. I didn't know what it was; I couldn't put my finger on it. He was drinking more...or he stopped drinking. I don't remember.

---

14 A round trip of about fifty miles.

An aerial view of the trailer park in Donna, Texas purchased by Bill.

Meanwhile, there were stirrings of another "rock and roll revival" in the U.K. and Europe. Rockabilly was center stage as a mainstream pop genre, launching acts such as Shakin' Stevens, Matchbox, and the Stray Cats. Major record companies began scouring their vaults for dormant 1950s product. In Philadelphia, Bill's old partner, Jack Howard, died on December 1, 1976, and his residual publishing and record businesses were taken over by Rex Zario.[15] Rex inherited a huge Bill Haley archive: a large number of reel-to-reel tapes from Bill's own recording studio, recordings by Haley from the 1940s, sheet music, songwriting contracts, photos, financial documents, etc. The archive was subsequently plundered by collectors and diminished over the years, though John Beecher, owner of the UK Rollercoaster Records label, would develop a working relationship with Rex Zario and, over the years, would issue the best of the material from the vaults.

---

15 Zario, true name Rosario Lafavi, was born January 3, 1926 in Catania, Sicily, and died in Philadelphia on April 15, 1991. He enjoyed local success as a hillbilly/country performer.

Rex Zario, who took over Jack Howard's Arcade music publishing and record company when Jack passed away. Rex had been an entertainer in his own right in the 1950s. During his stewardship of Arcade many previously unknown Haley recordings were released, but ultimately none of the interested parties (writers and performers) believed that they had received their fair share of royalties.

James E. Myers contacted Bill to invite him to join a tour with the "Original Comets" (Franny Beecher, Johnny Grande, Marshall Lytle, Joey D'Ambrosio, and Dick Richards), but Bill declined. Myers was insisting it would be billed as "James E. Myers Presents Bill Haley and His Original Comets" and Bill felt lingering bitterness towards the "defectors" who quit the band to form the Jodimars in 1955. In any event, he was already under contract to Patrick Malynn in Europe. He also resisted regular encouragement from Hugh McCallum, who was pushing for a return to the band's original instrumentation with upright bass, steel guitar, and piano.

Bill, meanwhile, took steps to sort out the flow of royalties through his publishing company, Valley Brook Music. In 1968, all songs had been transferred out of Valley Brook into Jack Howard's Arcade Music Publishing Co. but these instructions had not been acted upon by ASCAP. Bill wrote to Zario to re-authorize the transfer. Bit by bit, Zario managed to generate a flow of royalties for re-issues of Bill's 1940s recordings. In the process, Bill and Rex often spoke by telephone. Rex recorded their conversations, which started out as being about business, but became increasingly personal and distressing. Sadly, these recordings illustrate what appears to be the decline of Bill's mental health over the next three years.

In 1978, an Australian LP entitled *Golden Country Origins* made available for the first time a number of hillbilly and cowboy recordings that Bill had made in the late 1940s. Finally, in October and November 1978, Haley appeared to be getting interested in a comeback, as Jeff Kruger's Ember Concerts Division and Patrick Malynn began discussions about a possible U.K. tour.

Bill and Martha are seen on May 15th, 1974, passing through Customs on their way home after a hugely successful two and a half month tour of the U.K. Haley's career at this point had been buoyed up with "Rock Around the Clock" being chosen as the theme music for both the film *American Graffiti* and the TV series *Happy Days*, and by its resultant entry into the pop charts in several countries.

CHAPTER 11
God Bless Rock 'n' Roll (1979-1981)

In late October 1979, Bill and Martha flew to Amsterdam for a European tour which would culminate in a Royal Command performance in London for Her Majesty Queen Elizabeth II, in what is commonly (but unofficially) known as "The Royal Variety Show."

The mostly British band, recruited by Mal Gray, had two long days of stage rehearsals. Bill enjoyed a final surge in the applause at the end of the show, and was later photographed bowing before the Queen, who allegedly told him "It reminded me of when I was young."[1]

In May 1980, Bill took what would be his final bow, in South Africa. Two weeks at the Coliseum Theatre in Johannesburg were followed by five days in Durban and three in Cape Town. *En route* home, Bill and Martha stopped in London, where Haley told Hugh that, despite poor press reviews, he had "won in the end" and had been invited to return in 1981. Patrick Malynn was now claiming that filming of Bill's life story could begin in August, with Jeff Bridges as the front runner for the part of Bill Haley.

---

1 There are several hints from history that the Queen was something of a Haley fan. In 1956, during her annual summer holiday at Balmoral, she had a copy of the film *Rock Around the Clock* sent to her, which she watched in place of *The Caine Mutiny*. A delightful story from a gardener at Sandringham in the 1950s describes her and the Duke of Edinburgh being seen through a window dancing to "Rockin' Through the Rye." In 2002, she celebrated her Golden Jubilee at Buckingham Palace. When the opening firework display had finished and the party began, the first song to be played was "Rock Around the Clock." The British rock star Elton John has fond memories of being asked by the Queen to dance with her to "Rock Around the Clock" during a celebration at Windsor Castle.

Bill shakes hands with HRH Queen Elizabeth II after the Royal Variety Show at the Theatre Royal, Drury Lane, London on November 26, 1979.

```
OCTOBER/NOVEMBER 1980 EUROPEAN TOUR

Planning for this began as far back as last December with some of the proposed dates being
set as early as May/June this year. Here is the intinery as it stood a week ago.

October 31    - Stadthalle, Bremerhaven      (West Germany)
November 1    - Ball Pompos, Kiel                  "
         2    - Ta Toff, Bremervorde-Bevern        "
         3    - Markthalle, Hamburg                "
         4    - Burgerhaus, Troisdorf              "
         5    - Macumba Club, Lille-Frankreich (France)  (or La Toff,Bad Bevensen, Germany)
         6    - Macumba Club, Nantes           "   (or Stadthalle,Offenbach, Germany)
         7    - Unknown Venue, Paris           "   (or Stadthalle,Stuttgart, Germany)
         8    - Nurenberg Merstensingerhalle  (W/Germ) (or Rock-Cafe,Bonn)
         9    - Hotel Bachmair,Wottach Egern   "   (or Odeon, Kassel)
        10    -   "     "    "      "           "   (or Liberty-Bar, Stuttgart)
        11    - Schwabinger Brau, Munchen          "
        12    - Not yet known
        13    -   "    "    "
        14    -   "    "    "
        15    - Pavilion, Sandown, Isle of Wight
        16    - Fulcrum Centre, Slough
        17    - Diamond Club, Caerphilly
        18    -    "      "     "
        19    - Free date
        20    - Odeon, Hammersmith
        21    - Kings Club, Eastbourne
        22    - Pavilion, West Runton
```

-15-

```
        23    - Not yet known
        24    - Free date
        25    - Eden Court Theatre, Inverness
        26    - Magnum, Irvine
        27    - Pavilion, Hemel Hempstead
        28    - Royal Court,Liverpool
        29    - King George Hall, Blackburn
        30    - Webbington Country Club, Bristol

"Intercord" in Germany have received invitations for Bill to appear on no less than 5 TV
Shows - which will be played/when/where is as yet not clear. Similarly Patrick has secured
a Rdio One 3 hour "Special" on Bill as well appearances on the Michael Parkinson Show.
```

Hugh McCallum published this itinerary for a planned tour of Europe and the UK in October-November 1980, which would be cancelled as a result of Bill's ill health.

During 1980, attempts were made to have Bill record another album, but he would keep cancelling. The October 1980 *Haley News* began with the optimistic report that a Europe and U.K. tour was still scheduled to go ahead within two weeks. In those days, the production of the newsletter took many days, written from start to finish using a typewriter and stencils. Hugh's prognosis for the tour declined as he typed, to "tentative" and, by the end of the issue, "likely to be cancelled," with Bill "clearly not in the right frame of mind to undertake the tour."

For a glimpse of what kind of album project might have followed, we can thank Bill's youngest child, Gina Haley, who, some years later, "found a planner, with notes, and there he's got ideas for a gospel album, song titles, and so on. So, I think he was writing and preparing to look at a gospel album. That must have been 1980."[2] Bill's youngest son, Pedro Haley, believes that Bill might have pitched this idea to Sonet, but that they had rejected it. He was scheduled to record an album for Sonet in Memphis in the fall of 1980, but the sessions were pushed back and, before long, Bill Haley was gone.

Martha Haley's painful memories of this time would not support Hugh McCallum's pale optimism in the *Haley News* about Bill's future plans:

> [Bill] started going out in his car and driving around. Then he would come home and he wouldn't sleep, you know, he would stay up all night. I was so worried but I didn't know what to do. He started going to restaurants and he would say to people, "You don't know who I am? I'm Bill Haley." I sort of heard but they didn't declare what was going on. And I knew I couldn't tell him to go to see a doctor because I know he wouldn't.

> The house...we had had a swimming pool... no, we built it. He said, "We should have a pool for the kids." And on the side, there was a pool house and a garage, and there was a little cot and a chair or something like that, and a bathroom and shower and all that. He started to stay in the little room without coming into the house where our bedroom was. I didn't want to discuss it with him because I knew he wouldn't listen to me.

---

2 Gina Haley, interviewed by Chris Gardner, *Now Dig This,* No. 339, June 2011.

In a newsletter published after Haley's death, McCallum reported that Bill had suffered a suspected mild heart attack in the fall of 1980, which resulted in the cancellation of recordings and tours. However, this was a smokescreen, and the truth was more worrying. The Haley family had always lived a closely-guarded private life. While Bill and Martha valued their own and their family's privacy, Bill's new habit of calling old acquaintances at midnight and a visit from his first son, Jack, would reveal his trouble to the wider world. Bill had made contact with Jack in 1978, in the cause of a better father-son relationship. They spoke on the phone on a number of occasions and Jack began to worry that his father was mentally ill. Around Thanksgiving 1980, Bill asked him to come and visit. Jack found Bill alone (Martha and the children had left the house) and Bill, with black eyes and broken teeth, had been in a fight. Haley's hairdresser, George Martin, in conversation with Otto Fuchs, reported that Haley had visited his barber's shop at this time. "He looked horrid. He was missing his front teeth and had black eyes. He told me three guys in Houston had whapped him. Fights weren't new to him, but it was the first time something like this had happened to him."[3]

Jack spent four days with Bill and became scared by his drinking. Jack was later interviewed by National Public Radio about this visit:

> He would talk about his life in the Marine Corps, which he was never in... he said he was a Deputy Sherriff of Hidalgo County, Texas, which he wasn't. I'd go along with him. I knew he was lying, but I wouldn't dare say it... I never wanted to make him mad for fear that I would never hear from him again. [On the fourth day of the visit,] he was at the kitchen table with a bottle. I couldn't get him to put the bottle down. He didn't threaten me in any way, but he scared me with the way he was talking. He talked real loud and hollered. I called this Buddy Larimore, the captain of the police department. He's the one who came and got me, and he told my father, "You gotta quit the drinking. You're losing the people that you love the most. Your wife has left you and went with her family, and now your son wants to leave you again." He seemed then like he didn't care.[4]

---

3 Otto Fuchs: unpublished interview with George Martin, Harlingen, 1993.

4 Broadcast on National Public Radio, February 9, 1981.

Many parties had a vested interest in the success of the tour and Bill's condition was a becoming a concern. *Bild* (Germany) reported that he had a brain tumor, as did the The U.K. tabloid *News of the World*. *De Telegraaf* (The Netherlands) said he was dying and would never perform again, while *Berliner Zeitung* reported that Haley was going "cold turkey" to combat alcoholism. Patrick Malynn was quoted as saying, "We're very worried about Bill. He is seriously ill, but lawyers have told me to say nothing."[5]

Rex Zario's recorded telephone conversations with Bill at this time suggest that he was separated from Martha and living alone in a motel or an apartment in Brownsville. Haley had also told Zario that he had spent two weeks in the Rio Grande State Center for mental health, and was hiding from the police, who had a warrant out for his arrest. His rambling, sometimes bullying and abusive conversations would be were interspersed with quieter moments. The phone calls, however, leave no doubt that Bill's mental state at the time was incompatible with undertaking the tour.

Early in the morning of February 9, 1981, Bill phoned his sons, Jack and Scott, and had his last known conversations. He also made his usual "wake-up call" to Martha Maria. Martha Haley recounts that morning:

> He used to call Martha Maria in the mornings, every morning, for her to go to school [Martita may have been staying at a friend's home]. "Martita, get up, it's time for you to go to school." Every morning. One morning I went to the bank, but I had to wait for it to open, so this was before 9 a.m., I guess. I went to the bank and when I came back, I'm coming this way and I see people over there [at the poolside house]. Martha Maria was there already. A friend of mine, Norma, was and the police were there, and I said, "What's going on?" I go there and I get to where they are and from then on, I don't remember nothing. And then, later on, by then, they had already taken the body, right? [He died] in that little room. But, you see, they made mistakes because the coroner, the judge, they said that he died between six and...I don't know. But he died after that because he called Martha Maria at six o'clock in the morning.

---

5 *News of the World*, December 7, 1980.

Bill Haley was found dead in bed at home at 1902 South 1st Street, Harlingen, Texas. Death was officially recorded as being from "natural causes, probably a heart attack." Bill's cremation was delayed for twenty-four hours to allow Hugh McCallum to attend the memorial service. A Dutch TV company later highlighted the unmarked departure of the "King of Rock and Roll" using video footage taken by a friend on the day of the funeral. Bill's ashes were given to the family who placed them in a secret location. A message arrived from Cuppy with a bunch of Bill's mother's favorite flowers and the words,

"See ya later, Alligator. Love, Cuppy."

Martha and her children picked up the pieces of their lives and moved on as best they could. As she recalled:

After that, being alone, being by myself with all his things, people pestering me on the phone, and newspaper people calling and this and that, I stayed there a few more years because the house was big and [the children] hadn't finished school. Then Martha Maria went to Austin to go to college, and I still had Pedro, and Pedro was ten and my little one [Georgina] was five. And we stayed a long, long time. I didn't know what to do. I didn't want to get out of the house. I wanted to and I didn't want to. So finally, I made up my mind and I sold the house, and I bought a brand-new house in the same town, but in a new subdivision. I didn't want to see the old house anymore. And we stayed there about two or three years. [After college,] Martha Maria got married and then I moved to Arlington [Texas]. Her two little girls were born there. Pedro was in college. My younger one had taken up with an older man. And from then, I'm here.

Martha passed away at her home in Allen, Texas on June 29th, 2025, a week shy of Bill's 100th birthday. On July 13th, Gina Haley sent the following email to the authors, finally revealing Bill's resting place:

We had the cremation yesterday. I chose to play the beautiful aria *"Che gelida manina"* from *La Boheme* for her. It was epic and cinematic if one can call it that.

The trauma she experienced from my father's death made her want to hide my father's ashes away from the world. I will tell you now that they were always in the family catacombs of the Cathedral in Mexico City. About a decade ago she went and retrieved the ashes and they remained with us here at home. She did that because she wanted it to be easy for us to join them together when the time came. In her last days I rearranged the bedroom to make it as peaceful and beautiful for her. Next to her bed I placed my father's urn. He was with her when she passed. They will be placed in the columbarium at the church on July 26. It will no longer be a secret. I managed to convince my sister that we owe it to the fans who only wish to pay their respects and who have kept his music and memory alive all these years.

Lookin' through my window, my memory serves me well,
I go back to the places and all those happy faces under your spell,
I remember my first guitar that made me a rock 'n' roll star,
I traveled the whole world over, with fame and fortune in my hand.
I wanna thank you, rock 'n' roll, from the body, from the soul.
God bless rock 'n' roll, thank you, rock 'n' roll, God bless, rock 'n' roll.

I cannot tell you what it means to me,
I just love the rhythm and what it's given to me.
I wanna thank you, rock 'n' roll, from the body, from the soul.
God bless rock 'n' roll, thank you, rock 'n' roll, God bless, rock 'n' roll.
God bless!

God Bless Rock and Roll by Ronny Harwood & Nigel Jenkins. One of the last songs recorded by Bill Haley.

PART 2
Haley in Context

CHAPTER 12
Haley and Elvis

"The first three years were ours, all ours, till Presley came along." – Bill Haley[1]

In the late 1960s, famed composer and conductor Leonard Bernstein told journalist Richard Clurman, "Elvis Presley is the greatest cultural force in the twentieth century." Shocked and offering an alternative, Clurman suggested Picasso. Bernstein dug in. "No, it's Elvis. He introduced the beat to everything and he changed everything – music, language, clothes, it's a whole new social revolution – the '60s come from it."[2]

During Bill Haley's 1974 U.K. tour, British journalist Alan Watkins witnessed controversial politician Enoch Powell asking Haley if he could shake his hand. "Later I asked Powell: 'Why did you want to shake Bill Haley's hand, Enoch?' Powell replied, for one of his conversational tricks was to repeat the question before answering it, if indeed he ever came round to doing so. 'Surely the answer must be obvious. He is the most influential character of our age.'"[3]

From the 2011 *Texas Monthly* article "Falling Comet":[4] "Haley was increasingly bitter that all the credit for rock and roll had gone to Elvis. 'He talked and talked about how Elvis got so famous,' says [Sam] Charters. 'He couldn't get over it.'"

"He would be sober and happy for months, then something would happen (like when Elvis died) that triggered a week or two-long binge," Pedro Haley said to researcher Otto Fuchs.[5]

---

1 Michael Lydon, "Wild Bill Haley", Rolling Stone, November 9, 1967.

2 Jon Meacham, "Elvis in the Heart of America", *Time,* August 10, 2017.

3 Alan Watkins, *The Independent*, August 6, 2000.

4 Michael Hall, "Falling Comet", *Texas Monthly*, June 2011.

5 Fuchs, p.929.

In the history of rock and roll (as well as blues, jazz and other genres), fans, promoters, journalists, and historians have thrown around terms like "father of," "king of," or "creator of" to elevate the artist of their affections above their peers. Due to the chronology of their first fruits and their ten-year age difference, Haley has often been dubbed the "father" or "daddy" of rock and roll (look at the titles of the extant biographies) and Elvis Presley, because of the height and longevity of his career, is commonly dubbed the "King."[6] As we stated at the end of this book's Foreword, we the authors are not interested in bestowing such honors on Bill Haley or anyone else. That being said, Haley and Presley were significant early figures in popularizing what would come to be known as "rock n' roll" and Haley seems to have had a life-long obsession with Presley, considering him at once a protégé of sorts and a rival that torpedoed his career. Haley does not speak of other early successors (i.e. Jerry Lee Lewis, Little Richard, the Everly Brothers) in the same way or to the same degree in his autobiography, so we deemed it appropriate to repeat Haley's accounts and thoughts about Presley from the biographical section of this book and put them in context here. Also, in the spirit of Charlie Gillett's "five styles of rock 'n roll,"[7] it is enlightening to compare how Haley and Presley arrived at their particular brands of the music.

Haley outlived Presley by nearly four years. Presley's death haunted him and, to Haley's mind, imposed another burden. In the preface to his autobiography, Haley explained that he came out of retirement in the spring of 1979...

> ...only through the urging of promoters and fans and people like Hugh McCallum and my wife, Martha, and finally through Patrick Malynn who convinced me after Elvis Presley died that, unless I once again began to do tours, that everything that Rudy [Pompilii] and I had worked for would be forgotten.

Like many fans and friends of Elvis, Haley played the "what if?" game in regards to whether the tragedy of August 16, 1977, could have been averted. "After Elvis died, in 1977, Bill told me, 'If I could've gotten in to see Elvis, I could've helped straighten him out,'" said Russell Dota, a Houston Lincoln dealer, in the 2011 *Texas Monthly* article. "You had to sympathize with the poor guy [Haley] — he just seemed a little bit lost." The *Texas Monthly* article continued: "At some point in 1978 he began to think about another comeback, maybe because Elvis had

---

6 There are numerous live recordings in which Haley is introduced as the "King of Rock and Roll," a title also bestowed upon the likes of Chuck Berry and Little Richard by their promoters.

7 Discussed in Chapter 13.

recently died and everyone was saying he was the guy who had started rock and roll."

There were definitely parallels in Haley and Presley's upbringings and musical journeys. Both grew up in poverty with doting mothers and Southern-born fathers who scraped by either farming or working menial jobs. Both developed an early and insatiable passion for music that they would pursue at all costs. Both voraciously absorbed and synthesized all kinds of music, defying the strict stylistic and cultural categories established by the music industry of the day. Both were influenced by broadcasts of the *Grand Ole Opry* every Saturday night. Both more or less had their "coming out" at fairground-type settings — Haley unwittingly performing "Has Anybody Seen My Gal?" in 1943 at the Booths Corner Auction Mart and ten-year-old Presley singing the Red Foley tearjerker, "Old Shep," in 1945 at the Mississippi-Alabama Fair and Dairy Show in Tupelo, Mississippi.

Particularly significant to the history of the beginnings of rock and roll is the fact that, early in their recording careers, both Haley's and Presley's record producers (Dave Miller and Sam Phillips, respectively) experimented with having these hillbilly music artists make records with a "black song" on one side and a country song on the other, based upon the producers' perception that each were white men with a black sound that could break the tight style-category barriers set up by the industry in the late 1940s and early 1950s.

In his autobiography, Haley recalled his first meeting with producer Dave Miller at WPWA in Chester:

When Dave arrived at the station, I found him to be a young man full of enthusiasm and a real eager beaver and he told me that, when he first heard me sing, he thought I was a black singer doing country songs, and that his idea was to record me doing cover records of black songs. We finally came to an agreement. We decided to do one side a black song and a country tune on the other. He said he would only use the name Bill Haley and not allow any pictures of me as he wanted to sell me to both black and white audiences.[8] I agreed to this because it was a way to further my ideas about selling to all people — not just one set of fans. The first record we did for Dave was a cover of Jackie Brenston's record of a song called "Rocket '88'" and on the other side we did "Tearstains on My

---

8 This is similar tactic that was used by RCA in debuting black country singer Charley Pride in the mid-1960s. His image was not included on his records until he built a sizeable following. By then, as Pride himself stated, "People didn't care if I was pink."

Heart."[9] The initial reaction was not overwhelming, but we sold about 10,000 copies in the Eastern markets. This was enough for Dave Miller to record other tunes with us.

Similarly, Sun Records producer Sam Phillips' most famous quote was, "If I could find a white man who had a Negro sound and the Negro feel, I could make a billion dollars." Phillips seems to have found his man when nineteen-year-old Elvis Presley came to his Memphis studio in June 1954, and it's easy to see the parallel between what Miller heard in Haley and what Phillips heard in Elvis. As noted earlier, both producers initially used the strategy of recording a "black" song on one side and a country song on the other to cross over and blur the lines between pop, country, and rhythm and blues. For Presley's first recording for Sun, Phillips paired Arthur "Big Boy" Crudup's "That's All Right" on one side and Bill Monroe's "Blue Moon of Kentucky" on the other. (Monroe reportedly hated Presley's rockabilly interpretation of his gentle waltz tune until the royalty checks started rolling in!)

Then there are the differences. The difference that always comes to the fore is that Elvis was young, single, and undeniably attractive, a decade younger than the more fatherly-looking, married Haley, whose spit curl made him look, at best, like the 1930s-era Superman. Haley's presentation was all about the band, not about himself as the front man. Presley was always a singular attraction; he did not have a band as such, no Elvis Presley and the Whatevers, at least after his initial Sun recordings that were labeled "ELVIS PRESLEY" with "SCOTTY and BILL"[10] in smaller type.

Haley, by comparison, stood steadfastly on his mark; the only real bodily movement was his "singer's march" in place. He left the stage acrobatics to other band members. Presley was in constant and sensual motion, hence his nickname, "Elvis the Pelvis." It was this unbridled physical accompaniment to his singing that prompted the camera operators on CBS television's *Ed Sullivan Show* to cut Elvis off at the waist. Haley and the Comets only got bit parts in a couple of movies, even in *Rock Around the Clock*, in which they got top billing; Presley became a film star with a run of films spanning almost fifteen years.

---

9 These recordings were made on June 14, 1951, very soon after Brenston's recording began to catch on. Brenston, backed by Ike Turner's band, had recorded the song at Sam Phillip's Sun Studio in Memphis and the competitive versions remain key subjects in the argument as to what the "first" rock and roll record was.

10 His sidemen, guitarist Scotty Moore (1931-2016) and bass player Bill Black (1925-1965). In early concerts, the duo, plus drummer D. J. Fontana (1931-2018), were billed as the Blue Moon Boys, but this was phased out as Elvis' star began to rise, though all three continued to back him on recordings.

There were also great differences in the capabilities of their respective management. "Lord" Jim Ferguson was out of his league when it came to managing Haley's career, particularly when it hit its peak. Jolly Joyce, Haley's booking agent, was even worse, booking the Comets as a cheap lounge act in Holiday Inns and similar venues. Martha Haley said, "Jolly Joyce prostituted him...If it hadn't been for Jolly Joyce, his pride would not have dropped so much."[11] Martha thought better of Bill's later manager, Paddy Malynn. "Paddy, in my time, he was the best." Malynn was adamant about getting Bill and the Comets back out on the international stage where he had sustained a fervent fan base, even among young people who were not of Haley's era, and demanding big money for the appearances. "And that's what Paddy started to do," Martha stated. "He was already getting like $20,000 a performance." Latter-day Comets guitarist Bill Turner, who did his best to keep the group together after the death of Rudy Pompilii, had a darker view of Malynn. In his interview with Otto Fuchs, he said that Malynn "was doing everything he could to undermine the band — he was a real instigator."[12] He not only accused Malynn of trying to break up the band, but even driving a wedge between the members of Haley's three families.

Presley, on the other hand, was under the management of the savvy and experienced "Colonel" Tom Parker. Presley was equally loyal to his manager, but unquestioningly deferred to Parker's decisions. Many critics thought that Parker took an unusually large cut of Presley's income, but he made them both multi-millionaires and sustained Presley's career at a high level, passing him into popular culture mythology even before his death in 1977. "Let's face it, Colonel Parker was a genius, he really was," Bill Turner said. "I don't care what people say about him, Elvis approved of him all the way, whatever their financial 'split' was. It's interesting to see what would have happened if Bill Haley had had Colonel Tom Parker on his side."[13]

Haley attempts faithfully to elevate Ferguson to the same sphere of significance as Parker in his autobiography although, as stated below, he calls Parker "the greatest manager of our time" and says that Ferguson "took lessons" from Parker while they were on tour in 1955: "Without the Lord Jims and Col. Tom Parkers of

---

11 Interview with David Lee Joyner, October 16, 2018.

12 Fuchs, p. 740.

13 Fuchs, p. 749.

that day, there would not have been the Bill Haleys & Elvis Presleys. So much credit goes to these people."[14]

Now to the musical comparisons, focusing at this point on Presley's stylistic roots. In his liner notes for the Bear Family Records Bill Haley CD set, *The Decca Years and More*, Colin Escott compares Haley and Presley thusly:

> Where Elvis Presley drew upon the scary intensity and sparse instru-mentation of hillbilly music, Haley drew upon the country music he heard in Michigan, Pennsylvania, and the eastern seaboard. Where Elvis Presley drew upon the rawness and unsophistication of back country blues, Bill Haley drew upon the slick jump combos like those led by Louis Jordan and the Trenier brothers.

Escott's view of Haley's style is fairly accurate, as is his comparison of the styles of blues that influenced him and Presley. However, Escott's description of scary hillbilly music and unsophisticated country blues as the basis for Presley's style really misses the mark. In focusing on the wild-man exuberance of Presley, Escott and most Haley biographers completely miss the origin of Presley's and Jerry Lee Lewis's unhinged style — Southern gospel music.

In his two-volume Elvis Presley biography, *Last Train to Memphis*, Peter Guralnick unequivocally states: "There was probably no type of music that he didn't love, but [male gospel] quartet music was the center of his musical universe. Gospel music combined the spiritual force that he felt in all music with the sense of physical release and exaltation for which, it seemed, he was casting about."[15] Presley grew up in the fundamentalist Assembly of God church, with an emotional and boisterous style of worship that was reflected in its music. The white male gospel quartets that were bred from this style of church were a staple of radio, television, recordings, and the stage in the South. Like a barbershop quartet on steroids, the singers gave breathtaking displays of tight harmonies and virtuosic technique at the outer extremes of the male vocal range.

Elvis Presley ate this stuff up. He was a frequent patron of the marathon gospel quartet concerts at Ellis Auditorium's North Hall in Memphis that would attract up

---

14 Johnny Grande, interviewed for the DVD documentary *Rock and Roll is Born* (Universal Music Operations, 2008), explained that the band had been stuck in one place and getting stagnant. They asked Ferguson to take over the management. Initially dismissing them as a "bunch of hillbillies," he agreed on the basis that, if he increased their earnings from the current approximately $260 a week to $1,000, he would be made a partner. Grande said that Ferguson achieved this within a month or two.

15 Peter Guralnick, *Last Train to Memphis: The Rise of Elvis Presley* (Boston: Little, Brown and Company, 1994), p. 47.

to five thousand people per performance. The well-established Jordanaires quartet sang background vocals on many of his RCA records[16] and live shows. Most of Presley's all-night jam sessions at his Graceland mansion in Memphis were gospel music sessions. When Elvis performed, his conditioning in the evangelical church put him "in the spirit," manifesting itself in physical movement that many mistook for vulgar, sexual display. A gospel-quartet technique adopted by Presley was a way of delivering a lyric that gave a percussive shuffle beat to an ensemble that usually did not have drums. For instance, if you listen to Elvis on the Otis Blackwell song, "All Shook Up," he sings, "A-well-a bless-a my soul-a what's-a wrong-a with me..." where the "a's" provide an upbeat kick aligning with the right hand of the piano, characteristic of a shuffle groove.

That same evangelical background would plague Presley as to the morality of his music. Jerry Lee Lewis, who also grew up in the Assembly of God Church (in Louisiana) had a similar inner turmoil. Bill Haley never wrestled with such a moral dilemma, but he was also light years from the gravitational pull of gospel music and the Southern Christian hellfire and brimstone that was Presley's cultural core. Haley always felt his music was just music and devoted a lot of time and energy trying to convince authorities of his viewpoint. He could see that his rock 'n' roll excited youngsters, but could not wrap his head around his music actually being of the Devil, even with clergy and civic officials throwing those accusations in his face.

It is now time to revisit Haley's autobiography and get his own account of his memories of Elvis and his relationship to him. Always paternal in tone, he refers to "my boy Elvis" when recounting their shared Cleveland concert in 1955 and "my old pal Elvis" in his title for his proposed Chapter 9. He remains cordial and objective when obviously recognizing Presley's advantages of better looks and better management, but truly — and rightfully — takes pride in whatever part he played in offering guidance and encouragement to a young man who was in awe of him. However, there is no doubt that Haley saw Presley as a commercial adversary in his memoir, twice speaking of Elvis "challenging me for the King of Rock 'n' Roll title."

Here is Haley's story of his first encounter with Presley, confident of his own dominance in rock and roll — and even his established place in country music — at this point in time. From Chapter 4 of Bill's autobiography:

In October of 1955, Lord Jim received a phone call from Colonel Tom Parker, who was then managing Hank Snow. We were scheduled to do a short tour of the Midwest and Oklahoma with Hank Snow, Marty

---

16 Vocal group backing was part and parcel of the "Nashville Sound."

Robbins, and acts from the *Grand Ole Opry*. I was anxiously looking forward to this, because I knew these were great entertainers and I would be right at home with my own people, the country music fans. Tom explained to Jim that he was going to sign a young man from Memphis, and that he wanted to bring him along on the tour to give him some experience and exposure. He wanted to ask Jim if it would be all right with me. The young man Tom was referring to was named Elvis Presley, and I told Jim that we would be glad to have him with us.

And so, we travelled to Omaha, Nebraska, for the opening night of the tour. We arrived in the afternoon and I went to the auditorium for the sound check, and to say hello to Colonel Tom and Hank Snow and the rest. I talked for a while with my old friends. They all had a lot of praise for this new young kid, and so I was quite interested to hear him do his show. The first night was a sellout, and, after Hank and Marty had been on, and I was back in my dressing room I heard them announce Elvis Presley. As I watched the tall, good-looking youngster do his show, to only mild applause, I could see great potential, but he seemed not to be timing his tunes. We went on and did our part of the show.

When I returned to the dressing room, there came a knock on the door and in walked Elvis, and he introduced himself. He was, and would remain all the years I knew him, a very shy, polite young guy. He told me that I was his favorite singer, and, for many years, Elvis would repeat this.[17] Whether he meant it or not, I never really found out; but, anyway, he told me of his ambitions and how thankful he was to be on the tour. He asked if I would help him with any advice I could. I promised I would. For the next two or three nights, as the tour rolled along to great business, Elvis and I had more chance to get to talk and joke and kid each other. As I got to know him better, I realized that here was a very intense and determined young guy who really was intent on making it big in show business. Please remember those were the days before Elvis had had big exposure, or any big records, and on this show were the giants — Hank Snow, an idol of mine, and Marty Robbins, a giant in the business, even then, and of course our group with the #1 record, "Shake, Rattle and Roll." So, it wasn't easy for this young man, just starting out, to go out every night

---

17 Haley made it a point to include a Presley quote at the beginning of his autobiography: "No matter how big I get to be, he will always be the King." (Allegedly spoken by Elvis to Lord Jim backstage during Bill's performance in Frankfurt, Germany, in October 1958.)

to packed houses and entertain a crowd, there to see other artists, and impatient as the audience always is, while waiting for the feature attraction. Nevertheless, as the tour progressed, Elvis held his own every night.

One night after he had done his show, I saw him standing backstage looking kind of down. I called him to my dressing room and asked him what was wrong. He told me that he was worried because he didn't seem to be able to get the audience where he wanted them and couldn't figure out what he was doing wrong. I encouraged him and explained that he was fighting all the hit records of Snow, Robbins, and myself. I assured him of how proud we were of him, because he was indeed holding his own. I also suggested that he take out some of the slow ballads and add more up-tempo songs such as his "Blue Moon of Kentucky" and "That's All Right, Mama." He did change some of them, and, whether it helped him or not, I don't know. However, years later, in Germany, he was to recall our days here and he thanked me.

October 20, 1955. Bill shakes hands with Elvis Presley on the occasion of filming a concert which would come to be known as The *Pied Piper of Cleveland* but has never seen the light of day.

In his later references to Elvis, Haley tries to maintain his place as mentor or even peer, but recognizing that the young man from Memphis would knock him off the gold-medal podium in the Olympics of rock and roll. Notice that he refers to Presley as both challenger and friend in the same sentence, perhaps to assert his confidence or to recognize Presley's growing stature and to have the reader believe that their personal relationship was closer than it really was. Haley's narrative continues:

We finished our tour, and I didn't see Elvis again until Cleveland. As he was to go on to challenge me in the next few years for the "King of Rock" title, our paths were not to cross as much as we, as friends, would have liked to. But more of that later in the story. It is with great warmth that I remember this tour and young Elvis in his pink Cadillac, tremendous raw talent, and ambitions. I was indeed proud of him as he climbed the ladder of success. Also, all through this tour, Lord Jim was taking lessons from the greatest manager of our time, Colonel Tom Parker. Tom and Jim smoked many a cigar together. Those were indeed happy days for all of us.

After leaving Lubbock, we went on to Cleveland, Ohio, to do a show called A Sock Hop for my good friend, Bill Randle. The show was to be held at the Brooklyn High School and featured Bill Haley and the Comets, the Four Lads, a young Pat Boone, and my boy, Elvis Presley. We arrived, and, before the show, had a grand reunion with Elvis, who in one short year was really on his way. Colonel Tom had signed him to RCA Victor[18], and, as we laughed and talked that evening, Elvis told me of all his plans and how helpful Bill Randle had been. Elvis was shortly to do *The Jackie Gleason Show*,[19] and, as we parted that evening, wishing each other good luck, we were both shortly to be swallowed up in the publicity, clamor, and rush of the hectic first days of big-time Rock and Roll. We had talked that night of doing a tour together, but it was never to be.

---

18 Haley is one month out here. The concert he describes took place on October 20, 1955. Elvis was being considered by RCA at the time but was not signed to them until November 20 (from the official Graceland website, https://www.graceland.com/1954-1957, accessed on March 26, 2021).

19 Haley is actually referring to the television variety program *Stage Show*, produced by Gleason, but not starring him. In fact, when Presley appeared on the program in January 1956, it was hosted by brothers and swing band leaders Tommy and Jimmy Dorsey.

Bill's story of travelling with Elvis for several days and passing on fatherly advice is exaggerated. In truth, they only performed together on two dates, firstly at the Municipal Auditorium, Oklahoma City on October 16 and secondly at the "Sock Hop" at Brooklyn High School in Cleveland on October 20. Local DJ Bill Randle, a great supporter of rock 'n' roll and Bill Haley in particular, organized the afternoon show on October 20, 1955, at Cleveland, Ohio's Brooklyn High School, in which Bill and Elvis were joined by Pat Boone, the Four Lads and Priscilla Wright.[20] Filming continued later in St. Michael's Hall (East 100th and Union Avenue). Bill Randle described the hall as a "local ethnic dance hall." Various problems beset the film's post-production process: the poor sound quality made all but forty-eight minutes of the film unusable, and there were disputes with fourteen different workers' unions over memberships and fees. Publishers and record companies started asking questions, and, over many years, the whole thing eventually descended into mystery and farce. The whereabouts of the reels of film today are either being kept secret or are unknown.[21] The eyewitness accounts, including Bill Randle's own, leave no doubt that Elvis stole the show from Bill. Local WERE disc jockey Tommy Edwards took a photograph of Haley and Presley together and Haley hung it on the wall in his office in Chester and his home, Melody Manor, in Booths Corner. The *Sound and Glory* biography refers to this gig as a "freebee," indicating the respect that the Comets and the other major acts had for Randle, including the young and nervous Elvis, making his first appearance in the North. Prior to taking the stage, Elvis turned to Comets bassist Al Rex and said, "I hope these Yankees like my music."[22]

In Haley's next reference to Presley, he recognizes the upper hand Elvis has, not only in the superior management of Colonel Tom Parker, but in the aggressive marketing, distribution, and support of their artist exhibited by RCA in Nashville compared to Haley's label Decca in New York. From Bill's Chapter 5:

> Now, for the first time, I was being challenged for the title "The King of Rock & Roll" as another artist had exploded on the scene to challenge me. Guess who? Yes, my old buddy, Elvis, had come on like gangbusters, as they used to say. RCA Records had mounted a tremendous publicity campaign and Elvis Presley records were bombarding the charts. I felt that Decca should match the RCA promotion, so Lord Jim and I went to New York to have a conference with the powers that be at Decca. We

---

20 A young Canadian singer who had one hit with "The Man in the Raincoat."

21 Trevor Cajiao, *Elvis – The Man and His Music* magazine, September 2018.

22 Haley and von Hoelle, p. 109.

pleaded our case, but ran up against a stone wall. We were told that the company had a policy of treating all their artists equally, and, if they gave us extra promotion, they would have to do this for all the others. I had great respect for my record company, and especially for Milt Gabler, and, although I still felt that they should match the promotion of RCA for Elvis, there was no other choice for me but to go along with their decision.

The next Presley account finds Haley coming to the realization that the rock and roll race track now had lots of drivers, and he was not necessarily the pace car. The music he felt he invented was now morphing into a number of substyles, including that of the commercially manufactured teen idols. From Bill's Chapter 6: "Elvis was really hitting his stride. Such new acts as Jerry Lee Lewis, Ricky Nelson, Bo Diddley. The Everly Brothers and Tommy Sands were bursting upon the scene, and we worked with many of them."

Perhaps the most celebrated meeting between Haley and Presley was during the Comets' European tour in 1958. Elvis had been drafted into the U.S. Army and was stationed at a base near Friedberg, Germany, when Bill and the Comets arrived in Frankfurt on October 23 for a series of concerts in major German cities.

Bill was waiting backstage before the show when he became aware of a commotion outside his dressing room. He then heard his name called and instantly recognized Elvis' voice.[23] He was ushered in and they talked for a while and had photos taken. It was a fleeting visit (Bill had to get to another show that night in Wiesbaden.) There is a famous photograph of Elvis, in full uniform, hanging out in the dressing room as Haley tunes his guitar in preparation for his performance, and a second shot of Haley smoking a cigarette, apparently engaged in conversation. Comets drummer Ralph Jones recalled Elvis telling members of the band, "You know, if it weren't for you boys, I'd still be driving a truck back in Memphis."

---

23 It is important to realize at this point that Bill Haley and the Comets were an established international sensation. Elvis, at this point, was only in Germany as a soldier. Outside the U.S., he had been heard on record, but not seen in person.

October 23, 1958, backstage at the Frankfurt Film-Palast before the show. L to R: Kurt Collien (the tour promoter), Kurt Edelhagen (whose big band was the support act) Elvis Presley in US Army uniform, Franny Beecher, Bill Haley, Rudy Pompilii, Jim Ferguson, Heinz Hoffmeister (the tour manager) and Billy Williamson (partially in view).

As above, Bill & Elvis backstage.

Elvis made a second visit to a Comets show in Mannheim on October 24, where he was photographed (out of uniform this time and wearing a suit and tie) by well-known photographer Günther Thomas. As we move through the 1960s, Haley and Presley, in a way, shared a similar conundrum, but enjoyed respective "revivals" toward the end of the decade. While Bill and the Comets were languishing away playing joints for low pay and recording largely unimpressive fodder, Elvis was basically trapped into making a series of mediocre movies and recording equally mediocre songs written for them.[24] Elvis came back out into the light of day with his December 3, 1968, comeback TV special for NBC about the same time that Bill surfaced again in a big way through the Nader rock 'n' roll revival concerts and Patrick Malynn's European tours.

Elvis, in civilian clothes, visits Bill again. October 24th, Mannheim.

---

24 Legend has it that, during the 1966 recording sessions for his excretable comedy, *Easy Come, Easy Go* — a film that featured such compositions as "Yoga Is As Yoga Does" — Presley was heard to mutter, "What are you supposed to do with shit like this?" (Roy Carr and Mark Farren, *Elvis: The Illustrated Record* (New York: Harmony Books, 1982), p. 107).

In the wake of the special's success, Elvis and Colonel Tom Parker knew that he had not performed a live stage show in years and, in 1969, Presley was contracted for a four-week residency at the International Hotel in Las Vegas for a whopping $500,000 a week. Performing for a sold-out crowd of 2,000 at the first show on July 31, 1969, Presley ultimately performed more than seven hundred sold-out Vegas shows through 1976 and became synonymous with this city, much as one of his heroes, Frank Sinatra, had.[25]

Bill Haley was making his way back to Las Vegas as well, though on a significantly smaller scale. The Comets did a revival show at the Flamingo Hilton Hotel in late August/early September 1972, but sharing the bill with a number of other revival acts. Elvis was also in town, performing at another Hilton. Bill Turner remembers seeing a photograph of Elvis with Bill. It is not known whether Elvis was visiting Bill, or the other way around, and the photograph has disappeared into the mists of time and remains purely a memory and a tantalizing footnote to this story.[26]

Coinciding with his multiple seasons in Las Vegas, Elvis undertook a relentless tour schedule throughout the 1970s. At the end of June 1977, he returned to his home in Memphis, the Graceland mansion, to rest up and prepare for another concert tour. It was never to take place. He died in his home in the early morning hours of August 16. The year before, Haley's dear friend and colleague, saxophonist Rudy Pompilii, died, an event that led Bill to enter retirement. The news of Elvis' death impacted Bill with the same dichotomy as the "buddy/competition" view he had of Presley all through their careers. Haley and Presley's careers had gone so far apart in their level of success that Elvis' death certainly didn't open any doors of opportunity for a Comets comeback, but Bill did take it upon himself to come out of retirement in early 1979 to carry the torch as *the* representative of early (to him, *real*) rock 'n' roll now that "the King" was dead. To the end of his days, even in his ramblings on his solitary trips to Sambo's Restaurant in Harlingen, Bill continued to both proudly align himself with Elvis and to cast his bitterness.

To exhaustively compare Haley and Presley's musical output would be a vast undertaking so, to find common ground, we will compare two songs identified with or originally recorded by another artist and covered by both Bill and Elvis to see how their approaches differ. It is interesting to note that Elvis steered clear of covering Bill's signature "Rock Around the Clock" on a recording and Bill never

---

25 One of Presley's final films, 1970's *Elvis: That's the Way it Is*, features excerpts from some of his early Vegas performances and showcased the preparation that went into them.

26 In correspondence with the authors, Comets guitarist Johnny Kay said that Bill had spoken to Elvis "by phone."

covered iconic Elvis material such as "Don't Be Cruel" or "Heartbreak Hotel."[27] Nevertheless, Elvis did record "Shake, Rattle and Roll," initially in Lubbock, Texas, on January 6, 1955, as a radio demo during his Sun Records era. A live recording, captured by an Alabama radio station on January 19, sees Elvis using Haley's lyrics throughout the song. Presley would use Haley's opening lyric for his TV appearances on *Stage Show* (January 1956) and *The Milton Berle Show* (April 1956), but Joe Turner's on his February 3, 1956, RCA recording, though alternate takes of this track — ironically, the first new Elvis recording not to make the Billboard chart — reveal he also considered using Haley's lyrics. In any event, it is clear he was familiar with both recordings of the song.

"I Got a Woman" was first recorded by Ray Charles in 1954 as "I've Got a Woman," becoming his first big hit and marking the real beginning of Charles' rollicking, gospel-flavored rhythm and blues style, with him as the "preacher" and the band riffs (or backing singers) as the responding choir or congregation. His opening word, "Well..." is chant-like, like a minister deep in the spirit or reminiscent of a "field holler" from a solitary plowman.

Elvis recorded "I Got a Woman" as the first song of his first session for RCA in Nashville on January 10, 1956. For the opening "Well," Elvis utters it in his lower, more masculine range, creating a persona of menacing threat; he doesn't draw it out as Charles does. He continues in this lower register, only switching to his young, breathless high voice halfway through each verse and only for a moment, like a brief eruption. The style of the accompaniment is pure rockabilly. Over a brisk tempo, drummer D. J. Fontana plays a tight "doo-whacka-doo" pattern on his hi-hat along with a crisp backbeat snare drum, a sound that complements the slap bass that Bill Black often uses. The underlying riff, heard prominently in Floyd Cramer's piano, is a classic for early rock and roll:

The country flavor of the backing comes from the combination of strummed acoustic guitar and twangy electric guitar, provided by Scotty Moore. Moore's guitar solo takes the place of the sax solo heard on the Ray Charles recording, a definite transposition from R&B to rockabilly. Elvis retains the stop-time format of Charles' arrangement but, whereas Charles' record has a fade-out ending, Elvis employs one of his signature finishes — an abrupt pause, followed by the slow

---

27 That being said, Presley did perform "Rock Around the Clock" in early *live* performances. Elvis historians have confirmed at least three late-1955 performances on *Louisiana Hayride* radio broadcasts, and the hunt is ongoing for any surviving recordings.

"bump-and-grind" tempo. In live shows, this is where Elvis "the Pelvis" would break into his brow-raising moves such as those seen during his performance of "Hound Dog" on NBC's *The Milton Berle Show* in June 1956 that led to a flood of complaints against the network. The recording of "I Got a Woman" is pure Elvis, created before the Nashville Sound had a chance to morph his style closer to its own image.

Bill Haley and the Comets recorded their version of "I Got a Woman" for Decca at the Pythian Temple studio in New York on January 29, 1959. Their rendition is equally effective, yet maintains a distinctive Comets style. Like Elvis, Bill opens the song in his lower register, breathier, but no less intense. The band is likewise soft and spare, but with great energy and anticipation. Drummer Ralph Jones plays a very subdued sound with brushes instead of sticks. Guitarist Franny Beecher plays in a similar manner, with soft, muted chords. In contrast to the country-ish feel and texture of Elvis' Nashville band, the Comets generate a quasi-Caribbean beat, similar to the clavé pattern used by Bo Diddley on his self-titled signature song. After the first twenty seconds, everything changes gear. Bill leaps into his upper register full voice and the band shifts into a gospel two-beat feel that may reflect the flavor of Charles' recording. Where the Comets' version seems to tip its hat to the Elvis version is the drastic rise and fall of range and intensity throughout the verses. In the solo spot of the song, the Comets don't lean toward the guitar solo on the Presley recording or the sax solo on the Charles recording, but offer something in between, and a signature sound for the band, an ensemble riff with Rudy Pompilii's sax lead over Franny's guitar and Billy Williamson's steel guitar:

In a similar manner as the Charles recording, the Comets end their recording vamping into a fade-out. This version of "I Got a Woman" is that successful combination of awareness of the previous versions by Charles and Presley, while adding distinctive and identifiable stylistic elements, the goal of any good cover version. It is also a refreshing addition to the Comets' catalog in that, compared to the flat-out and consistent sound of their previous recorded performances, this record shows a tremendous range of dynamics, vocal, and accompanimental color and orchestration.[28]

---

28 Haley faithfully recreated his version of "I Got a Woman" for his 1976 Sonet album, *R-O-C-K,* recorded at Muscle Shoals' FAME studio. The only alteration in 1976 was the addition of a guitar and sax solo.

"(Now and Then There's) A Fool Such as I" was a country and western ballad composed by Bill Trader in 1952. Later that year, it was recorded for RCA Victor in Nashville by Canadian country star Hank Snow, who was managed by Presley's future manager, Tom Parker. The record rose to No. 4 on the *Billboard* charts in early 1953. It became enough of a staple in the country music canon as to be covered, not only by Haley and Presley, but by artists as wide-ranging as Jo Stafford (Columbia, 1953), Petula Clark (in a French version in 1960), Bob Dylan (1967), and Baillie & the Boys, whose 1990 version peaked at No. 5 on the Country charts.

Snow's version has typical accompaniment for country records of this era, with steel guitar, acoustic guitar, fiddle, bass, and no drums. Snow's voice is rather nasal and strident, but appropriately tender as suits the lovelorn lyrics, a classic country ballad. His enunciation is somewhat exaggerated to make the words understandable in large or loud venues, but a bit over the top as it comes off on a studio recording. For the instrumental break in the middle of the song, the fiddle and acoustic guitar take turns playing the melody while the other ad libs an obligato part, sometimes resulting in a rather mutually intrusive counterpoint. The song ends with a slow and deliberate ascending arpeggio from the steel guitar.

Bill Haley and the Comets recorded "A Fool Such As I" for Decca at the same session as "I Got a Woman," January 29, 1959. It was a fairly rare occasion that Bill got to sing a ballad at Decca, since the Comets' stock and trade at this time were energetic rock 'n' roll numbers. In a similar manner to earlier Comets ballad recordings, such as "It's a Sin" from November 19, 1957, Bill and the band render "Fool" in the "doo-wop" style of the day, but with distinctive touches that would set them apart from doo-woppers such as the Platters.

The recording opens with a solo saxophone cadenza by Pompilii that is much closer in style to the sophisticated jazz style of Ben Webster than a more R&B saxophonist such as King Curtis. Once the song goes into tempo, Beecher, Haley, and Jones (again on brushes) blend into a silky, but danceable two-beat groove, with pianist Johnny Grande maintaining the signature doo-wop triplet chords throughout. There are also light "*aah*" vocal harmony pads (presumably by members of the band) that were a typical feature of doo-wop groups.

Bill masterfully blends vocal mannerisms of a soothing and poised country balladeer like Hank Snow and the "crying" vocal style of a doo-wop singer like the Platters' lead, Tony Williams, but synthesized through the filter of a mature Bill Haley vocal style, with distinctive features like his slowly rounded diphthongs on words like "I'll" and hard "r's" on words like "dear." On the instrumental break, Pompilii brings back the jazz ballad sensibility with his free and flowing rendition of the melody with a breathy and romantic saxophone tone in the lower register of the horn.

When Bill's vocal returns on the bridge of the song, Jones introduces a subtle tension-building riff typical of doo-wop songs:

The Comets do a "tag" ending, capped off by one more luscious jazz ballad-flavored saxophone run and a rich jazz chord played by Beecher's guitar, a sophisticated tip of the hat to the steel guitar final chord in the Hank Snow recording, and a reminder that the Comets band was packed with veteran jazz musicians.

Elvis Presley recorded his version of "A Fool Such as I" at RCA Victor's Nashville Studio B on June 10, 1958, during his final formal recording session before his Army duties took him to Europe for the next year or so. He was backed, among others, by legendary Nashville session guitarist Hank Garland (sitting in for his usual guitarist, Scotty Moore), bassist Bob Moore (replacing Bill Black, who had recently left Presley's employ), drummer D. J. Fontana, and the Jordanaires vocal group. In a departure from the tender versions by both Snow and Haley, Elvis' version is raucous and energetic. The track opens with Garland's bluesy rock and roll guitar over a rocking groove, clearly heard in the piano, that we would now be easily associated with reggae:

Before Elvis makes his entrance, Jordanaires bass singer Ray Walker sings the tag line of the song in characteristic extreme low range (down to a low C). This common showcase of a gospel quartet's bass singer is not meant to be pretty (it isn't), but to be sensational. The rest of the vocal group can be heard offering different accompanimental effects throughout the recording: soft string section-like "*oohs*," rhythmic, percussive "*bops*," and harmonized echoes of portions of the lyric.

Over the top of the rocking band backup, Elvis and the Jordanaires overlay a tender, yet impassioned presentation of the song. Garland's rocking guitar returns for the instrumental break, the "reggae" groove of the rhythm section shifts into more of a honky-tonk shuffle, and the Jordanaires scat more aggressive rhythmic patterns to help turn up the heat. When Elvis comes back in on the bridge of the song, he locks in to the increased energy that has built up over the course of the guitar solo, but slowly guides the ensemble toward a more subdued demeanor, a process enhanced by the long fade-out during the repeat of the song's tag line.

The handling of both "I Got a Woman" and "A Fool Such As I" turned out to be a serious business miscalculation for Bill; Haley's "Fool" gained only regional success, while "Woman" was lost as a potential hit. Elvis' recording of "Fool," on the other hand, went platinum and reached No. 2 on *Billboard*'s Top 100 charts (June 7, 1959).

Artistically, both the Haley and Presley recordings of "Fool" are superb and well-matched to each of their musical worlds. Commercially, Elvis had the upper hand because his version was more at the vanguard of where rock 'n' roll and its young audience was by this time. Haley's version was too steeped in jazz balladry and doo-wop lyricism of the early 1950s, whereas Presley's version was able to retain a crooning tenderness while undergirding it with a more energetic and aggressive accompaniment that put Hank Snow and Haley in the shadow of a new and exciting concept that resonated with the emerging second generation of rock and roll fans.

In comparing Bill Haley and Elvis Presley, we can conclude that each has a distinctive and rightful place in rock 'n' roll and that each developed their own version of it. While growing up in two distinct regions of the United States, both had similar early musical influences but, through different circumstances and shaping by managers and record producers, came up with unique musical products that would capture the imagination and devotion of a generation. Bill had the historical advantage in that he was older, got into the rock 'n' roll game earlier, was the first to take it international, and was actually an inspiration and influence on young Presley. Presley had the advantage with his youth, good looks, and better management, both in personal promotion and in the recording studio.

Even though they only met a couple of times over the span of their life and careers, Bill Haley and Elvis Presley will always be linked in rock 'n' roll history, to some, as "The Father and The King."

CHAPTER 13
The Melting Pot (1945-1956)
The Musical and Cultural Evolution of Rock 'n' Roll

The *Wikipedia* entry for "Rock and Roll" states that "The origins of rock and roll have been fiercely debated by commentators and historians of music," and goes on to explain that:

> The immediate roots of rock and roll lay in the rhythm and blues, then called race music in combination with either boogie-woogie and shouting gospel or with country music of the 1940s and 1950s. Particularly significant influences were jazz, blues, gospel, country, and folk. Commentators differ in their views of which of these forms were most important and the degree to which the new music was a re-branding of African-American rhythm and blues for a white market, or a new hybrid of black and white forms.[1]

In the 1940s the "jump blues" style was dominated by Louis Jordan and His Tympany Five. At a time when dance music was the domain of the big bands, Jordan's music was powerful competition. The band had been under the wing of Milt Gabler at Decca Records since 1938. Sometime after Jordan left Decca in 1954, Gabler signed Haley and the Comets to the label. Whilst big bands like Count Basie's and Lionel Hampton's were quite capable of blasting out jump blues, it would be the smaller bands who triumphed, if only for the obvious reason that they could pack the same punch at a fraction of the cost. Although Haley's autobiography does not specifically acknowledge the influence of Louis Jordan, during his time at WPWA Haley would no doubt have heard a lot of Jordan's music in the program Judge Rhythm's Court that broadcast a daily offering of black blues

---

1 Wikipedia, "Early Rock and Roll," accessed October 3, 2023.

Louis Jordan, leader of the Tympani Five (right), with his long-time producer, Milt Gabler. c. 1954.

recordings, and preceded his own show on WPWA Radio. One intriguing paragraph from *Variety* magazine (December 2, 1953) announces "The Treniers [an all-black outfit] are waxing Bill Haley's 'Rock-a-Beatin' Boogie'[2] with Haley switching from his own outfit, to sing the lilt." Apart from the possibility that this was simply a misprint or mis-understanding, the statement is somewhat intriguing. Until then, Haley's steps across the racial barrier had been simply to produce "white" versions of "black" recordings.

With America being a large and diverse country, Rock 'n' Roll developed with regional stylistic differences, later described by Charlie Gillett as the "five styles of Rock 'n' Roll":[3]

- Northern band rock 'n' roll (exemplified by Bill Haley and partly deriving from Decca producer Milt Gabler who had been responsible for Louis Jordan and the Tympany Five);

- New Orleans dance blues (Fats Domino and Little Richard);

- Memphis Country Rock or "Rockabilly" (based on the vision of Sam Phillips at Sun Records);

- Chicago Style Rhythm and Blues (Chuck Berry & Bo Diddley);

- Vocal group vocal harmonies "doo wop" (epitomised by the Clovers)

Gillett goes on to define "Northern Band Rock 'n' Roll" as a type of rock that "exemplified high spirits and feelings of togetherness. The tempo was almost always fast and the music was meant to get people excited. Lyrics usually never

---

2 Mis-spelled as "Haley's-a-Beatin' Googie."

3 Charlie Gillett, *The Sound of the City: The Rise of Rock and Roll* (Souvenir Press, Ltd.,1971).

centered around heartbreak or solitude but instead were typically about the music itself or partying."

This describes Bill Haley and His Comets to a "T", and, musically speaking, they can now be seen more as the end of an era than the start of a new one. With few exceptions, such as Boyd Bennett and His Rockets, and Britain's Tony Crombie and His Rockets, the Rock 'n' Roll artists who followed Bill did not copy his style. Rock 'n' Roll would be dominated by younger stars and stylistically, it moved on quickly. Haley effectively was a musical "dead end" and his style of Rock 'n' Roll would eventually cease to be popular. Over the decades, and with an ever-changing line-up of musicians, he would continue to produce remarkable and accomplished music, but he found it more and more difficult to sell, and sustained commercial success, as well as his live performing career, would be based largely on performances and re-issues of the band's core 1954 -1957 output.

With the assistance of the Marshall Plan, Western and European economies recovered quickly after the World War II and would enter something of a "boom" period. Families became wealthier and leisure time increased. Children would grow up more quickly, with increasing independence as teenagers, and new musical tastes. The fundamental shift in popular music at this point was towards the styles known generically as "the blues," "rhythm and blues," "African-American" or "race music." The first disc to bear the label "Blues and Rhythm" was issued by RCA Victor in 1948. The same year saw the invention of the long-playing record ("LP"), which allowed jazz musicians to escape the limitations of the 78rpm disc and rise to new levels of improvisation and artistic expression. However, as jazz became more adventurous, sales began to fall, whilst small band Rhythm and Blues gained popularity, not only with its black audience, but increasingly with young white consumers. One person who saw the potential in these developments was Leo Mintz, owner of "Mintz's Record Rendezvous" a record shop on Prospect Avenue in Cleveland, Ohio. In the years after the War he had seen a decrease in sales of jazz and an increase in rhythm and blues ("R&B") records. In a bid to fuel his business, he courted, and convinced, a local radio disc jockey (Alan Freed), to play R&B on the air. Encouraged by Mintz, Freed would move in 1951 to Radio WJW, hosting "The Moondog House," and billing himself as "King of the Moondoggers."

Over the next few years, Mintz sponsored a number of live concerts compered by Alan Freed. The first was *The Moondog Coronation Ball* at the Cleveland Arena on 21 March 1952. Headlined by Paul "Hucklebuck" Williams and Tiny Grimes, and now generally recognized as the first "rock" concert, it featured The Dominoes, Danny Cobb and Varetta Dillard, and promised "many others!". The next day the *Akron Beacon Journal* reported that,

The Moondog Coronation Ball drew a crushing mob of 25,000. The huge crowd broke Arena doors to crash the gate, bringing forty extra policemen and thirty extra firemen to the scene. Battalion Fire Chief Bernard Mulcahy said he would seek arrests on grounds the hall was deliberately oversold. "He's the guy I want," Mulcahy snapped, accusing Freed and associates of violating fire laws. Freed... when he was finally located... admitted that the dance was "a mistake."[4]

Leo Mintz's Record Rendezvous store at 300 Prospect Avenue, Cleveland, Ohio.

Advertisement for Alan Freed's radio show, broadcast on WJW, Cleveland Ohio from July 1951.

Scheduled to run from 10 p.m. to 2 a.m., the event was closed by order of the Fire Department at 11 p.m., even before the opening act had finished. Nevertheless, Freed had gained momentum and was not going to fall at the first hurdle. A clear indication that music was evolving elsewhere too, was, that at almost the same time (c. March 1952), Bill Haley recorded his cover version of Jimmy Preston's "Rock the Joint." Haley had found that R&B was popular with the sailors who frequented his nightly performances at the Twin Bar in Gloucester, New Jersey.

While Freed would go on to create the legend that the early audiences for his music was mixed white and black, his biographer, John A. Jackson highlights that,

before he [Freed] consciously set out during his heyday in the late 1950s to revise his past, [he] admitted in a more candid moment that during his

4 *Akron Beacon Journal*, March 22, 1952.

first years as "Moondog" his program at first attracted an audience that was all Negro. Only as time went on did more whites listen.... Freed later confirmed that it was only after a rock & roll dance in New York City in January 1955 at which it was estimated up to 70 percent of the audience was white did he have the first inkling that white people enjoyed rhythm and blues.[5]

In March 1953, and shortly before Bill Haley would record his first hit record ("Crazy Man, Crazy"), *Billboard* would highlight the tremendous success of the Clovers, a black vocal harmony band who were dominating the R&B chart at the time.

The Clovers, the sizzling hot rhythm and blues vocal group who turn out wax for Atlantic Records, continued their unbroken string this week when their latest slicing, "Crawlin'," hit The *Billboard* Best Selling R&B charts. This marks the sixth time in a row that the group has made the charts with their disks. This record, a rare one in a field where artists much too often find it tough to follow up one hit, is even more imposing when it is noted that three of the Clovers' waxings to date have been hits on both sides rather than one.

The strength of the Clovers in the r&b marts is pointed up by the fact that every cutting by the group to date has sold more than 175,000 apiece, and a number of their hits have sold well over 200,000 platters, a record that would be solid even in the pop field. Their present disk, "Crawlin'," has hit close to 100,000 since it was released three weeks ago. In addition, nearly half a dozen of the tunes waxed by the Clovers have been recorded by pop artists or bands after the vocal combo made the tunes hits in the r&b market.[6]

Nevertheless, many now acknowledge that the first example of a Rock 'n' Roll recording was the Crows' "Gee," which was recorded in New York in February 1953 but which would not become a hit until 1954, scoring both on the pop (#14) and rhythm & blues (#2) charts.

---

5 John A. Jackson, *Alan Freed and the Early Years of Rock and Roll* (Schirmer Books, 1991, p. 34).

6 *Billboard*, March 14, 1953.

The Clovers, one of the most successful early progenitors of Rock 'n' Roll.

As "Moondog," Alan Freed's popularity increased over the next few months with WJW billing his show "the nation's number-one rhythm and blues show."[7] However, in April 1953 he would fall asleep at the wheel of his car whilst driving home. With major, life-threatening injuries, he was taken to hospital and underwent major surgery. His recovery was almost miraculous and after only a short hiatus, in June he was home and broadcasting from his bedroom. Meanwhile, another white Cleveland DJ was stealing some of his thunder, introducing white Rock 'n' Roll into the potent musical mix.

When Freed returned to WJW he did so looking over his shoulder. On June 5 WERE's Bill Randle, Cleveland's top-rated pop DJ, promoted a local rhythm and blues dance starring Billy Ward and his Dominoes (with new lead singer Jackie Wilson), ex-heavyweight boxing champion Joe Louis and his band, and Bill Haley and His Comets.[8]

Freed was fully back in action by July and, assisted by Leo Mintz and Lew Platt, he put on the *Biggest Rhythm and Blues Show*, which starred Ruth Brown, and featured Wynonie Harris, the Clovers, Joe Louis,[9] the Lester Young Combo and Buddy Johnson's Orchestra. The show toured for a month, with the show at the Cleveland Arena reported as drawing an audience of 20,000. *Billboard* highlighted the plans for future "Moondog" events:

Alan (Moondog) Freed, WJW, Cleveland r.&b. jockey who has attracted crowds ranging from 3,000 to 25,000 at his monthly "Moondog" dances, has given up on holding dances in armories. For his next affair *The Moondog Jubilee of Stars Under The Stars*, which will be held here in

---

7 Jackson, p. 48.

8 Ibid., p.53.

9 Like Sugar Ray Robinson, a boxed turned entertainer.

August, he has hired Ebbets Field, the 30,000-seat home of the Brooklyn Dodgers.

The date will be set within the next week. The nut for the show will run about $25,000 with about $15,000 laid out for talent. Talent being set for the show includes the Clovers, the Dominoes, the Orioles, the Count Basie and the Buddy Johnson orks and six combos, including Muddy Waters, Fats Domino and Little Walter.

Freed this week set the talent for his portion of "Star Night," the massive three-city, one-nighter package set by promoter Bud Arvev of Chicago, which will play Cleveland, Chicago and Detroit on June 23, 24 and 25. Freed will emcee the part of the show which will star Ruth Brown, the Clovers and the Tiny Bradshaw ork.[10]

This hybrid music, on the verge of being named "Rock 'n' Roll,"[11] was gathering momentum. In September 1954, close on 12,000 people would attend a show headlined by Bill Haley at the Painsville Armory, Clive, Ohio, again hosted by Bill Randle. In January 1955, Alan Freed's "Rock 'n' Roll" Ball played for two nights at St Nicholas Arena NY,[12] where half the audience (12,000 over two nights) was reported as "white." Artists featured included Big Joe Turner, The Clovers, Clyde McPhatter & The Drifters and the orchestras of Buddy Johnson and Red Prysock. This sort of show burgeoned during 1955 and just two weeks' later the *Top 10 Rhythm and Blues Review* would begin a long tour (the exact length of which is lost in the mists of time) of the Northern and Southern States with an exclusively black line-up of artists. The show was promoted by Lou Krefetz, a white man, record sales distributor and the manager of the Clovers, and very much in the mold of Alan Freed as a prime mover of the new music. In the music press, the audiences were described as "Blues Fans."

A second "Top 10 Review" tour was mounted from late August to the end of October boasting 16 states, 50 cities and 66 consecutive days of performances. Joe Turner stated that "all other styles of music will have to take a back seat in 1955 and let the Blues take the spotlight in the pop music world."[13] On this tour some

---

10 *Billboard* June 5, 1954.

11 On December 4, 1954, *Billboard* Magazine would report that Alan Freed had changed the name of his radio show to *The Rock n Roll Show*.

12 Derek Coller, *Big Joe Turner: Feel So Fine* (Hardinge Simpole, 2023), p.116.

13 *New York Amsterdam News,* August 6, 1955.

venues had segregated areas for white spectators, while others held separate performances for black and white audiences.

The addition of Bill Haley and His Comets as headliners for the concerts at The Syria Mosque, Pittsburgh, Pennsylvania on October 20, 1955 and the Mosque, Richmond, Virginia the following night was a major milestone in the evolution of Rock 'n' Roll into a multi-racial musical style. The enormous success of this bold move would lead, in January 1956, to Haley headlining eleven nights of a tour by otherwise black performers, which would include Birmingham, Alabama. The mixing of races would challenge and provoke the cities and states that the shows visited in the next couple of years. The city of Birmingham, Alabama was notorious for its application of and adherence to the "Jim Crow" laws, and described by Martin Luther King as "the most segregated city in the States." In 1956, Bill Haley started a diary, and his entry for January 29th in Birmingham is significant. "Afternoon show for whites and night show for colored. Not allowed to appear on stage at same time as any colored person. I hope soon the South will do away with its ideas on segregation."

Opening night of the Feld Brothers' *The Biggest Rock 'n' Roll Show of '56* at the Hershey Arena on April 20, 1956.

Advertisement for the May 7, 1956 show at the Olympia Stadium in Detroit, Michigan.

In April 1956, a seven-week tour headlined by Haley began and would travel the country widely. His diary tackles the influence of the music on teenagers, and the racial aspects head on, with some forthright opinion. In White Plains, New York, he notes that the organisers "had to turn away 5,000 people and they were unruly and hard to control. Kids danced in the aisles and wouldn't behave... They mobbed me after the show and I got hit again."

In Newark, where all went well, Bill penned a reminder to himself that "we have to... prove this music can be played right and not barbaric as *Variety* says." When 13,000 fans showed up in Toronto on April 30th, he notes that "newspaper, magazine, radio and TV interviewers all ask me the same thing: is this music hurting teenagers? My nerves are getting bad." He complains of feeling tremendous pressure from critics accusing him of inciting juvenile delinquency. By contrast, in Buffalo, New York Bill wrote that "Everything went fine, proving so far that rock'n'roll does not cause riots." In Richmond, Virginia on April 22nd he notes that "This tour is like sitting on a keg of dynamite. The show is all colored but our act. With the racial situation in the South broiling...I hope my nerves hold up."

His anxiety was well-founded. A few weeks earlier, on April 10th, Nat King Cole had been beaten up, onstage, at the Municipal Auditorium in Birmingham by five members of the Northern Alabama Citizens' Council. Even though arrests had followed the incident, some resentful and vocal blacks in the area had vowed revenge. Things were starting to heat up on both sides. Bill Haley, Jr. notes that,

While the Comets travelled in style, driving their Cadillacs, and a Decca van carrying their instruments, they followed the same route as the bus carrying the other acts on the tour. It bothered them that the black entertainers on the same tour would not be served in white establishments. They'd have to settle for sandwiches served from the back door, and eat – and often sleep – on their bus.

Such treatment was not confined to the South. On May 4th, after a performance in Columbus, Ohio, the tour drove off toward Canton, Ohio, for a show at Memorial Auditorium. Bill and the band stopped and ate at a restaurant on the Ohio Turnpike. While some of the black acts on the tour tried to buy meals at the same place while the Comets were still there, however, they were refused service. "They got in a fight, and we left in a hurry," Bill wrote. "Bill and the band sympathized with their colleagues and were angered by the injustice, but other than getting food for them, they felt powerless to change firmly entrenched prejudices held by others."[14]

In Birmingham, Alabama, members of the local White Citizens' Council picketed the show, and attendance was low. The Council's vitriolic tirades made front-page news all over the country. After an "anti-rock 'n' roll" rally the previous month, they had started campaigning to force radio stations and jukebox owners to "boycott this immoral music." The Council's spokesman called Bill a "Judas goat" who'd "betrayed for thirty pieces of gold the youth of America by white-washed nigger music." The whole town was in uproar. "These people are fanatics," Bill wrote. He wrote that all touring bands should stop visiting the south "until the race situation is straightened out." Bill Haley, Jr. adds that,

> Chuck Berry, a late addition to the tour, was chased by an angry mob after one show when he was seen with a white woman: The mob tracked him to the bus the Comets had rented and tried to board it, but Bill got them to back off by assuring them that whoever they were looking for wasn't there. "Do I look like a nigger lover to you?" he asked the mob. More than once on this tour, Cuppy had to feign kinship with Berry's white girlfriend to avoid potentially violent confrontations.[15]

Cuppy's memories of her few days on the road, as related to Bill Haley, Jr., included receiving death threats, anonymous notes, and Bill ultimately telling her

---

14 Haley Jr. & Benjaminson, p.113.

15 Ibid., p.114.

to remain in the hotel rather than travel to the concert. Cuppy also had memories of the tension caused by segregation of the audience, and the black compere of the show having to announce the Comets from the wings as he was not allowed on stage with white people.

During the first show in Greenville, the police were informed that a bomb, with a timer, had been placed under the stage. The *Greenville News* recounted the incident the next day, reporting that an anonymous tipster had phoned the police to say a time bomb had been placed. Haley and the Comets were on the stage when the call was received, and had to leave the stage immediately. The hall was evacuated, the second show cancelled. The next morning the local newspaper reported that no bomb had been found.

At a night show at the National Guard Armory, Washington D.C., *Newsweek* magazine reported that,

> Even before the joint began to jump there was trouble... 5,000 people, mostly teenagers, poured in for some rock'n'roll. Knives flashed and one young man was cut in the arm. Inside, twenty-five special officers waited for Bill Haley & His Comets to swing into the big beat.

"What next?" Bill wrote in his diary. For the rest of the tour, he would carry a gun. In Savannah, Georgia, black audiences began resisting segregation at Comets performances. "The Negroes refused to come to the second show," Bill wrote in his diary. "Results: 2,500 people first show, second show cancelled."

Twenty-five years later, writing his autobiography Bill glosses over the big issues and talks about the "great camaraderie" between the performers, saying "we not only did not have any racial tension among the entertainers, or the working people on the tour, we never even thought or talked about it." However, to make a fair assessment of his actions, one has to consider things he does not mention: the disparity in pay between the headliners and the other acts; that it would be wealthy white promoters who would benefit more from the success of the tour than the black performers; how often the black performers would spend the night or eat a meal in a bus rather than a hotel; the segregation that was involved in simply eating a meal, and the rules about black and white people not sharing the stage.

During 1955 Bill was, without doubt "The King of Rock 'n' Roll," but there is little or no sign of his using his status or influence to challenge the *status quo*. Conceivably, he could have used his exalted position at that time to make a major statement about racial inequality and segregation, but he chose to be happy that some of the concerts went off without trouble and the reassurance (one assumes) that the music was therefore not the problem.

There would another Feld Brothers tour in late 1956, with Bill and the Comets again headlining. Bill merely mentions it in passing it in his autobiography. He was no longer keeping a diary at this time, so we have no insight as to whether his views might have changed. In the final analysis he simply distanced himself from the issue with these words in his diary, written at the end of the first Feld Brothers' tour: "This race problem is not mine. I'll be glad to finish this tour and let the South alone for now."

Some black musicians were resentful of the success of "White" Rock 'n Roll and Louis Jordan, in an uncharacteristically outspoken interview from 1973, stated that:

> There is nothing that the white artist has invented or come along with in the form of jazz or entertainment...Rock 'n' Roll was not a marriage of rhythm and blues and country and western. That's white publicity. Rock 'n' Roll was just a white imitation..."[16]

Count Basie, interviewed by British pop singer Tom Jones, highlighted the difference that money could make:

> Basie: "The blues records that old black people used to do, they didn't have any money, so they'd just stick a bloody microphone in the middle of the room and whoever was playing would pick it up." Jones: "Rock Around the Clock...was so hot because they miked every instrument. That's the difference: it *sounds* different. It's only twelve-bar blues."[17]

Little Richard biographer Jordan Bassett goes on to note that the real shift was yet to happen with the arrival of Elvis. "He was ten years younger than Haley, much better-looking and, with his faster, shuffling tempos, happier to break the chains of the swing years that preceded them."[18]

In the UK, Jones explained that it was simply a matter of white acts "capitalising on a lot of black songs...with Elvis Presley being the example with his early stuff." He also ascribed the commercial success of white records to the fact that they were more available than the originals. "We didn't hear them, you see."[19]

---

16 Jordan Bassett: *Here's Little Richard*, (London: Bloomsbury Academic, 2023), p.40.

17 Ibid. p.42.

18 Ibid. p.43.

19 Ibid. p.109-110.

CHAPTER 14
Country Roots

"But mostly I remember the evenings when I would enjoy listening to Dad and Mom, our songs, and, on the radio: Big Slim from WWVA in Wheeling, West Virginia, the *Grand Ole Opry* from Nashville [WSM], and The *National Barn Dance* from Chicago [WLS]. Hence, I began to sing some of the songs, secretly practiced in front of a mirror, and I decided, at the age of seven, I would someday be a singer." – Bill Haley[1]

View of the Grand Ole Opry from the back of the stage in the War Memorial Auditorium sometime between 1939 and 1943.

---

1 This text has been repeated from Bill Haley's Chapter 1.

Bill Haley's reminiscence of his childhood in 1930s Booths Corner, Pennsylvania gives us insight into his musical awakening and the source and medium of his first stylistic influences. It is worthwhile to explore how "hillbilly music," as it was first called commercially, a culturally and geographically distant product from the Northeast, found such a faithful audience there and inspired many of its budding native musicians, including Haley.

Historian Bill C. Malone describes the expansion of country music at the beginning of the 1930s: "The once modest hillbilly business began to take shape as an industry with booking agents, promoters, advertising firms, publishers, music licensing agencies, and motion picture representatives recognizing the gold that might be mined from this new territory."[2]

Country music's dissemination through radio enabled it to reach beyond its geographical origins in the South to entertain audiences, influence

Harry C. McAuliffe (1899-1966) worked under the stage name of "Big Slim," appearing for close on thirty years on WWVA in Wheeling, West Virginia.

fledgling musicians, and become the voice of rural and working-class people throughout North America. Radio was more effective and immediate for reaching a large audience than phonograph records or live appearances by artists. If a household could afford to purchase a radio set, their entertainment thereafter was free, up-to-date, and delivered to their home, no matter how remote, as long as it was within range of the station's broadcast transmitter. With the advent of clear-channel stations that were licensed to transmit powerful signals of around 50,000 watts, local stations could have an even

---

2 Bill C. Malone, *Country Music U.S.A.*, revised and expanded (Austin: University of Texas Press, 1985), pp. 93-94.

broader reach, without the assistance of national networks such as NBC or CBS.[3]

WLS (AM 870) and WSM (AM 650), the host radio stations of the shows mentioned by Haley above, were clear-channel stations and two of the greatest forces in popularizing country music; both stations continue to operate today. WLS is based in Chicago and was founded in 1924 by its local retail powerhouse, Sears, Roebuck, and Company. The call letters stood for "World's Largest Store," touting the company's nationally distributed catalog and mail-order business.[4] WSM is based in Nashville and was founded in 1925 by the local National Life and Accident Insurance Company. Its call letters stood for "We Shield Millions." WLS went clear-channel in 1931 and WSM in 1932. Part of their programming strategy was to provide entertainment that would resonate with rural dwellers. To that end, both stations benefited from the talent and ambition of the father of country music radio, George D. Hay.

George Dewey Hay (1895-1968), an Indiana native, began his career as a newspaper reporter for the *Commercial Appeal* in Memphis, Tennessee, and as an announcer for the newly established radio station the paper owned, WMC. In 1924, he moved to Chicago to work for WLS. Recognizing the need to take "old-time music" to the large rural radio audience and catering to his own enthusiasm for the music, Hay founded the *National Barn Dance*, a program that quickly attained monumental success and became a home for many legendary artists that Haley cites as his idols and later co-performers.

Moving quickly, Hay went to WSM in Nashville the next year. He began programming a couple of hours of "old-time music," hosting as "The Solemn Old Judge" and, in parallel to his WLS creation, called his show the *WSM Barn Dance*. Already affiliated with the NBC network, WSM's show followed a classical music and opera-appreciation program from New York. In December 1927, as a humorous acknowledgement of the jarring stylistic switchover, Hay announced to his radio audience, "For the past hour, we have been listening

---

3 The so-called "X" radio stations had an even wider reach than the clear-channel stations, but were out of the mainstream. The first letter in a station's name indicated the region of transmission ("W" for east of the Mississippi River, "K" for west of the Mississippi, "C" for Canada, and "X" for Mexico). Crafty station owners in the Southwest United States found they could get around Federal Communications Commission limits on transmission range by placing their stations on the Texas side of the border and the transmission tower on the Mexican side. Blasting a signal at up to 150,000 watts, stations like XERA could blanket most of North America. The Carter Family, one of Ralph Peer's discoveries in Bristol, Tennessee (discussed later in this chapter), found widespread fame on "border radio."

4 It is also worth noting that these catalogs advertised the same phonograph records in all areas of the country, bringing hillbilly music to the attention and availability of consumers everywhere. In his Chapter 1, Haley describes first seeing the guitar he wanted in the Sears and Roebuck catalog.

to music taken largely from Grand Opera. From now on, we will present the Grand Ole Opry."[5] The program would forever be known by that name and continues to draw fans from all over the world and serves as the mark of validation for any artist privileged to appear on its stage and its airwaves.

The next thing to consider are the musical influences within Haley's own household. His English-born mother had some degree of formal training as a pianist, occasionally taught lessons in the neighborhood, and is said to have played organ at the Baptist church in nearby Marcus Hook. Maud Haley's purveyance of church hymnody and perhaps English folk balladry, a major progenitor of American country music, was her contribution to young Bill's musical development. Equally nurturing was her tolerance, sometimes defense, of her son's own musical pursuits. In a famous account, a neighbor complained about the raucous and frequent family jam sessions next door, to which Maud responded, with proper English poise, "As you well know, Mrs. Booth, the Bible tells us to make a joyful noise unto the Lord, which this family surely does!"[6]

Bill's father, William Albert Clifton Haley, brings a different aspect to the family musical and cultural dynamic and another clarification as to why we find an audience for southern old-time music in the North. Bill the Elder moved from his native Firebrick, Kentucky, to Michigan in pursuit of a better job. Many histories, including those on the topic of jazz and blues, describe the "Great Diaspora" or "The Great Northern Migration" of the 1920s, where thousands fled the dead-end agricultural, coal-mining, and textile-mill economy of the South for the more thriving and promising industrial jobs in the North. These accounts can lead the reader to believe that this migration only applied to African-Americans, not realizing that many poor southern whites were in the same boat. Like economic refugees of today, some would move north temporarily, leaving family behind and sending them money regularly. Others settled permanently, synthesizing their southern, rural ways with the culture of their new environment. This was the case with the Haley family.

We can, therefore, deduce that transplanted white southerners in the North and their influence on the northerners cultivated an audience for country and western music in that region. Also keep in mind that there were vast rural areas in the Northeast as well as blue-collar industrial areas, with inhabitants that related more to the fundamental expression of country music than the effete

---

5 Louis M. Kyriakoudes, "The Grand Ole Opry and the Urban South," *Southern Cultures*, Vol. 10, No. 1, 2004.

6 Haley & John von Hoelle, p. 22.

songs of Tin Pan Alley. Many historians recognize the outbreak of World War II as a catalyst for spreading country music. Southern soldiers were sent to military bases and ammunition plants in the North. Northern soldiers were sent to the same in the South. Detroit jukebox managers in 1943 reported that hillbilly records were the most popular stock in their machines. Southern merchant marine Ferlin Husky, who later became a major country music star, entertained his fellow sailors with his hillbilly fare. He observed, "Some of the most enthusiastic people were those who came from parts of the country where this kind of music was almost unknown."[7]

Bill Haley, Sr. played banjo and mandolin to an admirable level, according to his friend and fellow worker, James Otis: "I guess you would call him a real hillbilly at heart, but I tell you, he could play both the mandolin and banjo...He had an ear for good country music. I think that's where little Billy got his ear for them foot-stomping hillbilly tunes."[8]

Jimmie Rodgers, widely thought of as the "Father of Country Music," was hugely influential but his life was cut short by tuberculosis.

We can only speculate what Bill, Sr.'s repertoire was since none of the accounts name specific tunes, but it is a safe bet that it was mostly traditional music handed down through oral tradition and first-hand tutelage, though "picking out" tunes off of records or radio could factor in, as well. As both witness to and participant in music in the home, as well as the family activity of tuning into radio programs, "old-time" music made an indelible impression on young Bill Haley.

In advance of naming the legendary country and western musicians who influenced Bill in live appearances, radio, records, and movies, it is important to acknowledge the person who is the stylistic and inspirational root of the music, Jimmie Rodgers. James Charles Rodgers (1897-1933) was a native of Mississippi and grew up around white and black railroad workers. In this context, he absorbed blues, railroad songs and lore, and traditional cowboy songs and yodeling. Ralph Peer, representing the Victor record company, made a scouting trip to Bristol, Tennessee, located in the northeastern corner of the state and bordering

7 Ian Whitcomb, *After the Ball: Pop Music from Rag to Rock* (New York: Limelight Edition, 1986), p. 199.

8 Haley and von Hoelle, pp. 19-20.

Virginia and North Carolina in search of new "hillbilly" talent. In August 1927, Rodgers auditioned for Peer (as did the Carter Family) and was recorded the next day. He followed up with a session at Victor's studio in Camden, New Jersey. Rodgers' fame skyrocketed for the rest of his short life before he succumbed to his tuberculosis in 1933.

Known as "The Singing Brakeman" and "The Blue Yodeler," Rodgers' songs are an indication of his musical eclecticism and his shifting persona. Some of his songs were classy, Tin Pan Alley-like tunes such as "Miss the Mississippi and You." He performed songs about cowboys and the West, but Rodgers' real wheelhouse was his fusion of blues songs with cowboy yodeling, creating a series of songs known as "blue yodels" that were numbered similar to opus numbers by classical composers. Historically, Rodgers acquired yet another title, "The Father of Country Music," due to his influence on innumerable future country music artists, including those who would influence Bill Haley: Elton Britt, Gene Autry, Ernest Tubb, Hank Snow, and Hank Williams.

This leads us to a substyle of country music that so influenced Haley: the movie singing-cowboy "western" style. Like vaudeville blues, the music of the singing cowboy was manufactured by urban song-writers, but performed by some genuine descendants of Rodgers. Movie westerns had been a big part of motion picture history since their silent movie beginnings. As soon as "soundies" came into being in the late 1920s, music became an available and essential new offering in movies of any genre, including westerns, and movie cowboys were expected to sing as well as talk. Some of the earlier stars could do neither.

Gene Autry

Westerns of the 1930s were a wonderful distraction for audiences suffering through the Great Depression. They were a world of fantasy and adventure for young boys such as Bill Haley, who followed their heroes with their handsome horse buddies, pretty romantic interests, unquestionable virtue, fighting and gun-slinging skills, and, above all, their spectacular delivery of a song. One of the earliest of these new singing cowboys and arguably the greatest was Gene Autry. Orvon Grover "Gene" Autry (1907-1998) was born in the tiny town of Tioga, Texas. Early in life, he worked the graveyard shift as a railroad telegrapher, fighting the boredom and loneliness by singing. This distraction ultimately got him fired, but, before long, none other than Will Rogers, the legendary cowboy humorist and occasional partner with Jimmie Rodgers, discovered him.

Autry ultimately appeared in dozens of movies and television shows. He made almost 650 recordings and wrote or co-wrote more than three hundred songs. Highlights include his first hit, "Silver Haired Daddy of Mine" (co-written with Jimmy Long), "Back in the Saddle Again" (by Ray Whitley), and a series of classic Christmas songs, some composed by Autry himself ("Rudolph the Red-Nosed Reindeer," "Here Comes Santa Claus"). Autry was a regular on the WLS Barn Dance for four years early in his career and went on to host his own CBS radio show, *Gene Autry's Melody Ranch*, for sixteen years beginning in 1940, so Haley would have experienced him on radio, on records, in the movies, and in live appearances.

This survey and etymology of Bill Haley's musical roots ultimately leads us to the art of yodeling, something Haley excelled at, even though, when he mentioned it in many interviews as a Rock 'n' Roll artist, interviewers often erupted into laughter as if it were a joke. Haley would chuckle along politely, but it must have cut him to the core for something he had invested in so deeply to be ridiculed. Yodeling, as employed in the western music style, is believed to be of German and Swiss origin. It requires incredible flexibility, a relaxed throat, unique articulations, placement of the tongue, shape of the mouth cavity, and laser-like precision with pitch.

A singer and yodeler who quickly succeeded Gene Autry as king of the movie cowboys was Roy Rogers, born Leonard Slye near Cincinnati, Ohio, in 1911 (died in 1998). He began his musical career in 1931, joining the Sons of the Pioneers, famous for songs such as "Tumbling Tumbleweeds" and "Cool Water." Rogers began his film career in 1935, but it really took off in 1938 when Autry de-manded more money and Republic Pictures looked for a cheaper alternative. Rogers soon equaled Autry as both as a cowboy actor and as a singer, especially with his breathtaking yodeling technique.

Roy Rogers

Elton Britt (1913-1972) took yodeling to a whole new level. Born James Elton Baker in

Marshall, Arkansas, he moved to Los Angeles in 1930 to become one of the Beverly Hillbillies (not the family of the 1960s television series), the brainchild of KMPC station manager Glen Rice. Britt first rose to fame as a soloist in 1942 when he recorded the World War II hit, "There's a Star-Spangled Banner Waving Somewhere," written by Bob Miller, with lyrics by Paul Roberts and David McEnery. Within two years, the song about a disabled mountain boy who longed to serve in the war sold more than a million copies. The topic probably resonated with Bill Haley, who had similar sentiments over rejection by the military due to his bad eyesight. In his autobiography, he wrote:

Elton Britt

> In December of 1941 came Pearl Harbor and the Second World War. My two buddies and I went to enlist. They were both accepted; I was rejected because of my eyesight. This was crushing news for me. I still remember my mother talking for hours in an effort to cheer me up. Although I worked in defense plants, did hundreds of shows for U.S.O. and service bases, the disappointment I felt at that time was a long time wearing off.[9]

Throughout the last half of the 1940s and into the early part of the 1950s, Haley and his different ensembles wrote or covered songs that would address the images and sensibilities of country and western music. Songs such as "Ten Gallon Stetson," "The Covered Wagon Rolled Right Along," and "My Palomino and I" are firmly in the tradition of the romanticized West. Haley recorded sweet, perfumed love songs including "A Sweet Bunch of Roses," "Candy Kisses," and "My Sweet Little Girl from Nevada," whereas others such as "Icy Heart" and "I'm Not to Blame" address the heartbreak of love gone wrong.

---

9 Bill registered for the draft on July 7, 1943, the day after his eighteenth birthday. His draft registration gave his place of employment as the Baldwin Locomotive works in Eddystone. The registrar recorded him as being 5'11½" tall, approximately 165 lbs. in weight, with blue eyes, brown hair, and with a scar on his left leg. According to Bill himself, this was a knife wound from tackling an armed burglar (Haley, Jr. and Benjaminson, p. 42). His impaired vision would have been discovered at the subsequent medical exam.

Bill Haley in Cowboy gear, date and location unknown, c. mid 1940s, and before the Four Aces of Western Swing.

Haley and his colleagues also produced sentimental moralistic and patriotic material that was popular with their audiences, such as "Too Many Parties, Too Many Pals," a monologue featuring Tex King (a member of Haley's Western Aces, who sounds astonishingly like Willie Nelson when he sings) in which a lawyer pleads for lenience on behalf of his defendant who turns out to be his own daughter. There was also "Stand Up and Be Counted," a rallying cry for those who are "on the side of peace and freedom" and "on the side of the Lord."

As Bill Haley set his sights on a younger audience going into the 1950s, musical material of this type, sometimes called "old-time music," would gradually be either abandoned or signi-ficantly pepped up for the emerging Rock 'n' Roll crowd. One example is "Farewell, So Long, Goodbye," which, by the lyric alone, could pass for a bitter "cry in your beer" honky-tonk love song. In the 1953 Comets re-cording, however, it is on its way to being a rollicking, full-fledged Rock 'n' Roll number, its lively beat and exuberant vocal styling belying the sentiment of the words. In the years to come, it would be a rare occasion that Haley would get to sing a ballad or wear his heart on his sleeve as he increasingly sang about parties, dance beats, youthful slang, and novelty nonsense. He would attempt to turn back to his country roots in later years when Rock 'n' Roll seemed to have failed him but, in many cases, he would live out the adage that you can never really "go back home."

These three pictures are undated, nor can the location be identified. The item that Bill is holding is the volume of *Bill Haley's Down Home Melodies*, published by the Dixie Music Publishing Company in 1946.

CHAPTER 15
Jazz and R&B

"They were all World War II guys. They either were in the service, experienced that, or they were alive during that time. And we know the popular music, everything that was on the radio, was big band. Probably a faraway second was country music." – Pedro Haley

"I remember the Tiny Hill, Count Basie, and Big Joe Turner records used to fascinate me. I kept feeling the need for a style of my own in music." – Bill Haley (from Chapter 3)

"Bill Haley had this big acoustic Gibson with a pickup stuck on it, but Frannie [sic] Beecher was the most un-believable guitar player of all time. He must have come out of the jazz field; you had this thing happening where it was swing and rock simultaneously together on those rock 'n' roll records. I think a lot of those players were jazz players and Bill Haley & His Comets were quite an interesting combination, with the big upright bass, sax and Frannie Beecher. If you listen to the solo on 'Rock Around the Clock,' it's incredible playing." – George Harrison[1]

At the outset of this chapter, it is important to emphasize Haley biographer John Swenson's point that, "Haley may have been the focal point, but the Comets were the show. Haley spread the spotlight out among the other members of this group."[2] In the childhood and early adult years of many of the Comets, swing and bebop were ever-present and no doubt influenced their musical development to various extents. To understand the shadings of jazz styles found in the music of the Comets, it is worthwhile to take a broad view of what was happening in the jazz world from circa 1935 to 1955.

---

1 Interview in *Rolling Stone*, March 9, 1996. Harrison mistook Franny Beecher for Danny Cedrone, but his point is no less valid, given he would have likely been familiar with Beecher's other work with Haley.

2 Swenson, p. 63.

Tiny Hill, dance band leader and the innovator of the use of sanding blocks to create an exciting dance rhythm.

The commonly accepted watershed moment for the rise of swing was the Benny Goodman Orchestra performance at Los Angeles' Palomar Ballroom on August 21, 1935. This "new" style of big band jazz for a new generation had actually been gestating since the early 1920s with bands like Paul Whiteman's, Fletcher Henderson's, Glen Gray's, and Bennie Moten's. For about ten years after the Goodman event, hundreds of swing bands mushroomed and flourished through the World War II years. After 1945, however, changing post-war mainstream culture and economic realities took their toll, leaving the next generation of teen-agers devoid of an exciting new music they could call their own.

Beginning in the early 1940s, a cloister of jazz musicians in New York, weary of the constraints of commodified swing, began pushing the music forward in technique and complexity. Jamming, working, and experimenting in venues like Minton's Playhouse in Harlem and a row of clubs on 52nd Street, a new music blossomed. Derisively dubbed "bebop," its founding fathers were trumpeter Dizzy Gillespie, saxophonist Charlie Parker, pianist Thelonious Monk, and drummer Kenny Clarke.

By the time bebop saw the light of day around the end of the war in 1945, the jazz audience had split into three parts. Many young jazz musicians were intrigued by the instrumental technique and sophisticated melodic and harmonic language of bebop and went with it, though most of the listening public would reject it as strange and abstract. Another segment of jazz critics, musicians, and fans had taken up the cause of a "New Orleans revival," a movement that had started in the late 1930s. They not only rejected bebop, but swing as well, insisting that the only "real" jazz was what came out of New Orleans and Chicago in the 1920s. In fact, Milt Gabler, who would produce all of Bill Haley and His Comets' recordings at Decca Records, started his career in the mid-1930s at the Commodore Music Shop in New York, reissuing vintage early jazz records on his own label. He also promoted early jazz artists as part of the revival movement, resuscitating their careers on records and at clubs on 52nd Street that featured "traditional jazz" such as those of Jimmy Ryan and Eddie Condon.

The third segment of jazz fans in the 1940s, mostly black, went with rhythm and blues. Within the jazz world, this substyle grew out of the simpler and danceable

Milt Gabler with Bill Haley and a new equipment van, presented to Bill by Decca Records.

riff and blues-based swing of the Southwest, represented in bands like Count Basie's, Lionel Hampton's, and Jesse Stone's.[3] Smaller combos with a rhythm section and a couple of horns were better suited for the burgeoning jukebox recording market. Once again, we can point out Milt Gabler as an active participant. Gabler was recruited by Decca in 1941, where he oversaw what some might consider the prototype for R&B, Lionel Hampton's May 26, 1942 recording of his "Flying Home," with nineteen-year-old Illinois Jacquet's famous solo that set the standard for bar-walking R&B tenor saxophone, imbued with a robust tone that descended from the Coleman Hawkins school of that instrument. Gabler also made a star out of former Chick Webb Orchestra saxophonist Louis Jordan with

---

3 Under the name "Charles E. Calhoun," Jesse Stone was the writer of Bill Haley's first Decca hit record, "Shake, Rattle and Roll" and his 1955 hit, "Razzle-Dazzle."

recordings like "Choo Choo Ch'Boogie" and "Ain't Nobody Here but Us Chickens."

We can surmise from Bill Haley's own testimony that he had an average interest in big band swing, music that would have been at its peak when he was about ten to twenty years old, but he was obviously more into country and western music at this time. In his WPWA days as, among other things, the station librarian, he reported his interest in the more R&B and bluesy-swing bands like Basie's. As far as bebop is concerned, Haley showed no hostility towards it or its proponents, but probably just didn't understand it and saw it as a commercial kiss of death. He rightly saw it as the music of the time (the mid-1940s and early '50s), but a music that stood no chance of attracting most young people, thereby providing him with an opportunity to cook up something that *would* attract youngsters. (In his autobiography, he certainly laments the failed attempts by his promoters to book the Comets in jazz clubs.) Keep in mind that there *was* a sizeable youth following for so-called "cool" jazz (Dave Brubeck Quartet, Gerry Mulligan, etc.), or even the experimental Stan Kenton Orchestra, but that was the older college crowd. It was the less-mature high schoolers that Haley was aiming for, a demographic longing for something simple and energetic that they that had only been able to find by listening to black rhythm and blues.

Being that Haley was primarily plying his craft in the Northeast — Philadelphia, New York, and New Jersey — it is correct to assume that bebop, country, and R&B acts were working cheek by jowl in clubs next to each other. Stylistic allegiances vanish when you are just looking for a gig, and musical crossbreeding occurred. Jazz-trained session musicians that Haley recruited for his recordings and live performances knew going in that a lot of the newer "weird stuff" that had become their *lingua franca* needed to be thrown out for Haley's purposes, but their sophistication is still evident in Comets' recordings, and this is what sets the group apart from other early rock and roll bands.

For this look at the jazz influence on Bill Haley and the Comets, we will focus on the earliest musicians that shaped the band's sound: guitarists Danny Cedrone and Franny Beecher, and saxophonists Joey D'Ambrosio and Rudy Pompilii. Drummer Ralph Jones will be mentioned several times along the way, as well.

To begin a survey of jazz-influenced guitarists who played with Haley, it is essential to look at the first real pivotal figure in jazz guitar, Charlie Christian (1916-1942). Born in Bonham, Texas, he grew up in Oklahoma City. By 1936, he had taken up the new amplified electric guitar, a technological innovation that had spread east from West Coast innovators like Adolph Rickenbacker, Leo Fender, and Paul Bigsby. The louder and more commanding sound of the amplified guitar, combined with the Christian's dazzling technique and improvisational prowess, turned the instrument into a front-line contender with the louder wind instruments.

The majority of Christian's recordings we are left with are the collaborations with Benny Goodman's sextet commercially recorded for Columbia. Outside of that, there are the rare and precious amateur recordings made by Columbia University student Jerry Newhouse in Minneapolis in 1939 and at the legendary jam sessions at Minton's Playhouse in Harlem, New York, in 1941. Tragically, Christian died of tuberculosis on March 2, 1942, at only twenty-five years of age. In his short life, he raised the bar for what guitarists would be expected to do moving forward, not only in the jazz world, but out into the blues world of B. B. King (who left no doubt of Christian's influence in interviews) and, as we will see, rock and roll. In fact, Charlie Christian was inducted into the Rock and Roll Hall of Fame in 1990.

The electric guitar found its initial acceptance in the American Southwest where Christian cut his teeth. Bob Dunn, a member of the Texas-based western swing band, Milton Brown and His Musical Brownies, is credited with playing the first amplified steel guitar in 1934. In the jazz world of Southwest "territory" bands of the 1930s, guitarist, trombonist, composer, and arranger Eddie Durham took up the amplified guitar and may have influenced Christian to do so. By the 1940s, emerging Texas honky-tonk bands, such as Ernest Tubb's, were featuring electric "take-off" guitars to take the solo spots between verses. In the blues world, electric guitarist Aaron "T-Bone" Walker, composer of "Stormy Monday," brought the commanding electric guitar to the fore as a lead instrument with horn section accompaniment, rather than the other way around. Amplified instruments would soon make their way into blues recordings generated at Sun Records in Memphis and Chess Records in Chicago with the likes of Muddy Waters and Howlin' Wolf.

If Christian was the pillar of jazz guitar in the 1930s, Django Reinhardt was the post. Born Jean Reinhardt in Belgium in 1910, he was of Romani heritage and was self-taught on violin, banjo, and guitar. Around 1930, Reinhardt discovered American jazz through recordings. In 1931, five Parisian university students formed The Hot Club of France, a fan club of young French record collectors and promoters of jazz in Europe, including sponsorship of a new jazz string band, the *Quintette du Hot Club de France*, that included Reinhardt (who went by his nickname, "Django") and French violinist Stéphane Grappelli. The recordings made by this ensemble made their way back to the United States and Reinhardt's powerful, flashy, Romani-flavored acoustic guitar style made a huge impact on guitarists prior to the arrival of Charlie Christian and long afterward. Reinhardt died in Paris at the age of 43 in 1953.

Bill Haley's first great rock and roll guitarist was Danny Cedrone. Donato Joseph Cedrone was born on June 20, 1920, to parents who had emigrated to the U.S. from Italy in 1912. Cedrone was conversant with country music, blues, and jazz and flourished as a performer and session musician in the Philadelphia area. Eventually, he and Haley crossed paths. Cedrone never appeared on live gigs with the Saddlemen or the Comets, but did contribute to their landmark recordings, including "Rock the Joint," and, of course, "Rock Around the Clock." Cedrone's most famous solo, in fact, was first recorded on 1952's "Rock the Joint" before replicating it on 1954's "Rock Around the Clock." He had also deployed bits of it on the Esquire Boys' 1952 recording of "Rock-a-Beatin' Boogie."

A marvelous and detailed analysis of Cedrone's solo can be found in a feature article by Wolf Marshall in *Vintage Guitar*.[4] Marshall rightly lists the many influences of guitarists past that can be heard in Cedrone's playing. Particularly evident in the two versions of the solo is the musical language of Reinhardt. The famous descending run in the ninth measure that admirers find so technically elusive is remarkably similar to the descending run heard in Reinhardt's recording of his composition, "Minor Swing," recorded with the *Quintette du Hot Club de France* on November 25, 1937. It was a common device of Reinhardt's style and admirers of Cedrone's solo should give due acknowledgement to him.

Cedrone formed his own group, the Esquire Boys, to whom Haley supplied his composition "Rock-a-Beatin' Boogie." Another Esquire Boys recording, "Caravan," Juan Tizol's classic jazz composition for the Duke Ellington Orchestra with its exotic rhythm and minor key, really brings out the Reinhardt side of Cedrone's style, and his version of Arthur Smith's "Guitar Boogie Shuffle" leans more toward the country and rhythm and blues side.

There is no doubt that Cedrone was present for some of the most important recordings that marked the trajectory of the Comets as *the* rock and roll band of its day.[5] After the band gained traction in 1954, it would be interesting to know if Cedrone would have become a permanent member of the band, both for recording and for live performances. We'll never know, because he died suddenly on June 17, 1954, just ten days after playing on Haley's versions of "Shake, Rattle and Roll" and "A.B.C. Boogie." Most accounts say he had a heart attack. Others, including his daughter, Marie Cedrone Vanore, say he fell down a flight of stairs at

---

4 Wolf Marshall, "Danny Cedrone: The First Guitar Hero," *Vintage Guitar* (March 2019), pp. 64-68.

5 It seems likely that Cedrone was Haley's first choice for the guitar chair on his recordings. Cedrone's commitment to his own band during 1953 meant he was not always available, and his place would be taken by Art Ryerson.

a restaurant, breaking his back and his neck and dying instantly.[6] He was only thirty-three years old.[7]

Cedrone's successor, Francis Eugene ("Franny") Beecher, was born in Norristown, Pennsylvania, on September 29, 1921. That means he would have been nineteen when Charlie Christian came on the scene. Beecher became a disciple of the guitarist and, Haley historian Jim Dawson proclaimed, "he could play every lick by ... Charlie Christian."[8] As it turns out, Beecher would himself play at one time in the very band his hero had graced a few years earlier, that of Benny Goodman.

In the mid-1940s, Franny Beecher teamed up with Philadelphia pianist and singer Armando "Buddy" Greco (1926-2017) as a member of the Three Sharps. Greco was an accomplished bebop pianist in the manner of Bud Powell but, like Nat "King" Cole, his singing was pushed to the forefront. After an unsuccessful year or so and a few recordings for the Musicraft label, both Greco and Beecher ended up in the Benny Goodman band in 1948. At this time, some established swing bands were experimenting with setting the new combo-oriented bebop into a big band context. Bandleaders Claude Thornhill, Boyd Raeburn, and Woody Herman were including the new music in their repertoire. Goodman threw his hat in the ring, as well. As early as 1940, he had grown restless with the commercial swing numbers and crooning ballads that brought him to prominence and began exploring the probing compositions and arrangements of writers like Mel Powell and Eddie Sauter. By the time Greco and Beecher arrived in 1948, Goodman's band was plunging into the now-entrenched bebop movement with compositions and arrangements by Chico O'Farrill such as "Bop Hop," recorded in Hollywood for Capitol Records on April 12, 1949. The personnel on that disc included some luminaries in the jazz world, including saxophonist Wardell Gray and trombonists Billy Byers and Eddie Bert. Bebop is in full flower here. O'Farrill's composition features the flowing lines of bop phrasing and prominently and frequently features

---

6 *Rock 'n' Roll is Born: The Story of Rock Around the Clock and the Dawn of the Rock 'n' Roll Era* (director and writer, Barry Barnes; Universal International Music, 2008). Cedrone died in the early morning of June 17, 1954. He had been playing at Palumbo's, a fashionable nightclub in the South Philadelphia area, and was on his way home with his partner, Bob Scale. His death certificate describes his death as "an accident" and that he fell down four steps from the restaurant above the Tap Room on Snyder Street, suffering two broken vertebrae and transection of the spinal cord. Time of death was given as 5:15 a.m., although the family legend is that he had gone out to get some sandwiches for supper.

7 Recognition of Cedrone's importance within the band and in the early development of rock and roll, despite having played on only a few Haley recordings and never an official member of the group, came when he was posthumously included with the Comets when they were belatedly inducted into the Rock and Roll Hall of Fame in 2012.

8 Jim Dawson, *Rock Around the Clock: The Record That Started the Rock Revolution* (San Francisco: Backbeat Books, 2005), p. 135.

the "flatted 5th" that is the style's clarion call. After a fine trumpet improvisation and a tenor sax solo by Gray, Greco plays a virtuoso piano solo before Goodman tries his hand at improvising over the strange new chords.

Unfortunately, we don't get to hear Franny Beecher "stretch out" his jazz chops on the Goodman recordings. Buried deep in the rhythm section, we hear the usual swing-era rhythm guitar "chonk-chonk." In fact, Beecher found his year with Goodman constraining and dull. He told John Swenson he had "no liberty whatsoever, except for some things that were inserted at my request. I came back home quite disgusted." Greco, for his part, went on to become a popular singer, taking his place among other crooners of the 1960s such as Vic Damone, Jack Jones, and Steve Lawrence.

Frank "Franny" Beecher, who would become the Comets' first full time guitarist, but here very much in the background with the Benny Goodman band. Buddy Greco is the pianist.

After Cedrone died in June 1954, Beecher worked occasionally with the Comets while working a day job and playing gigs in the Philadelphia area with accordionist Larry Wayne's trio. His first recording session for Bill Haley was for the Decca single, "Dim, Dim the Lights" and "Happy Baby" on September 21, 1954. However, there was a learning curve.

Beecher told Swenson how he was briefly admonished by Haley during the recording of "Happy Baby": "We came to an ad-lib guitar solo and I started playing with a jazz feel...Haley said he'd never sell any records if I played like that. I had to stick to major scales, no flatted fifths or anything like that."[9] Beecher not only had to "change his tune," but also change his equipment. His hollow-body Epiphone Emperor was a guitar with a sound more suited to jazz, so the Gibson guitar company supplied him with their latest Les Paul[10] solid-body guitar, which was better suited for the rocking sound and higher volume of the Comets. Beecher commented on this in 1973 interview with *Guitar Player* magazine: "Loud wasn't the word for it — Jeez! ... The feedback was tremendous ... at the volume we played, [the Emperor] just wasn't suitable."[11]

With the success of "Rock Around the Clock" the next year, Haley needed a guitarist with enough chops to at least approximate its iconic Cedrone solo that was *also* on "Rock the Joint," and, a full year after making his first recordings with the group, Beecher was offered full-time band membership in September 1955.

Even before this, Beecher had quickly established himself as far more than the keeper of Danny Cedrone's flame. On "Happy Baby," Beecher's licks over the opening riff are deft and swinging. His solo has a requisite amount of blues inflection suitable for rock and roll, but also reveals the influence and melodic vocabulary of Charlie Christian.[12] However, it also important to understand that Beecher was far from being a card-carrying bebop musician. With country and western music enjoying significant popularity in this region of Pennsylvania and New Jersey, Franny was also conversant with that style of music. Prior to his stints with Buddy Greco and Benny Goodman, he was the guitarist with The Buckaroo Ramblers, so he certainly came into the Comets with a shared affinity and skill for cowboy fare. This is clearly evident in his feature solo number, "Goofin' Around," recorded on March 23, 1956, and featured in the film *Don't Knock the Rock*. His

---

9 Swenson, p. 59.

10 Les Paul (1915-2009) was a guitarist admired by generations of jazz and rock guitarists, but was also a pioneer on the technical side of music, including multi-track recording and the development of his Les Paul guitar for Gibson that is still in great demand to this day.

11 Bob Berman, "Frank Beecher: The Bill Haley Years," *Guitar Player* (September 1973), reprinted in *Rock Guitarists* (New York: Guitar Player Books, 1975), pp. 12-15.

12 This solo is notated in Chapter 18.

style here is more in line with some of the more dazzling country session guitarists such as Nashville's Hank Garland or Los Angeles' Jimmy Bryant. Just the fact that his opening riff, difficult enough itself, is repeated in three different keys would have left most rock and roll guitar contemporaries in the dust:

Colin Escott rightly points out, "By any standards, Beecher was the most technically accomplished guitarist regularly on the charts...Few of the kids who took up the guitar in the wake of rock 'n' roll chose Beecher as a starting role model."[13]

Beecher would remain with the Comets throughout the Decca "golden years" of 1954-59. In 1960, he temporarily quit the band along with sax player Rudy Pompilii and drummer Ralph Jones and, as the Merri-Men, the three recorded one single before Beecher and Pompilii returned to the Comets in 1961, in time for the start of the band's Mexican recording contract (discussed later in this book). Soon after, however, Beecher received what he described to *Guitar Player* magazine in 1973 as an "ultimatum" from his wife, telling him to come home, and he quit the Comets again. In 1962, he was invited to rejoin the Comets to record a live album in New York City; by this time, Beecher was back working a day job in a factory and, in his 1973 interview, said eleven days of commuting to New York for the evening sessions left him exhausted and falling asleep on the job.

In 1966, Beecher formed a four-piece combo that performed at The Inn of the Four Falls in West Conshohocken, Pennsylvania, playing a "unmodified" Gibson ES-350. By 1973, he continued to play the historic venue with his band by night, while working as a foreman in a Halloween mask factory by day.[14]

By the late 1970s, Beecher was back in the Comets' orbit, at one point performing with a version of the group that toured c.1977, during the hiatus Haley took from performing.[15] In 1981, within days of Haley's death, Beecher appeared with an ad hoc Comets reunion group that performed on NBC's *Tomorrow* talk show before touring and recording a single (the B side of which, "The Hawk Talks," was an instrumental built around Beecher and Cedrone's famous Haley solos). In the late 1980s, he reunited with members of the Comets from 1954-55

---

13 Colin Escott, liner notes to *The Decca Years and More* (Bear Family Records, BCD 15506).

14 *Guitar Player* (September 1973).

15 See Chapter 10.

and toured and recorded with them until his retirement in the mid-2000s. He died on February 24, 2014, at the age of 92.

As Bill Haley and his producers made the band's transition from a cowboy country band to a rock and roll band while at Essex Records, it was decided that the addition of a saxophone (and drums) was crucial. According to "Rock Around the Clock" historian Jim Dawson, Haley first tried Anthony Liguori (stage name Tony Lance) to play baritone sax, certainly a common accoutrement to rhythm and blues bands, and the instrument we see soloing and writhing around in a mid-1950s "musical short" of the Ralph Marterie band,[16] but Lance was not a "honker," familiar with the walking-the-bar style of the prominent R&B saxophonists of the day. At the end of 1953, Bill went with an 18-year-old teenager from Philadelphia, Joey D'Ambrosio, who performed under the stage name Ambrose.

Born on March 23, 1934, Joey first studied saxophone with a local former prizefighter, Carmen Spagnolia, when he was about fourteen years old. He played in his high school band and went on to study with Mike Guerra (1888-1976), principal clarinetist and saxophonist with the Philadelphia Orchestra. Guerra also taught jazz tenor legends John Coltrane and Michael Brecker, and baritone saxophonist Gerry Mulligan. Joey grew up listening to the bebop greats, among them the "Four Brothers" of the late-1940s Woody Herman Orchestra: Al Cohn, Zoot Sims, Herbie Steward, and Serge Chaloff. He was also influenced by tenor man Wardell Gray, mentioned earlier as a member of the Benny Goodman "bebop" band with Franny Beecher. As all jazz learners do, Joey copied great improvisations off the records, but had no real idea of the chords underneath.

At the same time, Ambrose was also deeply into the great jazz/R&B crossover saxophonists. He was particularly impressed with tenor man Red Prysock's stunning solo on the Tiny Bradshaw 1953 recording of "Heavy Juice."[17] After all, he was a teenage boy at the time and teenage boys were crazy about bar-walker tenor players and their showboating. Mastery of that style was particularly handy when he was playing in strip clubs. "I was fifteen. I couldn't drink in there, but they let me play," Joey remembered. On one occasion, he was playing with his own band next door to a club the Comets were playing. Joey considered them a hillbilly band and was not that interested in playing with them but, when the offer was made, he followed up and auditioned at Comets drummer Dick Richards' house. Starting out only part-time, his authentic R&B sound and stage routine sent the teenage

---

16 *Ralph Marterie and His Orchestra* (1955), directed by John Sherwood (Universal-International). Information (incomplete) accessed on the Internet Movie Database (imdb.com) on January 27, 2021.

17 Much of the information in this portion of the chapter, and quotations, are from a phone interview with Joey D'Ambrosio by David Lee Joyner on October 24, 2019.

audiences into hysterics and Haley promoted him to full-time. Having a real teenager in a band of middle-aged musicians helped as well.

Joey's first recording with the Comets was made while they were still with the Essex label. "Straight-Jacket," released in 1954 with Bill Haley given the song-writing credit, is considered the precursor to Rudy Pompilii's 1956 "Rudy's Rock." While intended to be a rocking showcase for the tenor saxophone — and the group's first-ever instrumental release — D'Ambrosio's solo is buried beneath the band's ceaseless and overbalanced group vocal, repeating "straight jacket!" for the duration of the recording. Joey recalled the session as Haley or someone telling him and the band "just play some blues." Fortunately, his playing is more at the forefront with the Comets' appearance in the film *Round Up of Rhythm*, in which the song is performed with the backing vocals restricted to only one part of the tune.

Joey d'Ambrosio, here pictured late in his life and still active as a saxophone player. Joey would leave the Comets to form The Jodimars in 1955.

Dick Richards told Hydra Records owner Klaus Kettner,[18] in an interview for Germany's *Rock 'n' Roll* magazine, "All instrumentals and arrangements from that time were worked out by Joey...Without Joey's influence, we probably would have stayed an unknown western swing band." Indeed, it is a common belief that Joey cooked up the "shout chorus" ensemble riff on "Rock Around the Clock," powered by his tenor saxophone lead over the guitars.[19]

After the band moved to Decca, Joey was present for all the landmark recordings that helped establish rock and roll between April 1954 and the fall of 1955, including "Rock Around the Clock," "Thirteen Women," "Shake, Rattle and

---

18 Klaus Kettner is a well-known Haley afficionado who lives and works in Munich. He has acquired a significant collection of Haley-related artifacts and memorabilia for his Bill Haley Museum, which was located in Munich, but now enjoys a nomadic and part-time existence. Kettner was a major promoter of European tours by the Original Comets (a.k.a. the 1954-55 Comets) who reformed in the late 1980s and toured widely until the late 2000s. Kettner authored the book *Rockin' Around Europe 1958*, detailing the Comets' historic European tour.. (English Edition, Munich, Germany: Hydra Records, 2024)

19 Fuchs, pp. 127-8. This belief, however, is not supported by the fact that the basis of the riff appears in the middle of the guitar solo in the earlier recording of the song by Sonny Dae and his Knights.

Roll," "A.B.C. Boogie," "Happy Baby," "Dim, Dim the Lights," "Birth of the Boogie," "Mambo Rock," "Two Hound Dogs," and "Razzle-Dazzle."

After an internal pay dispute at the peak of their early success in 1955, D'Ambrosio, Richards, and bass player Marshall Lytle left the Comets and formed the Jodimars, a band that lasted until 1958. D'Ambrosio settled in Las Vegas in 1964, where he spent twenty-five years working at Caesars Palace.[20] Over the years, he played in a group with his brother-in-law, both as a stand-alone act and as a backup band for others. He deepened his knowledge of jazz theory performing and studying with faculty at the College of Southern Nevada, such as pianist Tom Ferguson, and the University of Nevada Las Vegas, such as pianist Stefan Karlson. In the late 1980s, as had Franny Beecher, he reunited with members of the 1954-55 contingent of the Comets (also including Richards, Lytle, and Johnny Grande) for a series of special concerts that led to the reformed group continuing to perform for many years after. When not playing Comets and rock and roll revivals, he was content to watch John Coltrane DVDs in the afternoon and play jazz sessions in the evenings. He died on August 9, 2021.

His successor, Rudy Pompilii, was not only the Comets' most famous saxophonist, but also Bill Haley's loyal partner who was often the only one that stood between the band and its demise. This is not the place to recount the many tales of Pompilii and his personal and business relationship with Haley over more than twenty years, but, instead, it is to chronicle his jazz background and what that contributed to the Comets' unique character in rock and roll.

Rudolph Pompilii[21] was born on April 16, 1924, in Chester, Pennsylvania, the place that remained home for him all his life. His Italian-American family was devoutly Catholic. He served as an infantryman during World War II.[22] He got his musical training in high school, starting on clarinet, as many saxophonists of the day did. In the early 1950s, he could be found in the Chester area playing jazz with the Four Horsemen, a group that included drummer Ralph Jones, who would one day also become a Comet.

As Bill Haley and the Saddlemen were catching on in the Chester area, they caught Rudy's attention and, much as the character of Steve Hollis does in the movie *Rock Around the Clock*, he thought he should drop in at Haley's gig to see

---

20 "Las Vegan Joe D'Ambrosio Among Rock Hall of Fame Inductees," *Las Vegas Review Journal*, April 15, 2012.

21 This issue of the spelling of Rudy's last name was addressed in Chapter 4, Footnote 30. In addition to using the spelling "Pompilli" as his stage name, he also occasionally signed his autographs "Rudy Pell." It is possible, but unconfirmed, that Rudy's use of the name "Pell" might have been a nod towards Dave Pell, a West Coast tenor player who led a "cool jazz" octet that was popular in the 1950s.

22 Rudy was known to have claimed to have been a prisoner of war. However, his military record is now publicly available and it is known to be untrue. He served as a bandsman in the 84th Infantry Division.

what was going on. Haley himself told the crowd at the Comets' 1969 Bitter End gig what Rudy's first impression was: "The saxophone players who at the beginning used to call us hillbillies ... this guy was one of them."[23]

Rudy joined trumpeter Ralph Marterie's orchestra in 1955, which survived the demise of the big bands with a hit on "Caravan," a dead ringer — albeit orchestrated for a larger band — of the Danny Cedrone/Esquire Boys version. Marterie also did a cover of Haley's "Crazy Man, Crazy" in 1953. After being a member of the Comets for two years, Rudy supposedly won the annual reader's poll for best saxophonist in the tenor/baritone category as listed in the December 26, 1957 issue of *Downbeat* magazine. This has been repeated in previous biographies[24] but, after looking at the poll listing in that particular issue, Pompilii is nowhere to be found. It is unclear who made the claim, perhaps Rudy himself, but it has been potent enough to be propagated through the ages without fact-checking.

Once Pompilii joined the Comets, now playing tenor saxophone, he towed the line and left his bebop vocabulary at the door, confining himself largely to saxophone licks more common to rhythm and blues. His tone did not have the fullness and edge of Joey D'Ambrosio's, perhaps due in part to his use of the traditional rubber or plastic mouthpiece, rather than the metal Berg Larsen or Otto Link mouthpiece used by D'Ambrosio, Red Prysock, and other R&B saxophonists.[25] When he played loudly (which he probably did most of the time), his tone became a bit unfocused and overblown and he was sometimes out of tune, but his specialty was his high range. Saxophonists call the upper extreme range the *altissimo* register,[26] which is achieved by unusual key fingerings and extreme control of the *embouchure*, or how the lips surround the mouthpiece and reed. At the other end of the tenor saxophone range, a player can generate great excitement by playing the lowest notes with great force: "honking." It is the saxophone equivalent of giving a good rap on a bass drum. These effects, combined with all of Rudy's on-stage physical "walking the bar" antics, made him a show in himself and he and the Comets saw to it that there were musical vehicles to bring it off.

The first replacement for Comets drummer Dick Richards had been a young Don Raymond. He turned out to be temperamentally unsuitable for the band and left after a matter of weeks. Ralph Jones was the next to get the call, no doubt at

---

23 *The Warner Brothers Years and More* (Bear Family Records BCD 16157).

24 Citations include Haley,, Jr./Benjaminson, p. 110; Swenson, p. 61, implied by Haley/von Hoelle, p. 109.

25 D'Ambrosio did indeed, at this time, play with a Berg Larsen mouthpiece. As of 2019, the 85-year-old was still playing the Selmer balanced-action tenor saxophone he played back in the day.

26 In the R&B saxophone world, alto saxophonist Earl Bostic (1935-1965) was a specialist in *altissimo* high notes.

Rudy's suggestion. Jones was a Chester resident, born in 1921. He was almost eleven when he first played drums in the band of the Immaculate Heart School in Chester. He told the story of how Clarence Cottman, an old ragtime musician passed by the school and heard the band rehearsing. Allegedly, he told Ralph "You're coming with me, son. I like your style." He joined Bob Talone's band whilst still a student at Chester High School, describing the experience as "playing the smooth riffs for several hundred dancing couples in St. Hedwig's auditorium." The temptation of a career in music became irresistible during his final year at high school when he grabbed the chance of joining a "hot combo" working on an ocean liner. He celebrated his sixteenth birthday on the ship whilst sailing to many places including West Africa, the West Indies, and Europe.

At first inspired by the work of Louis Armstrong and Earl Hines, he would then discover the blues. "The music was changing in those days. The two beat was changing to a four beat and soon the rage was swing." In 1938 he would join Len Mayfair's swing band, based in Chester, which he described as a "strictly four-beat". Whilst this put food on the family dining table, Ralph's biggest thrill was sitting in with famous bands visiting his hometown. "At the El Rancho it was a thrill to sit in with Wingy Manone's jazz band. I also substituted in Leon (Louis's brother) Prima's outfit.... Gee, it was always swell to play jazz with the old New Orleans kick."

During the war, in which he spent three years as a radio operator, his biggest thrill had been appearing in "War Bond" shows. Asked "Are you still playing old time jazz?," he replied with a grin, "The truth is, you know, I've switched. I've switched to bop. You know, bebop. The newest thing. You can describe bop as a shock treatment or a brassy *blitzkrieg*, whatever you wish. But the trouble is you don't understand it. The truth is that bebop really is jazz. It's progressive jazz."[27] In 1947, Ralph was a member of "Little Ernie's Four Horsemen," a band in which Rudy Pompilii was also a member. Ralph & Rudy would revert to this band when they quit the Comets in 1960.

The most famous and successful of the Rudy feature numbers was "Rudy's Rock," which also showcased Jones's drumming. With the composition credits given to Pompilii and Haley, it was the successor to Joey D'Ambrosio's "Straight-Jacket." It's really more of a riff than a composition, but it is strikingly reminiscent of the riff in Lester Young's famous "Lester Leaps In," recorded for Columbia on September 5, 1939, one of the most influential and landmark recordings in jazz. In Rudy and the Comets' recording of "Rudy's Rock" at Decca's Pythian Temple New

---

27 Much of the material for the two paragraphs comes from the *Delaware County Daily Times* of August 12, 1949.

York studio on March 23, 1956,[28] we hear a much more jazz-influenced version of the tune than in the countless later versions. First of all, drummer Ralph Jones, Rudy's former bandmate in the Four Horsemen who joined the Comets in the fall of 1955, starts with a standard jazz ride pattern on the cymbals.

The sound and vocabulary of "Prez" Lester Young is readily apparent in Rudy's playing. After he plays the introductory riff, he leads into the main theme with a classic Young lick over an augmented chord:

Another Young trademark is playing the same note (the saxophone's "C") repeatedly, but using alternate fingerings to get a different sound for each repetition of the note.

In the middle of the piece, Rudy's saxophone cadenza is introduced by Jones playing a tom-tom lead-in that is an obvious tip of the hat to Gene Krupa's famous beat on "Sing, Sing, Sing" with Benny Goodman's band. Rudy's solo here also puts forth Young stylings, as well as a well-rehearsed pattern over the aforementioned augmented chords that is more in line with modern bebop vocabulary:

Now and then, the big band music of the Comets' youth would appear in their own recordings, such as on the *Madison* album recorded for Orfeon in Mexico in late 1962 during a period of the band's history in which instrumental performances dominated. With Pompilii still with the group, here we find Mercer Ellington's "Things Ain't What They Used to Be," Duke Ellington's "C Jam Blues," and the Glenn Miller band's "Tuxedo Junction," though highly stylized to fit the dance crazes of the time.[29]

On September 15, 1962, Bill Haley and the Comets recorded a special radio program for the Armed Forces Network (AFN) in Germany while doing a successful run at The Star Club in Hamburg. Instead of being a run-through of their greatest hits, the program ended up being, at least in part, a history of jazz. Haley

---

28 The first had been on the Columbia Films soundstage in January 1956, for the film *Rock Around the Clock.*

29 These standards were retitled for local consumption. For example, "Things Ain't What They Used to Be," "C Jam Blues," and "Tuxedo Junction" became "El Madison," "Madison en Azul," and "Reunion de Etiqueta."

is interviewed and introduces songs and performances well out of the norm for a Comets presentation (indeed, the only song associated with the group is a rendition of their roll-call number, "The Saints Rock 'n Roll"). Aside from Pompilii, the band at this point included Johnny Kay on guitar and Dave Holly on drums, along with Billy Williamson on steel guitar, Al Rappa on bass, and Johnny Grande on piano. Haley and Williamson step to the sidelines for most of the jazz numbers performed. The recording of this broadcast gives us a rare and thrilling glimpse into Pompilii's marvelous jazz abilities on both clarinet *and* tenor saxophone. Two performances from the broadcast are worth detailed examination.[30]

"The World is Waiting for the Sunrise," composed by Ernest Seitz and Eugene Lockhart in 1918, was a high-speed tour-de-force for the Benny Goodman Trio and Quartet in the 1930s. The Comets render an excellent recreation of the Goodman small group, and Rudy gets to show off his superb clarinet playing, closely replicating signature Goodman licks effortlessly.[31] At the end of the performance, the announcer actually names the members of the Comets as "Benny Goodman, Teddy Wilson, Gene Krupa and all the boys in the band" in tribute.

Bernie Miller wrote his classic "Bernie's Tune" in 1952. It was first brought to prominence by the West Coast recording of baritone saxophonist Gerry Mulligan and trumpeter Chet Baker. Dave Holly, Johnny Kay, and Rudy are definitely in their element, swinging like mad while Johnny Grande lays low and hangs on for dear life on piano. With his buttery tone and bouncy swing phrasing, Rudy conjures up the tenor saxophone greats of the day — Al Cohn, Zoot Sims, and Stan Getz — and the AFN performance shows he had the potential to stand among them as the jazz great *Downbeat* poll voters saw in him. After playing the song's melody, he plays a wonderful solo break leading into his first improvised chorus, chock full of bebop language such as the last two notes here:

---

30 The sessions were released on the CD *On the Air* (Hydra Records BCK27112) in 2001.

31 In a conversation at her home on April 24, 2021, Martha Haley told David Lee Joyner that Rudy practiced clarinet all the time, even though it was of little use in a rock 'n' roll band like the Comets. It is worth noting that many saxophonists in the early years of jazz got their formal training on clarinet, and it was a common double in swing bands. Rudy obviously maintained a love for the instrument that is on full display here.

More bebop *lingua franca* is heard in the fifth bar of his first chorus:

Like the Haley guitarists, Pompilii had a bit of country music in him, inspired by an unlikely tenor man. In the late 1950s, the Nashville studio stable welcomed "Boots" Randolph, born Homer Rudolph Randolph III in Cadiz, Kentucky, on June 3, 1927 (he died in 2007). Randolph's calling card was his composition (along with James Rich), "Yakety Sax." The song was modeled after the staccato "chicken tenor" solo by R&B saxophone great King Curtis on the Coasters' recording of "Yakety Yak," a novelty doo-wop song written by Jerry Leiber and Mike Stoller and released on the Atco label in 1958.[32] "Yakety Sax" kept the country two-beat feel of the Coasters recording and Boots expanded the style of the King Curtis solo to create a cross between a tough Texas tenor and a fiddle. The novelty song included quotes from the circus classic, "Entrance of the Gladiators," and the English folk fiddle tune, "The Girl I Left Behind."

After first recording it unsuccessfully in 1958, Randolph re-recorded it for a single released in April 1963 that rose to No. 35 on the rock charts. According to Hugh McCallum in his *Haley News*, Pompilii was a great admirer of Randolph. This is corroborated by mid-1970s Haley guitarist Bill Turner in an email to David Lee Joyner on November 1, 2019: "Rudy *did* like Boots Randolph's playing — and had this style down cold, too. He knew that *this* was the exclusive style they used in Nashville recording studios, so he made sure he had Boots' playing style totally mastered."[33]

Rudy and the Comets recorded a cover version of "Yakety Sax" in Las Vegas in 1964.[34] There are also live recordings of Pompilii playing it in Sweden in June 1968 and at The Bitter End in New York on December 16, 1969. In most cases, Rudy

---

32 Adam Bernstein, "Boots Randolph, 80; Versatile Musician Recorded 'Yakety Sax'," *Washington Post*, July 4, 2007.

33 It is worth noting Randolph's considerable jazz side. He recorded with New Orleans trumpeter Al Hirt and was part of a Nashville "all-star" group that played jazz standards, including guitarists Chet Atkins and Hank Garland, and budding jazz vibraphonist Gary Burton. This group was to play at the 1960 Newport Jazz Festival, but was cancelled due to a riot (shades of the Comets in England and Germany in 1957-58!). Instead, they made an album for RCA in Nashville of the music they would have done, appropriately entitled *After the Riot at Newport*. Randolph's tenor on "Riot-Chorus" is similar to Duke Ellington's Paul Gonsalves. His alto sax on "Relaxin'" reminds the listener of West Coast alto men Dick Nash or Bud Shank.

34 Guest Star LP GS-1455, *Boots Randolph*, issued under Boots Randolph's name only..

does not replicate the short, "ricky-ticky" articulation of Randolph, but brings a slightly more relaxed jazz and R&B phrasing to the song.

Despite Rudy's fine playing and his prominent role in the Comets' stage shows, he had no real following of his own. The idea for Rudy to record his own album seems to have originated in July 1974, when Bill first announced it on stage at The Oaks Club in Sacramento, California. The album was to be Bill's "thank you" to Rudy for those years, and, as the tour progressed, they discussed the concept, whether it should be jazz, rock and roll, or a mixture of the two. Sadly, completing it would become a race against time. After complaining of chest pains and congestion, Rudy was diagnosed with lung cancer. He knew that he now had limited time to make his own album.[35] At the final moment, Bill was to let Rudy down, and played no part in its making. It was a thrown-together affair, recorded for the European-based Sonet label in 1975.[36] Sam Charters, who produced it, as well as two of Haley's albums for Sonet, wanted to keep costs to a minimum and used a local studio near Rudy's home to save him the travel time. Though the cover of the album bills it as by Rudy Pompilii & The Comets, the only official Comet to take part was bass player Jim Lebak, who had only joined the band the previous year. The remainder were local session musicians: Tom Keel (piano), Herb Hutchinson (guitar, later to become a Comet), and Bill Pfender (drums, who had been a member of Ernest Tubb's Texas Troubadours and also a band run by Ray "Pudge" Parsons, who was a rhythm guitarist and featured vocalist with the Comets for much of the 1970s). As Charters recalled, "Sadly enough, the musicians weren't right. [Rudy] knew it, I knew it, and they knew it."[37]

Released in 1976 after Rudy's death, the album, with the verbose title *Rudy's Rock: The Sax That Changed the World*, was indeed a disappointment, a present-ation little better than a hotel lounge band, neither good rock and roll nor good jazz. The jazz aficionado might have hoped to hear an unencumbered Rudy Pompilii returning to his swing and bebop roots, interacting with a stellar group of New York or Philadelphia jazz luminaries. Sonet contributed to the debacle by failing to get any sort of wide distribution and by mastering the tracks so that they were a half tone flat. The record was only sold in the U.K. and, as a result, it is now a rare collectors' item. In a dream world, with today's technology, someone would take Rudy's sax tracks and add new backing tracks played by first-rate jazz and

---

35 This information was received in e-mails to Chris Gardner from Bill Turner.

36 The exact date appears to be uncertain.

37 Swenson, p. 149.

rock and roll musicians. Until that happens, the album is a worthwhile testament to Rudy's musicianship, but it could have been so much better.[38]

With no proper recorded documentation of Rudy Pompilii's jazz playing, we will have to settle for reliable testimony that he indeed continued to actively perform jazz, classical, country, and even polkas back in his hometown of Chester, Pennsylvania. In a November 2019 email, Bill Turner recalled:

> When I'd spend time at Rudy's house, he'd bring me to these afternoon gigs he had —and they were *all* big band-style jazz. He had a *lot* of friends who were *great* musicians — great pianists, horn players and when they played together it was fantastic. The guy who owned the local sandwich shop, Mike, was a fabulous jazz trumpet player. When I first went to Chester, PA, I thought there would be a lot of Bill Haley's music being played everywhere ... but I was wrong — it was jazz and the music of Frank Sinatra that was everywhere ... but that was the kind of crowd that Rudy hung out with.
>
> As far as I know, Rudy's two favorite sax players were Stan Getz and John Coltrane. When I played in the local clubs with Rudy, he did a lot of commercial music, rather than heavy jazz. Another Boots Randolph song he played and sang was "Big Daddy's Alabama Bound," which really tore the house down. He also played terrific polkas on both sax and clarinet. Seriously, the *only* music I never heard Rudy play ... was the modern "funk" style ... but I'm sure he could certainly do it. Back then, disco was just starting to come in (in New York), but it hadn't caught on in Chester, PA, yet — so nobody was playing it yet.

Even though the jazz nuance was subtle in the music of Bill Haley and the Comets, it was nevertheless present and helped to establish Northeast rock and roll, as rock historian Charlie Gillett labeled it, as a distinctive approach compared to, say, Elvis Presley in Memphis or Buddy Holly in Lubbock, Texas. So-called "jazz-informed" elements in rock and pop music have always opened new possibilities and enriched a musical milieu that tends to favor simplicity and technical conservatism. Cream's drummer, Ginger Baker, was heavily influenced by jazz drummer Art Blakey. Jazz alto saxophonist Phil Woods' solo on Billy Joel's recording of "Just the Way You Are" is considered as much a part of the song as the composition itself, as is jazz tenor saxophonist Pete Christlieb's sumptuous solo on Natalie Cole's recording of "Unforgettable."

---

38 There is a detailed appraisal of this album in Chapter 22.

Bill Haley's son, Pedro, is correct in insisting that his father's band didn't just happen to have some jazz musicians in it; jazz is indeed a key element in defining what the Comets were all about.

The "Classic" Comets' line up during the period 1955-1959. L. to r. Al Rex (Piccirilli), Johnny Grande, Frank Beecher, Bill Haley, Billy Williamson, Ralph Jones & Rudy Pompilii.

Franny Beecher with Benny Goodman and legendary saxophonist Wardell Gray.

Ralph Jones with organist Frank Mingus.

CHAPTER 16
Into the 1970s

The dawn of the 1970s brought about a new era in popular music. Rock was now mainstream music; it was entering its third decade and so was its audience. The kids that were thrilled by Bill Haley's "Rock Around the Clock" were now the age he and most of his band were when they introduced the song in 1954. The rock and roll revival concerts of the late 1960s, in which Haley and the Comets played a big part, brought their music back like a ten-year class reunion, but also gave the second-generation rockers a chance to check out 1950s rock and roll for themselves.

The youth of the 1960s created and/or followed a significant evolution in rock music. Though rock and roll demonstrated great diversity from its beginnings, as Haley witnessed from the first Feld Brothers' revue tours he made with LaVern Baker, Big Joe Turner, and others, the music of the time was still largely simple, short, danceable, and light in subject matter.[1] This continued into the first half of the 1960s with the rhythm and blues/soul music coming from Ray Charles, Aretha Franklin, and Stax and Motown Records, or the surf music of the Beach Boys and the Ventures. Beatlemania and the First British Invasion added a new wrinkle, but the music remained, in the eyes of the older music establishment, "greasy kid stuff." Though they can't take all the credit, a flashpoint was the Beatles' retreat from live performance into the studio to produce the ambitious *Sgt. Pepper's Lonely Hearts Club Band* album, released in 1967. Rock music had grown up. By then, even the adult pop music stalwart Columbia Records acquiesced and started releasing rock and rock-like artists such as Simon & Garfunkel, Blood Sweat & Tears, Chicago, and Janis Joplin.

---

1 However, Bill Haley's 1956 recording of "Teenager's Mother (Are You Right?)" (Lewis, McFarland) is probably a worthy candidate for the title of rock and roll's first message song, tackling the thorny subject of the relationship between parents and teenaged offspring.

As the 1970s dawned, rock (increasingly no longer associated with "roll") appeared in many forms to appeal to a diverse audience encompassing the aging and the young. Whereas Bill Haley and the Comets had filled stadiums around the world in the 1950s, that kind of draw was now commonly expected for performers in the '70s — inspired by the unexpected success of the Woodstock festival in 1969 — as were record sales in the multi-millions. In the aftermath of the Vietnam War, the edgy counterculture music gave way to big-business pursuits and the rock music industry was growing by twenty-five percent a year. Though 1970s culture and its music might be viewed as superficial and money-grabbing — author Tom Wolfe famously dubbed it the "Me Generation" — the decade also produced a wide range of styles. Singer-songwriters such as Carole King and Neil Diamond, second-generation British invader Elton John, and former jingle-writer Barry Manilow offered a softer side of rock, whereas heavy metal and hard-rock artists like Led Zeppelin and Black Sabbath purveyed music with more hair and fangs.

British bands carrying on the lofty goals implied by the latter-day Beatles created a classical/rock fusion commonly labeled "art rock" that could be heard in the music of King Crimson, Yes, and Emerson Lake & Palmer. However, from the same country, the class consciousness that gave us the Haley-loving and riotous Teddy Boys in the 1950s gave us Johnny Rotten and the Sex Pistols, fervently pushing back against the polished and erudite rock music status quo with their in-your-face "punk" music. In the second half of the 1970s, a dance craze reminiscent of the Twist in the early 1960s grew out of the urban clubs in the form of disco.

Meanwhile, the country music industry was certainly not living in a vacuum and neither was its audience. Young musicians far outside the Nashville industrial complex were conjuring up a country/rock hybrid. In the 1960s, Buck Owens had already challenged Nashville with his more electric-sounding country music out of Bakersfield, California that must have had some part to play in injecting rock sensibilities into honky-tonk music. By the end of the 1960s, also in California, Gram Parsons, Linda Ronstadt, the Flying Burrito Brothers, and the Nitty Gritty Dirt Band claimed a new type of country music for a new generation. Back in the American South, the Allman Brothers Band and Lynyrd Skynyrd came out with a fusion labeled "southern rock." Texas native Willie Nelson, who had composed monumental hit songs for other artists in Nashville (such as Patsy Cline's "Crazy"), never really got any traction there as a performing artist, so he returned to his home state and reinvented himself, arrayed with jeans, a bandana, long hair, and a beard, and nurturing a uniquely Texas cowboy-hippy culture with his "redneck rock" or "outlaw country."

The country music version of soft rock was heard in the music of artists like Barbara Mandrell, a multi-instrumentalist and singer who was the female country version of Las Vegas headliner Wayne Newton. Canadian Anne Murray reached No. 1 on the *Billboard* Hot 100 chart with "Snowbird" in 1970. Kenny Rogers, formally of the California-based First Edition, former R&B singer Ronnie Milsap, and former jazz and rockabilly pianist Charlie Rich all crossed over to the country side to offer similarly soft music. Elvis Presley also tapped into this new kind of country music to greet the 1970s. His 1970 hit, "Kentucky Rain," was written by "new" country singer Eddie Rabbit. He also covered Willie Nelson compositions, as well as a number of country music classics in his later career.[2] In mainstream pop, this type of music was eventually labeled "adult contemporary;" in the country music sphere, this wide-appealing music became known as "country-politan."

By the 1970s, Bill Haley was enjoying being hidden away with his third family in Mexico, content to make an occasional revival appearance, repeatedly recreating the music of his glory days in the 1950s. Following the failure of his efforts for J. D. Musil and United Artists to generate any success in 1967-68, he didn't seem particularly interested in pursuing any kind of musical innovation or attempt to recreate himself. He would turn fifty in 1975 and, like most people his age, musician or not, he did not feel compelled to keep up with or give much comment about current trends in popular music. When he did comment, it was usually along the lines of how far newer rockers had strayed from his "real" rock and roll. In his interview with Otto Fuchs, Pedro Haley gives insight as to his father's musical tastes at the time:

> There has been some criticism that my dad didn't keep up more with rock music, and that's mostly true, but I know that he kept up more with contemporary country music than rock. He was a great admirer of Willie Nelson. Another major factor in Dad's drinking, I believe, was his unrequited aspirations to sing country music again. Time and time again, I can remember his love of country music. He stayed true to his original love and he wanted to go back to it. As anyone can see from the recording history, he did try to record country music, but it was never strongly promoted. I think no one could put Bill Haley back into the country music scene. He was rock and roll, not country. That's what the average person would immediately pigeonhole him into.[3]

---

2 Alan Hanson, "Elvis Presley…Is He 'The King of Country Music'?", Elvis History Blog.com (January 2012).

3 Fuchs, p. 953.

While it is true that Haley did not have the confidence of Milt Gabler or other producers and managers to return to country music, it is also clear that he also had his own doubts about letting go of his threadbare rock and roll lifeline and diving back into country music with firm commitment. Repeatedly, he would retreat from his chance to make a country music comeback, such as the case with his recording of "That's How I Got to Memphis" for United Artists in 1968. Written by Nashville songwriter/storyteller Tom T. Hall, it was a perfect fit for Haley at this point in his musical life, but not in his view. His guitarist Johnny Kay remembers:

Tom T. Hall, composer of "That's How I Got to Memphis".

He didn't particularly like the song, and the producer only let him do one take. Without his knowledge, the producer replaced the band (except for my guitar) and added a harmonica and strings because he wanted a modern country sound. [Bill] was furious [and had] wanted it to be a Comets-style record. He screamed at the record producer, "It's not rock 'n' roll." No, it wasn't rock. It was modern country. I personally loved it and so did Rudy [Pompilii]. Bill sounded fabulous and the overall sound was up-to-date. I still feel it was better than anything he sang in the 1960s. In fact, on the strength of this recording, Bill had an offer to be a regular on the *Grand Ole Opry* shows in Nashville. He flatly refused, saying he would not revert to being a country singer. While Bill did the promotion that was required of him, he never sang it in his shows or went out of his way to push it. This song made it to No. 10 in the country charts without any promotion from Mr. Haley.[4]

Back in his days with Warner Brothers, Haley similarly refused to conform to the highly produced country format with strings and such; he was similarly wary

---

4 These quotes are a composite from liner notes from the CD *Johnny Kay: Tale of a Comet (Bill Haley and Friends Vol. 4)* (Hydra BCK 27139, 2009), and David Hirschberg's article in *Now Dig This*, June 2010. The authors have not been able to find supporting evidence for the claims regarding the *Grand Ole Opry* and the chart-placing, apart from a *Haley News* report of single listing as the tenth most played track on a local US radio station.

of such augmentations of his unreleased 1967 recording of "Jealous Heart."

As recounted previously, Haley signed with the Swedish-based Sonet label during his successful 1968 tour of that country, recording a studio album of remakes of Decca-era hits and two live albums. Oddly enough, according to biographer John Swenson, Haley himself suggested an album of country songs for his fourth Sonet release, under the production supervision of Sam Charters. The resulting album, *Rock Around the Country*, was recorded in Nashville in 1970. The views of both Charters and Swenson as to how successful this was may very well reflect Haley's own skepticism as to his future in country music, with Charters saying, "You don't know whether to continue the old direction or try something new. And Bill himself could never decide. Usually at the last moment he opted out and sort of scurried back to what he knew he could do and what he knew was successful."[5]

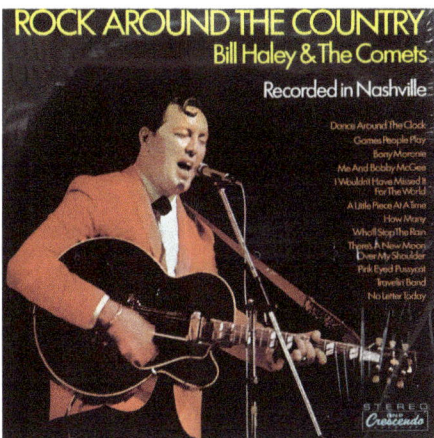

The cover of Bill Haley's *Rock Around the Country* LP, recorded for Sonet in 1968.

Echoing Milt Gabler's comment that Haley didn't have a good voice for country music (Chapter 12), Charters got down to specifics: "I didn't believe there was any hope for Bill Haley singing country and western ballads. Bill's voice is a high voice, it's kind of a light voice, and the great country singers have a much heavier voice. Bill had a wonderful cheeriness with that voice, and I couldn't see him doing the kind of ballads he wanted to do."[6]

It has always been the case that music directed at the youth market is more successful if the male singer has a higher range and a youthful voice that teenage boys and girls can relate to. Haley had made the successful transition from cowboy crooner and yodeler to the required sound of rock and roll and youth appeal by singing in his upper range in high keys (such as the key of A for "Rock Around the Clock"), but taking on country music of the 1950s and '60s required a different set of chops. The Nashville Sound vocal quality of Eddy Arnold or Jim Reeves was baritone in range and rich in timbre, as opposed to Haley's lighter, more reedy sound. On the other hand, honky-tonk singers like George Jones or Ernest Tubb had a grit and earthiness that was also beyond Haley's reach.

---

5 Swenson, p. 142.

6 Ibid.

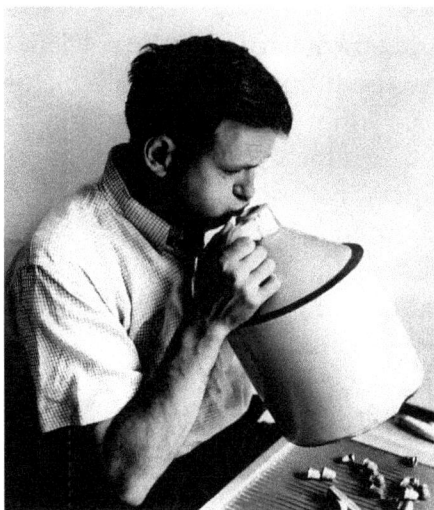

Sam Charters, the producer of Haley's album, pictured here in 1968 playing the jug.

Regarding marketability, we must also keep in mind that country music at this point was still aiming at the adult audience, be they the "sophisticate" consumers of the Nashville Sound or the working-class consumers of honky tonk. Neither group was attracted to men who sang with a high, emasculated voice. (A notable exception could be made for the "high lonesome tenor" of bluegrass or the screaming lead tenor in male gospel quartets.) Only after Elvis Presley and the Everly Brothers began lurking around Music Row did Nashville start to figure out that they had better start wooing the youth market, and that doubling down on the adult market would only carry them so far. Now Haley was in a real mess. His voice didn't match the Nashville status quo and, once they shift-ed their target audience, Haley was far too old to sell "young country." Yet, as he navigated his way through country music to find his niche, he occasionally hit on a song that at least offered artistic if not commercial possibilities.

Like the "That's How I Got to Memphis" single, *Rock Around the Country* yielded another convincing performance that held promise for Haley's return to country music, a version of Kris Kristofferson's "Me and Bobby McGee," the song made popular a few months after Haley recorded it when Janis Joplin's version was released posthumously. Like "Memphis," it was convincing to everyone but Haley himself. "He just didn't think he could do that one at all," Charters recalled, wist-fully.[7] However, much as *Rock Around the Country* was an artistic success (which will be discussed further in Chapter 22), it was a commercial failure, which only added to Haley's hopelessness and lack of direction.

Placing Bill Haley in the context of 1970s popular music reveals both sides of a coin. On the one hand, his instincts were probably correct, that he didn't have a viable commercial path outside of his 1950s revival act. He wasn't necessarily lazy or unambitious; he was just a realist. On the other hand, if he had been in better health and a better frame of mind, he might not have been as riddled with self-doubt as to his potential to return to the softer rock/country "country-politan" that was active at that time. If he had been afforded the good fortune that, say, Johnny Cash had in the final years of his life when he recorded a series of albums

---

7 Swenson, p. 143.

produced by Rick Rubin that reintroduced him to a new generation, the promise of what we hear in "That's How I Got to Memphis" and "Me and Bobby McGee" may have borne much more fruit.

Two pictures taken on November 23, 1979 at the Crawley Leisure Centre, the night after
Bill had taken part in the Royal Command Performance in London.

PART 3
Focus on Music

CHAPTER 17
Focus on Music (1946-1953)

The first known recordings involving Bill are transcription discs made by the Down Homers in the Spring of 1946 for WTIC, Hartford, Connecticut. Bill sings solo on "She Taught Me to Yodel" in the same key as Kenny Roberts's recorded version (D major), but with a significantly shorter yodel, and shying away from Roberts's astonishing falsetto finale. For the rest, Bill is on rhythm guitar and sings tenor in harmony vocals *á la* Sons of the Pioneers. It is a competent performance by a young man stepping up to a new level of music-making in a band that had a nationwide audience on network radio.

Bob Miller

In Chapter 14, we learned of another influence on Bill, in the shape of Elton Britt, who recorded the 1942 World War II hit "There's a Star-Spangled Banner Waving Somewhere." That, however, did not show off Britt's yodeling fireworks. For that, you would need to hear "Chime Bells," co-written by Bob Miller[1] recorded for RCA Victor in 1947. The song begins in Germanic style in waltz time. Britt gives an admirable yodeling display. Halfway in, the waltz tempo speeds up considerably and finally transforms into a quick two-beat rhythm. It is here that Britt unleashes his jaw-dropping technique, shifting from his falsetto to his chest voice with the speed of a

---

1 Miller also co-wrote "Star Spangled Banner" under the pseudonym "Shelby Darnell." Miller was discussed in Chapter 14.

drum roll. At the climax, Britt reaches a high F, a vocal cord-shredding note for any male singer, even in falsetto. He holds the note for about twenty seconds while the orchestra quotes a series of songs, including "Turkey in the Straw" and "There's a Star-Spangled Banner Waving Somewhere." After a brief tapering off, Britt goes to the high F for an additional five seconds while the band plays a swinging ending. The high-note bravura is a reflection of Louis Armstrong's Hot Five and Hot Seven recordings, where Armstrong would hit and hold spectacular high notes at the climactic points in the recording. Armstrong, in turn, probably borrowed it from high-note hot-shotting in opera arias.

Bill Haley studied Britt's performance of "Chime Bells" deeply, either from an earlier recording[2] or a live performance, and recorded a cover version on September 18, 1946, while with the Range Drifters. It has survived on an aluminum disc in the Country Music Hall of Fame Digital Archive in Nashville. Haley performs the song a half-step lower than Britt and only ventures up to the note B, about five tones lower than Britt's highest note, and then only in short bursts, and not the long note that Britt showcases.

Kenny Roberts

Kenny Roberts might also have sung the song as a member of the Down Homers and in later life, he would refer to it as his "most requested" song. His performance on the *Porter Waggoner* TV show, aired on February 2, 1972, is quite spectacular as, apart from the yodeling itself, there is a sudden increase in tempo for what Roberts referred to as a "galloping and mountain-climbing yodel." This is followed by a sustained display of high-note singing during which he reaches the same high F as Britt, and he does it whilst hopping up and down on one leg.

Back in Chester, Pennsylvania, in the fall of 1947, Haley landed a job with WPWA. As a disc jockey and record librarian, he would receive and hear the latest country recordings. During the late 1940s he recorded dozens of demos, acetates, and transcription discs, including many covers of contemporary country hits by artists such as Red Foley, Floyd Tillman, and Eddy Arnold, as well as original songs including "Rose of My Heart," "Cute Little

---

2 Britt recorded "Chime Bells" as a duet with Ezra Ford for the Banner label in 1934 and again as a soloist for the Bluebird label in 1939. These would likely be Haley's reference points from records.

Brown-Eyed Gal," and "Candy and Women." Most of his recordings would not see commercial release until after his death[3] While Bill was leader of the Western Aces,[4] all the members would take turns in the spotlight. Between 1947 and 1949 their commercial output consisted of just two discs on Jack Howard's Cowboy Records.

"Too Many Parties and Too Many Pals," released in August 1948 (Cowboy CR-1201), is sung and spoken by Tex King. The simple and repetitive accompaniment is probably played by King and Haley. A 1920s song by Ray Henderson, Mort Dixon, and Billy Rose, it would be most famously recorded in 1950 by Hank Williams in his persona "Luke the Drifter." Largely a monolog with a strong moral turn, the male speaker defends the promiscuous ways of a "lady of the night" at a trial. The lady turns out to be his daughter. *Billboard* criticized it for having a "dull draggy first chorus."

On the B side, Bill solos on "Four Leaf Clover Blues" (written by Bill and Shorty Cook c. 1946), with Barney Barnard providing vocal harmony on the chorus. It is the song of a habitual gambler who wants to "gamble all the time and never ever lose," but whose "baby needs a new pair of shoes." Far from being a "blues," it is up-tempo and played with gusto by the band (Al Constantine on accordion and Barnard on double bass). For *Billboard*, however, it was "too hard to sell."[5]

Barney Barnard sings Jimmy Work's "Tennessee Border" on the A side of the next release in the Spring of 1949 (Cowboy CR-1202). A number of artists covered the song including Tennessee Ernie Ford and Red Foley. On the B side, Bill sings "Candy Kisses," a recent No. 1 country hit by George Morgan. The overall effect is melancholy, in a song in which the singer's girlfriend finds "candy kisses"[6] more appealing than him. Bill plays basic rhythm guitar, with tasteful answering phrases from an unidentified steel guitar player and fills from Constantine on accordion, supported by Barnard on the double bass. It is competent, well-crafted, but ultimately unexceptional. *Billboard*'s verdict was, "Haley gets good feeling into the delightful folk torcher."[7]

These were years of consolidation, with Haley's daily routine revolving around the radio station. With radio being very much a "live" medium in those days, and

---

3 Bear Family *Rock 'n' Roll Arrives: The Real Birth of Rock 'n' Roll (1946-1954)* BCD 16509 EL Released in 2006. First released on *Golden Country Origins*, Grass Roots Records GR-1001 (Aus.), 1977

4 The name was not set in stone. As noted previously, the two Cowboy singles were billed as "Bill Haley and the 4 Aces of Western Swing." One can also find advertisements for the band listing them as "The Four Western Aces" and "The Western Aces," as well as a number of other variants.

5 Both reviews from August 14, 1948.

6 "Candy kisses" is a generic term for small American chocolates, perhaps Hershey Kisses specifically.

7 *Billboard*, April 2, 1949.

L to R: Tex King, Marshall Lytle and Merle Fritz, all of whom were members of Bill Haley's band at one time or another. The date of photo is unknown, but likely to be shortly before Marshall would join The Saddlemen.

Barney Barnard (left of picture) photographed c. 1949 outside the WPWA building with (L to R) Brother Wayne, Frances Chandler (a fan) and Bill Haley.

Al Constantine (far right of picture) with The Four Aces of Western Swing with (L to R) Rusty Keefer, Barney Barnard., and Bill Haley (front).

a far cry from today's format-based approach, WPWA provided a schedule of mixed programming. A day's broadcasting in January 1948, involved an early morning slot *Wake Up and Dream*, with the Western Aces doing half an hour at 7 a.m. They had another half an hour at 3:30 p.m. Other programs include *At Your Request* and a morning broadcast by a local priest. Xavier Cugat and Pee Wee Hunt are listed mid-morning, and there is an hour of classical music at lunchtime. The afternoon is occupied by *Bandstand*, the prototype for the later *American Bandstand*.

The band built an extensive repertoire from the gamut of country music hits, while no doubt also promoting their own songs. In the summer, they worked at Radio Park,[8] supporting visiting stars of country music on stage. They would play for barn dances, live gigs at open air auctions, school dances, as well as "bread and butter" work in Luke's Musical Bar and, later, the more up-market Maltone Melody Lounge.

The Western Aces saw many personnel changes and by the end of 1949 they had effectively disbanded. Bill was on the verge of giving up his aspirations of stardom, but was soldiering on at Luke's Bar in Chester as a solo performer when he met two musicians with high ambitions and eager to make a fresh start: Billy Williamson, an established steel guitarist, fiddler, and guitarist, and John Grande, a younger, promising accordion and piano player, who could read music. An article published in Grande's name in 1957 described how the pair came to work with Bill Haley:

> When it came time to go to work, we had settled on one thing — we both wanted to get into an outfit where the guys would stick together until we amounted to something. It should be a sort of musical family. To head that family, we needed a leader — not just a guy who could stamp out a beat, but someone we could look up to, that we could learn from.... We talked. The longer the huddle went on the more I liked Haley... Young as he was, this guy had something. Music to him was more than some notes on a page or sounds dragged out of an instrument. It was direct communication from one person to another... Haley clinched it by saying, "All my life I've been looking for something I haven't yet found in music. Maybe it's a sound, maybe it's a beat. I've always thought that if I could get together with some guys who felt the same way as I did, we might work it out." ... We shook hands on it. That's all the contract The Comets

---

8 Radio Park was located on Route 491 between Johnsons Corner and Booths Corner. Cousin Lee had operated it from the early 1940s until 1947. During 1948 & 1949, under the name "Haley-Barnard Enterprises," Bill and Barney took it over.

really have to this day. When we turned into big business, we had to formalize it with corporations, but we're still just a bunch of guys who trust each other.

The new four-piece band, now named "The Saddlemen" made its debut in the New Year of 1950. "Big Al" Thompson, the last remaining member of the Western Aces was on upright bass, but problems caused by his enormous weight led to him giving way first to Joe Piccirilli and then to Joe's brother Al, who used the stage name "Al Rex".

Two people would now become significant rivals in Haley's career: David Leonard (Dave) Miller and James E. Myers (aka Jimmy DeKnight). Both had served in the Second World War, Miller in the Navy and Myers with the Army in the Far East,[9] and both were entrepreneurs by nature, well able to identify and seize commercial opportunities. On demobilization they both chose the music industry. Miller had seen that a boom in jukeboxes and record sales would need manufacturing support, and opened the Palda[10] pressing plant in March 1947. Myers opted for publishing and recording, buying a share in Jack Howard's Arcade Records and publishing companies. Miller would also quickly establish record labels, the first being Palda, whose principal artists were the amateur Ferko String Band. When the American Federation of Musicians' strike took effect in 1948 and closed down professional recording activity, amateurs had been allowed to continue recording. Cowboy Records, for whom Bill recorded, had stockpiled recordings before the strike took effect and were able to continue releasing discs during the two years' of strike. Both companies thereby weathered the storm.

Dave Miller was something of a legend. In addition to his success in the music industry, there are stories of sex parties which he organised in which, allegedly, he participated. It has been rumored that he would take the Saddlemen there to get them excited for a recording session. There is little evidence, but Jimmy Myers did remember "there were a lot of parties. A few I was invited to, but I never went."[11]

Myers's first gambit involving Bill, around February/March 1950, was to sign a deal with Eddie Wilson to record four tracks for the Keystone label: "Deal Me a Hand," "Susan Van Dusan," "I'm Not to Blame," and "Ten Gallon Stetson." As well as being sold commercially, the discs were licensed to a hundred or so local movie theatres to be used as background music between shows.[12]

---

9 His story told in the autobiographical *Hell is a Foxhole*, Vantage Press 1966.

10 Named after the Miller brothers, **Pa**ul, **AL**bert and **Da**vid.

11 Swenson, p.35.

12 The lack of subsequent mention or expansion of this novel idea might indicate that it was a failure.

Myers' next idea (in October 1950) may have been prompted by the Korean War. Bill and the band (now under the pseudonym "Johnny Clifton and his String Band") recorded what seems to be a recruiting song for the Korean War, "Stand Up and Be Counted," backed by "Loveless Blues," both songs Myers Music, Inc. Publications. The disc was released on Center Records, known only to have released one other disc and it is possible that the label was owned by Myers himself.

Around the same time, we can see the first evidence of Haley crossing a musical boundary. Myers spied an opportunity in the shape of "Teardrops from my Eyes," recorded as an upbeat R&B number by Ruth Brown which was unpublished, but #1 on *Billboard*'s R&B chart for 11 weeks. The success of this song led to a flurry of bids from music publishers keen to take a share of the spoils. Jimmy Myers joined in, producing a recording of the song by Bill and the Saddlemen with a clutch of country-styled numbers that he leased to Atlantic Records. Up to this point, making a rhythm and blues record appears to have been far from Haley's mind and the recording is firmly at the "Western Swing" end of the spectrum, in a style the band would identify as "Cowboy Jive." Myers himself provides a subtle, but solid beat with brushes on a snare drum, while Johnny Grande lays down a classic "shuffle boogie" accompaniment on the piano:

Williamson, on steel guitar, ad-libs a series of florid phrases answering the vocal line. Haley's vocals are unexceptional, Jimmy Myers's drumming is workman-like, and Grande breaks out of the shuffle boogie for a simple "one-fingered" piano solo during which he abandons the left-hand pattern. This unassuming but ground-breaking performance was not destined to see the light of day until 2006.[13] Although Myers leased four tracks to Atlantic the label chose to release only one single "Why Do I Cry Over You?" and "I'm Gonna Dry Ev'ry Tear with a Kiss."[14] These up-tempo tracks feature Bill Borelli and Johnny Grande

---

13 On the Bear Family Records' boxed set *Rock 'n' Roll Arrives* (BCD 16509 EL)

14 Atlantic 727 (Green label), released October 1950.

duetting on piano. Meanwhile, Myers's bid for the publishing rights to "Teardops" failed and the song was bought by Simon Music.

Myers' last "throw of the dice" as Bill Haley's *de facto* manager was rather unusual. The disc ("My Palomino and I" and "My Sweet Little Gal from Nevada") and the sheet music were marketed under the name of the female cowboy movie star, Reno Browne, the songs being performed anonymously by Bill Haley and the Saddlemen. After a year or so of trying to develop Haley's career, Myers had achieved very little. The spotlight will now turn on Dave Miller...

In the Spring of 1951 a record by Jackie Brenston and His Delta Cats on the Chess label, "Rocket 88," was doing well on the R&B chart. Dave Miller recalled:

A 1951 poster advertising an appearance by Jackie Brenston and His Delta Cats, at the time that "Rocket '88'" was doing well, and about to be recorded by Bill Haley.

I was down in Richmond, Virginia, visiting a distributor - Richmond being just south of the then racial demarcation line in the United States, the Mason-Dixon line. And this fellow had said to me he was distributing the Chess record, he said "Son, it's a darned pity we can't get some of those black things done by a white boy," because the white stores down there would just not stock black product at that time. So he suggested that I found someone to cover black songs with a white artist, so that it would have acceptance in the white stores. I came back to Philadelphia with a copy of the Jackie Brenston record and checked with a friend of mine, a fellow named Jim Myers, who subsequently was the publisher of "Rock Around The Clock." He said he knew a country guy who could sing the blues. So, I said, well, it's not really blues, it's rock,[15] and he led me to Haley, who at that time was Bill Haley & The Saddlemen. I played the record for Bill, and he was quite reluctant to record it as it wasn't "his bag" - he being a country artist. But Billy Williamson and a few of the other fellows in the band said, "Bill, we have

---

15 This is unlikely, as the word "rock" was not then in use to describe the musical style.

nothing to lose," so Bill did make the cover of "Rocket 88," which sold very well locally.[16]

Miller went on to accept that his action had been "born in prejudice. I don't say that possibly Haley later wouldn't have been discovered, but the timing and the chances in this business, I somehow feel that if it weren't for prejudice within the United States at that time - programming prejudice - possibly Haley would have not been the world phenomenon that he turned out to be."[17]

Haley and the Saddlemen duly recorded the song on June 14, 1951 at the WCVH radio station in Chester, PA. They recorded it in the same key (Eb) as the Ike Turner original which meant Haley singing in a lower *tessitura* than usual. The vocal revolves around middle C, and the Eb, G & Bb below it, with the occasional excursion to the Eb above. This contrasts with the later "(We're Gonna) Rock Around the Clock" where Haley regularly reaches the G above middle C, and "Shake, Rattle and Roll" which demands a lot of high Fs in the vocal chorus. John Swenson summed up "Rocket 88" as:

> unlike anything else Haley ever recorded. The song opens with the sound effects of a car horn blaring followed by the screeching of brakes. Grande's piano leads off with a standard boogie-woogie blues pattern featuring hot right hand figures. Under this introduction Rex slaps a heavy, almost funk pattern on the bass. The rhythmic pace is certainly meatier than any uptempo material the group had previously recorded. The beat is dense and pronounced, a radical departure from their light, airy western swing style recordings.[18]

and goes on to describe Haley's singing on the recording:

> He gives the singing a thick sound against the booming bass line by emphasising the syllables in grunts and guttural expressions rather than singing in his usual clear diction. It's a technique he obviously picked up from r & b vocalists, and the surprising thing about it is how well Haley does it, considering he never later returned to even a close approximation of this style.

The addition of an electric lead guitar is another innovation, played by local guitar virtuoso Bobby Scales (Scaltrito), who trades solos with Billy Williamson on

---

16 Dave Miller interviewed by Stuart Colman, *Now Dig This Magazine* No. 204, 2000.

17 Dave Miller, interviewed by Stuart Colman on December 13, 1980 for BBC Radio London

18 Swenson, p.34. He is not quite accurate because Bill did give "I Got a Woman" similar treatment when recording it for Decca in the late 1950s and again for Sonet in the mid 1970s.

steel guitar. Johnny Grande, after his introductory solo which copies Ike Turner's original, sticks to a simple shuffle boogie pattern on the piano. A "slap bass" is deployed for the first time on a Haley recording, and is assumed to have been played by Al Rex, although Haley would later lay claim to it. The record was issued in the Summer of 1951, and Miller remembered sales of around 10,000. For their next recording the band would return to more familiar formats with "Green Tree Boogie" and "Down Deep in my Heart," both of them Haley originals.

Miller's hand might also have been behind the band's next Holiday release which was a back-to-back release in December 1951 of two Rhythm & Blues covers, under the moniker Bill and Loretta and the Saddlemen: "Pretty Baby" (closely based on the Griffin Brothers' recording which featured Margie Day on vocals) and "I'm Cryin" (Memphis Slim). On December 8th, *Cashbox* reviewed the disc, "Pretty Baby" as "an attractive country blues ditty given a strong reading by a boy-girl team. Has some sleeper potential," and "I'm Cryin," "a blues item derived from the R&B field is served up with country feeling from the pair."

On the face of it, this disc was somewhat "out of the blue." Bill's duet partner, the teenaged Loretta Glendinning, had been singing with Bill Haley for several years as a guest performer. Interviewed by the authors in 2022 by telephone at the age of 94, she had memories of happy times, performing occasionally with Haley's bands, The Texas Rangers, Four Aces of Western Swing and The Saddlemen. Her disc was released at the same time as Haley's 1951 Christmas disc[19] and Loretta, then aged 21, would later claim that she earned enough money from it to be able to buy a car.

At the end of 1951 Al Rex would leave the band and be replaced at short notice by Marshall Lytle. Describing how he had joined the band Marshall remembered,

> One day, Bill walked into WVCH[20] and told me his bass player had just quit and that he wanted me to join his band. I was a guitar player and I said, 'Bill, you know I'm not a bass player.' And he said, 'Hell, I'll teach you to play that thing in thirty minutes and I'll show you how to slap it.' He had an old bass fiddle at his Station and we rode out there and he showed me how to do a shuffle beat. I felt good with it, so Bill said, 'Get yourself a bass fiddle and come to work for me tonight.[21]

In February 1952, Miller's Palda Record label was in trouble, being deemed by the American Federation of Musicians as being "not of good standing," with claims

---

19 "I Don't Want to be Alone for Christmas"/"A Year Ago This Christmas" (Holiday 111).

20 A local radio station where Marshall was then working as a singer/guitarist.

21 Interview on *Out of the Attic* on FM 91 Radio in 2011.

that sales were being under-reported and the pressings were poor quality. Ever the business man, Miller was quick to react, setting up a new company, Essex Records, and signing Haley in April 1952. Haley's first recording for Essex was a cover version of "Rock the Joint," a song written by Harry Crafton, Wendell "Don" Keane, and Harry "Doc" Bagby which Haley had first encountered during his daily work at WPWA. Whereas Alan Freed usually gets the kudos from being the first white man to broadcast black music, the truth lies further back in time. In February 1949, Radio Station WVCH first broadcast *Judge Rhythm's Court*, which aired at lunchtime for half an hour. The show also had a daily slot on WHAT at 11:00 p.m, playing what were then known as "race records," more than two years before Alan Freed assumed his "Moondog" persona and broadcast rhythm and blues music on WJW in Cleveland.

"Judge Rhythm" was a white man named Jim Reeves (not to be confused with the singer of the same name). He would soon move to WPWA, where, for several weeks in 1950, his program immediately preceded Bill Haley's. His theme music was "Rock the Joint,"[22] pretty much the wildest thing on wax at the time. Reeves would hand over to Bill Haley at 2:30 p.m., so Haley would hear "Rock the Joint" as he was getting ready for his own program. He and the band would join in, "laughing and joking about it."[23] Haley is known to have introduced the song into his live show at the Twin Bar, reporting that it went down a storm with the sailors from the nearby navy yard.

The first record issued followed the formula of a country song, "Icy Heart," by local Philadelphia writers Morty and Meier Berk on the A side and "Rock the Joint" on the B side. "Icy Heart" is a conventional country weepie, but "Rock the Joint" comes as if from another planet, and simply leaps out of the grooves. The Saddlemen, augmented by Danny Cedrone on lead guitar are on fire. Although Marshall Lytle had joined the band on bass following Al Rex's departure in late 1951, it is apparently Bill's assertive slapping of the bass[24] that propels the band through what is effectively a prototype for "Rock Around the Clock," complete with Cedrone's trademark guitar solo.[25] Grande is once again reliable on the boogie shuffle, with a simple one-fingered solo, while Williamson weaves a beautifully crafted steel guitar solo. Bill's experience of playing for dancers told

---

22 Most likely the original recording by Jimmy Preston and his Prestonians.

23 Interview with Brian Matthew on "My Top Twelve" BBC Radio 1 1974 (date unknown).

24 Although the common perception of Bill was that he was a rhythm guitarist (and indeed that is what he did most of the time), he was also a competent on lead guitar, violin and double bass. Through the 1950s he would regularly play the bass on stage if Al Rex was on vocals.

25 Analyzed in detail in the next chapter.

him that they needed to know when a song was finishing. There is no mistaking the finality of what would become the standard "Bill Haley" ending!:

After a pair of "country boogies", "Green Tree Boogie" and "Sundown Boogie," it was with "Rock the Joint" that Bill and his band had finally put "lightning in a bottle." It was the sound and the style for which he and the band had been striving, containing the perfect mix of the musical ingredients from white country music and black rhythm and blues, while Cedrone's trademark solo would become the flag that all guitarists salute.

Following a summer residence at the Shelter Haven in Stone Harbor in 1952, where he had rubbed noses with artists such as The Treniers, Bill returned to the Twin Bar as Bill "Rock the Joint" Haley. In an interview with Red Robinson in Vancouver on May 31, 1966, he explained his view of the part he played in the evolution of rock and roll during these years:

> The flavor of our music was a mixture of country and western and rhythm and blues. I was working in a little night club called the Twin Bar in Gloucester, New Jersey, doing our style of music, which was a hand-clapping, stomping sort of semi-gospel type music, you might say, and we used to have the people jumping. There is a big naval base in Philadelphia and all the sailors used to come down. They used to love this kind of music. It became the rompin', stompin', rockin' club for all the Philadelphia area.

> Too much publicity has been given to the fact that rock 'n' roll is rhythm and blues music. It is not. It very definitely isn't, any more than it is western music. It is a combination of both. It is a rhythm. We changed the rhythm from just a shuffle-type rhythm to a heavy "two four" beat, which was "one, *two*, three, *four*." We emphasized the two and the four beat and we added to this the flavor of the old-time swing bands. We've talked a lot about the rhythm and blues end of it. Let's talk about the Spade Cooleys and the Tex Williamses and their western swing bands. This was the feel:

the combination of the two. It wasn't any more one than the other, that formed what is called rock 'n' roll music."[26]

The next two years with Dave Miller yielded ever more crazy and daring records, adding the elements that would finally crystallize in the 1954 recording of "Rock Around the Clock." One of these was Billy Gussak's drumming. He is first heard on the recordings of "Real Rock Drive" and "Stop Beatin' Round the Mulberry Bush," recorded in November 1952.

Samuel William "Billy" Gussak was born on September 9, 1906. His father, Solomon, had moved his family from the Ukraine to the U.S. in December 1905, settling in Brooklyn. Billy trained at the Juilliard School, becoming an accomplished pianist, although he would focus on the drums for his professional career. He worked for some years with Leith Stevens and the CBS Band, broadcasting regularly on the Saturday Night Swing Club, before moving on to join Charlie Barnet's band. He worked also for Johnny Green, Louis Armstrong, and Will Bradley, amongst others. As someone who could read music as well as improvise, he was a versatile and adaptable musician. Surviving footage of him in a pair of musical shorts with the Leith Stevens band reveals a drummer with an excellent, well-schooled traditional technique, impeccable timekeeping, and a real flair for punctuating the beat with an assortment of rimshots,

Billy Gussak in 1938, with a "guzzake," the first of his many percussion instrument inventions.

flams, and crashes. In later life, he moved to the West Coast and was still performing into his senior years.

In a press release from Lord Jim Ferguson on March 3, 1953, Earl Famous is named as the band's first drummer. Famous was a student at Upper Darby High School, two years senior to Johnny Grande. His connection with the band was probably a product of his being a related to Billy Williamson via Billy's mother, Sara Famous. He was replaced by Charlie Higler shortly afterwards. Haley and

---

26 *The Bill Haley Tapes* (Jerden Records, 1995).

his producers, Dave Miller and Milt Gabler would continue to use Gussak and other session drummers on recordings until December 1955. As a result, it was Gussak who announced the band's next record, "Crazy Man, Crazy," with a flurry of rim shots, flams, and rolls, very much in the style of Gene Krupa.

Promotional photograph of the band from early 1953, showing drummer Charlie Higler, bottom right of picture. Like Marshall Lytle (left of picture) he sports a pencilled-in "moustache."

"Crazy, Man, Crazy," recorded in March 1953, would become the band's first national hit record. Working free high school dances meant that Haley understood the musical tastes and needs of the younger generation. He picked up their phrase, "Crazy man, crazy!" for the insanely catchy chorus of the song ("Crazy man, crazy ... man that music's gone!"), and added a vital second element, a shout chorus of "Go, go, go, everybody!" that ushers in a party scene and a short but blistering solo from session musician Art Ryerson, who references "Dixie" and the traditional fife and drum tune "The Girl I Left Behind":

Of working with Haley, Ryerson remembered:

Art Ryerson, who played lead guitar on a number of the band's recordings in 1953.

I did a couple of dates with them. Their producer, Dave [Miller]... liked me and so I did these dates with Bill Haley. The group wasn't far away from being a hillbilly band. Don't think that I am a snob or anything, but I was just glad to get through those dates and get on....those Haley things were done on that first little Les Paul he came out with. I had one of those for eight or ten years and they allowed for a lot of facility and so forth, but I never cared for the tone of it or the sound of it..."[27]

Gussak, on drums, punctuates the song with his extensive repertoire of effects, patterns, and rim shots, opening out with strong off-beats in the instrumental solos. The inflection in Bill's voice suggests that he is actually smiling with enjoyment as he sings the second chorus after the guitar solo. The atmosphere in the studio was electric and there is little doubt that Miller was instrumental in generating that atmosphere. *Billboard* (May 9, 1953) was moved to report that Miller had hired a group to provide the "gang-sing shouts of 'go, go,

---

27 Jim Carlton, *Conversations with Great Jazz and Studio Guitarists* (Mel Bay Publications, February 2012). The solid-bodied Gibson "Les Paul" first came out in 1952. For his jazz recordings, Ryerson said he used mainly the hollow-bodied Gibson L-5.

go'" but that "The group didn't sound big enough to Miller and the engineer, so pressed into service...were Miller himself, his Essex label promotion man D. Malamud, distributor Jerry Blaine and the studio porter." So carried away was Miller that he seems to have forgotten to fade the ending which, on the original tape and on some releases, ends with an unmuted solo "cough."

Miller's publicity claimed 200,000 sales of the record in a month, by far the biggest Haley had so far enjoyed. In June, the song entered the "Honor Roll of Hits" Top 20, and was No. 1 in St. Louis. It would help Haley and the Comets to do a roaring trade at Wildwood during their summer residency, and ultimately it would inspire a number of international cover recordings, including one by Ralph Marterie and his Orchestra.

Marshall Lytle would maintain vehemently that he was the writer of "Crazy Man, Crazy" but that he had been fobbed off by Haley with a 50% share in "Fractured," while "Crazy Man, Crazy" was attributed 100% to Haley. To this extent, as well as in terms of musical style, Bill and the Comets had well and truly broken the Tin Pan Alley mold in which composers, lyricists, publishers, and record companies had had separate and distinct roles. The Comets and Miller were trailblazing a new way of working that would eventually become the norm for the popular music industry.

Dick Richards, here shown singing with the Comets c. 1955, became the band's drummer on Labor Day, 1953, although Bill would continue to use session players for recordings for the rest of Richards' time with the band.

Before the Fall of 1953, the drum chair passed briefly to Dean Tinker before being filled by Dick Richards (real name Richard Boccelli), but Miller would always use professional session drummers for recordings. "Crazy Man, Crazy" was followed by "Pat-a-Cake", a children's nursery rhyme with the novelty sound effect of a single strike bicycle bell, and "Fractured" (co-written by Haley and Marshall Lytle), which featured the sound of a ratchet,[28] presumably to copy the sound of something being "fractured." A simple and loose instrumental arrangement would be embroidered with comedic sound effects. Williamson's repertoire of lightning-flash effects is used to answer the voice (such as his replies to Bill's shouts of "I'm gone!" in the chorus of "Pat-a-Cake"). Unison shouting is often used to put over the vocal hooks, as on "I'll be

---

28 A noisy orchestral instrument once beloved of English football fans and known there as a "football rattle."

True". There are also intriguing and subtle changes to the instrumental sound with effects such as the use of brushes on the drums on "What'cha Gonna Do".

A baritone sax[29] features in the recordings of "Farewell, So Long, Goodbye" and "Live it Up!" in the fall of 1953. The former song was pitched in F and exploits the bottom of the instrument's range and with a quirky little harmonic shift down a tone in the chorus:

With the sax now featuring in their recorded output, the band needed a player for live appearances. They took on Joseph D'Ambrosio (stage name "Joey Ambrose") towards the end of 1953, at about the same time Dick Richards joined the band. He described his arrival to Otto Fuchs:

Joey D'Ambrosio (Ambrose)

I was 19 years old. I had my own band in Philadelphia and trying to find gigs, and Bill Haley had a band in the Philadelphia area at the time...I learned playing rock 'n' roll, then still rhythm and blues, backing up strippers when I was sixteen. Doing that, you'll learn how to play rock 'n' roll!... It was a different thing for me 'cause they were still a country band and I wasn't used to some of the keys they came up with. It was a lotta fun: everyone was a good player.[30]

In a 2007 interview for the *Las Vegas Review-Journal*, D'Ambrosio said: "We really turned it around. We came in with our own ideas of how to play this music. Bill wasn't too hip on that stuff. Bill was a hillbilly. But he had an ear."

He went on to pinpoint the difference between the Treniers, who were a big influence on the Comets, and the Comets themselves: "They were the swingingest

---

29 Believed to have been played by Tony Lance (Liguori).

30 Fuchs, p. 193.

rock band anywhere at that time. They were the best. But while the Treniers were content to focus on their live act Bill was always more conscious of recording. He knew the power of recording and he had an ear for songs."[31]

Haley remained faithful to the sound of a baritone sax on his Essex records, and Joey, a tenor player, did not get to play on any of them except "Straight-Jacket". Here Joey is revealed as an accomplished R&B-style player, whereas, on his other recordings with Bill Haley he was limited to simple, pre-arranged riffs.

Towards the end of 1953, the Comets covered Faye Adams's "I'll Be True" and while, musically speaking, they blew her original out of the water with their raucous "booting" rendition, the segregation of the charts meant that they had no chance of crossing over or even reaching the R&B market. Another innovation on this recording, as well as on its B side, "Ten Little Indians", was the use of an electric organ. The year would end with one more single remaining to be recorded under the contract with Palda.

Publicity picture for the Treniers, whom Bill encountered in Wildwood. He wrote the song "Rock-a-Beatin' Boogie" for them. They were highly influential in the development of the Comets' music and stage act.

31 Mike Weatherford, "Las Vegan Joey D'Ambrosio, Comet," *Las Vegas Review-Journal*, March 4, 2007.

CHAPTER 18
Focus on Music (1954-1959)

Haley and the Comets reached a crucial point in their career in early 1954, having failed to produce a significant hit since "Crazy Man, Crazy" in the Spring and Summer of 1953. Meanwhile, the story of "Rock Around the Clock" had been unfolding in the background, with Jimmy Myers one of the significant players.

In 1952, Max Freedman,[1] a postal worker and part-time songwriter living in Philadelphia, had penned a song entitled "(We're Gonna) Rock Around the Clock." A few years earlier he had had a reasonable hit with "Sioux City Sue," written under his wife's name, and recorded by Bing Crosby in 1946. His main publisher was James Myers' Myers Music, Inc. Ever the wheeler-dealer, the deal Myers did with Freedman would channel 50% of the proceeds to Myers Music, Inc., 25% to Myers himself as "co-writer," leaving just 25% for Freedman. When asked about his contribution to the song, Myers would tell a different story each time, but consistently

Max Charles Freedman (1893-1962), composer of "(We're Gonna) Rock Around the Clock"

characterizing himself as the main protagonist, with Freedman simply chipping in a few ideas. The evidence, however, strongly suggests it was entirely Freedman's work as the sole named writer on the handwritten manuscript, dating from 1952,

---

1 Max Charles Freedman (1/8/1893-10/8/1962).

is Freedman. The melody meanwhile is strikingly similar to Leroy Anderson's "The Syncopated Clock." This had become the theme music for CBS-TV's *The Late Show* in 1951 and is noted in *Wikipedia*[2] as "a piece that many Americans could readily hum or whistle, even if few knew the name of its composer." A comparison of the sheet music reveals the similarity. Firstly, "Rock Around the Clock":

Rhythmic

Fm $C^{7(\sharp 5)}$ C^7 C^7 *3*

One, two, three o' clock   four o' clock rock,   Five, six,   se-ven o' clock

Fm   Fm   *3* $C^{7(\sharp 5)}$ C^7

eight o' clock rock   Nine, ten, e-le-ven o' clock twelve o' clock rock, we're gon-na

$B\flat^7$ C^7 F^6 F

rock a-round the clock to - night!___   Put your   glad rags   on   and

F^7

join   me hon'_   We'll   have   some   fun   when the   clock strikes one,_

and secondly "The Syncopated Clock":

---

2 Accessed May 17, 2023.

Moderately (♩=132)

(clock ticking)

Sonny Dae and His Knights, the first band to record "(We're Gonna) Rock Around the Clock".

Another key player in the story was Paschal Vennitti,[3] another Philadelphian and the band-leading drummer of "Sonny Dae and His Knights." Their stock-in-trade was to take a song and give it a "boogie-woogie" treatment and they had been going down a storm at the Terrace Lounge in Indianapolis for much of 1953. Their success had attracted the attention of a local record company and Vennitti called his Philadelphia-based agent, Bob Bennett, asking him to send some songs for consideration. The batch he sent happened to include "Rock Around the Clock." However, Vennitti discovered that the record company was a "non-Union" opera-tion, pulled the plug on them and returned to Philadelphia for the Holi-days. In January he recorded the song for Arcade Records, owned by Jack Howard and James E. Myers. Myers,

3 Paschal Salvatore Vennitti (born May 24, 1928, died February 1987).

almost certainly for the first time, saw potential for giving it the "Haley treatment." This is how Vennitti handles the opening, against a boogie shuffle beat:

The resulting recording was quickly pressed on the Arcade label. The scarcity of the disc today suggests it was only a small, promotional pressing. *Billboard*'s review was unenthusiastic: "Effort has an insistent beat as the group chants of an upcoming night of pleasure. Could attract some juke coin." Of the wild instrumental B side, "Movin' Guitar" they were more positive: "Some fancy guitar work, briskly negotiated, and good support by the ork make this a listenable instrumental."

Jimmy Myers now had a song which he knew would suit Bill Haley. If he could persuade a major label to record it, he could finally be "in the money." As we know, since 1950, he had been trying to do great things with Haley's career. Myers had no love for Dave Miller, and with his 75% share in "Rock Around the Clock," and Haley's contract with Miller soon to expire, he moved into top gear.

What follows is conjecture...A plausible theory is that Myers took the disc to Haley to persuade him to record "Clock" as his final single for Essex. The eventual, somewhat strange choice of "Chattanooga Choo Choo" as the 'A' side suggests that Miller preferred to capitalize on the then current success of the film *The Glenn Miller Story*. The absence of "Clock," even as the B side, could well be down to the mutual dislike between Myers and Miller. The "made up on the spot" B side, "Straitjacket," however, seems to have been influenced greatly by Sonny Dae's "Movin' Guitar," (which was on the B side of the Sonny Dae disc) indicating that Myers might well have given Haley one of the promotional pressings.

Billboard reviewed the Essex disc on February 25th: "Haley gives the standard the razzle-dazzle treatment here, dressing it up in a bright new arrangement and providing an exciting beat. Potent for the boxes." Their review of the B side was encouraging: "The younger set could go for this novelty with its crazy lyric: two words, repeated hundreds of times before the end is reached. This is an instrumental built on a solid boogie figure and is infectiously rhythmic, and is aided by the monotony."

Haley had now fulfilled his contract with Palda and Miller had an option to renew. However, he had travelled to Europe in the cause of expanding his business. His eye was "off the ball" as far as Haley was concerned, and he simply forgot to invoke the renewal clause. Haley's contract was due to end on April 8th, leaving the door wide open for Jimmy Myers. Myers travelled to New York to visit various record company moguls and secured a contract for Haley and the Comets with Milt Gabler at Decca. "Rock Around the Clock" would become the B side of their first Decca single. Decca often used the Pythian Temple[4] in New York City

---

4 The Pythian Temple, located at 135 West 70th Street, was built as a meeting place for a fraternal organization called "The Knights of Pythias." Founded in the 1940s, it was leased to Decca as a recording studio and in the 1980s, converted to residential use.

The Pythian Temple, NYC.

for orchestral recordings, and its remarkable acoustic properties engendered both clarity and ambience in the record-ed sound. Gabler and his engineers used spatial separation expertly to balance the breeze that was Haley's voice against the gale that was the Comets in full flight. Pictures of their sessions show Haley on the floor of the hall and the band on the stage, with no acoustic screening between the instruments. The ten recordings made there in the first thirteen months of Haley's association with Gabler were the bedrock upon which Haley's success was built. Every one of his first five singles placed in the U.S. Top 20, two of them in the Top 10, and "Rock Around the Clock" became an international #1 record.

Myers' lack of involvement in the creation of the song became a matter of public record in October 1955 when Irvin Ballen, owner of Gotham Records, threatened him with a lawsuit, claiming plagiarism of "Rock the Joint," written by Harry Crafton, Don Keene, and Doc Bagby and recorded for Gotham by Jimmy Preston and His Prestonians in 1949. As recounted by music historian Jim Dawson, "Myers' attorney, Edward D. Werblun, answered Ballen by stating for the record that the song was 'written by Max Freedman, a freelance composer and song-writer, who sold the song to Myers'",[5] thus establishing that Myers was *not* the co-writer and could not be accused of plagiarism. It did not, however, stop him from telling the world forevermore that he had written the song with just a little help from Freedman.

As we saw earlier, Haley was specific in saying he had been given the song in 1952, during one of his summer residencies at Wildwood. He claimed he had tried to record it for Essex a number of times, but that each time, Miller had stopped him. Miller refuted this story when interviewed by Stuart Colman on BBC Radio London in December 1980: "I didn't actually turn it down. I was over in Europe

---

5 Jim Dawson, *Rock Around the Clock – The record that started the rock revolution!* (San Francisco: Backbeat Books, 2005) p.62-63.

and Bill's option came up, in my absence basically; we didn't pick up the option on Haley."[6]

The evidence we have presented suggests it is unlikely that anyone would have seen the potential in the song "Rock Around the Clock" until Sonny Dae had recorded it and revealed its potential for "rock 'n' roll" treatment. In 1954 Myers might well have attempted to have Haley record the song at his last Essex recording session and been thwarted by his rival, Dave Miller. Haley does seem to have used Sonny Dae's B side, "Movin' Guitar" as inspiration for the B side, "Straitjacket," so he would at least collect some writer's royalties from the disc. Myers then moved behind Miller's back and negotiated "Clock" onto the B side of Haley's first Decca single. Haley signed a one-year recording deal with Decca Records on March 29th, a few days before his contract with Palda was due to expire. Haley and the Comets had to move quickly to be ready for their first session with Decca, which was booked for April 12th. During their later career from 1989 onwards, the "Original Comets" (a reunion of the band which included several musicians who had been present on April 12, 1954) would describe rehearsing the song the night before

Frank Pingatore (on left) with Bill Haley and "Two Hound Dogs." Behind them is Harry Broomall, Bill Haley's factotum and bodyguard. (Picture dates from 1955)

the session. However, on April 11, they were advertised with an evening performance at Vito's in Mount Holly, New Jersey, where they had a weekly residency. Don Vanore, Danny Cedrone's grandson, tells a more plausible story about the preparation for the recording:

---

6 Dave Miller, interviewed by Stuart Colman on December 13, 1980 for BBC Radio London

A couple days before the recording session, Bill Haley came to Danny's house in South Philly[7] (as he did many times), hung out there for a while, had dinner, and then they picked up a couple guitars and started an informal rehearsal for the upcoming session (in the parlor, mind you). From what my grandmother and mother told me it wasn't real long before grandpop started using his now legendary solo (it had always been a favorite of his wife and daughters). So Rock & Roll history was decided that night, in a little row home, up a little street in South Philly with Danny's wife, his daughters, his sister (Mary), and Bill Haley there to witness it.[8]

The significant changes in the Haley recording of the song are a change of key from F to A, the introduction and chorus sung on an arpeggio rather than a scale, and the restructuring of the harmony in the introduction. Whilst various band members who lived longer than Bill would be eager to press their claims to coaching Billy Gussak on the art of drumming, telling Danny Cedrone to reuse his "Rock the Joint" solo, and choosing a riff rather than a saxophone solo, one man who claimed to have made the fundamental changes to the fabric of the song itself was Frank Pingatore.[9] Frank was a barber, the owner of Frank Pingatore's Haircut Shop at 12th and Market Street in Wilmington, Delaware. He played the trumpet and led a dance orchestra and a Dixieland band in the Wilmington area on a part-time basis in the early 1950s. He claimed a musical education at the Juilliard School and, for a time, was responsible for maintaining the Haley "kiss curl." The obituary written by his family and published in the *Wilmington News Journal* on December 18, 2012, described his contribution to the recording of "Rock Around the Clock" thus:

> In 1953, Frank was presented a song, "Around the Clock," to revise, arrange, and rehearse with Bill Haley and the Comets. He arranged the union of country with rhythm & blues, wrote a new intro and revised the lyrics giving birth to "Rock Around the Clock."

In an interview in the *News Journal* on January 7, 1986, Pingatore stated that Decca had thought "Bill Haley was black," and that Myers had employed Pingatore "to make him sound that way." He went on to explain that the song had been "a hit

---

7 1922 S. Jessup St.

8 Sleeve notes for the CD *Danny Cedrone: Guitar Virtuoso* (DJC Records E-00821)

9 Born August 8, 1930, died December 17, 2012.

on the burlesque circuit because it meant a guy and girl going around the clock, if you know what I mean." Myers had "cleaned up the lyrics and called it 'Dance Around the Clock'." Then they changed the title to "Rock Around the Clock." These observations conflict with all the other accounts, and we are left with two silent voices, those of Bill Haley and Danny Cedrone, and the fact that it might have been they, with their memory of "Rock the Joint" from two years' earlier, who wrought the important changes.

Another divergence from the story told in Haley's autobiography emerged when John von Hoelle and Jack Haley interviewed members of the Comets for their book, *Sound and Glory*. According to the musicians, Gabler was more interested in the other song scheduled for the Pythian session, Dickie Thompson's "Thirteen Women (and Only One Man in Town)," because he "owned a piece of it."[10] *Sound and Glory* relates that Gabler was angry that the band was late (due to the sandbar incident related by Haley in his autobiography), that "Thirteen Women" had taken the lion's share of the studio time, and that everyone was disappointed after the day's work, feeling that they had blown their chance.[11]

Haley's autobiography says Gabler was relaxed about their lateness, "Clock" was recorded first, and Haley left with a feeling of satisfaction and excitement. The official Decca documentation, however, confirms the Comets' version of events. A double session had been booked, but did not begin until after the band arrived, at 1:20 p.m. "Thirteen Women" was completed in three hours and, after a short break, "Rock Around the Clock" was recorded in just fifty-five minutes, the session ending at 5:40 p.m.

There is so much to say about this game-changing recording, Billy Gussak's drumming being one of the more remarkable elements. Gussak had played on many of the Comets' Essex recordings, though he was never a member of the band. His musical response to playing with a slapped bass is to abandon the off-beats and deploy a variety of crashes, flams, and rim shots as punctuation on the last beat of every other bar, using a different and distinct pattern for each verse, chorus or solo. He launches the song with three cracking rim shots, the "wake-up" call for a new "Rock 'n' Roll" generation. In Haley's own words, many years later, "We were so ready when we walked in there. We had the feeling. It was a case of, I think, the greatest rhythm band of the last thirty years."[12]

The precise "stop" chords that punctuate the vocal introduction indicate a band on fire and meaning business. The popular guitarist's key of A major, puts the

---

10 Haley and von Hoelle, p.94.

11 Haley and von Hoelle, pp.93-97.

12 Talking to Roger Scott on LBC Radio, UK, March 2, 1974.

vocal right in Bill's *tessitura.* He sings the introduction on an A major arpeggio. When he reaches the note E ("Nine, ten, eleven o'clock, twelve o' clock rock, we're gonna rock..."), the band moves to the dominant 7th chord (E7), punctuating the offbeat to wind up the harmonic tension, as surely as Beethoven had done more than a century and a half earlier at the climax of the development section in his *Eroica* symphony. The resolution of this tension fires the starting gun for the song proper:

clock to-night. Put your glad rags on and join me hon'_ We'll

have some fun when the clock strikes one,

After two verses, Danny Cedrone steps forward for his solo, one of the most famous in rock music history. He opens with a formidable display of rapid tremolo picking:

On the IV chord, he deploys a repeated pattern redolent of the playing of the earlier generation of jazz guitarists who had been his inspiration:

The final downward scale over the V chord, played on the six strings of the guitar in turn, is a *tour de force* that has been admired by generations of guitarists:

This solo was something of a Cedrone trademark and he had used it on "Rock the Joint" in 1952. After two more vocal choruses, Joey D'Ambrosio, on tenor sax, leads a simple, but classic riff (similar to the one on the Sonny Dae recording), played in unison with the steel guitar (Billy Williamson) and Cedrone's lead guitar:

Haley's trademark ending signals the end of the song with a "falling off the drum stool" routine from Gussak as the last word.

The band only needed two takes to get a master. Different stories persist as to how they were edited together. Grande said Gussak had fluffed the ending and it was merely a case of splicing the ending of one take onto the other. Gabler, on the other hand, described a more elaborate and technically unlikely approach: Haley's voice had been inaudible on the first take and a second take was made, with the band playing off-mike. The two takes were played in synchronization on two tape machines and "bounced down" onto a third machine.[13] The recording of "(We're Gonna) Rock Around the Clock" was the crowning glory of more than three years of musical evolution that had begun in November 1950 when Bill and the Saddlemen recorded Ruth Brown's R&B hit, "Teardrops From my Eyes." However, it failed to reach the Top 20 and a cover of Big Joe Turner's "Shake, Rattle and Roll," recorded at the Comets' second Decca session in June, did much better. Haley and Gabler removed most of the innuendo from the lyrics (although the "one-eyed cat" was still "peeping in the seafood store") and replaced the instrumental solo with a unison riff based on the song's opening instrumental riff. It was a massive hit, making No. 7 on *Billboard*, selling a million copies, and charting in the U.K. in late 1954.

Like "Crazy Man, Crazy," the success of "Shake, Rattle and Roll" is based on simplicity and catchiness. The "Crazy Man, Crazy" hook is unforgettable, and you didn't need to be a trained singer to join in with "*go, go, go everybody!*". "Shake, Rattle and Roll" was even simpler, with the chorus line also being used for the instrumental chorus. The recording didn't have an instrumental ending, and the last shout of "Roll" simply falls over the edge of a cliff (a gimmick later used at the close of "See You Later, Alligator").

Haley would plow this groove for most of the next three years, the period of his greatest success. In hindsight, we can clearly determine the template that delivered Bill's biggest hits. The key was simplicity, and the lyrics could be pretty much meaningless. The main thing was a "hook," often shouted rather than sung. Bill had been doing this since 1953: "*Crazy man, crazy!*" Shout it or sing it, it doesn't matter and the verse is just nonsense. Before the guitar solo comes the shouted chorus of, "*Go, go, go, everybody!*" Go and do what? One might wonder, but it really doesn't matter — just "Go!"

So it continued with other early Decca tracks such as "Mambo Rock" ("*Hey mambo, Mambo Rock*"), "Happy Baby" ("*Happy, happy baby....*"), "R-O-C-K," and so on. In the case of "See You Later, Alligator," Bill would acknowledge the

---

13 Dawson, pp. 85-86. This sounds improbable given the technology then available.

formula himself as he once introduced the song as "a tune that we did which we hoped would become a saying for young people all over the world." [14]

Following Cedrone's premature death in the summer of 1954, guitarist Francis "Franny" Beecher was brought in by Gabler for his first session with Haley to record "Dim, Dim the Lights" (Julius Dixon and Beverley Ross) and "Happy Baby" (Frank Pingatore). Beecher was a versatile guitarist, with a foot in both jazz and country camps, having worked with Benny Goodman and Buddy Greco, as well as Shorty Long's Texas Rangers. As recounted in Chapter 7, Beecher recalled he was admonished by Haley for playing one of his first solos, for "Happy Baby," with too much of a jazz feel and, he said, "I had to stick to major scales." [15] The solo he ultimately recorded for his Comets debut indicates how well he followed his master's orders without compromising the quality of his improvisation:

---

14 In the Belgian TV film *Vijf Jaar Vlaamese*, broadcast during the Comets' European tour in 1958.

15 Swenson p.59.

Five sessions for Decca in 1954 and 1955, produced five hit singles and it seemed the World was at their feet as "Rock Around the Clock" became a No. 1 hit in June 1955. However, the salaried members of the band had seen the partners growing rich, buying houses and Cadillacs and, in September 1955, Dick Richards, Joey D'Ambrosio, and Marshall Lytle quit. Lord Jim Ferguson had apparently told Bill they were bluffing, but his late desperate offer of a raise was turned down. They had already negotiated a deal, with an advance, from Capitol Records and would record for them as "The Jodimars."[16]

The Jodimars, during a rehearsal for their first public appearance. L. to R: Jim Buffington (drums), Charles "Chuck" Hess (guitar), Dick Richards (vocals and drums), Marshall Lytle (bass guitar), Joey D'Ambrosio (tenor saxophone), Bob Simpson (piano, on stage).

---

16 From their names: JOey, DIck and MARShall

Bill now had the draw and the money to take on top-flight musicians. Rudy Pompilii (tenor sax) and Franny Beecher (lead guitar) joined Billy Williamson (steel guitar) and Johnny Grande (accordion and piano), while Al Rex (a former member of the Saddlemen) returned on bass. Don Raymond was hired on drums, but quickly replaced by Ralph Jones.

The new Comets' line up, post September 1955. L to R: Bill Haley (on double bass while Al Rex takes a vocal solo), Johnny Grande (accordion), Rudy Pompilii (tenor saxophone), Ralph Jones (drums), Franny Beecher (lead guitar), Billy Williamson (steel guitar).

Haley realized early on that his bubble could easily burst and he set about building a business which would outlive the rock and roll. He established an empire that included music publishing companies, record companies, real estate, and the band began to generate much of its own musical material. As a vital component of the group's success Gabler benefitted and it became standard practice for the homegrown material to carry the writing credit "Haley, Gabler, Keefer, Cafra." While Rusty Keefer might well have been the primary writer, we also see Billy Williamson being recognized (his share being in the name of his wife, Catherine Cafra). This approach was to become typical in the music business, with writing, performing, and producing being intertwined and inextricably linked, and rewarded accordingly.

Gabler's memories of how he worked with the band reveal that he was closely involved in the process of creation.

> None of Bill's boys — except Johnny Grande... could read [music]. So you'd have to hum riffs to them and they'd play a line and get their beat going, and Johnny would be shuffling on his piano... I'd just use all the tired old riffs I'd known all my life from R&B records, and Jordan's backgrounds and things... [If they goofed] you'd have to go back to the intro again because they could never pick up on bar seven or the second eight, or the middle eight. They had to take it from the top and go through each step and figure out how they'd get it right. But after three hours, they knew it. And the band rocked![17]

There were a number of people on whom Bill had turned his back when the Jodimars defected. These included Frank Pingatore, who wrote the Jodimars' first single, "Well Now, Dig This," a song that, in different circumstances, could have been the Comets' next hit. It has all the elements, from the crazy and inconsequential lyrics ("Lots of chocolate bars, and Jaguar cars, and a trip to Mars, among the moon and stars. If you're in your teens, and you like blue jeans, movie magazines, pretty moonlight scenes...") to simple riffs and a catchy hook line:

---

17 Milt Gabler quotations are taken from an article written by Ralph J. Gleason in *Rolling Stone*. Publication date could not be located.

Now dig this!

Now dig this! etc.

While the Jodimars struck out on their own, the new Comets got to work quickly and recorded four dynamite numbers at their first two sessions, on September 22nd and 23rd, 1955: "R-O-C-K" (credited to Haley, Rusty Keefer, and Rusty's wife, Ruth), "Rock-a-Beatin' Boogie" (written by Bill in 1952 for the Treniers and the Esquire Boys), "The Saints Rock 'n Roll" (credited to Bill Haley and Milt Gabler, a "traditional jazz" favorite that was ideal for introducing the new members of the band, all of whom took solos), and "Burn That Candle" (a cover of the R&B recording by the Cues, written by Winfield Scott). Stuart Colman described the revised band's first recording session thus:

> The Decca engineers pushed the limiters into overdrive on the first song, "R-O-C-K." The resulting distortion was just within their tolerance levels, but they made doubly sure that the problem was ironed out before they cut the thunderous "Rock-a-Beatin' Boogie" ... As an exercise in craftsmanship, this is where all the elements of Rock 'n' Roll come together. The gale-force impact of Rudy's sax raises the hairs on your neck like a hastily removed Band-Aid. From there on, the spirit of the song gnaws its way into your consciousness as Bill treads out his recipe for rock 'n' roll. Some careful planning, fueled by that abundant level of confidence, results in a truly audacious instrumental break. Tenor and guitar trade glissandos like sparring heavyweights, paving the way for a clutch of flattened thirds as Frank Beecher charges headlong into his solo. In the emphasis department, guest drummer Cliff Leeman[18] highlights a series of sporadic off-beats on his floor tom and the whole band neatly pulls out of the solo, right on the penultimate bar. The fusillade of "Rock, rock, rock, everybody" hook lines never lets up

---

18 Cliff Leeman (September 10, 1913 – April 26, 1986) was a legend in jazz circles. His immaculate time-keeping earned him the moniker "Mr Time."

until the lead guitar finally draws a cascade conclusion to punctuate the excitement."[19]

On "The Saints Rock 'n Roll", Rudy takes his first full-fledged solo, announcing his presence with an astonishing three octave glissando down from an altissimo top F:

These four tracks all achieved *Billboard* chart placings, but significantly lower than those recorded by the original Comets. The formula had been diluted in small but crucial ways, before re-emerging with "See You Later, Alligator," a cover of an original by Bobby Charles. John Swenson described how Gabler had "heard a regional hit version of 'See You Later, Alligator' and recognized the connection right away," and went on to write, "Gabler laughs when he recalls 'See You Later, Alligator', It was covering a record, and Haley hadn't heard it until he came into the studio.'"[20]

In the 1960s, *Haley News* published a slightly different version of the story, told by Bill. He had been visiting Milt Gabler to discuss future recordings, saw a test pressing of the Decca recording of Roy Hall's cover version of the song, lying on top of a pile of records on a coffee table. He played it on Gabler's hi-fi and immediately identified it as the next song he wanted to record.

"Alligator" was a typically tight and neat arrangement with two catchy riffs alternating in answer to an equally strong vocal hook. It became the band's third

---

19 Stuart Colman, *Now Dig This,* No.179, February 1998.

20 Swenson, p.70.

million-seller. In his account of the session, Colman highlights Bill's addition of a few "e's" into the word "See" at the beginning of the chorus, which, transforming it into a multi-syllable word, just adds to the song's winning qualities. So, too, does Beecher's opening falsetto, "See you later, alligator."

Until now, Ralph Jones had only played on gigs and not on recordings. As he later told Swenson, Gussak had come to a live gig to check him out and told Haley, "I see no reason why this boy can't play on your records." Jones said he knew that Gussak's "secret sauce" was an extremely tight snare drum for his signature rim shots, and adjusted his snare accordingly. In the studio Gabler called out, "Lemme hear that rim shot!" Jones hit a few to everyone's satisfaction, and Haley's use of session drummers came to an end.

The Comets were soon asked to make an album. *Rock 'n' Roll Stage Show* was the perfect solution. Recorded in three sessions in March 1956, it reflected the band's live performance and could be described as a "concept album." Nine of the tracks had been written by band members and would be published by their own Valleybrook Company.

The cover of Big Joe Turner's "Hide and Seek," sung by Williamson, makes an interesting comparison with Haley's earlier recording of Turner's "Shake, Rattle and Roll." The musical reins are looser. Jones' drumming is more "jazzy" than Gussak's, the bass, still slapped, is lower in the mix. The instrumental riffs are more elaborate and quieter during solos. It is tight, the playing of the highest quality, but energy and urgency has been reduced. The musical style was evolving and reflecting the talent, experience, and influence of the new musicians.

A real oddity on the album is Grande's accordion solo, "A Rockin' Little Tune" (written by Grande and Williamson). A neat little melody is built on a "*IIm⁷, V⁷, I*" harmonic "turnaround", with a middle eight based on the cycle of fifths. Franny and Rudy take the number by the scruff of its neck in their solos. By now, Franny is well used to working within the permitted stylistic range, while the structured and delicate interplay between guitar and sax illustrates the band departing from the template established by the original Comets in 1954:

Towards the end, Johnny Grande reveals his musical pedigree by working in a short passage from Liszt's 2nd Hungarian Rhapsody:

Rudy's feature number, "Rudy's Rock," was the successor to "Straight-Jacket" and also recorded for the album. The concept and the antics involved would have been familiar to Rudy, who had been a member of the Ralph Marterie Orchestra, which featured a similar number.[21] This Decca recording of "Rudy's Rock" was

21 "Dubba Dubbin' with Hank"

predated by an earlier recording, made on the soundstage at Columbia Film Studios in Los Angeles for the movie *Rock Around the Clock.* Away from Gabler's influence, the first thing to strike the viewer is the tempo, which is considerably up on the Decca version. It features the rich sound of Johnny Grande's accordion filling out the harmony and a series of simple ad. lib. riffs from Franny Beecher. Rudy's playing is less florid than on the Decca recording, being based largely on simple riffs. By the time he gets to the second chorus, he emerges as a full-fledged "honker" in the same vein as Big Jay McNeely, Red Prysock, or Joe Houston:

This priceless gem of a film clip, mimed over a track recorded "live" in the film studio, gives insight as to how the band sounded on stage. By contrast, on the recording for the *Stage Show* album, Rudy slows the tune down and expresses himself in terms that are more worthy of be-bop.

"Calling All Comets," the hastily cobbled-together stablemate of "Rudy's Rock," opens the *Stage Show* album. Like many follow-up or "answer" songs it is less memorable than its predecessor. Rudy's opens with economical re-use of the riff from "Rock Around the Clock":

This number does, however, feature two remarkable key changes, firstly from B flat to E flat and then to A flat. Stuart Colman observed that "such inventiveness in rock 'n' roll totally by-passed the music's detractors at the time."[22] This is also heard on the Comet Trio number, "Tonight's the Night" (Haley, Cafra), with its surprising key change up a semitone for the third verse, and a return to the home key of G for the instrumental chorus.

No doubt as a nod to his producer, Haley recorded Louis Jordan's "Choo Choo Ch'Boogie" (Gabler was one of its three credited writers, the other two being Vaughn Horton and Denver Darling). The tempo comes down and the performance lacks Jordan's sassy wit and well-oiled fleetness of foot. On this track and some others, there are hints of a band "going through the motions," but *Rock 'n' Roll Stage Show* remains one of the most musically accomplished albums ever made by a pop band.

The chart placings achieved by the singles released from the album were a pale shadow of former triumphs. "Hot Dog Buddy Buddy" #60, "Rockin' Thru the Rye" #78, while "Rudy's Rock" did best with #34.

A few months later, the Comets were signed for a second film, *Don't Knock the Rock*. They recorded and rush-released a cover version of Little Richard's "Rip it Up," which became their biggest hit (#30) since "See You, Later, Alligator". Haley and Little Richard's recordings were neck-and-neck for a long time, with Richard's ultimately fairing a little better. Alarm bells should have been ringing when "Don't Knock the Rock," the theme song, did not chart in the U.S.

The tours to Australia and the United Kingdom, described in Haley's autobiography, followed and, on the band's return in March 1957, they launched a new single, "Forty Cups of Coffee" (recorded towards the end of 1956), on *The Ed Sullivan Show*. By now the musical formula was becoming tired and this recording (a cover of an R&B original by Danny Overbea with King Kolax and His Orchestra) attained a modest chart placing (#70). Having recently returned from the UK, Haley was talking widely about diversifying the Comets' business interests, which would include building a recording studio in the basement of their office building and the formation of their own record companies.

In March 1957, J. Leslie McFarland provided two songs for a single that reached No. 60 in the charts, "(You Hit the Wrong Note) Billy Goat" and "Rockin' Rollin' Rover," "cutest dog I ever did see," who entertaining the crowd by "wagging his tail to the rock 'n' roll" and "wiggling his ears to the rock 'n' roll." Bill does his best to sound enthused by the lyrics, but the musical arrangements, general lack of

---

22 Stuart Colman, *Now Dig This* No. 179, February 1998.

conviction were becoming obvious, and the steel guitar "lightning flashes" were now becoming a *cliché*.

In Chapter 6, Bill summed up the second concept album, *Rockin' the Oldies* as "we took some of the big tunes of the past and did them in the Comet fashion." At the time many people were decrying Rock 'n' Roll as a danger to civilization. The album reflected the theme (exploited in the film *Don't Knock the Rock)* of Rock 'n' Roll being no different to the music one's parents had enjoyed.

The band had difficulty rising to the challenge presented by this album. They were deprived of Rudy's services while he had an operation on a hernia, and his replacement, Frankie Scott, did a workman-like job. Some of the tracks bear the hallmarks of simply having been "thrown together" in a hurry, and the band lacks enthusiasm.

Toward the end of the sessions, they rallied somewhat to produce a creditable, neatly arranged and tight rendition of Fats Waller's "Ain't Misbehavin'." However, the album fell between two stools in attempting to interest both teenagers and their parents. The album was Haley's first excursion towards the "middle of the road," and the indications were that he had not gotten the correct mix of ingredients.

Bill was now no longer the cutting edge of rock and roll music, now spearheaded by Elvis Presley, Jerry Lee Lewis, Little Richard, and Chuck Berry. Bill had opened the gates but they were now closing behind him. A third feature film showcasing the Comets was mooted, but never came to be.

At a session in July 1957, Bill rekindled his lost spark with a return to his western-music roots, with "How Many" (Hal Blair and Howard Barnes), recorded in 1955 by Jim Reeves, and "Move it on Over", written and recorded by Hank Williams in 1947. The first is a polished arrangement with backing vocal harmonies, and the second, "rocked up" with a committed vocal performance from Bill. He re-recorded "Rock the Joint", as "New Rock the Joint." The Comets drive, Haley pushes the vocals, but it lacks the energy of the 1952 recording.

The LP *Rockin' Around the World*, was recorded in November 1957. Another concept album, it consisted of a dozen arrangements by Rusty Keefer of folk and popular songs from around the world (Gabler, Haley, and Cafra taking their usual writing percentages). The Comets display their instrumental and arranging prowess, employing an array of musical styles, instrumentation, foreign-sounding effects, as well as clichés. There is some inspired and imaginative playing from Rudy and from Franny, but the album veers between kitsch and the plain banal, with only the occasional rock and roll highlight.

Beecher's assessment of the situation was that,

They were struggling with the music. They were struggling for good material. They were trying to come up with hit records and they were trying to do it on their own, trying to write hit songs themselves. None of them were professional songwriters, so they started to run out of ideas. What they should have done, what I felt back then was to hire professional writers and have someone write some hit material that you could record. Some of the stuff they came up with was actually ridiculous... It wasn't thought out, it was just thrown together.[23]

Bill then made another a return to his roots, recording "It's a Sin" (Zeb Turner and Fred Rose), made famous by Eddy Arnold in 1947 and known to Bill from his early days. His performance on this number, the first in a song of this type since "Icy Heart" back in 1952, is convincing, but, as Colman observed, "he's trying to win over a new audience rather than converting his current one."[24]

In February 1958, the band recorded the impossibly catchy "Skinny Minnie," which charted at No. 22 in the Spring and provided a ray of hope at a time when their fortunes were waning. As Gabler told Swenson, "I really love 'Skinny Minnie' and [contradicting Bill Haley's version of the story told on page 114] the whole idea was mine, the basic gimmick — she's not skinny, she's tall, that's all. Then we put some verses together in the studio."[25] The song carried the *de rigeur* joint credit to Haley, Gabler, Keefer, and Cafra. Every element of this recording catches the ear and is instantly memorable, such as the use of the Mixolydian mode in the guitar intro:

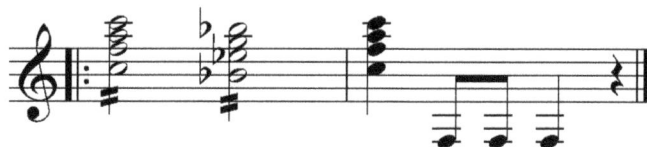

This was one of the few numbers recorded by the band at this time which used "straight eighths." It was a return to the classic hit formula with an impossibly catchy "hook," and made for dancing. With the right material the band could still sell records. It just missed the Top 20 and put some gas back in the Corporation's tank. It was followed by the similarly styled "Lean Jean" (credited to Stella Lee, John Grande, Ralph Jones, and Rudy Pompilii), which also charted (#67).

---

23 Swenson, pp.182-183.

24 Stuart Colman, *Now Dig This,* No.179, February 1998.

25 Swenson, p.112.

Bill endeavored to unlock the success that can come with a novelty dance number. He recorded Carl Sigman's "Don't Nobody Move" in a rock and roll version of "musical chairs" while Bill's fans were encouraged to invent a dance for "Skinny Minnie." Neither strategy seems to have yielded success, and it was left to "Tony and Joe" to score with their similar "The Freeze."

Bill had brought back two records from his South American tour in 1958, Joe Reisman's "Joey's Song" and Julio Gutiérrez's "*Un Poquito de tu Amor.*" These herald a move into the instrumental "easy listening" or "middle of the road" genre (to be discussed in Chapter 19). Reisman's original recording of "Joey's Song" was a full orchestration with lush strings and counter melody on the French horns. The Comets' version is closely modeled but inevitably simplified. The second song was retitled "Chiquita Linda (Un Poquito de tu Amor)." Gutiérrez's original, marvelously subtle Latin-styled take on the song was considerably distilled and simplified. It was released as the B side to "Whoa Mabel!" (Keefer, Haley, Gabler, Cafra), a hot number that is powered by a relentless paradiddle pattern from Ralph Jones on the snare drum. Rudy plays a spiky off-beat solo that portends Boots Randolph's "Yakety Sax" of a few months later:

This was their third "girl's name" single, but the formula had probably run its course and it failed to register as a hit. Despite this, the success of "Skinny Minnie" and "Lean Jean" inspired a "concept" album, *Bill Haley's Chicks*, recorded in three sessions in June 1958. It contained tracks recorded in stereo, a recent innovation in recording technology. One of the unfortunate effects was to remove the "guts" from Haley's recordings, which sounded better in mono: the album of course was also released in mono, still by far the more common medium.

The corporation's new and well-equipped recording studio was ready for action in the basement of 129 East 5th Street in Chester, Pennsylvania in early 1958, and the members of the band (both partners and employees) were busy as session players and producers for artists who had been signed to the corporation. The Comets, without Haley, made four instrumental recordings that they leased to the East West record label under the name "The Kingsmen." The Comets were under exclusive contract to Decca at the time. The cat was soon out of the bag, and the masters passed into Decca's ownership.

"Week-End" (Pompilli, Beecher, and Williamson), the particularly strong A side of the first of the singles, had significant airplay in the Philadelphia area, which led to a spot on Dick Clark's *American Bandstand.* The group, minus Bill Haley and Al Rex (then on the verge of quitting), mimed for their appearance on August 14. Within a couple of weeks, the record reached No. 35 in the *Billboard* chart, representing the band's biggest success for some time. *Billboard* got hold of the story and published an article, challenging their "hip" readers to name the band. Their wry conclusion about the episode was:

> As for the original group, here's the funny — or the ironic — part of the story; they had been less than warm at the box office before they cut the hit record 'Weekend,' but in spite of the hit, they are still having some difficulty getting work. For how can they go to club owners and theater bookers and say they are the ones who cut 'Weekend?' And if they did, who'd believe them?"[26]

On December 15, the Kingsmen were listed as No. 7 in the most promising instrumental group category for *Billboard*'s year-end round-up. Unable to capitalize on this rare success, and buckling down to fulfill his obligation to Decca during the first half of 1959, Haley continued manfully to search for a formula that would give him another hit record. His endeavors included an excursion to New York's Chinatown in the shape of "Dragon Rock" (Eddie White, Bill Haley, Mac Wolfson), an attempt at a children's "spelling bee" with "ABC Rock" (Fern Dougherty, Haley), another Louis Jordan cover, "Caldonia" (Fleecie Moore), and "Ooh! Look-a There, Ain't She Pretty" (Clarence Todd and Carmen Lombardo). It was all pretty lackluster, however and before long, Haley began searching for a new record deal to take him into the next decade, though his final obligation to Decca would see him, and his band, attempt a new musical direction.

---

26 *Billboard* Nov. 3, 1958.

Bill and the Comets on stage during the South American tour in April 1958. L to R: Al Rex, Johnny Grande, Rudy Pompilii/Pompilli, Bill Haley, and Ralph Jones.

CHAPTER 19
Focus on Music: New Directions
(Fall 1959-Winter 1960)

"At thirty-three [in 1958, Bill Haley] was too old to be a 'teen idol', too controversial to be welcomed into adult popular music, and too proud to quit while he was down." – John von Hoelle[1]

By the end of 1958, Bill Haley and the Comets' initial and highly successful rock and roll experiment had run its course. At first, youngsters were willing to overlook the fact that the band was twice their age[2] but, by 1958, their attention was turning to new, younger and/or more outrageous rock and roll artists who were offering up their own variations of the music. In interviews, Haley openly discussed his awareness that they were an ensemble of mostly middle-aged swing-era musicians and their position in pop culture was tenuous. It was time to come up with a new strategy — but what? His Decca producer, Milt Gabler, stated, "Rock music had progressed beyond Bill... I got him to do a two-part harmony thing with a guitar and a saxophone; it would be what you would have called a Billy Vaughn sound today. It was pretty and I thought I could get him to go in that direction because the Billy Vaughn sound had become very popular with the older buyers and Bill wasn't keeping up with what was happening with rock groups."[3]

This is but one stylistic strategy the Comets would pursue in the late 1950s and early 1960s but, to understand what the "Billy Vaughn sound" is and how the Comets reflected it starting in 1959, we need to look not only at its background and musical characteristics, but also Haley's producers' involvement with it. Very little has been discussed in any of the extant biographies and interviews about this

---

1 Haley and von Hoelle, p. 195.

2 It is also interesting that youngsters overlooked the label on the record of "Rock Around the Clock" designating the song as a "fox trot," a definition Decca applied to virtually all of its Haley releases.

3 Milt Gabler, interviewed by Rob Finnis, *New Kommotion Magazine*, No. 24, 1980.

aspect of the Comets' output, so much has to be left to speculation, but there are interesting associations and coincidences that guide our investigation as to how the band went down this road.

In the world of adult music, a distinct musical genre had been formulating over the course of the 1950s: the "easy listening" or "beautiful music" format. This format had strict guidelines for instrumentation that included heavy use of orchestral strings and minimized percussion, all awash in cavernous reverberation. The addition of a piano created a light parody of a classical piano concerto and allowed the listener to feel high-class, without the intellectual commitment that real classical music requires. The saxophone, associated with jazz and rock and roll, was usually excluded.

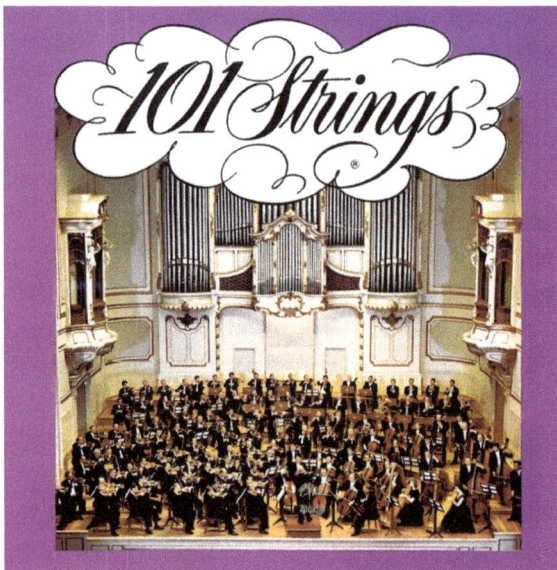

Promotional photograph of the 101 Strings Orchestra, usually used as their album cover.

Bill Haley's early record producer, Dave Miller, owner of the Holiday and Essex record labels (among others, including Somerset), vigorously turned his attention to the burgeoning easy listening style. He contracted the Northwest German Radio Orchestra of Hamburg to record soft popular music under the name *101 Strings*. (As will become very evident, connections with German musicians and audiences would play a big part in the production and popularity of easy listening music.) This project was what supposedly distracted Miller from his promotion of the Comets, allowing them to slip away to Decca. He sold the franchise in 1964, an enterprise that sold more than fifty million records worldwide in its 24 years of existence.[4]

Though easy listening stressed the strictly instrumental format, singers did eventually play a part. Choir-like vocal ensembles were added, singing romantic and novelty popular songs of the day. The Anita Kerr Singers were contracted to sing on many easy listening records and Nashville Sound productions, itself

4 *Wikipedia*: "101 Strings" accessed July 28, 2024.

designed to be an easy listening form of country music. Ray Conniff (1916-2002), a former trombonist and arranger for swing bandleader Artie Shaw, produced a winning formula with his choral/orchestral combination.

So, in the Gabler quote earlier in this chapter, was Billy Vaughn just a random name of an easy listening artist thrown out to make a point, or could this be someone that the Comets could specifically latch onto? There's a case to be made for the latter. Whereas the general instrumentation formula for easy listening was to exclude the saxophone, Vaughn was actually a saxophonist who became one of the most successful of the easy listening recording artists. Born in Glasgow, Kentucky, in 1911, Vaughn joined Nashville's Dot label as music director and had a hit single, "Melody of Love," selling more than a million copies. He had nineteen Top 40 hits with songs like his version of the Spanish ballad, "La Paloma." On this recording, we do indeed hear a saxophone duet, but with the sweet classical tone and warm vibrato of "Mickey Mouse" bands like Freddy Martin's or Guy Lombardo's. It is logical that saxophonist Vaughn would be the model for the Comets' venture into easy listening, since saxophonist Rudy Pompilii would be at the forefront of the many instrumentals they recorded during this stylistic period.

Billy Vaughn (1919-1991), photographed in 1958.

The last artist that should be mentioned as a probable link to the Comets' easy listening style is Bert Kaempfert, born in Hamburg, Germany in 1923. His 1959 composition "Wonderland by Night" features the lush ballad trumpet of Charles Tabor. (Kaempfert was a trumpet player himself.) The accompaniment has more prominent percussion and a "choke-string" electric guitar ostinato that would be a feature of the Comets' recordings in this genre. His compositions such as "A Swingin' Safari" (the theme of the TV game show *The Match Game*) and offered a peppier, bouncier type of easy listening music. His signature sound of paired trumpets shared a similar sound with the music of Herb Alpert and the Tijuana Brass and composer Burt Bacharach.

When Kaempfert couldn't find interest for releasing "Wonderland by Night" in Germany, he took the track to Decca Records, probably presenting it to Milt

Bert Kaempfert (1923-1980) whose influence, via Milt Gabler, would be felt strongly during the recording of the *Strictly Instrumental* album. Bill Haley at this point was under great financial pressure and would take very little part at all in the recording of this album.

Gabler, who released it in the U.S. in the fall of 1960. Gabler maintained a close relationship with Kaempfert, producing all his studio albums in Hamburg for the Polydor record label until Kaempfert's death in 1980. Gabler was the lyricist for the blockbuster Kaempfert composition, "L-O-V-E," the landmark recorded performance by Nat "King" Cole on Capitol Records in 1964. This is the strongest supporting evidence yet that Gabler would have been the one who steered the Comets in the direction of the easy listening genre while they were still under his supervision at Decca.

Finally, it is interesting to note that it was Kaempfert who hired the fledgling Beatles to back Tony Sheridan for the album *My Bonnie* for the Polydor label while they were performing in Hamburg in 1961. This album and the singles generated from it were the Beatles' first commercially released recordings. The concept involved rock and roll versions of old sing-along songs such as "My Bonnie Lies Over the Ocean" and "Ain't She Sweet." This effort bears a remarkable resemblance to the Comets' concept for *Rockin' the Oldies* that was recorded for Decca in 1957. Early on, the Beatles reached out to Decca to distribute their records in the U.S., but were refused (Capitol ultimately became their U.S. distributor). Could there still have been a connection between Gabler and the Beatles through Kaempfert?

The Comets' three contract-concluding easy-listening sessions for Decca occurred in September 1959. They are all instrumental tracks and mostly feature Franny Beecher's guitar or Billy Williamson's steel guitar and Rudy Pompilii's saxophone, either playing melodies in unison, harmonized in thirds, or alternating playing the melody. Though Pompilii is listed in the discographies as playing tenor sax, a careful listening reveals that he is obviously on alto saxophone for many of the recordings, achieving a lighter timbre suitable to easy listening music and a closer match to the Billy Vaughn sax sound. The guitar/saxophone pairing may have been conceived to emulate the saxophone pairing on Vaughn recordings or the trumpet duets utilized by Kaempfert.

The first session was on September 17. "Puerto Rican Peddler," written by British songwriter Johnny Brandon, is a Beecher/Pompilii pairing, a dreamy,

Caribbean-flavored song. Ralph Jones' drumming is subtle and is augmented by auxiliary Latin percussion, including bongos and claves. The natural ambience of Decca's Pythian Temple recording studio adds a pleasing warmth to the sound of the band and fits well into the easy listening formula of rich reverberation. The song gets a bit of a lift halfway through when it modulates up from the key of A flat to B flat and ends with the cliché three-stroke "cha-cha-cha" ending.

Also recorded was "(Put Another Nickel in) Music, Music, Music)." It was composed by Stephen Weiss and Bernie Baum and was a best-selling recording by vocalist Teresa Brewer in 1949 on the London label. (It is interesting to note that Baum later wrote songs extensively for many of Elvis Presley's movie musicals.) The Comets' version is more in the lively Kaempfert style and faithful to the peppy two-beat style of the Brewer recording. The guitar doubles the bass riff, and the staccato melody is reminiscent of "Joey's Song," recorded by the Comets the year before. In early 1960, it would be chosen as the A side of what would be the final single released under Haley's original Decca contract.

On the September 23 session, the Comets recorded "Skokiaan (South African Song)." As it turns out, this track and "Joey's Song" would be the last big hits for the band in the United States, and both were instrumentals, which may have been the hint that they needed to pursue this genre more aggressively in the future. Despite its subtitle on Decca, "Skokiaan" originated in Zimbabwe (Rhodesia at the time), composed by August Musarurwa (often listed as "Msarurgwa") and first recorded in 1947. The title refers to a local homemade moonshine. The song made its way to the U.S. in the 1950s. Cleveland disc jockey Bill Randle, to whom Haley gave so much credit for early promotion of rock and roll, was given a 1954 recording of the song by Musarurwa and was sufficiently enthused as to push it heavily. Cover versions quickly followed. Ralph Marterie, Pompilii's old employer, recorded one version of "Skokiaan" that soared to No. 3 on the *Cashbox* chart. Another 1954 version, with lyrics, was by Louis Armstrong, recorded for Decca and produced by Gabler on August 13, four months and a day after the Comets recorded "Rock Around the Clock." Every version of "Skokiaan" has its own take of the original African beat, from a gentle folk Cuban sound (Marterie) to a New Orleans second-line beat (Armstrong).[5] The Comets go for a more rock and roll-oriented riff, similar to the opening of their version of "Shake, Rattle and Roll":

---

5 "Skokiian" also appeared on Bert Kaempfert's 1962 album *A Swingin' Safari* (Polydor 273 639-9). All the songs on that album were influenced by South African music.

Common throughout the recordings of "Skokiaan" is the long, upward portamento on the saxophone at the outset of the melody, the signature gesture of the song. Given the close association of Haley and his men with Bill Randle, Ralph Marterie, and Milt Gabler, it is no surprise that the band would give "Skokiaan" a shot. The Comets recording reached No. 79 on the *Billboard* charts.

Another track recorded during the September 23 session was a Hawaiian song by Jack Ailau, "Drowsy Waters," also known as "Wailana Waltz." It was first recorded for Decca on September 10, 1937, by the Paradise Island Trio, three years after the label came to the U.S. from England and four years before Gabler came on board as its A&R manager. On the Comets' version, the feel is more like that of a Texas-style country waltz. In the tradition of Hawaiian guitar, Williamson's steel guitar is prominently featured, a rare treat on Comets records (and certainly at Decca) where he is usually folded into the overall ensemble sound. In the middle of the cut, Pompilii plays the melody on alto sax with a true Vaughn sweet tone and vibrato.

On the September 24 session, the Comets recorded four tracks. One of them, "In a Little Spanish Town ('Twas on a Night Like This)" (Wayne, Lewis, and Young) is performed at a vigorous tempo, with a fluent solo by Franny that finishes with a glorious flourish of high notes. Ralph makes good use of his high tom toms to punctuates a riff chorus, and Rudy finishes the number off with a raunchy sax solo competing with Franny for honors in the flourish stakes. Bill Haley might be heard in the background providing rhythm on unidentified Latin percussion instruments, as could Billy Williamson, whose steel guitar is not audible. Johnny Grande's fills on the piano sound under-nourished; they are low in the mix and he could have done with playing fuller chords. The song had been a hit for Paul Whiteman in the 1920s, Bing Crosby in 1956, and then came a knockout for Rosemary Clooney and Perez Prado in 1960, with a suitably gutsy rendition on their *A Touch of Tabasco* album (originally marketed with a free bottle of the fiery sauce). One cannot help thinking that Decca could have provided more support for the Comets' endeavor in the shape of added musicians and fuller orchestration.

"Two Shadows" is an original co-composed by Williamson and Johnny Grande. Judging from the title, the style, and the manner of recording, one might conjecture that the band is conjuring a scene of two lonely lovers, played by Beecher as the one remembering and Pompilii as the one remembered. If the idea was to make Pompilii sound like the far-away character, Gabler and the band overachieved their goal. With his heavy reverberation and distance from the microphone, it fully sounds as if poor Rudy had been locked out of the studio and was playing his part from the alley out back.

"Strictly Instrumental" would become the title track from the resulting album of these and earlier instrumental sessions. Credited to four writers (Eddie Seiler, Sol Marcus, Bennie Benjamin, and Edgar Battle), it comes about as close to Erskine Hawkins' "Tuxedo Junction" as you can get without being sued. Drummer Ralph Jones also comes as close to playing a swing beat as you will get on a Comets recording. In big band style, Beecher takes the role of the trombone section, Williamson takes on the trumpet section, and Pompilii doubles Franny as the sax section. During Rudy's bluesy saxophone solo, Beecher provides horn section-type background riffs over Jones' silky swing beat. There is also a big-band "shout" chorus with call-and-response between Rudy and Franny in character with the saxophone/brass antiphony common to most big band swing arrangements. This track would be released as the B side of "Music! Music! Music" in the spring of 1960.

The final recording on September 24 was a cover version of Kurt Weill's "Mack the Knife," written for 1928's *The Threepenny Opera* and, at the time of the session, heading to No. 1 on the charts in a version by vocalist Bobby Darin. At its beginning, it is the stiffest and least satisfying of the lot, stifled by square, wooden melody rhythms and a strict "country club two-beat" in the drums. As the tune progresses, however, there seems to be a mutiny against the Lawrence Welk-ish restraint the band has been put under. Over the number of choruses, they modulate upward from the key of C to the key of E flat (a typical practice when playing "Mack the Knife"). Williamson starts throwing in his brass-like "stabs" and the band gradually adds more demonstrative riffs, climaxing with the classic rock and roll riff famously used in "Rock Around the Clock", just so you won't forget with whom you are dealing:

By the time of Haley's September 1959 sessions for Decca, his rock and roll star had faded and he was looking for a viable way to stay in the popular mainstream. The *Strictly Instrumental* album was the Comets' attempt at the adult easy listening audience. Another idea Bill had in mind to regain musical relevance was a return to his country music roots, but this received little enthusiasm from Gabler. According to Jack Haley and John von Hoelle's biography, "Bill wants to move into the mainstream of popular music and also record some of his country-western songs. Gabler, wishing to stick to a winning formula, doesn't believe Bill has the voice to be a good country singer and tries to discourage Bill's rekindled ambitions."[6]

Just like he had to leave Essex Records behind in order to go to Decca to record "Rock Around the Clock," it looked like Haley would have to carry out his country music renaissance somewhere else. That opportunity was on the near horizon because, that same September, even as work had yet to begin on *Strictly Instrumental*, Haley might have already signed up with another record label, Warner Brothers.[7]

Warner Brothers, a film studio, launched its own record label in 1958. Not long after, George Avakian (1919-2017) was brought aboard as A&R man to get them on solid financial ground right off the bat; he was there from 1959 to 1962. His biggest success at Warner may have been producing an album by the young Bob Newhart, the first comedy record to win a Grammy for Best Album. He also signed the Everly Brothers, two of the fresher faces that were undermining Haley's popularity in rock and roll, luring them away from Cadence. In 1940, he was hired at Columbia Records (like Gabler at Commodore Records) to reissue recordings of earlier jazz artists. After World War II, he took on a greater production role and was part of a stunning array of recordings with some of the greatest names in jazz, classical, and popular music, including Louis Armstrong, Miles Davis, Dave Brubeck, Edith Piaf, and John Cage. He was also instrumental in establishing the 33 1/3 rpm. long-play record as an industry standard, the microgroove technology being developed at Columbia in the late 1940s.

A series of sessions was scheduled for Bill and the Comets at Bell Sound Studios between January and March 1960, with the intent to record enough material for two albums and some singles. One of the albums, simply named *Bill Haley and His Comets*, would be made up of unexceptional covers of well-known rock and roll songs (including some of his own hits, starting with the first re-

---

6 Haley and von Hoelle, p.169. Also, see Chapter 21 of *this* book for more discussion of this issue.

7 Date per Haley and von Hoelle, p. 197. However, there is no hard evidence to support this assertion. Negotiations are likely to have been clandestine, and could have taken place any time during the final three or four months of the year. The recording deal with Warner Brothers would be formally announced In the US music press in early January 1960. (See p. 135.)

recording of "Rock Around the Clock").[8] Haley, more likely, was mostly looking forward to fulfilling his ambitions of recording a country album, to be titled *Haley's Juke Box: Songs of the Bill Haley Generation*, and evidence of his preparation exists in the form of taped recordings of sessions held in his own basement studio in Chester ahead of the formal recording sessions. Bill's drummer, Ralph Jones, was quoted as describing the move to Warner Brothers as "a fiasco."[9] The choice of tracks for their first single certainly reflected the dilemma facing Haley as to what musical direction he should take.

Bill began his association with Warner Brothers by plowing the same "novelty instrumental" vein, with "Tamiami" (Mort Garson, Earl Shuman), a corny melody featuring Johnny Grande's jangly piano. This was very much a continuation of the easy listening style of the Comets' *Strictly Instrumental* project. The flipside, "Candy Kisses" (George Morgan), harkened back to Bill's roots. The song had been one of his Cowboy Records releases in 1949 and the new recording was an altogether more sophisticated and stylized musical arrangement, showcasing Beecher, Pompilii, and Grande giving refined and restrained performances. Warner Brothers nominated "Tamiami" as the A side, gave it a major promotional push, and *Billboard* welcomed it with the words, "Haley and crew bow on the label with a colorful reading of a catchy and cute instrumental theme. It's given a zestful and attractive treatment, and it appears a strong bet to score." The band performed it on the *Dick Clark Beech-Nut Show* (a prime-time variant of *American Bandstand*), miming to the record, and, as noted previously, the song almost became a minor Top 100 *Billboard* hit, ranked as "bubbling under" the Top 100 for four weeks in February and March.[10] *Cashbox*, meanwhile, acknowledged "Candy Kisses" as the bigger hit, in the bottom half of its Top 100. Apart from periodic reissues of "Rock Around the Clock," the *Cashbox* placing would be Bill Haley's last major U.S. chart entry.

---

8 Re-recording one's hit(s) for a different label was a common practice and motivated by various reasons. An artist and his/her new label may just want an updated performance by the original artist. The larger issue is probably ownership rights of the original recording master. Contemporary to this writing is pop artist Taylor Swift re-recording her entire catalog starting in 2019 to regain artistic and financial control of her material from her former label. Along with Haley, Chuck Berry, Little Richard, Johnny Cash, and other early rock 'n' roll figures used this practice. Notably, Elvis Presley did not because he was always with RCA and they had purchased the rights to his earlier Sun masters.

9 Swenson, p. 129.

10 "Tamiami" was released shortly after it was recorded and while "Skokiaan" was still on the charts; whether the timing was intentional is a matter of speculation. Similar speculation is possible regarding the fact that, soon after "Tamiami" reached its peak on the "bubbling under" chart, Decca chose to release its final Haley single, "(Put Another Nickel In) Music! Music! Music!" which, in terms of arrangement and sound, was similar to "Tamiami".

In February, he undertook a second set of Warner Bros recordings, making a full-blooded return to his roots as he launched into his planned album of country songs that included Hank Williams's "Cold, Cold Heart," Jimmy Walker's 1945 "Detour" (Paul Westmoreland), and Tex Ritter's "There's a New Moon Over My Shoulder" (Jimmie Davis, Ekko Whelan, Lee Blastic). The *Haley's Juke Box* album shows Bill pretty much at his best as a vocalist, and, for Grande and Williamson, also returning to their roots, it was no coincidence that they are more to the fore than on the Decca recordings, with lovingly crafted backing riffs and licks and the occasional solo. Williamson, in particular, reveals what he was capable of on steel guitar with an electrifying solo on "Detour." Avakian wrote in the sleeve notes: "...Bill Haley sings with warmth and understanding of a kind of music he knows and loves, handling with ease a range that goes from the impassioned style of the 'heart' ballads to the irony of 'Detour' and the rocking 'shout' style of 'New Moon.'"

As we saw in Chapter 15, Bill's relationship with Warner Brothers would quickly turn sour. His bold attempt to reinvent himself musically, epitomized by the combination of musical styles on his first Warner Brothers' single, had effectively failed and he faced a difficult road ahead.

CHAPTER 20
Focus on Music (1961-1964)

In March 1961, still signed to Warner Brothers, Haley was casting around for a winning formula and recorded "Hawk" (Ollie Jones/Joe Thomas). This was an uncharacteristic, breathy, finger-snapping number, in the same vein as Peggy Lee's "Fever." The instrumentation is sparse, with a female backing chorus. "Chick Safari," the A side, was an equally unusual track, credited to Haley, Keefer, and Cafra. *Billboard's* review read, "Bill Haley chants an interesting song idea, with near Eastern overtones. A mighty cute piece that could score with spins. 'Hawk' - An interesting sly rhythm job by Haley, this side could bring spins too."[1]

Variety predicted that "Chick Safari" was "headed for the hit lists because of the hot tempo and lyric angle that the teeners will go for in a big way, while "Hawk" also will pull the juke crowd's interest." *Cashbox* thought that both looked "like money-in-the-bank for all concerned." Despite these enthusiastic endorsements, the record did not sell in significant quantities. Disappointed with their promotion and caught in a battle between Warner Brothers' East and West Coast offices, Bill began to lose heart. He took to promoting the song himself in the music press: "For your copy of this new and great record — write to Valley Brook Publications Inc. 129 E. 5th Street, Chester, Pa."

Despite the Warner contract being for five years, the final single was made in April 1961, an exciting version of "Flip, Flop and Fly," featuring two saxophones, and backed by a punchy rendition of Bill Doggett's instrumental, "Honky Tonk." On July 5, 1961, Bill's diary notes that he had secured a release from Warner Brothers and, within a few days, while working a residency at Tony Mart's on the New Jersey shoreline, he negotiated a deal with George Goldner of Gone Records. With his eyes now on the possibility of working and recording in Mexico, his deal

---

1 *Billboard*, April 25, 1960.

with Gone excluded Spanish-speaking countries as his plan involved parallel, territory-specific releases in English and Spanish.

Having finished at Tony Mart's on July 14, Bill took a trip to Mexico City where Cèsar Alvarez (a Mexican promoter) took him to meetings with the local branches of RCA, Capitol, and Decca and the Mexican label, Orfeon, with whom Bill signed a deal to cover the Spanish-speaking world. He then attended a press reception in Mexico City on July 20. A couple of days later, the band travelled to New York City to record two titles for Gone Records: "The Spanish Twist" (Ann Thompson) — Haley's first venture into the new dance craze, and "My Kind of Woman" (T. Troob, M. Lane).

The origins of the Twist itself are speculative, with the term "twisting" being applied in African-American folk and popular music and even nineteenth-century minstrelsy, referring to a provocative bodily movement. Like many popular American dance steps, it was likely a watered-down version of a dance found in predominantly black dance halls and juke joints, much like the dances introduced by the pioneering couple Vernon and Irene Castle in the early twentieth century that helped usher in the popularity of ragtime and jazz.

As the story goes, Hank Ballard and the Midnighters had seen teenagers doing the dance in Florida. Ballard wrote a song called "The Twist," inspired by what they had seen. "The Twist" was released on the B side of a 1959 single. The ever-watchful host of ABC's *American Bandstand*, Dick Clark, noticed the spreading popularity of the dance among teenagers, but was reticent to promote the Midnighters' recording, as they had a reputation for rather bawdy repertoire. Clark suggested to Cameo Records that they re-record the song with the more family-friendly Chubby Checker (born Ernest Evans in 1941). His cover version on the Cameo subsidiary label, Parkway, became a No. 1 hit in both 1960 and 1962, eventually selling more than fifteen million copies and forever musically typecasting Checker as the king of "gimmick" dances. Since the modern, youthful version of the Twist was so associated with Florida, it was the site of a publicity stunt on October 11, 2012, when Checker sang "The Twist" live with four thousand dancers doing the dance step in the streets of the city of DeLand, breaking a Guinness World Record.

The Twist became a huge popular sensation all over the world and Mexico was no exception. Rock and roll had made a comparatively late arrival south of the border and twist music may have been Mexicans' first real taste of it. The lyrics to Haley and the Comets' "The Spanish Twist" (in both English and Spanish) obviously pander to the Mexican audience, granting them distinct ownership of the twist mythology. Texas-based Haley historian Denise Gregoire, declared that

Bill Haley "skyrocketed to fame in Mexico ... and has now been accorded the indisputable title of 'Creator of Twist and Rock 'n' Roll.'"[2] Over the course of the first few albums Haley recorded for Orfeon, he, his band members, and his songwriting team generated a number of original "twist" compositions and recycled older material converted to a twist beat and even "twisted" old standards such as "Twist Marie," an adaptation of the Italian popular song (by Eduardo di Capua) "Oh, Marie," popularized by Louis Prima.

The "twist beat" was a significant stylistic shift from the Comets' earlier music. Haley's extant music had a lopsided shuffle derived from boogie-woogie, swing, and rhythm and blues. By the time Chuck Berry came along, rock and roll took on a more even eighth-note pulse, as heard in Berry's "Johnny B. Goode" or "Roll Over Beethoven."[3] His "Sweet Little Sixteen" was reimagined by Brian Wilson and the Beach Boys as "Surfin' U.S.A.," which leads us to a related rock and roll style, "surf music." Surf music, as pioneered by the Beach Boys; Tacoma, Washington's the Ventures; and Glendora, California's the Surfaris, enhanced the twist beat with a snare drum pattern similar to the conga drum beat often played over jazz swing:

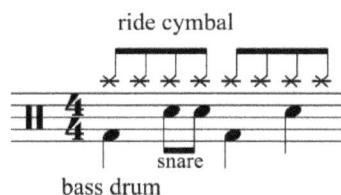

Linking West Coast surfing with Florida's twist beach party made for powerful rock and roll imagery, coupled with an infectious beat that led to other dance crazes, such as the Watusi, the Madison, and the Jerk. Haley and the Comets would adjust their beat accordingly to stay as current as they could.[4]

---

2 Cited in Chris Gardner's liner notes to the Bear Family collection, *Bill Haley: The Warner Brothers Years and More*. In an interview with David Lee Joyner, Martha Haley added that as far as the Mexican audience was concerned, Haley *was* indeed the "creator of the Twist." In 1961 and 1962, Checker appeared in two film musicals that took their titles from Haley's two major films, *Rock Around the Clock* and *Don't Knock the Rock*, substituting *Twist* for the word *Rock*. Like Haley's films, they were produced by Sam Katzman for Columbia Pictures.

3 Johnny Kay recounted his instructions to the band at an Orfeon session in Mexico: "I told the guys the twist sound was like a modified eighth-note beat, with a moving fifth under-rhythm." (Dave Hirschberg, "A Comet's Tale", *Now Dig This*, June 2010, p. 10).

4 After recording an album of Madison-style songs, they would take a stab at the surf genre with their 1964 Orfeon album, *Surf, Surf, Surf,* that includes the number "Surf de la Sandia," a cover of jazz pianist Herbie Hancock's "Watermelon Man" that appeared on his Blue Note album, *Takin' Off,* from 1962.

While appearing at the Oyster Barrel in Quebec City at the beginning of August, Bill recorded his first songs in Spanish for Orfeon: "Cerca del Mar" (Ezequiel Cisneros Cárdenas), "Twist Español" ("The Spanish Twist"), and an instrumental, "Riviera" (Ricardo Martinelli). Bill's diary noted, "Record not as good as studio was TV studio and sound was bad. I hope they accept it for release." Orfeon duly rejected the tracks and Bill re-recorded them in Mexico in October.

On October 13, the band recorded another version of "Riviera" and an original instrumental, "War Paint" (Billy Williamson) for Gone. Rudy Pompilii is in fine form for "War Paint," his sax subtly enhanced by a tape echo, while Franny Beecher's guitar solo also makes bold use of echo to produce multiple layers of sound. Musically and creatively speaking, the Comets were well up with many of their rival acts, but fundamentally hampered by being regarded as "yesterday's heroes."

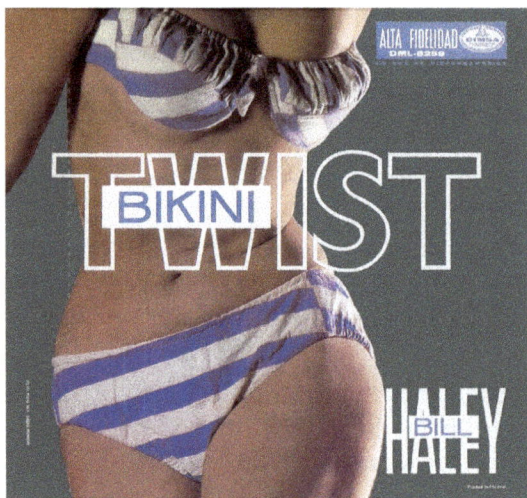

Bill Haley's second Mexican LP, Bikini Twist, tracks recorded in September 1961 and issued in early 1962.

Bill was steadily gravitating towards Mexico, both a new market for his music and a home for his third family. Whereas he had worked with top producers and major record companies he was now into mass production and exploitation of the market and "quantity" would soon get the better of "quality."

The first Orfeon sessions were held in Mexico City between October 23 and 25, 1961, yielding more than two albums' worth of tracks, of which only seven were sung by Bill. He was relying heavily on his musicians and the band became adept at writing, arranging, learning, and recording large numbers of tracks in a short space of time. It would ultimately be the Twist songs that were most successful in Mexico. Guitarist Johnny Kay observed that, "Twist music was all the rage in the States, and in those days music trends moved slowly from one country to another. Bill decided to introduce it in Mexico, and before long he became a superstar there. They called him 'El Rey de Twist'."[5]

Notable tracks from the October sessions include "Florida Twist," written by Philadelphia Music Shop owner Anthony Caruso and Rudy Pompilii, and

---

5 All quotes by Johnny Kay in this chapter come from "A Comet's Tale" by David Hirschberg, *Now Dig This*, No.327, June 2010.

"Caravana Twist" (Ellington, Tizol), both Top 10 hits in Mexico the following Spring. Bill also sang songs in Spanish: "El Quelite" (traditional), "Cerca del Mar" (Ezequiel Cisneros Cárdenas), and "Cielito Lindo" (Quirino Mendoza y Cortes).

Another October 1961 track, "Adios Marquita Linda" (Marcos Jiminez), stands out as a lovely Mexican ballad and a pleasant juxtaposition of 1950s rock and roll balladry and Latino romanticism. Haley, once again singing in Spanish, sounds very comfortable, dialing down his usual ebullient, high-range shouting voice into a more intimate, soft, and crooning sound. From the rock and roll ballad side, we hear the "choke string" bass riff in the electric guitar typical in many American popular slow songs of the time:

Over the top, Johnny Grande, on piano, plays high triplet chords typical of doo-wop ballads. The Mexican flavor comes from the *obligato* fills played by the second electric guitar, and lyrical melodies voiced in thirds, a typical sound in Mexican instrumental ensembles with either a pair of guitars or trumpets. Haley keeps this presentation simple and brief, just a chorus and a half with no instrumental solo section to speak of beyond the twin guitar introduction and a four-bar interlude between choruses. Bill also sings a couple of up-tempo numbers: "Mas Twist" — a Spanish translation of "Let's Twist Again" (Appell, Mann) — and "Negra Consentida," a well-known song by Joaquin Pardavé from a 1949 Mexican film, which he sings in Spanish over a Louis Prima, tarantella-style shuffle.

Of the instrumentals that comprised most of the early Mexican output, an original, titled "Bikini Twist" (Pompilii, Williamson), reminds us that Rudy Pompilii was an admirable clarinetist *and* flutist. He could probably never have gotten away with clarinet work on "Bikini Twist" on an American rock and roll recording at the time, but it was obviously acceptable to the Latin audience that was too new to rock and roll to have formed any set rules. Now being far removed from that era and the popular music trends therein, we can listen objectively and hear what a refreshing and successful sound it is. The clarinet doubles the staccato melody, with the electric guitar an octave higher. The percussive, high boogie-woogie piano fills, rather than crowding the melody, effectively weave in and out of it. On the bridge of each chorus, Rudy improvises a Benny Goodman-like solo, charming in its incongruity over the twist beat.

A rare picture of a Bill Haley recording session in Mexico. L to R: Rudy Pompilii, Johnny Grande and Al Rappa. The two figures in the background are unidentifiable. The picture reveals both how small the studio was, and also illustrates that Bill Haley was more often absent than present, as the Comets would record instrumental after instrumental which made up the majority of their Mexican output.

"Rudy's Flutey" (Pompilii, Haley) is a rare showcase for Pompilii's flute chops and an appropriate instrument for somehow giving this track a tropical flavor. One can almost picture a tanned, goateed, beatnik surf bum at a fireside clambake on the beach entertaining his friends. The character of the melody itself sounds like a mashup of Henry Mancini's "Baby Elephant Walk," the theme from Dick Clark's *American Band-stand*, and Moe Koffman's popular flute tune, "Swingin' Shepherd Blues."

Billy Williamson is not in great evidence on these recordings, while Johnny Grande can be generally heard tinkling on the piano discreetly in the background, but not taking a lead role (with the notable exception of "Actopan," an instrumental version of the dance standard, "The Hucklebuck" (Andy Gibson), where he takes a rare extended solo). The drummer is Ed Ward. The overall effect is that of high-class "lounge band," rather than the erstwhile Kings of Rock 'n' Roll. Johnny Kay was invaluable at this time in ensuring that the Comets played and harmonized in the established "twist" style:

> Bill was there only for his vocal parts. We made up most of the instrumentals right in the studio. I told the guys the twist sound was like a modified eighth note beat, with a moving five under-rhythm. Johnny Grande interpreted this to the engineer in standard musical terms. Rudy and Franny worked very well together and I sat back and learned. One time, Billy heard Franny play a chord progression, and said that he liked it, but it was jazz. So he came to me and said, "Twist this chord progression." So, I gave the feel to Franny and he played it as a twist. Then Billy added some whistling and stomping and called it "Whistling and Walking Twist" [a.k.a. "Silbando Y Caminando"]. So, these things were mostly a collaborative effort.

The October 1961 sessions resulted in two albums: *Twist*, issued in 1961, and *Bikini Twist* following in January 1962. These are probably the best of the Mexican recordings, having been made at a time when Mexico was still a new experience for the band, enthusiasm was high, and the challenges of working in the territory had not yet worn them down.

Orfeon's small studio in Mexico City was primitive and the resultant recordings are "lo-fi," rather than hi-fi. Kay remembers that, "They gave us an engineer who mostly recorded classic Mexican groups. He always wanted to turn down the volume, but we wanted to give it more punch." Orfeon pioneered Mexican TV pop in the form of the weekly *Discotheque Orfeon a Go-Go* TV from 1961 until 1969. The show mainly featured Mexican bands such as Los Locos del Ritmo, Los Hooligans, Los Rockin' Devils, and, on a few occasions, "Bill Haley Y Sus Cometas." This was pioneering stuff as only a small minority of Mexican homes had a TV.

Back in the States, Bill's relationship with Gone Records had not delivered on its promise, and, after two unsuccessful singles, he moved to Morris Levy's Roulette Records for a live album, *Twistin' Knights at the Roundtable,* in late March 1962. The rise of the Twist in the U.S. had been meteoric. By 1962, the craze had really taken off with thirteen *Billboard* chart hits, including Joey Dee and the Starliters' "Peppermint Twist" in January, while Chubby Checker became the first artist ever to get to No. 1 twice with the same recording when his "Let's Twist Again" returned to the top later in the year. According to syndicated press reports in early March 1962, Roulette was "ecstatic over signing Bill Haley and His Comets to a long-term contract." In reality, it was a slightly "grubby" deal involving one album and came about as a result of favors owed and being called in, and Bill needing money to keep his Corporation afloat and his debts paid. Bill would sing the songs he was told to sing.

These circumstances are illustrated in the story of one of the prescribed songs, George Shearing's "Lullaby of Birdland." In the early fifties, Levy had been operating the New York jazz club, Birdland. He was also starting a radio show and needed a theme tune. Levy asked Shearing to record a tune in which he (Levy) had a financial interest. Shearing found the music was too difficult to work with and composed his own tune. Levy would use it only on condition that he would get half of the royalties. In the Comets' case, they were handed a bundle of songs, including "Lullaby of Birdland," to turn into "twist" tunes. Another stricture placed on the band was that they would use "Sticks" Evans as their drummer. He had a jazz pedigree, but was presented to them as a "specialist" twist drummer. He was then working with Joey Dee and the Starliters, who were also contracted to Roulette.

Speaking with Hugh McCallum, Johnny Grande described the recording as "a total shambles." The engineers set a tape machine running as the band went on stage and switched it off (when they remembered) at the end. Some of the tracks were hastily edited, and when Bill is heard introducing Billy Williamson to sing Grandpa Jones's "Eight More Miles to Louisville," what we hear are only the last ninety seconds from a night when Johnny Kay sang the lead. However, it is possible to find semi-positive reviews, such as the one by Bruce Eder for the *AllMusic* website:

> ...there is decent, occasionally inspired sax and guitar playing (Rudy Pompilli and Franny Beecher were still aboard). The array of songs is entertaining, including a twist version of "Lullaby of Birdland" and other jazz/big-band standards, all stripped down for Haley's band to work with. Leader and group alike are a bit past their prime and sound it, but they're still tight and they still enjoy the work...

Johnny Kay remembers that "Roulette wanted us to use a very fast tempo, so we couldn't really get in the groove. To the record company, 'Twist' meant 'play everything fast.'"

The tracks are full of surprises. Despite Roulette demanding fast-tempo numbers, Bill "waltzes the twist" with "1-2-3 Twist" (Syd Wyche). He sings Big Joe Turner's "I Want a Little Girl" (Moll, Mencher) as a 12/8 blues, with an inappropriate country-style vocal delivery and a messy accompaniment by the band distinguished mainly by some stylish "noodling" from Beecher and some unusually improvisatory playing by Williamson on steel guitar. Rudy leads off a high-speed rendition of the Orfeon "Caravana Twist" arrangement, while Franny joins him in the solos, both of them stripping down their jazz stylings for a simpler, idiomatic approach. Several other Orfeon songs were featured, including "Florida Twist" and "Whistlin' and Walkin' Twist", both of which would have been brand-new to most American listeners.

There is little aural evidence of Grande on piano or accordion. Rudy and Franny carry the instrumental work, with Johnny Kay providing a solid and idiomatic rhythm guitar, and "Sticks" Evans is obviously completely at home in the music. The Comets did not believe he was any better than their regular drummer, Ed Ward, and it would be Beecher's final gig with Haley.

On return to Mexico, Bill found four of his records in the Top 20: "Caravan Twist," "Florida Twist," "Spanish Twist," and "La Paloma." The band had a number of recording sessions for Orfeon/Dimsa, yielding more than two albums' worth of material. The first album was *Twist Vol. 2*, with songs from many sources. The Glenn Miller catalog was raided for "Jarrito Twist" (Joseph Winner's "Little Brown Jug") and "De Buen Humor" (Joe Garland and Andy Razaf's "In the Mood"). Bill contributed two Spanish-language vocals: Louis Prima's "Hey Marie" (Prima, Di Capua, Mazzucchi, Russo), which came out as "Twist Marie" (a song he had previously recorded in English for the Roulette live album) and, in what is obviously a love song to his wife, "Martha," originally a rhumba written in the 1930s by Moisés Simon[6] and R. Gohin, on which Bill sings over a surf/twist even eighth-note beat.

The Comets created ten new instrumental numbers for their fourth album, *Twist en Mexico*. All were neat, catchy and idiomatic. The writing credits were shared between some of the members of the band, with credits also for Jack Howard and Charlie Le Vigne, two men who were back in Chester, managing what was left of the Comets' business empire. The tunes, such as "Vera Cruz", "Oaxaca Twist", "Mexicali Twist", and "Monterrey Twist", owed nothing to the locations named, but they exhibit a neatness and economy of writing that also demonstrates how well the musicians now understood the idiom:

Vera Cruz

---

6 Simon was a Cuban musician best known as the writer of "Peanut Vendor," a huge hit for Stan Kenton.

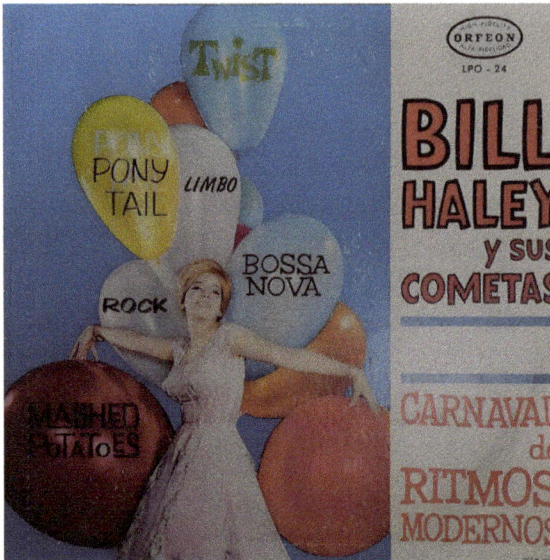

The LP *Carnaval da Ritmos Modernos*

By the end of 1962, the Comets consisted of Johnny Kay (lead guitar), Billy Williamson (steel guitar), Rudy Pompilii (tenor saxophone), Al Rappa (bass guitar), and newcomer Dave Holly (drums), with Johnny Grande now departed. They were back in Mexico City just before Christmas 1962 and recorded another two albums' worth of tracks. The only vocal by Bill was *"Que Pachanga"* ("What a Party" by Bartholomew, Domino, King). The albums were released in October 1963 as *Madison* and *Carnaval Da Ritmos Modernos*.

On the *Madison* album, the Comets go through the motions of making an album to appeal to fans of the "Madison," a dance craze that originated in 1958, and barely alive in 1963. They sound like a lounge band going through a tired routine, and even the indefatigable Rudy Pompilii finds it almost impossible to break free of the all-pervading lethargy. He manages to breathe some life into the Mercer Ellington tune, "Things Ain't What They Used to Be" (retitled *"El Madison"*), and, on *"Avenida Madison"* ("Madison Avenue," writers unknown), he shines briefly in his solo, throwing out a quick virtuoso arpeggio in the tenor sax's altissimo range. Williamson and Kay contributed "Tip Top", a number that consists of a couple of limp and obvious riffs, and two rather ordinary solos by Johnny. The track sounds unfinished, the band never getting around to overdubbing a melody or solos, apart from a couple of choruses by Johnny Kay. Orfeon brought in a local piano player who noodles somewhat aimlessly through most of the session, often sounding disconnected from the band.[7] Of all the Comets, Dave Holly appears to be the most subdued, and there is no aural evidence of Williamson's steel guitar at all.

Carnaval de Ritmos Modernos attempted to be something to fans of all dance crazes, involving the Limbo, the Pony, the Mashed Potato, and the Madison. The highlight is "Que Pachanga" ("What a Party" by Dave Bartholomew and Pearl King, first recorded by Fats Domino), an up-tempo number supported by a dotted

---

7 We do not know for sure who this is, but it could be Venezuelan musician Julian Ber't, who would go on to record for Orfeon as "Julian Ber't And His Beat."

shuffle pattern on the snare drum, with a female vocal chorus providing an effective counterpoint to Bill's vocals. Other tracks of interest on this album include Bill singing the ballad "Cerca del Mar" (Ezequiel Cisneros Cárdenas), (recorded in September 1961 and the first song he sang in Spanish), and "Teresa," a charming melody written by Rudy using a well-worn jazz chord progression and named for one of his sisters.

Bill's Orfeon contract would be renewed several times but he was still "label-hopping" in the States. Despite Roulette's publicity saying how pleased they were to have signed him to a long-term contract, there were no further recordings and Bill's next deal was with Harold B. Robinson's Newtown label in Philadelphia in 1963.

Haley recorded for Newtown some songs he had already recorded for Orfeon. "Tenor Man," although credited to "M. Levinson and R. Dicicco" on the label, was an adaptation of Fats Domino's "What a Party," also recorded by the Comets for Orfeon as "*Que Pachanga.*" Now it became a feature for Rudy with electric organ, the Cameos on backing vocals, and Rudy blowing a wild and free solo in his best style. The recording also makes much use of the famous "Rock Around the Clock" riff. In Europe it attracted significant radio play and record sales.

The Comets were augmented by Richard Rome and Bobby Martin on keyboards, with the Cameos providing the backing vocals. They also recorded two tracks backing gospel singer Carrie Grant, "Mish Mash" and "Let the Girls Sing," which were issued under the name "Carrie Grant and the Grandeurs." On these songs, the musical style reflects current U.S., and particularly Philadelphian, musical trends. The original issues on the Newtown, New-Hits, and Nicetown labels were poorly mastered, poorly promoted, and their rarity today indicates disappointing sales. Other Newtown recordings remained unreleased until the late 1990s. Little or nothing appears to be known about Marcia Levinson, the credited songwriter of many of the songs, one of which, "Dance Around the Clock" (a sequel to "Rock Around the Clock"), clearly resonated with Bill as he re-recorded it in later years for Orfeon (in Spanish), Buddah (a live performance in New York), and Sonet.

Orfeon sessions in November 1963 produced material for a jump onto the "surf" bandwagon; the resulting album, *Surf, Surf, Surf,* being released in Mexico in 1964. The production is of higher quality than earlier recordings, with a louder and more "present" mix. Bill again sings few numbers, but can be heard in several shouted interjections such as "*No no no, no te puedes sentar!*" on an otherwise-instrumental cover of "You Can't Sit Down," a 1963 hit for the Dovells. The presence of Rudy's sax does not fit the typical "surf" model, but the guitar is more prominent.

Haley plunges deep into traditional Mexican music and sound with the Marty Robbins-written ballad, "Jimmy Martinez," with breathtaking results. The Comets step aside and Bill joins an unidentified male chorus accompanied only by guitar. Singing lightly and lyrically, his voice blends beautifully with the characteristic rich harmony and high tessitura of the choir. Rather than affecting a Mexican balladeer, a rock and roll shouter, or a 1960s-style honky-tonk country singer, he taps into the cowboy balladeer of his youth. He sings most of the song in Spanish, save for where he sings "Jimmy the Mexican Soldier" in English. Had he not been so pigeonholed back in the U.S., and if American producers and listeners were more open-minded, Bill could have given Robbins and his better-known "El Paso" a serious run for his money.

"Movin' 'n' Groovin'" (Hazelwood, Eddy) (released by Orfeon as "Movendiose") is played with a modified beat, electric organ and sax. On "Washington Square" (Bob Goldstein, David Shire), Johnny Kay switches to banjo for this novelty hit by The Village Stompers. The Comets copy the original faithfully, complete with key changes with Rudy duetting with himself on clarinet and tenor saxophone. "Baby Elephant Walk" started life as a classic piece of light music, written by Henry Mancini in 1961 for the film *Hatari*. The Comets' version stands up surprisingly well against the original, greatly aided by Rudy's well-executed clarinet playing, though the organ playing pales by comparison. The Boots Randolph hit "Yakety Sax" (Rich, Randolph, "Sax Tartamudo" in Spanish) features Rudy's sax, with Bill calling out the English title periodically. Bill also has another go at "Dance Around the Clock" (in Spanish, retitled "Al Compas Del Reloj"), a song for which he clearly had some enthusiasm.

On January 22, 1964, Bill and the Comets took part in a clandestine session in Las Vegas for Guest Star Records. As discussed in Chapter 8, this was motivated by the urgent need for a new car.

In order not to compromise contractual arrangements with other companies, Bill's cover story was that it had been recorded in November 1962. The album was a product of business practices that were geared to generate revenue rather than producing good musical product. Guest Star was part of a network of labels that shared tracks that would be re-badged for maximum exploitation. Songs were acquired by scraping the industry's barrel of those that had failed to attract interest from major artists. As a result, the album, *Rock-a-Round the Clock King*, featured a number of songs that Haley never performed nor would he record again.

Bill *was* required to re-record two of his hit songs. "See You Later, Alligator" (Guidry) and "A.B.C. Boogie" (Russell, Spickol) were chosen. He demonstrates his ability to assimilate material quickly, putting in credible performances of songs that were completely new to him, such as "Altar of Love" (Conn, Werner) and "This is Goodbye, Goodbye" (Lenke, Corda). The Comets, meanwhile, drew on their ability to conjure up new numbers at the drop of hat with a riff-based instrumental that they named "I've Got News for Hugh" for Hugh McCallum. The record label applied the writing credit "copyright control" (a music industry convention meaning "writers and publisher unknown"), thereby ensuring that no money would be channeled away from the label and into Haley's publishing companies.

Rudy, meanwhile, needed little encouragement to revisit "Yakety Sax," at the request of the record company. He was a huge admirer of Boots Randolph, but Guest Star's motivation was rather less honest as the track was destined for a "Boots Randolph" album. The record company had acquired some little-known Randolph recordings for an album and needed "Yakety Sax" to make it more marketable. They padded the album with material from another sax player and added Rudy's "Yakety Sax" without making it apparent that it was not Boots's own recording. Guest Star later released some of Bill's tracks with the made-up name "Scott Gregory," to pad out another album, this time by Trini Lopez. The Comets' session was completed within a few hours and served its purpose, Bill leaving with the money for a new car.[8]

June 16, 1964 saw Bill return to the Pythian Temple for another throw of the dice with Decca and his old producer, Milt Gabler. Bill was sensing a revival of his fortunes, having played to massive crowds at open-air concerts in Germany, and "Rock Around the Clock" was riding high in the Australian charts.[9] Gabler augmented the band (Johnny Kay on lead guitar, Nick Masters on steel guitar, Rudy Pompilii on tenor saxophone, and Dave Holly on drums) with two local session players, Dave Martin[10] on piano and Abie Baker[11] on bass guitar. "The Green Door" (Davie, Moore), a cover of the 1956 hit for Jim Lowe, was chosen as

---

8 The business practices of Guest Star Records are detailed in *Rock Rarities for a Song* by Brian McFadden (Middletown, Del.: Kohner Madison & Danforth, 2015).

9 There was no national record chart in Australia at this time. The *Kent Music Report*, produced by music enthusiast David Kent, would later publish a "re-engineered" chart, aggregated from local radio record charts that had, in turn, been compiled from local sales reports. "Rock Around the Clock" peaked at No. 4 in the national report in 1964.

10 A New York-based bandleader of the 1940s and 1950s.

11 Session musician, arranger, and bandleader who worked on many R&B, jazz, and pop recordings in New York City in the 1950s and early 1960s.

the A side and Gabler's arrangement gives it the energy it never had in Lowe's hands.[12] Gabler's intention appears to have been to retain the elements of the classic Haley style, but couched in more contemporary terms.

The piano, a feature of the Lowe original, imitates the chimes of a clock and provides some colorful doubling of the melodic riffs which accompany the verse.

For the chorus, the band reverts to classic "Haley" riffs:

Into the instrumental chorus the band builds triplets, reminiscent of "A.B.C. Boogie" from 1954, while Rudy's solo reminds of his arrival in the band on "The Saints Rock 'n Roll" in September 1955, starting in the stratosphere and ending in the funky middle register:

---

12 The Comets had previously recorded an instrumental version of the song for Orfeon in 1962 as "Puerta Verde," and a comparison of the two recordings reveals the creativity, energy, and professionalism that Gabler injected into the remake.

Another high-pitched "scream" from Rudy introduces the second instrumental chorus before the band fades out and Bill vows to "get an axe and chop it down" whilst threatening to "drive a car through there." The hat is doffed to the earlier Haley sound: slap bass is overdubbed using drumsticks, and the glorious "lightning flashes" are in the capable hands of Nick Masters. A high-pitched Frank Beecher-style "little girl" voice can be heard laughing at one point, while the fade-out evokes the ending of "Crazy Man, Crazy."

The B side, "Yeah! She's Evil!" by Joy Byers, has a more contemporary feel. The song-pluggers had reached both Milt Gabler and Elvis Presley's management simultaneously, and Elvis made his recording of the song six days before Bill.[13] There are similarities, especially the paradiddle patterns on the snare drum and the rhythmic feel of Rufus Thomas's "Walkin' the Dog." Masters' steel guitar is constrained to riffs, Kay's playing is more pop-orientated than Beecher's, and there is a backing chorus to add excitement.

Of all Haley's recordings from the early 1960s, "The Green Door" was probably the one that could have been a hit, but his star had fallen too far for that to happen. While there was talk of a follow-up, a garnishee order on Haley's Decca royalties, in place following his failure to take part in an IRS audit in 1963, was a distinct disincentive to his recording again with Decca.

---

13 Retitled "The Meanest Girl in Town", it was featured in his 1965 film, *Girl Happy.*

The Caruso family was a long-time fixture in Philadelphia music making. Anthony Caruso, Sr. had founded the music business which sold sheet music, instruments and provided instrumental tuition. In 1925 he opened a music store in Chester at 113 E.7th St., where, over the next 34 years, more than 400 students were taught by a staff that included all five Caruso brothers. In 2021, Anthony's son, Vince (then aged 97) closed the business and retired. The illustration here is of Anthony Caruso's handwritten manuscript for the song, "Florida Twist," which, recorded for Orfeon, would become Bill and the Comets' biggest Mexican hit, and one of the all-time hits in that country.

CHAPTER 21
Focus on Music (1965-1967)

In 1965 Bill signed with ABC-Paramount's subsidiary, APT, which was looking for updated "go-go" versions of Bill's old hits. At the first session in February, he obliged by remaking his Decca tracks, "Burn That Candle," and "Dim, Dim the Lights." He also recorded "Stop, Look and Listen" (Joy Byers)[1] for the B side of his first APT single, backing "Candle."[2] The band was augmented by Panama Francis, who puts in a sledgehammer-like performance. Ernie Henry[3] on organ takes the solo, while Rudy Pompilii remains in the background on sax, putting in suitably groovy and rhythmic riffs during the verse. "Stop, Look and Listen" is punctuated by a male voice (most likely that of guitarist Johnny Kay) occasionally screaming and interjecting idiomatic "*ah-ha-hay*s" and "*yeah, yeah, yeah, yeah*s" taken directly from the arrangement of Ricky Nelson's original 1964 album version.

David Albert "Panama" Francis (1918-2001), renowned American jazz drummer who appeared on many Rock'n'Roll recordings in the 1950s.

---

1 Also recorded by Elvis Presley in February 1966 for the film *Spinout*.

2 This was a post-production decision as "Stop, Look and Listen" had originally been envisaged as the A side.

3 Presumably *not* the better-known saxophone-playing Ernie Henry.

At a second session later in the year, APT put forward a number of new songs. The top-class session musicians included Milt Hinton on bass, Everett Barksdale and Don Arnone on guitar, with Stan Free on piano. Rudy was the only Comets' musician involved. Bill pushed his musical boundaries with "Tongue-Tied Tony" (Peter DeAngelis and Jean Sawyer), a novelty comedy number that made good use of sound effects and overdubbed Alvin and the Chipmunks-style voices while Bill tells the story of a man who is getting married but who cannot say "I do." At the end, fleeing the bride's gun-toting father, he stammers, "I de dee dee, I de do do" with a final, desperate "I do! I do! I do!" and a fusillade of gunshots. The instrumental "Haley à Go Go" ("Samba Rag") by Ruth Roberts,[4] is performed as a stomping, rasping sax instrumental by Rudy, with a honky-tonk piano chorus from Free.

Neither single registered significant sales, and Bill would not record again until January 1966 when he signed a new contract with Orfeon. Following Bill's reunion with Big Joe Turner (see Chapter 9), Joe jumped at the opportunity to record with Bill in Mexico. Johnny Kay remembered that Bill, uncharacteristically, was in the studio the whole time and that "Joe made the room feel alive with his soul. He sang twelve-bar blues, and we just followed along. Some of the lyrics he made up while he was singing. Now that was art."[5] Most of the recordings, remakes of Turner classics, feature a chopping "back beat" on the electric guitar, very much in the vogue of the "British invasion" groups such as the Beatles. Despite the poor recording quality, it sounds as if the band are enjoying themselves and that the session was a labor of love. Pompilii had no difficulty crossing the stylistic divide, and he opens "Lonesome Train" (retitled "*Tren Solitario*" by Orfeon) with a brief exposé of his mastery of the altissimo range of the saxophone, while the piano captures a heavy blues groove. Kay puts in a handy solo and the ensemble cooks up a pretty decent climax, with a backing chorus singing wordless block harmonies throughout. In "Low Down Dog" (a.k.a. "*Perro Lento*") the introductory riff is strikingly similar to the one heard on the Beatles' "Day Tripper," and the band really cooks. The piano solo in the middle of the track,

---

4 Probably best known for the song "Mailman, Bring Me No More Blues," recorded by Buddy Holly and by the Beatles.

5 Johnny Kay, quoted by David Hirschberg in *Now Dig This,* No. 327, June 2010.

played by session musician Julian Ber't,[6] has some dazzling jazz-like "double-time" lines with Erroll Garner-esque chords to finish with, inspiring the band to get into the groove for a stomping finale. Eight of the twelve tracks recorded were issued on two EPs, which did not sell well and Orfeon left the remaining tracks unissued.

Bill had two albums of his own to record. In recording "La Tierra De Las Mil Danzas" ("Land of a Thousand Dances") by Chris Kenner, he was ahead of the game. The Kenner recording had only minor success in the U.S. charts, and Wilson Pickett's No. 1 hit version would not be recorded until later in the year. Appropriately for Bill, who had spent the last few years jumping on all the passing dance crazes, it was a song about all the dances in the world and was therefore a suitable finale to his Mexican recording career. It was also his last Top 20 hit in Mexico. Along with the other tracks featured on the first of the two albums, *Whisky a Go Go,* it featured overdubbed applause and audience screams in an attempt to simulate a live recording. Turner makes a cameo appearance at the start of "Dances," introducing the band to the imaginary audience: "And now, ladies and gentlemen, here's Mr. Go-Go *Beel* Haley and his Comets. Let 'em roll!"

Bill's final recordings for the second album, *Bill Haley a Go Go*, included many of his old hits including "Rock Around the Clock" and "Shake, Rattle and Roll" and gave Orfeon a commercial product that would be released over and over again around the world. The band continued to make appearances on the TV series, *Discotheque Orfeon a Go-Go.* Footage survives of them miming to both "Land of a Thousand Dances" and "Rock Around the Clock" while Big Joe Turner appeared on one episode to lip-synch "Feelin' Happy" with Bill Haley and the Comets backing him.

After these recordings, Bill and Martha would leave Mexico and move to Houston. Mexico had given Bill a shot in the arm and had revived his career, at least on a local basis. Now he would see about reviving his fortunes in his homeland.

In an interview with David Lee Joyner at her home in Texas on December 15, 2019, Martha Haley was asked which of his own recordings her husband liked most. Without hesitation, she said "Jealous Heart," the country and western standard he recorded with a local ensemble in Phoenix in August 1967. Given that, we can listen to this track confidently for pinpointing Bill's musical desires at this point in his life. It also gives us insight as to his heartbreak when it failed to impress any prospective producers, was in danger of Nashville Sound over-post-

---

6 Julian Bert, who worked under the name Ber't, was a versatile Venezuelan pianist and arranger who appeared in many guises including the 1960s pop band La Yenka, and as "Julian Ber't & His Beat." He played on the Comets' recording sessions after Johnny Grande left the band.

On stage in the TV Studio. Bill Haley (left) and Rudy Pompilii at the front, behind them (left to right) Mike Shay (guitar), Al Rappa (bass guitar) and Johnny Kay (lead guitar), Johnny "Bam Bam" Lane at the back (drums).

Another picture in the TV studio. Big Joe Turner's head is just visible behind the clapping man, Mike Shay, at the far left.

production, and, historically at least, was the center of a scandal where Chet Atkins allegedly "stole" the song and gave it to Freddie Fender.

Though discographies sometimes identify the local mariachi band on the track as a trio, there are clearly at least five instruments: rhythm acoustic guitar, lead/ *obbligato* acoustic guitar, electric steel guitar, bass, and a percussionist (none of the Comets are known to have participated). The bass plays a standard pattern for songs of this style, familiar to those who know the introduction to the Otis Redding recording, "(Sittin' on) the Dock of the Bay":

The percussionist (perhaps with a sidestick on the rim of the snare) overlays a pattern usually associated with a cha-cha:

The steel guitar is more subtle and violin-like than what is usually heard on country recordings and amply serves the role that a string section would serve in the bigger productions typical of the day.

Bill's vocal rendition is heartfelt and sincere, a performance that likely reflects his deep admiration for one of his Latin singer-heroes, Augustin Lara. He sings the song in the key of F, putting him on the high side of his range. While it gives his voice a lightness appropriate to the overall sound of the ensemble, he is also pressing his luck. As in much of his ballad singing, he sounds a bit strained and thin. From a vocal technique point of view, you can hear that his throat is tight, perhaps his lower jaw too extended, and his head pointed a bit too much upward to let his upper range flow out freely with a more complex tone. He also has a habit of singing long notes through hard "r's" in his enunciation, which further constricts his sound. This occasional lack of fullness of tone may be why his early and later producers, Milt Gabler and Sam Charters, thought his voice didn't fit in with the commonly accepted vocal aesthetic for male country singers at the time. All that aside, the sincerity and emotion of Haley's performance would strike any listener as one of the most profound moments in his professional career. "Jealous Heart" was recorded on August 22nd, 1967, but would not be released until 1999, when it was included on the Bear Family Records box set *The Warner Brothers Years and More*.

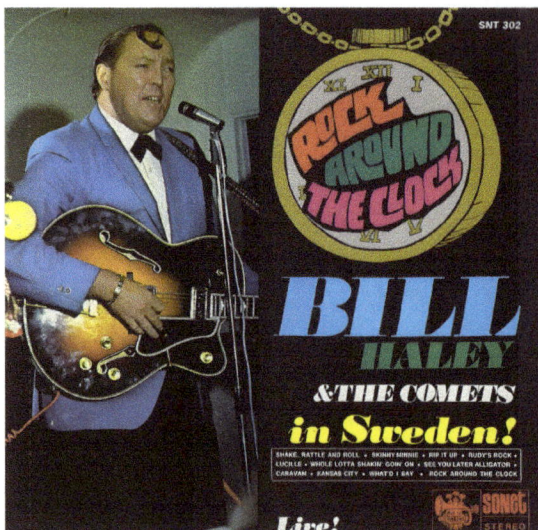

Bill Haley's first LP for Swedish Sonet Records in 1968.

By the time Bill next visited a recording studio, the rock and roll revival was under way, at least in Europe. During a tour of Sweden, he signed a contract with Sonet Records and went straight into the studio to record three albums' worth of tracks, based on his current stage show.

The most interesting song choice for the venture was "Cryin' Time," a song that had started as a country hit for its composer, Buck Owens, and then for Ray Charles in 1967. Charles was known to be a favorite of Bill's (his 1962 country album, particularly). Bill's performance avoids the honky tonk country character of the Owens original and blues overtones of the Charles version. Bill is simply dead-center on this record — the man who brought country and R&B together to make rock and roll and, in his hands, the song is a cosmopolitan hybrid of the two styles.

The studio album, recorded the very next day at the Europa Film Studio, consisted primarily of Decca-era remakes, and featured Haley's second cover of Big Joe Turner's "Flip, Flop and Fly" (previously recorded in 1961 for Warner Brothers). During "Skinny Minnie," Bill slips in the Turner phrase "double diveeney" to describe a beautiful girl, remembered from their time together in 1956.

The Comets by this time were Nick Masters/Nastos (lead guitar), Rudy Pompilii (tenor saxophone), Al Rappa (bass guitar), and John "Bam Bam" Lane (drums). These recordings, being cheap and readily available in many countries, quickly became the entry point for a new generation of Bill Haley fans.[7]

---

7 Including one of the authors of this book.

CHAPTER 22
Focus on Music (1968-1979)

The country-flavored tracks Haley made in the late 1960s and early 1970s are recordings that, historically, everyone agrees were highlights of his canon, even if he didn't believe it himself — nor did, apparently, promoters and audiences at the time.

In October 1968, Haley undertook a recording session for United Artists. The producer was Henry Jerome and the musical arranger Hutch Davie. The fact that Haley reportedly didn't particularly like Tom T. Hall's "That's How I Got to Memphis" may have actually worked to his advantage. With none of his stylistic or vocal tricks to fall back on in this context, Haley just went with his gut and unconsciously hit the nail on the head. Rather than trying to sing the song lyrically, bel canto-style, he rendered it in a half-spoken, storytelling mode that was perfect for the lonely, wistful mood of the lyric. Though Bill vehemently condemned the post-production addition of harmonica and strings, it wasn't a bad idea; it was just executed badly. No doubt the added instrumentation was in line with the country pop of the day, similar to the Glen Campbell recordings of songs by John Hartford or Jimmy Webb ("Gentle on My Mind" and "Wichita Lineman," respectively), adding a "lonely wanderer" flavor to the mood. However, in the hands of this producer, the harmonica being panned hard left in the stereo mix and the strings panned hard right sound detached from the original tracks and indeed come off as an add-on. The harmonica line sounds too repetitious, pre-planned, and controlled, and the string writing is just plain bad; fragmented and intrusive, it does not provide the usual lush padding or well-placed countermelodies one usually expects from their application on a pop recording.

The Comets line-up for this session was Bill Miller (lead guitar), Rudy Pompilii (tenor saxophone), Johnny Kay (rhythm guitar), Bud Sharp (bass guitar), and Bobby Monk (drums). An unidentified harmonica player and Moe Wexler on piano were added session players. The B side was "Ain't Love Funny, Ha Ha Ha" (F. Burch). The remaining time was filled by "Jingle Bell Rock" (Joe Beal, Jim Boothe) and "Rockin' Around the Christmas Tree" (Johnny Marks), and a single blistering take on "Flip, Flop and Fly," with an unbridled, supercharged piano solo by Wexler.

In December 1969 and in the wake of his triumphant return at the Felt Forum, Bill was quickly booked for a week at The Bitter End at 147 Bleecker Street in Greenwich Village and signed with Buddah Records. Three shows were recorded for the album, *Bill Haley's Scrapbook.* The band was Nick Masters (lead guitar), Rudy Pompilii (tenor saxophone), Rey Cawley (bass guitar), and Bill Nolte (drums). Haley was now attracting interest from "long hairs" and he has fun during the performances telling them the story of rock and roll while re-recording his greatest hits and padding the show out with well-known songs and instrumentals from the band. For the first time in years, he revives the songs "Crazy Man, Crazy," "Dance Around the Clock," and "Skinny Minnie."

It is interesting that, as he was being rehabilitated as the "King of Rock 'n' Roll" in his homeland, Haley next chose to make an album of country music. Sonet paired him with Sam Charters. His brief was to update the Haley sound to the modern vernacular. The sessions took place at Woodland Studios in Nashville in early October 1970. The Comets were augmented by session men Karl Himmel (drums), Curley Chalker (steel guitar), Jimmy Riddle (harmonica), and Hargus "Pig" Robbins (piano). In discussion with John Swenson, Charters opined:

> On Bill's side there was the continual belief that if he were to sing country ballads, that would be his breakthrough. There was always a continual stream of suggestions about ballads, about country songs, about country and western material from Bill. It was very close to his heart. He recognized, in a way, that he had reached a dead end in what he was doing and he was looking around for new things to do. I didn't believe there was any hope for Bill Haley singing country and western ballads. Bill's voice is a high voice, it's kind of a light voice. Bill had a wonderful boyish cheerfulness with that voice, but I couldn't see him doing the kind of ballads he wanted to do.[1]

Though Comets' drummer Bill Nolte felt the Nashville session wasn't what it could be, the artistic success of "Me and Bobby McGee" (Kris Kristofferson) is hard to deny. The key of E flat eases the high-range vocal tension sometimes apparent in Bill's singing and gives him a meatier sound. He settles into a more authentic Southern twang in his enunciation that is congruent with the country

---

1 Swenson, p.142.

rock flavor of his accompaniment and sets him apart from the Janis Joplin recording. If Charters is to bear any blame (and there was plenty from Nolte[2]), it might be that the backup band needed a bit of taming. The fills between vocal phrases get a bit overbearing at times, coming off as more of a freewheeling jam session than a cohesive group performance. The unison group vocal on the chorus of the song is also a bit questionable, dialing the stylistic clock backward to the *Hootenanny* urban folk revival sing-along style of the late 1950s. If the story is an intimate portrait of two lone hoboes (one male, one female in Haley's rendition), the sound of a large group of singing comrades shatters the imagery of the story.

There were two songs on the album that appear to be first recordings and not covers: the ballad "A Little Piece at a Time" (Neal Merritt and Walter Hall)[3] and a novelty song, "Pink-Eyed Pussycat" (Merritt).

Despite Charters' reservations, "A Little Piece at a Time" was a successful foray into the world of ballads. However, for each ballad Bill wanted to do, Charters would trade an up-tempo number to keep a balance. Charters was pushing "Me and Bobby McGee" for the single, and Bill was pushing "A Little Piece at a Time." *Billboard* was less than impressed when it reviewed the LP on September 23, 1972:

> Considering the current mania for 1950s rock & roll it is quite appropriate that the art form's granddaddy Bill Haley should cut a new LP. Amazingly, Haley's band and indeed his own vocals sound incredibly like they did in 1955. Instrumentally bare and unembellished the album might have fared better if the pattern set by "Dance Around the Clock" were followed rather than trying interpretations of "Games People Play" and "Me and Bobby McGee."

Yet again, Bill's attempt to return to his country music origins had fallen on barren ground. He did not promote the new songs on his live shows, and he retired once more to the safer ground of his greatest hits from the 1950s. He was experiencing how difficult it can be for an established performer to reinvent himself.

In the process of choosing tracks for the album, Sam Charters sent Bill a list of songs previously recorded by Elvis Presley. They Included "Walk A Mile in My

---

2 "I do not think that Sam was the right man to produce that album. It should be done by somebody out from Nashville...by someone who knew how to produce country music; like Shelby Singleton..." (Fuchs, p.677).

3 These two had their biggest copyrights (via Cliffie Stone at Central Songs) with Jimmy Dickens' "May the Bird of Paradise Fly Up Your Nose" and Elvis' "It Ain't No Big Thing (but it's Growing)."

Shoes," "Polk Salad Annie," "I Need Your Love Tonight," "Hound Dog," and "Guitar Man." Bill's reaction was simply to cross through them all.[4]

It is probably no surprise that, for his next Sonet album — recorded toward the end of 1972, again at Woodland Studios in Nashville with Charters as producer — he played it safe with well-known rock and roll hits, including his 1953 hit, "Crazy Man, Crazy." Charters' sleeve notes for *Just Rock & Roll Music* describe the making of the album:

> The arrangements were put together as we went along — everyone adding ideas — remembering old riffs and harmonies. We'd put it together, see if we liked it, make a few changes, then get it down on tape while it was grooving. It was like the old days of rock recording, before the machines in the studio started taking over from the musicians. The songs were everybody's favorites — the great rock songs that Bill hadn't recorded, but that had always been part of Bill's life. Every one of them had personal memories for him.

By any standards, the album was unexceptional, if still interesting, since songs associated with other rock and roll artists such as Chuck Berry and Fats Domino were interpreted by an artist from the country side of things as well as major Nashville session musicians, including Lloyd Green (steel guitar and dobro), Jerry Shook (rhythm guitar), and Bobby Wood (piano). In the process of being "updated," however, "Crazy Man, Crazy" had all its "in your face" craziness removed and became a sterilized Nashville version of itself.

To describe the album, *Rudy's Rock: The Sax That Changed the World*, recorded in February 1975 for Sonet, is to put forth a litany of adjudication and criticism as to everything that is wrong while grieving for everything that could have gone right. Sadly, Haley kept his distance. He could have been Rudy's advocate by insisting that everything about the production, overseen by Charters, met Rudy's wishes and specification, and would be the fulfilment of his musical dreams. This was not to be, and the venture is a tragic epitaph for a dying man who had so much more to offer.

The recording sounds terrible. The drums have the dead tone that was in vogue in the 1970s. The tom-toms, in particular, sound like drummer Billy Pfender is beating on cardboard boxes. Herb Hutchinson's guitar is too loud in the mix, while Tom Keel's piano is generally dialed back. Aside from the sound, the ensemble is mismatched. Billed as "The Comets," it was no such thing, but primarily a throw-

---

4 Klaus Kettner *Bill Haley - Rockin' Around Europe*, Hydra Records, June 2024.

together band of unknowns. The one current member of Haley's band was Jim Lebak (bass guitar), who had gathered the group from his musical circle. Rudy was badly served by piano, bass, and drums that were simply out of their element. Keel's chord voicings are simplistic, Lebak's walking bass lines are rudimentary and clipped, and Pfender plays plodding backbeat snare that robs the swing of its natural flow. Six of the ten tracks are twelve-bar blues, but the band can never decide how elaborate the chords will be. Some players stick with the "bread-and-butter" three-chord blues progression while others (usually Hutchinson on guitar) will extemporaneously throw in more advanced passing chords or chords with upper extensions from the bebop jazz tradition. Except for perhaps "Midnight at the Oasis" (David Nichtern), there seems to be no sign of awareness as to what pop music in 1975 sounded like. The offerings here are clueless and far from contemporary.

Anyone with perfect pitch might marvel at how well Rudy handles this repertoire in the unfriendly saxophone keys of A, E, and F sharp. The album was mastered at the wrong speed. Such carelessness is really unforgiveable.

The album opens with a clunky swing hi-hat pattern, and Rudy is introduced: "Here's a cat that'll put you in the mood. He's got his sax, it's Rude the Dude!" A band chant of the song's title, "Rude the Dude!" alternates with the riff of the melody and party sounds of handclapping and cheers create a convivial atmosphere that hopes to promise a festive listening to the next nine tracks. (The opening song is credited to Pompilii and Charters.)

Other blues-based numbers are "Annie Bananie" (Pompilii; previously recorded for Orfeon Records as "Rudy's Flutey")[5] and "Slippin' and Slidin'" (Little Richard Penniman), that are set to a dated boogaloo beat that might have flown in 1962, but not in 1975. The group's interpretation of Gordon Lightfoot's "Same Old Loverman" is a blues as well, and borrows its chord progression from the portion of Jerry Gray's "A String of Pearls" that trumpeter Bobby Hackett solos over in the famous Glenn Miller recording.

"Midnight at the Oasis," a 1973 hit for singer Maria Muldaur, is the most contemporary selection on the album and the one the band is obviously most comfortable with, but it is still not without problems. It should have been in a higher key for the tenor sax. The melody played is incorrectly, repeating the first phrase when the second phrase is actually different. It has an interesting jazz-like chord progression and would have been a great vehicle for Rudy to improvise over but the only soloist is the pianist, playing the melody. The most oddball choice for the album is "Saxophobia" (Rudy Wiedoeft), a confluence of Scott Joplin ragtime

---

5 This was renamed and re-recorded for Rudy's soon-to-be wife, Ann Swan.

and Boots Randolph's "Yakety Sax," with a corny, staccato melody and occasional wood block "tap dance."[6]

The brightest moment on the album was Rudy's signature tune, "Rudy's Rock." Rudy lights up compared to his performance on the rest of the album and offers some rich musical moments. Listeners familiar with "Rudy's Rock" have been programmed, once they hear the "Sing, Sing, Sing" tom-toms lead-up, to listen for Rudy to play an unbridled, unaccompanied cadenza where he is free to throw in all the jazz complexity and bravura he wishes, without leaving the rest of the Comets in the dust. Over the course of his fifty-eight-second cadenza, he plays his usual growls and bluesy riffs, but downplays all the showboating *altissimo* high notes he usually offers. He offers complex jazz patterns, as if he knew this might be his last shot. Among them, ascending patterns built on a diminished scale (though he falters on it a bit):

Rudy also plays a wonderful descending pattern outlining a series of minor ninth chords:

---

6 "Saxophobia" had been an early success for Rudy Wiedoeft in 1919. Wiedoft became a major star with his unusual playing style. He played a C-melody saxophone with a playing style based on lyrical *legato* phrases interspersed with fast articulated passages involving double and even triple-tonguing. In later years, Boots Randolph had great success emulating the Wiedoeft style with tunes like "Yakety Sax," a favorite with Pompilii.

Finally, we can lament that Rudy didn't get a chance to show his softer side. The lovely Ted Grouya standard "Flamingo" should have been an ideal setting for Rudy to play a luscious ballad performance with a rich Coleman Hawkins or Ben Webster sound. Instead, it was stuck over a cliché rock and roll riff and builds to the classic "Rock Around the Clock" shout chorus riff that continues way too long into Rudy's second improvisation. That beautiful Hawkins style was instead used on the Pompilii original, "Groovin' at the Nightcap," but, unfortunately, the style is mismatched with a 6/8 doo-wop-style rhythm instead of a smooth jazz ballad texture in the rhythm section.

In 1976, Charters hooked Haley up with the marvelous musicians at Rick Hall's FAME Studios in Muscle Shoals, Alabama, to make the album *R-O-C-K*. The studio had been the site of legendary recordings by Aretha Franklin, the Allman Brothers Band, and many others.[7] Bill took Ray Parsons and Jim Lebak to the session, but he just didn't click with the local players.[8] Being that this session took place shortly after Rudy's death the preceding February, his enthusiasm seemed to be completely gone.

According to Swenson, Charters wanted Haley to record new songs, but had difficulty in finding suitable material. "In Nashville we went down publishers' row asking if anyone had a song for us. Bill's kind of songs were so unique and there

---

7 FAME (acronym for Florence Alabama Music Enterprises) Studios was founded in the 1950s by Rick Hall (1932-2018). With its famous house band, known as the Muscle Shoals Rhythm Section and the Swampers, it created a unique sound and style that brought famous acts from all over to record there. It was a turning point for the "Queen of Soul" Aretha Franklin when she recorded her famous early hit there, "I Never Loved a Man (The Way I Love You)." Other famous visitors were Wilson Pickett and Percy Sledge.

8 It is important to note here that the personnel of the Swampers left FAME in 1969 to start a rival studio, Muscle Shoals Sound Studio, in nearby Sheffield, Alabama, and copyrighted the name "The Muscle Shoals Rhythm Section." (The Swampers was their more casual nickname, attributed to either Leon Russell or his producer, Denny Cordell). Hall hired a new stable of house musicians at the time that he names the FAME Gang. To date, no one has been able to determine who the local musicians were on Haley's 1976 album. The FAME Gang II, the next round of Hall's hires, was the group on Haley's 1979 album, discussed later in this chapter.

was really no one else doing Bill's kind of songs in the 70s. Bill had a sense of the kind of thing he could do. It wasn't so much of a formula, but you had to find something that was up-tempo, cheerful, optimistic, didn't make much sense, and there couldn't be anything sexual in what Bill did."[9] As a result, Haley revisited less-familiar repertoire that he had recorded for Essex and Decca Records, in some cases more than twenty years previously. Listening to the thick southern rocking sound of the FAME session musicians, Haley's voice is overwhelmed, and his old songs, such as "R-O-C-K" and "Dim, Dim the Lights," had to be taken down in pitch. The only "new" song on the album (at least in terms of a Haley vocal) was a cover of the early

This picture shows Mal Gray on the right, with Bill Haley and Susan Simmons. It dates from Mal's time as lead singer of the British rock 'n' roll band The Wild Angels in 1968. Susan Simmons was a Wild Angels' fan. Mal would be employed by Patrick Malynn in 1979 as Bill Haley's road and band manager.

Charlie Rich hit, "Mohair Sam" (Dallas Frazier), a desperate attempt to wring a viable single out of the album. Ultimately, no singles emerged.

In March 1979, Bill came out of retirement for a tour of the UK and Europe. Patrick Malynn persuaded Bill to replace his American band (save for Lebak and Parsons) with a mostly British band that worked with Mal Gray, who acted as road manager, general factotum for Bill, and featured guest vocalist. Gray had ambitions as a songwriter and also produced and appeared in a number of cabaret and stage shows styled on the American rock and roll revival/parody act, Sha Na Na. The tour took in a number of major British cities. Haley's show at the Royalty Ballroom in North London was filmed for the film *Blue Suede Shoes*. Bill also spent time with Hugh McCallum, working on the proposed life-story film.

While in the U.K., Haley recorded songs at a studio in Wembley for his next Sonet album. These included the first song he had written in years: "Let the Good Times Roll Again," as well as the autobiographical "God Bless Rock and Roll" by British songwriter Ronny Harwood. The Comets' Gray-recruited drummer, Steve Murray, contributed a new song, "Hail, Hail Rock and Roll." It was very much in the image of "Crazy, Man Crazy," with trivial lyrics and an absurdly simple "hook." In 1979, this approach fell far short of causing the same sensation as it had in 1953.

---

9 Swenson, p.150.

After the single of "Hail, Hail Rock and Roll" was released by Sonet in May, the normally supportive British DJ, Stuart Colman, criticized the song on air.

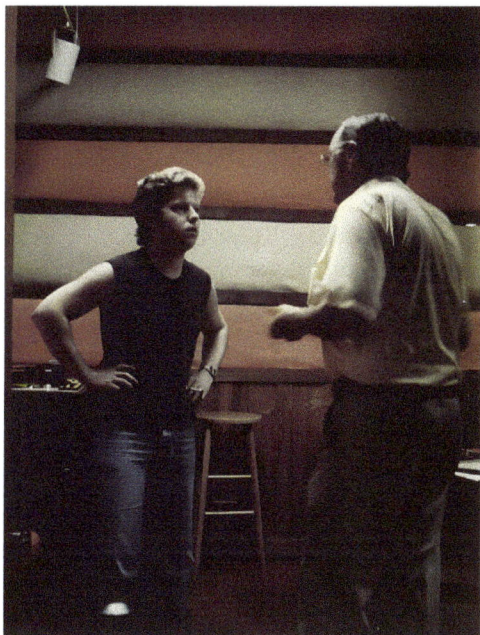

Kenny Denton, a British record producer, cut his teeth at Pye Recording Studios in London in 1969, and in 1971 joined the staff at the newly built De Lane Lea Studios in Wembley.

Kenny Denton, the session's young British producer, encountered several problems:

After the initial introductions, we were soon running through the first take, what a mess! Straight away it was obvious apart from Bill's vocal, which was hard to fault, the only professional studio musician was [session piano player] Pete Wingfield. The rest of the musicians were all competent players, but live performing is quite different from playing under the microscope in the studio. It's easy when playing the songs on stage night after night, to perfect all the imperfections that won't really be noticed at a live gig.[10]

At this point, like Gabler and Charters before him, Denton took control. He simplified the musical arrangements and endured what he called a "hideous" song by Gray ("I Need the Music"). Bill ditched another by Gray called "The King," in which Bill would have sung about himself as the "King of Rock 'n' Roll." The band's sound and feel are regimented and stiff, obviously under the strict control of Denton trying to keep flaws to a minimum. It is notable that there is a return of the baritone saxophone. The seasoned studio musician Pete Wingfield offers some impressive piano work. Geoff Dailey's tenor saxophone solos, over-dubbed later and applied to "Hail, Hail Rock 'n' Roll" and "I Need the Music," offer another bright spot.[11] All the tracks end with studio fade-outs over too long of a stretch. This suggests that no one thought up endings and that the long fade-outs were to stretch a short song to a respectable length.

---

10 Quoted from Kenny Denton's unpublished autobiography, *There Ain't No Rules in Rock 'n' Roll* (Chapter 10, "The Fifties: Rock n Roll & Bill Haley") which exists in part on the Internet; accessed July 24, 2019.

11 Though Geoff Driscoll is credited with being a saxophonist (tenor) on the session, the authors are fairly certain that his parts were replaced entirely by Geoff Dailey (baritone *and* tenor) in the overdub sessions.

One of the more remarkable occurrences was meeting Dave Miller, Bill's old Essex Records boss. Kenny Denton, the producer of the new album, remembers:

My good friend Dave Miller came out of Studio 1, where he was producing the recording of a full orchestra. I told him Bill was in Studio 4. "You're kidding me, can I go in?" he asked. Dave and I walked into the studio. Dave stood quietly for a moment just looking at Bill, who was receiving his gold record. He asked Kenny, "Shouldn't Max Freedman get one of those?" Bill looked over. "Dave, is that you?" Dave replied, "I can see you're busy. I'll catch you later," then left the room. The reunion lasted less than two minutes. They never met again.

Dave Miller's association with Bill went back to the early 1950s and is detailed is in the relevant chapters of the book.

According to Denton, Bill spent a lot of the rest of the evening talking about Miller.

In April, Hugh McCallum travelled to Harlingen, Texas, to continue working on Bill's life story to support the plans for a biographical film. Malynn worked on the idea for several years, and, although scripts were (apparently) commissioned and well-known actors "reserved," nothing material ever came of it. It is understood that the backers finally got "cold feet" when a similar film about Jerry Lee Lewis, starring Dennis Quaid, was a disappointment at the box office.

Two days of working on the Sonet album with the band in London back in March yielded three usable tracks, and work on the album would continue in June at FAME Studios in Muscle Shoals, Alabama. Kenny Denton used local session musicians, collectively known as "The FAME Gang II," including Jimmy English (guitar), Walt Aldridge (guitar synthesiser), Ed Logan and Ronnie Eades (saxophones), Dave Baroni (piano), Wanda Hale (backing vocals/harmonica), Chalmers Davis (bass and piano), and Owen Hale (drums). Saxophonist Ed Logan was a member of the famous Memphis Horns that accompanied many recordings on the Stax and Hi labels. This group was a stark stylistic contrast to the musicians in the U.K. The natural "southern-fried" element is there, capable of handling the neo-rock 'n' roll Sha Na Na style of the late 1970s and more country leanings, as required for "Jukebox Cannonball" (Cliff Rodgers, Arrett "Rusty" Keefer, Gordon

Barrie), and the touch of banjo on the cover of country singer Johnny Horton's "The Battle of New Orleans" (Jimmy Driftwood). Ed Logan has complete command of the "yakety yak" style of saxophone pioneered by King Curtis, and Wanda Hale provides impressive harmonica work. There is a harpsichord on the Harlan Howard song, "Heartaches by the Number," bringing in a bit of the flavor of Brian Wilson's orchestration on the Beach Boys' *Pet Sounds*. The group vocals are well done and seem to be to Haley's satisfaction. Denton recalled having no problems working with Haley.

What would be Haley's final album, *Everyone Can Rock and Roll*, was the product of a lot of careful work. The tracks combined newly written songs such as "Everyone Can Rock and Roll" (Wilson), with well-known songs such as "The Battle of New Orleans," along with songs from Bill's extensive "back catalog," individually selected by Hugh McCallum, such as the aforementioned "Jukebox Cannonball."

Another back catalog track was "That's How I Got to Memphis," almost eleven years after Bill had first recorded it. Haley had not performed it on his live shows, nor did he push the recording. It appeared on the composer Tom T. Hall's 1969 album, *Ballad of Forty Dollars & His Other Great Songs* (Mercury Records) around the same time that Haley's recording was released, but neither recording gained much attention. At Nashville's Bluebird Cafe on March 11, 2011,[12] Hall said he never released "Memphis" as a single, but buried it in the compilation album cited above. Country singer Bobby Bare discovered it and recorded it in on his 1970 Mercury album, *This is Bare Country*, and it spent sixteen weeks on the Hot Country charts, reaching No. 3. It was covered by Scott Walker in 1973 and Lee Hazlewood and Eddie Mitchell in 1976. Hugh McCallum's involvement in the selection of tracks led to Bill re-recording the song. In the October 1980 *Haley News*, Hugh declared that the original United Artists recording was:

> the best record Bill has ever recorded... I have again exhorted Bill to cut this again for quite some time... When Bill phoned me to say he was re-cutting it "just for you and [McCallum's wife,] Ruth," I was really pleased though inwardly I must admit I had doubts it could possibly re-capture the "feel" of the original... Though I think the original is still the best cut, the Sonet version is not far behind.

This later version is fairly faithful to the 1968 recording with no concerted effort to capture the stylistic developments of the intervening years. However, the acoustic rhythm guitar is more present, giving this version a folksier, troubadour-

---

12 Video posted on YouTube, April 11, 2011.

ish character. Haley obviously came to terms with the harmonica and strings sweetening on the 1968 recording and they appear again here. We can probably assume the "strings" are from a synthesizer keyboard, as that technology was readily available by 1979. There is also the distinct sound of the Yamaha electric grand piano that was briefly in use in that period. Haley seems to sing with more energy and enthusiasm, as in his days of old, and his riffing over the vamp/fade at the end is particularly satisfying.

For the man who had introduced rock and roll to the world in the first place, an album containing songs like "God Bless Rock and Roll," "Everyone Can Rock and Roll," and "Hail, Hail Rock and Roll" simply summed up his life's work. His music had made people happy and it got them up on their feet and dancing. During the years 1952-1954 he had played fundamental part in the creation of music for young people. With his band, The Comets, he had presented music that they could call their own, and which would continue to evolve in the hands of later generations of musicians. In short, he had invented pop music, and the World would never be the same again. Those who were his original fans in the early 1950s were still buying records and going to his shows, through the 1960s and 1970s, and until his death in 1981.

PHOTO GALLERY
From the Haley Family Collection

A lovely Martha Valasco singing with the Comets in Mexico. (p. 134)

Bill and Martha with the Lincoln Continental they bought in Las Vegas. (p. 144)

Photo Gallery

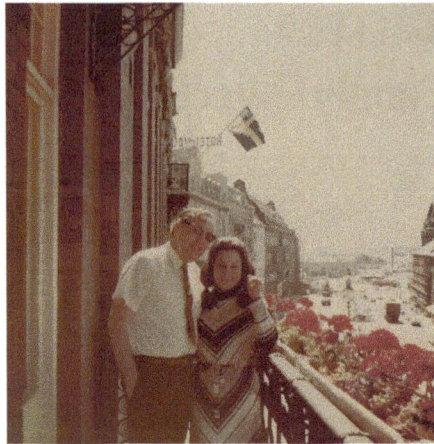

Bill and Martha on various Comets tours.

Photo Gallery

A gathering of Martha's extended family.

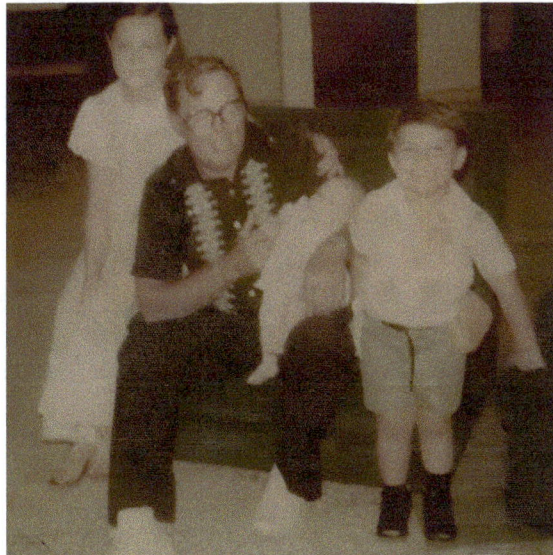

Dad Bill Haley with Martha Maria, Gina, and Pedro.

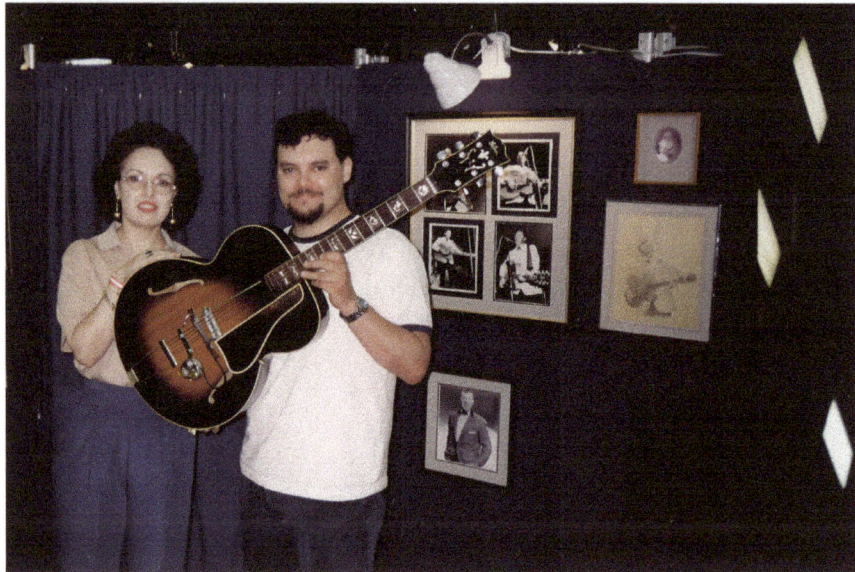

Pedro Haley and Bill Haley collector and researcher Denise Gregoire at Bill Haley Day in Harlingen, Texas, probably in April of 2003. Pedro told David Lee Joyner (5/4/2025) that the guitar in the photo was in his dad's collection, but not one he played very much. Bill probably purchased it from another musician when he was touring either Hawaii or Australia. Martha loaned it to a man with a small museum in Richardson, Texas who kept it for twenty years. Pedro got it back in his possession around 2014.

SELECTED BIBLIOGRAPHY

Bassett, Jordan. *Here's Little* Richard. (London: Bloomsbury Academic Press, 2023).

Cajiao, Trevor. "The 40th Anniversary of Rock Around the Clock." *Now Dig This* No. 133, April 1994.

Carlton, Jim. *Conversations with Great Jazz and Studio Guitarists*. (Fenton, MO: Mel Bay Publications, 2012.)

Colman, Stuart. "A Detailed Analysis of Bill Haley's Decca Recordings." *Now Dig This* Nos. 179 and 180, February & March 1998.

"Repeating Echoes: Dave Miller on Radio London" (transcription of interview) *Now Dig This* No. 204, March 2000.

—. *They Kept on Rockin': Giants of Rock 'n' Roll*. (London: Blandford Press, 1982.)

Cornelsen, P. and H.D. Kain. *Bill Haley*. (Cologne, Germany: Bastei Lübbe, 1981.)

Cullinan, James F. *Bill Haley King of Rock 'n' Roll*. (Folkestone, England: Finbarr, 2009.)

Dawson, Jim. *Rock Around the Clock: The Record That Started the Rock Revolution!* (San Francisco: Backbeat Books, 2005.)

Driver, Dave. "Shake Rattle and Roll: Big Joe Turner and Bill Haley in Mexico 1966." *Now Dig This* No.38, May 1986.

Selected Bibliography

Escott, Colin and Chris Gardner. *Bill Haley & His Comets*. Booklet published with the CD box set, *The Decca Years and More.* Bear Family Records, BCD 15506, 1990.

Ford, Peter. *"Rock Around the Clock and Me."* *Now Dig This* No. 255, June 2004.

Fuchs, Otto. *Bill Haley: the Father of Rock 'n' Roll*. (Gelnhausen, Germany: Wagner Verlag, 2014.)

Frazer-Harrison, Alex. "Rock Around the Clock-a-Thon." *Now Dig This* No. 270 September 2005.

Gardner, Chris. *Bill Haley and His Comets.* Booklet published with the CD box set: *Rock 'n' Roll Arrives... The REAL Birth of Rock 'n' Roll 1946-1954.* Bear Family Records, BCD 16509, 2006.

—. "Bill Haley Day by Day: 1958." *Now Dig This* No. 450, September 2020.

—. "Bill Haley Day by Day: 1974." *Now Dig This* No. 433, April 2019.

—. "Bill Haley: My Top Twelve (BBC Radio transcript from 1974 with extensive commentary)." *Now Dig This* No.434, May 2019.

—. "Bill Haley's UK Tours." *Now Dig This* Nos. 249-253, December 2003- April 2004.

—. *Bill Haley: The Warner Brothers Years and More.* Booklet published with CD boxed set of the same title. Bear Family Records, BCD 16157, 1999.

—. "Taking Care of Bill: Lifting the Lid on Bill Haley's Business Practices." *Now Dig This* No. 321, December 2009.

Gardner, Chris and Alex Frazer-Harrison. "Bill Haley Day by Day: 1953." *Now Dig This* No. 335, February 2011.

—. "Bill Haley Day by Day: 1954." *Now Dig This* No. 417, December 2017.

—. "Bill Haley Day by Day: 1960." *Now Dig This* No. 384, March 2015.

—. "The Sax That Rocked the World – A 30th Anniversary Tribute to Rudy Pompilii" *Now Dig This* No. 275, February 2006.

Gardner, Chris and Steve Winter. "A Comets Diary: Eyewitness Account of the First UK Visit by the Comets & The Jodimars." *Now Dig This* No. 81, December 1989.

Grande, Johnny. "Bill Haley – Shooting Star of Rock 'n' Roll." *TV Radio Mirror*, February 1957.

Selected Bibliography

Guralnick, Peter. *Last Train to Memphis: The Rise of Elvis Presley* (Boston: Little, Brown and Company, 1994).

Haley, Bill. "Bill Haley's Diary: 1956." *Now Dig This* No. January 154, 1996.

—. "Bill Haley's Diary: 1957." *Now Dig This* No. 166, January 1997.

Haley, Bill Jr. and Peter Benjaminson. *Crazy Man, Crazy: The Bill Haley Story.* (San Francisco: Backbeat Books, 2019.)

Haley, John W. and John von Hoelle. *Sound and Glory: The Incredible Story of Bill Haley, the Father of Rock 'n' Roll and the Music that Shook the World.* (Wilmington, DE: Dyne-American Publications, 1990.)

Hall, Michael. "Falling Comet." *Texas Monthly*, June 2011.

Hirschberg, David. "'Bill Haley Day!" *Now Dig This* No. 92, August 1990.

—. "Comets/Jodimars: The Brean Reunion 30th Anniversary." *Now Dig This* No. 440, November 2019.

—. "The Jodimars Story." *Now Dig This* Nos. 75-77, June-August 1989.

—. "The Reunion of Haley's Comets, Parts 1 & 2." *Now Dig This* Nos. 63-64, June-July 1988.

Hirschberg, David and Johnny Kay. "A Comet's Tale." *Now Dig This* No. 327, June 2010.

Jackson, Fred and Hugh McCallum. *Haley News*. The Bill Haley International Fan Club, 1959-1964.

Joyner, David Lee. *American Popular Music.* (New York: McGraw-Hill, 2008.)

Kamitz, Herbert. "The Comets in Europe." *Now Dig This* No. 107, February 1992.

Lytle, Marshall and Michael Jordan Rush. *Still Rockin' Around the Clock.* (Philadelphia: Michael Jordan Rush, 2009.)

McCallum, Hugh. *Haley News.* The Bill Haley International Fan Club, 1964-1981.

McCarrick, Elizabeth and Faith McCarrick-Diskin, with the Bethel Township Preservation Society. *Bethel Township, Delaware County.* (Mt. Pleasant, SC: Arcadia Publishing, 2013.)

McFadden, Brian. *Rock Rarities for a Song: Budget LPs That Saved the Roots of Rock 'n' Roll.* (Middletown, DE: Kohner, Madison and Danforth, 2015.)

Myers, James E. *Hell is a Foxhole.* (New York: Vantage Press, 1966.)

Selected Bibliography

Robinson, Red. "Bill Haley interviewed by Red Robinson." *Now Dig This* No. 359, February 2013.

Shaw, Arnold. *The Rockin' 50s.* (New York: Hawthorn Books, 1974.)

Smaine, Jean "Charles". *Bill Haley*. (Paris, France: Editions Horus, 1981.)

Swenson, John. *Bill Haley, The Daddy of Rock and Roll*. New York: Stein and Day, 1983.

Unattributed. *Bill Haley and his Comets Souvenir Programme.* (Chester, PA. 1955).

Unattributed. *Bill Haley's Comets Scrapbook.* (Munich, Germany: Rock It Concerts, 2001.)

Unattributed. *Bill Haley* (songbook). (Jack Howard Publications Inc., 1950.)

Unattributed. *Bill Haley's Down Home Melodies* (songbook). (New York: Dixie Music Publishing Co., date unknown.)

Unattributed. *Bill Haley and His Comets* (songbook). (Chester, PA: Valley Brook Publications, Inc., 1956.)

Various Authors. *Remember Bill Haley Tour 2011.* (Germany: CultConsult Show Productions International, 2011.)

Winter, Steve and Jason Pittham. "The Bill Haley Story." *Now Dig This* Nos. 7-9, October-December 1983.

ACKNOWLEDGEMENTS

In one way or another, research for this book has been going on for more than forty years. In that time, many people have freely shared information and memories with the authors.

Martha Haley and her three children, Martha Maria, Pedro, and Georgina: It was Pedro who took charge of reviving and preserving the legacy of his father's life and work and who first reached out to us to write this biography. After so many years of silence, save for the 2011 *Texas Monthly* interview with Michael Hall, Martha put her complete trust in us to tell her and Bill's story, welcoming us into their personal life. Not only did she and her family give David Lee Joyner hours of interviews, but they accepted him as a family friend. They enjoyed many non-working social visits whenever David was in the Dallas area to visit his daughter who lived nearby.

Alex Frazer-Harrison is a lifelong Bill Haley fan and a professional journalist and editor for more than twenty-five years. He has produced a comprehensive "Bill Haley Who's Who" on the Internet, which aims to provide information about everyone who worked or purported to have worked as a musician with Bill Haley. This combination of skills led to his being the natural choice as a third collaborator and editor of our first draft, guiding our text along appropriate style lines, as well as adding facts we had forgotten and correcting facts we got wrong.

Hugh McCallum published *Haley News*, the magazine of the International Bill Haley Fan Club from 1964 to 1981. Hugh enjoyed a lasting friendship with Bill and his family, gaining Bill's confidence and trust. The biographical chapters covering the period 1959 to 1969, are built on the text he produced with Bill in 1979 for a proposed motion picture of Haley's life. Hugh has responded to our requests for information and provided unique insight into Bill's character and events in Bill's life.

Acknowledgements

We have had direct contact with Johnny Grande, Joey D'Ambrosio, Francis "Franny" Beecher, Dick Richards, and Johnny Kay (all now deceased), and Bill Turner, a member of the band in the 1970s has provided many helpful email exchanges.

We have had contact over the years with John "Jack" Haley, Bill Haley Jr., and Barbara Joan Cupchak. Jimmy Myers, a key figure in Haley's career in the early 1950s, gave two substantial interviews to Chris Gardner in the late 1970s, while the late Patrick Malynn was helpful during the period when he was developing plans for a stage musical based on Bill Haley's life and music.

Haley fans, many of them members of informal online groups have been an invaluable source of information. Amongst Bill Haley fans David Hirschberg (at one time the manager of the band Bill Haley's Original Comets) stands out and we must also remember Herbert Kamitz, whose premature death in his fifties was a great loss to Haley fandom. Herbert had unearthed a treasure trove of pictures, recordings, and artifacts. In professional life, he travelled widely and met many of the worldwide fraternity of Bill Haley fans.

We have been preceded by a number of people whose published work has been valuable. They include Stuart Colman (now deceased), John von Hoelle, and Otto Fuchs. As a musician and record producer, Stuart's insight into the process of recording, coupled with his enthusiasm for rock and roll — and particularly Bill's part in it — produced much material over the years which has supported our own endeavours. His producer's ear has provided much insight into how the "Bill Haley sound" was created in the 1950s. John von Hoelle collaborated with Jack Haley in the late 1980s to write the biography *Sound and Glory* and interviewed many of Haley's colleagues and acquaintances, including some who had been involved in providing the finances for Haley's failing career in the early 1960s. Otto's enormous "fanography" (a compendium of articles and references about Bill Haley) was particularly useful for the many interviews it contains. We also owe a lot to John Swenson, who wrote the first Haley biography, in 1982, and was able to interview many key people who are no longer alive. He uncovered the inner workings of the Haley organization. We also thank Bill Haley Jr., another biographer, who benefited from exclusive input from his mother, Cuppy, and Bill Haley's senior employee, Sam Sgro.

Four men were instrumental in discovering and publishing Bill Haley's recorded legacy. The late Rex Zario of Arzee Records inherited what was left of Haley's business empire from Jack Howard in 1976. The assets included discs and tapes of unreleased recordings.. In collaboration with John Beecher of Rollercoaster Records, many were released on vinyl in the late 1970s. Richard Weize, founder of Bear Family Records, with Beecher, gathered all the known early recordings for a 5CD set, *Rock 'n' Roll Arrives... The REAL Birth of Rock 'n' Roll* in 2006. Two other boxed sets covered the 1950s and the 1960s. Klaus Kettner of Hydra Records worked through the Bill Haley legacy locating and releasing recordings that had lain dormant for decades, including a complete live Comets' performance from April 1955, and two radio broadcasts in Germany from 1962. We thank Trevor Cajiao, whose magazine, UK magazine *Now Dig This*, has long been the standard bearer for rock and roll appreciation, with many articles about Bill Haley over more than forty years. Trevor also secured us an audience with Pete Guralnick, the doyen of Presley biographers.

Dr. John Hasse, curator emeritus of American Music at the National Museum of American History at the Smithsonian Institution in Washington, D.C. gave much sage advice on how to pursue this project.

A special thanks to Athena Robbins for the digital restoration of the many photos in this book.

Finally, to anyone who helped us and whose name we have omitted, "thank you!"

David Lee Joyner and Chris Gardner, May 2025

INDEX

Index

Index

Index

Index

Index

Index

Index

Index

Index

Index

Index

Index

Index

Index

www.ingramcontent.com/pod-product-compliance
Ingram Content Group UK Ltd.
Pitfield, Milton Keynes, MK11 3LW, UK
UKHW050807220925
8007UKWH00005B/67